Cryptanalysis for Microcomputers

Cryptanalysis for Microcomputers

CAXTON C. FOSTER

University of Massachusetts

HAYDEN BOOK COMPANY, INC.
Rochelle Park, New Jersey

To Walter and Georgia

Unprovided with original learning, unformed in the habits of thinking, unskilled in the arts of composition, I resolved to write a book.

Edward Gibbon

Printed in the United States of America

1	2	3	4	5	6	7	8	9	PRINTING
82	83	84	85	86	87	88	89	90	YEAR

Preface

In this book we are going to explore the fascinating world of secret writing called *ciphers.* We will learn how to use many standard ciphers and possibly how to invent new ones. There are several good texts available on *cryptanalysis* (the "breaking" of somebody else's cipher) so that you may wonder why the world needs another one. The answer is that the best available texts were written in the late thirties before the computer was invented and certainly before they became cheap enough for a person to have one in his own home.

As one delves into cryptanalysis, one soon discovers that a great deal of counting and building tables of letter frequencies and letter-pair frequencies is required. A computer is, naturally, quite good at counting and does it much faster and with many fewer mistakes than a human being. Thus we have an ideal marriage between two previously separate "hobbies," solving cryptograms and using a home computer.

We are not going to be able to solve cryptograms entirely by machine. Perhaps that can be done by the giant computers available to the National Security Agency; perhaps not. They aren't saying. Nevertheless, we can let the machines do a lot of the dogwork and leave the rest of us free to use our trained intuition.

In the course of this book we will look at a number of types of ciphers. In each case we will first look at the methods of enciphering and deciphering messages when we know the secret of the system involved. Next we will examine standard hand methods of solving these ciphers when we don't know the secret, and then we will explore how these hand methods can be revised to take advantage of computers. Finally, we will try to find out if there are things we can do with a computer that would have been too time-consuming to do by hand.

I am going to assume that you know the fundamentals of programming a computer in some higher level language. The language to be used here is BASIC. I am going to assume further that you have a computer with a video display. Although hard copy would be better, it is still quite expensive and I will therefore proceed as if it didn't exist. I am also going to assume that you have about 8K of RAM to work with. More would be better, but you can actually get along with less if your finances are strained. You will need at least a cassette recorder, and a disk would be ideal. Sometimes I will consider how to tackle a problem given no hardware limitations. We poorer types will just have to eat our hearts out when this situation comes along.

As I said before, I am going to assume that you know what a computer is and the fundamentals of how to program it, but I will do my best to lead you through each algorithm presented. They will be written in BASIC for the PET computer. Since this is quite close to the original Dartmouth Basic and doesn't have many extensions, most of the algorithms will be directly applicable to any home system.

This book grew out of a course offered at the University of Massachusetts in the spring of 1978—a course I enjoyed teaching immensely and one that seemed to elicit a similar reaction from the students. I've included lots of sample crypts to test your prowess on. Some of them have solutions in the back of the book but some don't. Personally, I find the temptation of an available answer irresistible. If anybody gets really stuck, drop me a line and I'll send you the answer.

You won't finish reading this book and be automatically ready for a job with NSA, much less to unlock the secrets of the ancients, but you just might have a lot of fun along the way and even become an addict who is scarcely able to wait for the next issue of *The Cryptogram.* It has certainly happened to some other poor souls I know of.

I particularly want to thank Ruth Morrell for typing the manuscript with such accuracy. She is a secretary *sans pareil.*

CAXTON C. FOSTER

Contents

Cryptanalysis for Microcomputers

1

Introduction and Definitions

Cryptography is the science of writing messages that no one except the intended receiver can read. *Cryptanalysis* is the science of reading them anyway. As long as most of the world was illiterate, any form of writing would do to convey a message from its source to its destination with reasonable certainty that, should the message fall into the wrong hands, it could not be read. As soon as it became probable that the interceptor of a message could read and hence understand the message, ciphers and codes became necessary.

Stating the problem more formally, suppose that there are three people, A, B, and C. Suppose that A wants to send a message to B and that C has a way to intercept or eavesdrop or otherwise obtain a copy of the message. Now suppose that A wants to tell B something and that he doesn't want C to know it. If you happen to be marketing a homestudy course entitled "Secret Writing for Fun and Profit, or Selected Unbreakable Ciphers," Mr. A looks like a potential customer. If you have a second course called "Breaking the Unbreakable," and if C really cares about what A is saying to B, then you might have another sale in the offing.

We can summarize all this with a diagram (see Fig. 1.1). A composes a message in his native language, which for convenience we will assume to be English. This original message is couched in what is called *plaintext*—a text in plain (that means "everyday," not necessarily "clear") English. He puts this plaintext message through a process known as *encipherment*. Out of this comes *ciphertext*. It is the ciphertext that gets sent to B. B receives the ciphertext and puts it through another process known as *decipherment* and recovers the plaintext, which he presumably reads and acts upon. If he doesn't, A has gone to a lot of work for nothing.

Meanwhile, C, the dastard, has obtained a copy of the ciphertext. He would probably have preferred to get a copy of the plaintext, but

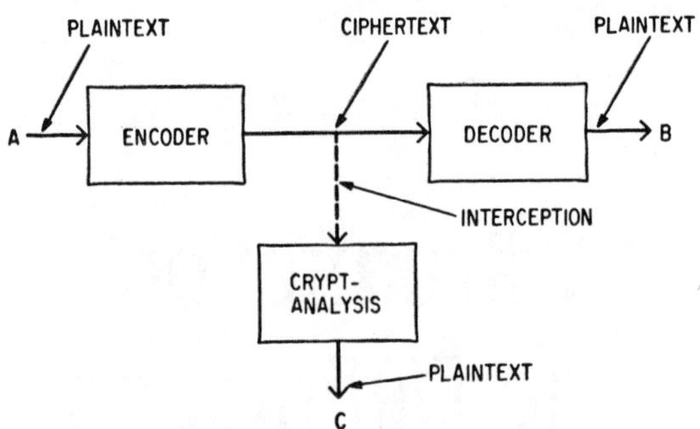

Fig. 1.1 The general picture.

that would spoil the game. How he intercepted this copy is of little interest to us. He might have steamed open A's letter or tapped A's phone or listened in to A's radio broadcast or lured A's carrier pigeon to land by making appropriately sexy cooing noises. However he gets it, we must assume that he is able to get it. (If, speaking technically, the channel between A and B had been "secure"—that is, untappable—then there would have been no need for a cipher, for if C can't get a copy of the message, he would be hard put, no matter how clever he is, to decipher and read it.)

The process that C now applies to the ciphertext is known as *cryptanalysis.* Before we go into any details of cryptanalysis, let us see if we can frame any guidelines for A so that he can use the best cipher possible. To begin with, we must recognize that there is no such thing as an unbreakable cipher.* All that A can hope for is to delay C's reading of the message long enough so that the contents will be useless when he finally does decipher it. Suppose that A wants to tell B to ship five tons of marijuana to him the day after tomorrow. If C represents the Federal Narcotics Bureau and it takes them a week to decipher the message, the cipher is resistant enough for A's purposes. If, on the other hand, C can decipher the message within an hour of its receipt, A is in deep trouble.

The problem of breaking a cipher has been referred to as the "chastity belt problem." In the so-called age of chivalry when knights rode off to war, they sometimes locked iron belts about their wives to ensure marital fidelity. No matter how complicated the lock, if the war was long enough and the wife attractive enough. . . . Today, even the manufacturers of vaults rate their products as being only one- or two- or n-hour burglar-resistant.

*There is one exception to this flat statement—the "one time pad," which we will discuss in some detail in a later chapter.

So, too, with ciphers. If the goal (in this case, knowledge of the plaintext) is valuable enough and the cryptanalyst has enough time, no cipher is unbreakable. This statement obviously has to be qualified to some extent. Paul Revere's famous "one if by land and two if by sea" couldn't have been cracked by the British even if they had had the best of modern computers on their side. There simply wasn't enough data there to work on. Similarly, several systems that we will consider require a considerable body of text for the analyst to work with. One could use these systems sparingly and have a reasonable expectation that they could not be cracked. In many real life situations, however, the volume of traffic cannot be arbitrarily restricted. The classic example, of course, is the problem of the military, where daily, intimate contact must be maintained between different units. Kahn (1)* estimates that German communications during the second World War reached a volume approaching 400 million words per day, most of it in cipher. Consider also any one of today's multinational corporations with operations in every major country and tens of thousands of employees. Consequently, in any real world application of cryptography, the amount of traffic is large and one cannot rely on scarcity to provide security.

Applications in Modern Computing

That computing is a rapidly changing field may classify as the understatement of the decade, if not the century. At the present time, it looks as if remote computing (the manipulation of numbers from a distance) will soon be passe. Microcomputers are dropping rapidly in cost and increasing in power and availability. It is probably true that present local micro- or home-computers can compete economically if they have telephone access to a large central machine, but what an isolated machine can't do locally is to interact with a common data base. Some one central point must know how many seats are presently available on the 6:10 flight from Hartford to Miami. Each local travel agent's terminal must be able to access that information in the central location in order to make reservations and cancellations. Data of this type (number of seats available) does not need to be *private* (indeed, we often go to great expense to make it public), but it must be *secure*. That is, we do not want any idiot with a terminal to be able to get at and manipulate this data. Only certain "authorized" people should be allowed to make reservations or cancellations.

The problem of *data security* is quite separate from that of *data privacy*. In the first case, we are concerned with who may modify the

*Numbers in parentheses following an author's name should be consulted in the Bibliography at the end of the book.

data; in the second case, with who may read it. We will not be greatly concerned in this book with data security. Instead, we will concentrate on issues of data privacy. Even after our old enemy C gains access to our data bank (by suitably nefarious means, of course) we want to keep him from being able to understand what he has. This is the realm of cryptography. In order to know how to create strong ciphers that will cause C as much heartache and pain as possible, we will study the tricks and techniques he can bring to bear. But enough of this preamble. Let us get to the meaty stuff.

2

Types of Ciphers and Practical Considerations

Conventional wisdom categorizes methods of private communication by a succession of dichotomizations. First, we distinguish between *hidden messages* and *visible messages.* The former constitute the branch called *steganography* and include such things as invisible inks, microdots, hollow shoelace tips, and other such wonders out of a James Bond movie. We will not consider them in this book because it is not immediately obvious how computers could be applied to such a field.

We next separate the branch of nonhidden messages into *codes* and *ciphers.* Codes deal with words or phrases as units whereas ciphers deal basically with letters. For example, in a code we might have:

AVECI = I (we) are now in San Francisco
BALIN = Diamond(s)
CORBO = Price is lower than expected

Thus, the message AVECI BALIN CORBO would mean that the agent is in the bay area and the jewels he is trying to fence won't bring as much as he had hoped.

Codes require large code books, which, for security, are divided into two parts, one for encoding and the other for decoding. In the encoding section, words and phrases are arranged alphabetically and codes are assigned to them at random. The need for randomness is readily apparent. Should the enemy discover that

BALIG = diagram

and

BALIT = diaphram

he won't be able to deduce that BALIN means diamonds. In the second half of the book, the code groups are arranged alphabetically to ease the task of the legitimate decoder, and the translation to English follows them. When a code such as this is used in telegrams purely for brevity and not for secrecy, a one-part book with words and code groups assigned in regular order will suffice. When constructing a code book the maker usually tries to ensure that no two code groups differ by only a single letter so that no one mistake can convert one phrase into another.

One meets codes in modern time-sharing computers in the guise of *passwords*. Each user selects a code group of some standard number of letters (often 4 or 5) and communicates it to the computer installation manager. After a suitable delay, this information is entered into the computer. Then, when the user dials up the time-sharing service, the machine asks him for his account number and password. The assumption is that only he knows the secret password and hence if what is presented matches what is stored he must be who he says he is and therefore entitled to all the rights and prerequisites of that person.

A popular form of code is the *book code*. A and B agree on some book and each buy a copy of the same edition. To encode a word, A pages through the book until he comes on the desired word. He writes down the page, line number, and word number. With much paging, he builds up his message in triples of numbers and then sends this set of triples to B. If C doesn't know which book is in use and if A is careful never (or very seldom) to use the same occurrence of a word again, this is a good code and almost impossible to break. Its drawback is that only words appearing in the chosen book can be encoded. Some words may occur so rarely in the book that they will have to be reused time and again. Some desired words may not occur at all, and they will have to be either given in "the clear" or spelled out using some agreed-upon convention. Also, if the parties decide to change code books, you might be amazed at how hard it can be to find a copy of the 1938 edition of "Gone With The Wind" in Central Afghanistan.

Making reference again to a certain Boston silversmith, it is obvious that his signaling system was a code, that is,

One = by land
Two = by sea

We will not spend any more time on codes in this book, if only because the amount of material that must be stored exceeds the size of most home computers by at least an order of magnitude.

Ciphers

Ciphers break down into two different varieties. These are called *transposition ciphers* and *substitution ciphers*. In the former, letters stand for themselves, but the order of the letters in a word or sentence are rearranged (transposed) so as to confuse the enemy. A simple form of such a cipher is shown in Fig. 2.1. It is called the *railfence cipher*.

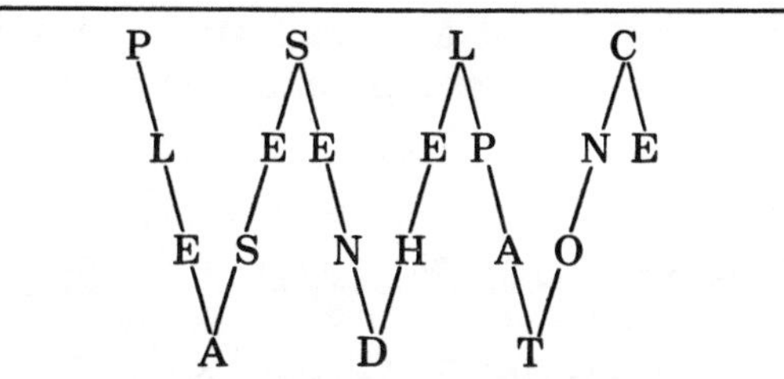

Ciphertext: PSLCLEEEPNEESNHAOADT

Fig. 2.1 A railfence cipher.

The plaintext message is written in a series of "V's" as shown, and the ciphertext read off in horizontal rows. We will devote considerable space to the study of transposition ciphers.

In a substitution cipher, the order of the plaintext is not changed, but new letters or symbols are substituted for the ones of the plaintext. Figure 2.2 shows a *Caesar cipher*, in which each plaintext letter is replaced by the letter that occurs three positions later in the alphabet.

Plaintext:	H a v i n g	a	w o n d e r f u l	t i m e
Ciphertext:	KDYLQJ	D	ZRQGHUIXO	WLPH

Fig. 2.2 Caesar cipher

Substitution ciphers come in four basic varieties. We will explore each in detail later on, but they may be outlined briefly as follows:

1. *Monoalphabetic:* Letters are treated as the basic unit of encipherment, and each symbol of the ciphertext stands for a unique plaintext letter. There may (or may not) be more than one ciphertext equivalent for a given plaintext letter.
2. *Polyalphabetic:* Again single letters are the basic unit, but in this case several substitution alphabets are utilized in rotation (or by some other scheme) to encipher successive letters of plaintext. Thus, in one part of the ciphertext, the letter "X" might stand for plaintext "k" while at another place the cipher letter "X" might stand for plaintext "r."
3. *Polygraphic:* Two or more plaintext letters form a unit of encipherment. In the *Playfair cipher,* pairs of plaintext letters are used to generate pairs of ciphertext letters. In so-called "algebraic schemes," each ciphertext letter may depend in a complex way on several plaintext letters.

4. *Fractionating:* These schemes are usually thought of as a form of substitution cipher in which fractions or sub-parts of letters are treated as the units of encipherment. Actually, they are perhaps more easily understood as combinations of substitution and transposition (see the description of the *bifid cipher* in a later chapter).

Complicated and very resistant ciphering schemes can be constructed by successive application of two or more of the simple schemes outlined above. For example, the proposed National Bureau of Standards "Data Encryption Standard" consists of sixteen stages of polyalphabetic substitution, each followed by a transposition.

The Requirements on a Cipher System

About the end of the last century, Auguste Kerchoffs published a book called *La Cryptographie Militaire* in which he laid down six general rules for the design of a military cryptographic system. These rules, which are still valid today, are as follows:

1. The system should be unbreakable in practice, if not in theory. At the least, it should provide sufficient resistance so that messages cannot be read until after the execution date of any orders contained therein.
2. We must assume that the enemy knows the system in its entirety except for the "key" being used.
3. The key should be easily remembered.
4. The ciphertext must be transmittable by telegraph or teletype.
5. The apparatus must be portable and operable by one man.
6. The system must be easy to use without lots of complicated rules or attendant mental strain.

Let us consider these rules one by one. The first is obvious. A cipher system that cracks under light pressure is no use whatsoever. Most military (and much civilian) information is time-dated. For example, until the day of his big show in Paris, Gucci's designs for a spring wardrobe are guarded from the competition with a zealousness that compares with the AEC's concern over the plans for an atomic bomb. "Does Macys tell Gimbels?" Not on your life! Nor does Ford tell GM what its new cars are going to look like. But once the cars are in the showrooms, the troops on the move, or the clothes in the salon, the enemy has better and simpler ways of discovering the truth than by solving some dusty cryptogram. Thus we don't need infinite resistibility. We need only delay the enemies' cryptanalysts long enough to make a solution come too late to change the course of events.

We have to assume that the enemy knows the general method we are using. Overrunning of an advanced position, desertion, subversion, or plain mischance will assure that the system falls into his hands quite early in the game. Since installing a new system involves training of personnel and the logistics of distributing the system, we cannot change an entire system every day or even every week. What we can change is the key.

Assume that we are using a transposition system in which the plaintext is written in rows of six letters each and then read out one column at a time. The key to this system is the order in which the columns are read out (see Fig. 2.3). With this system, we can "easily" change the key and read out the columns in a different order, say 243516, and thus maintain privacy even if the enemy knows we are using a transposition and knows the key we were using yesterday. Since

B	L	A	N	K	S	
3	*5*	*1*	*6*	*2*	*4*	*Ciphertext*
A	L	L	U	N	I	L M V S L S N S N A A I A T A
T	S	M	U	S	T	E I P L I T C P S B L S D A D
A	D	V	A	N	C	O E U U A R Y S
E	A	S	R	A	P	
I	D	L	Y	A	S	
P	O	S	S	I	B	
L	E					

Fig. 2.3 A columnar transposition.

a key like 351624 or 243516 is somewhat hard to remember, people often replace straight numeric keys with words that, presumably, can be remembered more easily. The method used is to pick a word of the appropriate length (in this case, six letters) and then read out first the column corresponding to the alphabetically earliest letter in the keyword, then the next earliest, and so on. If the keyword is "BLANKS," one reads out the third column, then the first, then the fifth, then the second, and last of all the fourth. If the keyword has duplicate letters in it, such as "LETTER," you take the E first, then the second E, and similarly with the T's, giving 251346 as the order of columns for the readout.

The interoffice memo was invented, despite what cynics may say, because human memory is fallible. Similarly, a military organization must share the memory of events, orders, and reports via the written word. Human understanding of the spoken word relies heavily on context and redundancy. For example, if I say "les squeet," you may not understand me unless you know that I am hungry. Since ciphertext is unfamiliar and of low redundancy, it can be transmitted with far fewer errors in written form than in spoken form. Besides, unless the receiving cipher clerk is extremely fast, he will have to write down the message as it is received and decipher it later. Even if we use a telephone, the message must be capable of being written down. Consequently, all cipher systems in use today restrict their ciphertext to letters, numbers, and symbols that can be transmitted by telegraph (in Morse Code) or teletype (in ASCII).

We welcome this restriction because we are going to want to enter our ciphertext into a computer, and also print it out by computer, and it would be rather tedious, to say the least, to try to get our computer to accept or generate Mayan hieroglyphics. If one is faced with symbols of an unfamiliar form, Poe's "dancing men" for example, the wise cryptanalyst replaces each unique symbol by a letter from the ordinary Roman alphabet, or if there are more than 26 symbols, by a number between 1 and 99 or 1 and 999, if that is necessary. Analysis then proceeds as if the message had been written in ordinary letters originally.

For an army that moves, portable apparatus is a must. Every army wishes to advance and at some time every army has to retreat. In retreat, it is not generally a wise idea to leave one's cryptographic material behind and hope that it will remain unnoticed and unmolested by the enemy during his occupation of the premises. Also, a system that requires only one trained operator is to be preferred over a system that requires two or more. For businesses like Ford or GM, which do not move their offices from Detroit to Chicago all that often, portability is not such a strong requirement. For a lonely spy deep in enemy territory, small size and ready concealment are essential. For any user of a cryptographic system, the old song which says that "a good man (read person) is hard to find" sums up staffing problems most succinctly.

Finally, Kerchoffs suggests that the system can't afford to be too complicated. Human beings make mistakes. Indeed, as someone recently remarked, "To err is human; to foul-up completely requires a computer." Many supposedly secure cipher systems have been compromised by operator error. A message is sent in cipher and then again in the clear, or perhaps in an old and broken cipher. If you enjoy tales of other's stupidities, read Kahn's book (1), which offers many examples.

Before you state too categorically that you wouldn't make dumb mistakes like those idiots did, remember that the majority of them were probably only partially trained, they were often working in miserable physical conditions, they were many times without sufficient sleep, they were rushed and overloaded, and above all they were very likely being shot at with intent to kill, which is not known to improve a person's ability to perform intricate mathematics flawlessly.

Operations carried out by hand are especially prone to human error. When they are carried out on mechanical or electrical equipment, there can always be dirt in the gears or water on the connections. When they are carried out inside a microcomputer, however, the sky (or your programming ability) is the only remaining limit on complexity. If accuracy is all important and you doubt the infallibility of your favorite micro, then set three of them in parallel doing the job and accept the results of their computation only if they all agree.

To the requirements of Kerchoffs, we can add two more modern ones:

1. The enciphering system should not cause a large expansion of the text.
2. Small errors caused by operators or by ordinary electrical "noise" should not wipe out large portions of a message.

The first is necessary because, for military communications at least, the number of messages is already so high that the capacity of the communication channels is strained. Adding to the burden by doubling or tripling the length of enciphered messages is strictly out.

Certain of the modern ciphers we will look at later cause each ciphertext letter to depend on several plaintext letters. In deciphering, therefore, each recovered plaintext letter will depend on several of the ciphertext letters. In such systems then, a single "E" changed to an "F" by miscopying or by static on the line will wipe out several letters in the deciphered message. The human mind is good at using the redundancy of a message to correct occasional errors in a text, but if a single burst of static should wipe out an entire message by reducing it to gibberish, it will add substantially to the traffic problem by necessitating a lot of retransmissions. There are such things as "error correcting codes," but the more efficient these are at correcting errors, the more they expand messages with increased redundancy.

Let us keep these points in mind as we look at the various cipher systems in the remainder of this book.

3

Transposition Ciphers

One of the earliest forms of cipher, one known to the ancient Greeks, is called the *skytale*. It is a form of transposition cipher and one of the very few that employed a mechanical aid for enciphering and deciphering at the very beginning. The originator of a message took a straight rod, and around this rod he wrapped a long, thin, narrow strip of parchment in spiral fashion with the edges of the spiral touching. Next, he wrote his message on the parchment with the text running along the rod, successive lines of the message following each other around the rod. If he wrote without regard to the joints of the parchment, unrolling it revealed only bits and pieces of letters with the information from successive lines more or less shuffled together. The unrolled parchment was then sent to its destination, where the recipient rewrapped it around another rod of exactly the same diameter. The broken pieces miraculously reassembled themselves into letters and the letters into words and sentences. Figure 3.1 shows in schematic form how the method works.

If the ciphertext message of this figure is rewritten into rows of six letters, as follows:

```
E V E D Y -
M A S R A -
O H U O L -
C - C B E -
```

the plaintext can be read in ascending columns from left to right. Of course, if the blanks are not marked out and the letters fall across the edges of the strips so that I appears on one and < on another, it becomes somewhat harder to put the letter "K" back together but by no means impossible or very forbidding to one who knows the system. (The Skytale, incidentally, is used as part of the logo of the American

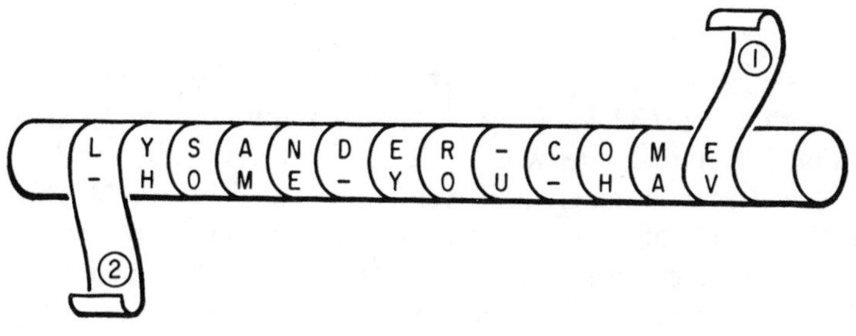

l	k	j	i	h	g	f	e	d	c	b	a	①
L	Y	S	A	N	D	E	R	-	C	O	M	E
-	H	O	M	E	-	Y	O	U	-	H	A	V
E	-	B	E	E	N	-	A	C	C	U	S	E
D	-	O	F	-	I	N	S	U	B	O	R	D
I	N	A	T	I	O	N	-	D	E	L	A	Y
-	F	A	T	A	L	-	-	-	-	-	-	-
②	l	k	j	i	h	g	f	e	d	c	b	a

Points a–a are connected behind the rod as are b–b, c–c, etc. When unrolled, the "ciphertext" beginning at 1 reads EVEDY-MASRA-OHUOL-C-CBE—UCUD-ROAS—EY-NN-D-NIOLENEE-IAAMEFTT SOBOAA YH—NFL-EDI-

Fig. 3.1 A Skytale message.

Cryptogram Association, a group of amateur cryptanalysists who enjoy solving crypts as a hobby.)

Another cipher of the same general class is the *railfence,* which was discussed briefly in a preceding chapter. Again, as with the Skytale, there is little difficulty in reading a message once the scheme is known. With the railfence, the only uncertainty is the height of the "V's." They may be of any height in theory, but in practice they range from perhaps 3 to 10. Suppose we assume that the V's are of height H. Then, each V will contain 2(H − 1) letters. For example, if H = 4, as shown in Fig. 3.2, then each V will contain 2(4 − 1), or six letters.

1						7					
	2				6		8				12
		3		5				9		11	
			4						10		

Fig. 3.2 V's of height 4.

So, if the message consists of M letters, we can try to write it out in V's of various heights until we find the height that makes it read in plaintext.

A message will always consist of some number of complete V's followed by one partial V. Suppose that we have received the ciphertext of Fig. 2.1, namely PSLCLEEEPNEESNHAOADT, and that we wish to see if it was generated by a railfence of height 5. There are eight letters in a V of height 5; therefore, if 5 is the correct height, our twenty-letter ciphertext should be written in two full V's with four letters left over in the partial V. That gives the pattern shown in Fig. 3.3. The ciphertext should then be written a row at a time into spaces 1, 9, 17, 2, 8, 10, 16, 18, etc., as shown in Fig. 3.4, which produces the somewhat ambiguous PCPND HNLS EEATOEE LESA as a purported plaintext. Eventually, of course, we get around to trying V's of height 4, yielding three complete V's and two letters left over that provide the plaintext "Please send help at once" after we reinsert word spaces.

```
1                 9                       17
  2            8    10                 16     18
    3       7          11           15           19
      4   6               12     14                 20
        5                    13
```

Fig. 3.3 V's of height 5 for 20-letter ciphertext.

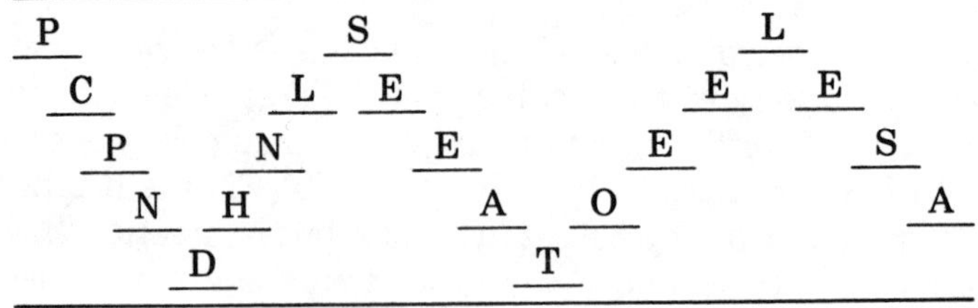

Fig. 3.4 Placement of ciphertext.

It is conventional in cryptography to remove word spaces (except in the amateur amusement known as "the Aristocrat") and then break up the ciphertext into groups of five letters. Word spaces give away lots of information, and it is somewhat easier to keep your place with groups of five letters than with a long string of letters with no spaces.

As our first computer exercise, let us construct a program for reading in plaintext and printing out a railfence encipherment of that text in blocks of five letters. Since we are going to need both the reading and printing parts of this program in many of the other exercises, we will write them as subroutines.

Before we pick up our pencil and start coding, it might be wise to think ahead and plan out exactly what we are going to be doing. Let's start with a list of the operations to be performed:

1. Read in the plaintext
2. Translate into cipher
3. Print out the ciphertext

This list is general enough to be used to describe any of the enciphering problems we will tackle; only step 2 will vary from one cipher to another.

But wait. This railfence cipher requires a parameter: It needs to know the height of the V's. We could, of course, write a program especially tailored for V's of height 7 and another for V's of height 6, and another for . . ., but you probably have the idea already that this might entail quite a bit of work. What we need is to add a step that will read in the parameter of the enciphering method and use it to specialize a general program that can handle any height of fence. Thus our list becomes:

1. Read in the height of fence
2. Read in the plaintext
3. Translate into cipher
4. Print out the ciphertext

We could interchange the order of steps 1 and 2, but let's do it in the order shown.

Now we have to begin to ask some questions about how the internal representation of the message should look so that it will be convenient to manipulate. This information will tell us how to construct the input and output steps. For example, do we want to represent the letters internally as ASCII characters or as numbers between 1 and 26? Do we want to squeeze out blanks on input, as part of the enciphering program, or as a separate subroutine entirely?

It is going to turn out that at various times we will want various combinations of these different operations, sometimes one and sometimes another. Perhaps the best solution, therefore, is to break down each task into as many logically separate tasks as we can and code up each one independently. This approach provides two major advantages. First, it gives flexibility. Second, it makes our programs easier to understand because we can either grub around in the details of how blanks get squeezed out or just say "here the programmer squeezes out blanks" and let it go at that. If we are going to use this subroutining technique, however, we must be very careful to keep track of what each subroutine expects in the way of inputs and what it generates in the way of outputs. We must also keep track of any side effects that our subroutines generate. For example, in the subroutine to squeeze out blanks, we must make sure to update the variable that represents the length of the string.

We still have some more decisions to make before writing a line of code. We must decide how long an input text we will allow and how we are going to tell the computer when we have entered it all. We must decide about punctuation characters; are they permitted or not? I personally have chosen to allow up to 500 characters per message. That seems long enough for most cryptograms and still short enough not to use up too much space. Since many BASIC compilers get indigestion when you try to input commas and semicolons, it seems safer on the whole to eschew punctuation entirely and avoid any such problems. My BASIC compiler being quite happy to accept slashes (/) as an ordinary character, I use the slash as an "end of text" indicator. A little experimentation should tell you if you can use that character or must invent another. You don't want to use Carriage Return because you need that if your message is more than one line long. You would like to have a printing character so that you can be sure if you have entered the end of text indicator or not.

To tackle this problem, we have made up a collection of subroutines that are called from a Railfence Master program (see Program 3.1). This master program first reserves five hundred slots for an input buffer, T%, and a similar number for an output buffer, S%. In BASIC for the PET 2001, the % sign indicates that the variable is restricted to integer values with a range from approximately −32000 to +32000. The reason for using integer variables is that they take only 2 bytes per element as opposed to 5 bytes per element for floating-point numbers. If your BASIC doesn't support integer variables, you can easily cut down the size of T and S if necessary for space reasons.

Program 3.1 Railfence Master Program

```
1  DIM T%(500),S%(500)
10 REM RAILFENCE MASTER PROGRAM
20 PRINT "INPUT NUMBER OF RAILS 3 TO 20"
30 INPUT H
35 REM GET PLAINTEXT OR CIPHERTEXT
40 GOSUB 10000
45 REM SQUEEZE OUT BLANKS
50 GOSUB 10200
55 REM DO THE ENCIPHER OR DECIPHER
60 GOSUB 200
65 REM PRINT RESULTS
70 GOSUB 10300
80 PRINT
90 GOTO 20
```

The enciphering program (Program 3.2) is made up from the master program; the input, squeezing, and output subroutines; and the enciphering subroutine. The deciphering program (Program 3.3) replaces the latter with a deciphering subroutine. The master program calls the input subroutine and squeezes out blanks and all punctuation; it then calls the enciphering or deciphering routine. Finally, it calls the subroutine to print out results and loops on itself.

Program 3.2 Railfence Encipher Routine

```
200  L=0
210  D=2*H-2
220  REM DO TOP RAIL
230  FOR I=1 TO J STEP D
240     L=L+1: S%(L)=T%(I)
250  NEXT I
260  REM DO RAILS 2 THRU H-1
270  FOR R=1 TO H-2
280     L=L+1: S%(L)=T%(R+1)
290     FOR I=D+1 TO J STEP D
300        L=L+1: S%(L)=T%(I-R)
310        IF I+R > J GOTO 330
320        L=L+1: S%(L)=T%(I+R)
330     NEXT I
340  NEXT R
350  REM DO LAST RAIL
360  FOR I=H TO J STEP D
370     L=L+1:  S%(L)=T%(I)
380  NEXT I
390  RETURN
```

Program 3.2 (cont'd) Railfence Encipher Comments

We do this program in three parts—first the top rail, then all the middle rails, and finally the bottom rail.

200 L is a pointer to a slot in the output buffer S% where we are going to assemble the ciphertext letter by letter.

210 D is the distance between peaks of the V's.

230 - 250
We pick off every Dth letter from the input buffer and move it to the output buffer. This processing takes care of the top rail.

260 - 340
Here we do the middle rails. At each peak of the V's we are going to pick off two letters, one to the left of the peak and one to the right.

270 R is one less than the number of the rail we are working on. For example, when we are working on rail 2, we want to take the letters oc-

curring one space before and one after the peak. On rail three we want the letters occurring two spaces before and two after the peak. Rather than running the loop from 2 through H−1 and then continually having to subtract one from the rail number each time we use it, we have run the loop from 1 through H−2. Consequently, we don't have to subtract one all the time. This is a pretty standard trick if not altogether kind to the reader.

280 Since the leftmost peak (at letter 1) has only one letter following it, we move that letter by itself.

290 - 330
I is the number of the peak we are working at. The first "half peak" is at 1; the complete peaks are at D+1, 2D+1, etc.

300 If the peak exists and we haven't dropped out of 330, then the letter R to the left of the peak surely exists; we therefore move it to the output buffer.

310 Since the letter R to the right of the peak may not exist if we are working on the last peak, we test to see if I+R is greater than J.

320 The letter exists and so we move it.

360 - 380
We take out the bottom rail just as we did the top one.

390 We go back to the calling program.

Program 3.3 Railfence Decipher Routine

```
200  L=0
210  D=2*H-2
220  REM DO TOPRAIL
230  FOR I=1 TO J STEP D
240     L=L+1:  S%(I)=T%(L)
250  NEXT I
260  REM DO RAILS 2 THRU H-1
270  FOR R=1 TO H-2
280     L=L+1:  S%(R+1)=T%(L)
290     FOR I=D+1 TO J STEP D
300        L=L+1:  S%(I-R)=T%(L)
310        IF I+R>J  GOTO 330
320        L=L+1:  S%(I+R)=T%(L)
330     NEXT I
340  NEXT R
350  REM DO LAST RAIL
360  FOR I=H TO J STEP D
370     L=L+1:  S%(I)=T%(L)
380  NEXT I
390  RETURN
```

Program 3.3 (cont'd) Railfence Decipher Comments

The method is identical to the encipher routine except that we take successive letters of the ciphertext and " spit them out " in the output buffer according to the rules.

The enciphering routine expects the squeezed plaintext in the vector T% and expects the variable J to be equal to the number of characters in the input buffer. It generates the ciphertext (in vector S%) in three stages: the top rail first, then rails 2 through H-1, and lastly the bottom rail. The pointer to the last character entered in the output buffer, L, is incremented before a new character is added to that buffer. The distance between letters on the top rail, D, is equal to 2*H−2. For the top rail, we step along taking every D^{th} letter, starting with the first. For the middle rails, we take two letters on each step, one left of the "peak" and one to its right. Finally, on the bottom rail, we take every D^{th} letter again but start with the Hth letter.

To decipher, we take successive letters from the ciphertext and place them in the proper slots of the plaintext buffer. To read in the text, we input a string (line 10050) and then step across each of its letters (Program 3.4). LEN(A$) is the length of the string. MID(A$,I,1) gives the Ith letter from string A$ and ASC (letter) gives the ASCII representation of that letter as a number. ASCII representation of the letter A = 65, B = 66, etc. Subtracting 64 from these representations gives us the values, A = 1, B = 2, . . ., Z = 26. After this conversion and translation, the slash becomes "−17"; therefore, if we find a slash,

Program 3.4 Subroutine to Read in Text

```
10000  REM READ IN TEXT
10010  J=0
10020  F=0
10030  PRINT
10040  PRINT "ENTER TEXT.AS MANY LINES AS YOU LIKE.END
       WITH A SLASH(/)"
10050  INPUT A$
10060  FOR I=1 TO LEN(A$)
10070     B=ASC(MID$(A$,I,1))-64
10080     IF B=-17 THEN F=1
10090     J=J+1
10100     T%(J)=B
10110  NEXT I
10120  IF F=O GOTO 10050
10130  J=J-1
10140  RETURN
```

Program 3.4 (cont'd) Subroutine to Read in Text Comments

10010 J is a counter of the number of characters that appear in the input text. It is also used as a pointer to the slot in the buffer T% where we put the next letter.

10020 F is a flag. When we encounter a slash, we set the flag to 1 and don't go back to get any more input.

10050 Get a line of text from the keyboard.

10060 - 10110
Pick off the letters from the input line (A$) one at a time, translate them, and put them into T%. LEN (A$) is the number of characters in A$.

10070 This line translates a character to a number. As shown, the letters take the values, A = 1, B = 2, . . . , Z = 26. Other characters are outside the range, 1–26.

10080 A slash will get translated to a negative 17. If we see a slash, we set the flag F to 1.

10090 - 10100
We bump the pointer and put the number into T%.

10120 If we haven't seen a slash yet we go back for more input.

10130 We put the slash into T% and count it in line 10090. Since this is wrong, we subtract 1 from J to get the correct count of characters up to, but not including, the slash.

---

we set flag F to 1. In line 10130, we set J back by 1 so that the slash isn't included in the count of letters in the buffer T%.

The blank-and-punctuation squeezing routine tests to see if the character is outside the range, 1–26 (Program 3.5). If so, the character is skipped; otherwise it is moved to the left as required. Finally, the count of characters, J, is corrected (line 10270), and the subroutine does a return to the calling program.

Program 3.5 Squeeze Out Blanks Subroutine

```
10200  REM SQUEEZE OUT BLANKS
10210  I=0
10220  FOR K=1 TO J
10230     IF T%(K)< 1 OR T%(K) > 26 GOTO 10260
10240     I=I+1
10250     T%(I)=T%(K)
10260  NEXT K
10270  J=I
10280  RETURN
```

Program 3.5 (cont'd) Squeeze Out Blanks Comments

This routine is going to go through the buffer T% and remove everything that isn't one of the letters A through Z and then squeeze the letters that remain.

10210 I is a pointer to the place where we are going to *put* the characters.

10220 - 10260
K is a pointer to the character we are presently examining. It runs from 1 through J.

10230 If the character is not a letter, we ignore it and look at the next character.

10240 Since it turned out to be a letter, we bump the pointer I and put the Kth character into the Ith slot.

10270 We set J equal to the pointer I because J is supposed to indicate to the rest of the world how many characters there are in the buffer.

The printing routine is a double loop that prints out five blocks of five characters per line for all the letters in the buffer S% (Program 3.6). If you want to print some other buffer, you will have to change the variable name in line 10360. The function CHR$ (number) converts a number to a character, but the number must be in the range, 0–255.

Program 3.6 Print Out Results Subroutine

```
10300 REM PRINT IN BLOCKS OF FIVE
10310 PRINT
10320 I=0
10330 FOR K=1 TO 5
10340    FOR L=1 TO 5
10350       I=I+1
10360       PRINT CHR$(S%(I)+64);
10370       IF I=J THEN RETURN
10380    NEXT L
10390    PRINT " ";
10400 NEXT K
10410 PRINT
10420 GOTO 10330
```

Program 3.6 (cont'd) Print Out Results Comments

This routine prints out the buffer S% in five blocks of five characters per line. Since BASIC subroutines won't accept parameters, you have to change line 10360 if you want to print some other buffer.

10330 K counts the blocks on the line.
10340 L counts the letters within a block.
10350 I points to a letter in the buffer that is going to be printed.
10370 If I = J, we have done all the letters in the buffer and we return to the calling program. Since this exits from inside the K and L loops, it is often considered to be poor programming practice, but it would appear to be more intuitively obvious and less complicated than a clumsy arrangement with flags and tests.
10390 Print the space between the blocks.
10410 Print the carriage return after five blocks.
10420 Go back and do another line.

Since the railfence can readily be solved by exhaustive search of all possible heights, we present a program that uses the decipher subroutine (among others) to list all possible decipherings and allow the user to read out the one that makes sense in English (Program 3.7).

Program 3.7 Rail Search

```
  1  DIM T%(500),S%(500)
 10  REM SEARCH ALL POSSIBLE HEIGHTS
 20  REM GET CIPHERTEXT
 40  GOSUB 10000
 45  REM SQUEEZE OUT BLANKS
 50  GOSUB 10200
 60  FOR H=3 TO 20
 65     REM DECIPHER FOR HEIGHT H
 70     GOSUB 200
 80     REM PRINT RESULTS
 90     GOSUB 10300
100     PRINT "-";H;
110  NEXT H
120  GOTO 10
```

Program 3.7 (cont'd) Rail Search Comments

40 We get the ciphertext.
50 Squeeze out the blanks and punctuation.
60 - 110
Loop on H.
70 Decipher, assuming that the height is H.
90 Print the results.
100 Print the height H of this decipherment.
120 Allow the user to enter new ciphertext.

4

Complete Columnar Tramps

A second form of transposition cipher is called *columnar.* In this chapter we will examine the simplest form of columnar cipher, in which all columns are of equal length; it is called a *complete columnar.* In the next chapter we will look at the more complicated problems brought out by having the columns of unequal length.

The classic way to construct columnar tramps is, of course, with pencil and paper. As usual, you should first construct and then solve several ciphers by hand before you attempt to write computer programs for doing them. Suppose that the message you wish to send is "Arrive harbor at midnight with fifty bales" and that you and your confederate have agreed that you will use the keyword "Smokes." Since the keyword has six letters in it, you write the message in six columns as follows:

```
A R R I V E
H A R B O R
A T M I D N
I G H T W I
T H F I F T
Y B A L E S
```

It turns out, by coincidence, that this message has six rows as well as six columns. Had the message been longer, it would have had more rows. The only requirement for a complete columnar is that the last row come out even so that all columns will be of the same length.

Examining the keyword, we find that when the letters of the word SMOKES are rearranged in alphabetical order, we have EKMOSS. Putting numbers over the letters in their proper alphabetical ordering, we have:

```
5 3 4 2 1 6
S M O K E S
```

with 1 over E, 2 over K, 5 over the first S, and 6 over the second one. If we had a keyword like WHISKEY, we would write:

```
6 2 3 5 4 1 7
W H I S K E Y
```

Repeated letters are numbered from left to right as we did with SMOKES. Thus, we find that the keyword has two distinct functions:

1. It helps us remember how many columns to use.
2. It gives us a set of numbers to write over the message block.

Writing the numbers from SMOKES over the message block, we get

```
5 3 4 2 1 6
-----------
A R R I V E
H A R B O R
A T M I D N
I G H T W I
T H F I F T
Y B A L E S
```

and we are ready to encipher the message. We read out the columns in the order of the numbers above them—1, 2, 3, 4, 5, and 6—to get:

VODWFE IBITIL RATGHB RRMHFA AHAITY ERNITS

and this is the message we send to our confederate. It is usual to divide the message into groups of five letters, each with a space between them, so that we would probably send the message as

VODWF EIBIT ILRAT GHBRR MHFAA HAITY ERNIT S

The reason for doing this is that if all messages are sent in five-letter groups, it gives an interceptor no clue about the structure of the message.

When our confederate receives the message, he first counts the number of letters in it and gets 36. Dividing 36 by the number of letters in SMOKES, he comes up with six letters per column. Then he writes down the key numbers derived from SMOKES and, starting in the column labeled "1," writes down six letters and then six more in the column labeled "2," and so forth, until the block is reconstructed:

```
5 3 4 2 1 6
-----------
      I U
      B O
      I D
      T W
      I F
      L E
```

Almost at once we receive the reply,

ADLEA OWSEE VYTOE RNLTI RDTCI RNRFE
AEYAO LCDRG MX

This has 42 letters or seven per column. We write down the key numbers and reconstruct the message seven letters at a time, as follows:

5	3	4	2	1	6
F	E	D	S	A	L
E	R	T	E	D	C
A	N	C	E	L	D
E	L	I	V	E	R
Y	T	R	Y	A	G
A	I	N	T	O	M
O	R	R	O	W	X

This reads, "Feds alerted. Cancel deliver. Try again tomorrow. X." The X is not a signature but a "null" or meaningless letter added to the last row of the block to make the row come out even. Since X is used so often as a null (along with Q and K and J), our confederate would have been wiser to use a vowel or common letter like S or T. That way he wouldn't have given any clue as to location of the last column of the cipher.

Try the following ciphers for practice to make sure that you understand the method involved:

1. Keyword = JONES	Message: ETTSU OTROA HSBOE IQION BTETO THTEN
2. Keyword = SMITTEN	Message: ILREG XTADH SEUHE WYHTO EDEXO IVEAT OVTOT RNEHL OX
3. Keyword = CLANDESTINE	Message: MTSUA ECAHA ITTRA IDOOD NNWMT YNROS GKSSL TOFUB PBEEB SNHHM OTNSN ADEIE IRISL S

Programs

We now need a program that will read in a keyword and then read in plaintext and output ciphertext. Before we attempt this program, it will be helpful to look at columnar transposition in a slightly different fashion. Suppose that the key number sequence (derived from the keyword PLAY) is 4213 and that the plaintext is

ABCD EFGH IJKL MNOP QRST

Rewriting this as a block, we have

A B C D
E F G H
I J K L
M N O P
Q R S T

Let us replace the letters with numbers since that may make the point a little clearer,

1	2	3	4
5	6	7	8
9	10	11	12
13	14	15	16
17	18	19	20
21	22	23	24

and suppose that we are going to read out the third column first. We will get the third, seventh, eleventh, fifteenth, nineteenth, and twenty-third letter of the plaintext. Since we are reading the third column, we begin with the third letter of the plaintext, and, since the key is four letters long and hence the block consists of four columns, we will take out every fourth letter following the third letter. In general, for column C and keyword of length N, we will take out letters C, C+N, C+2N, . . . to the end of the plaintext.

Suppose now that we have a table telling which columns to read out. Call it the "order table." For example, if the keyword is

	M	O	N	D	A	Y
Order:	3	5	4	2	1	6
Column No.:	1	2	3	4	5	6

we first read out column 5, then column 4, and so on. The order table will then consist of the numbers,

5
4
1
3
2
6

Given order table OT, we can easily generate the ciphertext, as follows:

```
10  FOR I = 1 TO N
20     C = OT(I)
30     FOR R = C TO J STEP N
40        L = L+1 : S%(L) = T%(R)
50     NEXT R
60  NEXT I
```

In line 10, N is the number of the columns, that is, the number of letters in the keyword. Line 20 selects the column to read out, as determined by the order table. Line 30 selects successive rows down the column, stepping N letters at a time until we get to the end of the plaintext.

If we should happen to have ciphertext in buffer T and be building plaintext in S, then line 60 should read

```
60  L = L+1 : S%(R) = T%(L)
```

Now all we need to do is generate the order table from the keyword (Program 4.1), and we will have programs for enciphering and deciphering both complete and incomplete columnar transpositions (Programs 4.2 and 4.3).

Program 4.1 Subroutine to Generate Order Table

```
    2  DIM OT(30)
10500  REM GENERATE ORDER TABLE FROM KEYWORD
10510  PRINT "INPUT KEYWORD UP TO 30 LETTERS-WITHOUT
       SPACES"
10520  INPUT A$
10530  N = LEN (A$)
10540  FOR I = 1 TO N
10550  T%(I) = ASC(MID$(A$,I,1))-64
10560  NEXT I
10570  FOR I = 1 TO N
10580  M = 200
10590  FOR J = 1 TO N
10600       IF T%(J) <M THEN M=T%(J) : T2=J
10610  NEXT J
10620  T%(T2) = 100
10630  OT(I) = T2
10640  NEXT I
10650  RETURN
```

Program 4.1 (cont'd) Generating Order Table Comments

This routine will generate an "order table" from a keyword.

10520 Get the keyword up to 30 characters.

10530 N is the number of characters in the keyword.

10540 - 10560
Translate the characters to numbers: A = 1, B = 2, . . . , Z = 26.

10570 - 10640
I is the slot in the order table we are going to fill.

10580 M is the "minimum" we have found. We start with a large number in M.

10590 - 10610
J scans all the letters of the keyword, looking for the smallest value—the alphabetically earliest letter.

10600 If the Jth letter is less than the smallest we have found up to now, we put J into M and a pointer to the place we found J into T2.

10620 T2 is pointing at the "smallest" letter remaining in the keyword. We "wipe out" that letter by setting it equal to 100; thus we won't select it again. Since 100 is greater than 26, the number representing Z, any real remaining letter will be less than 100.

10630 Now we copy the pointer (to that smallest letter we just wiped out) into the Ith slot of the order table. Thus, if the keyword was BLANK on the first pass, the smallest letter will be A in slot 3. We erase the A and set OT(1) to 3. Since the next pass finds B in slot 1, OT(2) = 1, and so on.

Program 4.2 Enciphering Columnar Tramps

```
 10  REM COLUMNAR TRAMPS
 20  GOSUB 10500
 30  GOSUB 10000
 40  GOSUB 10200
 50  L = 0
 60  FOR I = 1 TO N
 70     C = OT(I)
 80     FOR R = C TO J STEP N
110        L = L+1 : S%(L) = T%(R)
120     NEXT R
130  NEXT I
140  GOSUB 10300
150  PRINT
160  GOTO 20
```

Program 4.2 (cont'd) Enciphering Columnar Tramps Comments

20 Generate an order table.
30 Get the plaintext.
40 Squeeze out blanks.
50 L is a pointer to a slot in the output buffer.
60 - 130
N is the number of letters in the keyword and hence the number of columns.
70 C is the column we are to do.
80 - 120
R is the letter to be plucked out of the plaintext. We are going to take the letters from slots C, C+N, C+2N, . . . until we hit the end of the plaintext.
110 Bump the pointer L and move the letter.
140 Print out the ciphertext.

Program 4.3 Decipering Columnar Tramps

This program is the same as Program 4.2 except that

```
110  L = L+1 : S%(R)=T%(L)
```

Program 4.3 (cont'd) Deciphering Columnar Tramps Comments

These comments are the same as those for Program 4.2 except that in statement 110 we move the Lth letter from the input buffer (the ciphertext) to the Rth slot of the output buffer (the decoded plaintext).

From Keyword to Order Table

Since translation from keyword to order table is a common task for many transposition-type ciphers, we will perform this task as a subroutine, as shown in Program 4.1. Statements 10500 through 10560 get the keyword and translate A's to 1's, B's to 2's, . . . , Z's to 26's. N is the length of the keyword.

Now, consider lines 10590 to 10610. J is a pointer to a letter in the keyword and ranges from 1 to N. We are going to search the keyword for the smallest (alphabetically earliest) letter remaining in the keyword. M, which is the value of the minimum, starts at 200, and since the letters go from 1(A) to 26(Z), that value won't remain long as the minimum. When we find a letter less than M, we put its value into M and set pointer T2 to point at the place we found that letter in the input keyword.

When we exit from 10610 the very first time into the program, T2 will be pointing at the smallest letter of the keyword; if there are two or more occurrences of that letter, it will be pointing at the first such occurrence. Since the position of that smallest letter also indicates the number of the first column to be read out, however, we put its location (T2) into the first slot of the output table (line 10630). To make sure we won't keep on getting the same letter over and over again, we effectively "erase" it from the keyword by overwriting it with the number 100. We repeat this until we have done all N letters of the keyword and then return to the calling program.

Solving the Complete Columnar Without a Keyword

Suppose now that you are the interceptor and have received the following message:

LEAWX YNLTR IPOIU TOLCT EAIHR ETOQA BLEUT

For various reasons, you are certain that the message is a complete columnar but have no idea of the keyword. The first thing to do is count letters. Here we have 35 letters that can make up a block either 5 by 7 or 7 by 5. At this point it is just luck which block we pick to work with. If one doesn't seem to work out, we try the other. So, by pure chance, let us try 5 columns by 7 rows. We write seven letters in a column and a total of five columns, as follows:

```
L L U A Q
E T T I A
A R O H B
W I L R L
X P C E E
Y O T T U
N I E O T
```

It is helpful to write each column on a separate strip of paper, making sure that letters in corresponding rows line up. Quadrille paper is very handy for this. What we are going to do is shuffle the strips around, trying first one combination and then another until the rows begin to make words or (in the beginning) likely pairs of letters. In this example, we are going to take advantage of the fact, which everybody knows, that in English we never find a Q unless it is followed by a U. Right there in the first row we find column 5 beginning with Q and column 3 beginning with U; we therefore set these two columns next to each other in the order 5, 3:

5	3
Q	U
A	T
B	O
L	L
E	C
U	T
T	E

If this is the correct alignment, most of the pairs of letters should be common combinations in English. Since all these pairs are very common, we have no hesitancy about accepting this alignment. One or two uncommon pairs can be excused as coming at the joints between words, but the easier it is to imagine words for each pair, the more likely the alignment is to be correct.

Next, looking in row 5, we find an X. If this is not a null or a substitute for a period, we can take advantage of the fact that X is almost always preceded by an E. Since there are two E's in row 5 (columns 4 and 5), let us try column 1 preceded by column 4 (since column 5 is already followed by column 3, it can't be followed by column 1):

4	1
A	L
I	E
H	A
R	W
E	X
T	Y
O	N

Every pair here is fairly common except the RW of row 4. let us tentatively accept this pairing and now try to fit in the remaining column (2) somewhere. There are four places it could go: before column 4, after column 1, before column 5, or after column 3. Lacking any obvious clues, let's try them all:

	(A)			*(B)*			*(C)*			*(D)*		
	2	4	1	4	1	2	2	5	3	5	3	2
1	L	A	L	A	L	L	L	Q	U	Q	U	L
2	T	I	E	I	E	T	T	A	T	A	T	T
3	R	H	A	H	A	R	R	B	O	B	O	R
4	I	R	W	R	W	I	I	L	L	L	L	I

	(A)			*(B)*			*(C)*			*(D)*		
	2	4	1	4	1	2	2	5	3	5	3	2
5	P	E	X	E	X	P	P	E	C	E	C	P
6	O	T	Y	T	Y	O	O	U	T	U	T	O
7	I	O	N	O	N	I	I	T	E	T	E	I

For starters, we can eliminate *(D)* because QUL is not part of an English word and there is no way to make it out as the junction of two words. (A) is somewhat suspect because LAL in row 1, although possible, is rare. Moreover, rows 3 and 4 of *(A)* are both unusual enough to cause slightly raised eyebrows. *(B)*, on the other hand, is acceptable. Row 4 of *(B)* might be "earwig" or it might be a word junction. Row 6 is also a likely word junction. If we assume temporarily that *(B)* is correct and that 5, 3 is a correct pair, then we have only two possible choices for arranging the columns:

41253 or 53412

The first of these makes the message "All quiet at harbor. Will expect you tonite."

The following message was intercepted in a military situation:

MKBOH RSNAN FUFNY IRNRC NANOT EEOEC ARSOT
TGAXI MWETO DRNE

Since it has 49 letters, this message, if it is a complete columnar, must be 7 × 7. Reconstructing the block, we get:

	(1)	(2)	(3)	(4)	(5)	(6)	(7)
1	M	N	Y	A	E	T	E
2	K	A	I	N	C	G	T
3	B	N	R	O	A	A	O
4	O	F	N	T	R	X	D
5	H	U	R	E	S	I	R
6	R	F	C	E	O	M	N
7	S	N	N	O	T	W	E

In row 4 we find an X but no E to precede it; perhaps this X is a sentence separator. Scanning the rows for letter pairs with strong affinity, we find no TH or EX or QU possibilities, but in row 2 we do find both C and K, which often go together. Lacking anything better to try, let us write out column 5 followed by column 1. With paper strips this is the work of a moment, and if it doesn't pan out, we can abandon it with small loss of time.

5	1
E	M
C	K
A	B
R	O
S	H
O	R
T	S

All these pairs are plausible. If CK in row 2 is correct, it should be preceded by a vowel. There are two in this row—namely, A and I—but it might be the case that columns 5, 1 stood at the beginning of the row and the vowel preceding CK came at the end of the previous row. That might be the A from column 4 or the E from column 7. Before we try those, let's try the two possibilities from the same row, giving the following partial blocks:

2	5	1
N	E	M
A	C	K
N	A	B
F	R	O
U	S	H
F	O	R
N	T	S

3	5	1
Y	E	M
I	C	K
R	A	B
N	R	O
R	S	H
C	O	R
N	T	S

Since either of these would be acceptable, there is not much help here. Notice, however, that the first combination leaves INGT unused in row 2, while the second leaves ANGT. Now, although ANG is possible, ING is much more frequent a combination. If we set that triple up, we get:

3	4	6
Y	A	T
I	N	G
R	O	A
N	T	X
R	E	I
C	E	M
N	O	W

YAT is unusual and will require a word boundary; ING is a very common triple; ROA is acceptable; if X is a null used as a sentence terminator, then NT will come at the end of a word and that is a very common word ending; REI is a bit strange, but not impossible; CEM is conceivable; and NOW is a word in its own right.

If we have 251 set up and 346 also set up, it might be natural to put them side by side, which gives us

2	5	1	3	4	6
N	E	M	Y	A	T
A	C	K	I	N	G
N	A	B	R	O	A
F	R	O	N	T	X
U	S	H	R	E	I
F	O	R	C	E	M
N	T	S	N	O	W

We will leave it to you to find a happy home for column 7 and read off the message.

Selecting the Correct Block

In the foregoing discussion we sidestepped the problem of selecting the correct block dimensions. Sometimes nature is not quite so kind, however, and we are faced with two or more blocks that we would like to choose among without having to spend a lot of time making up and shuffling strips for those that will never work out. There is a method, which while not infallible, often gives guidance. It is called the *vowel distribution method.*

Studies have shown that very nearly 40 percent of all letters occurring in English are vowels: A, E, I, O, U, and Y. This is true not only in the large but also in the small; that is, it is true not only of long paragraphs, but of short sentences and even groups of contiguous letters extracted from sentences. Of course, we seldom find vowels in a row of a block totaling exactly 40 percent, but usually the percentage falls close to that figure.

Consider the example of 56 letters arranged as a 7 × 8 block (correct) and as an 8 × 7 block (wrong), as shown at the top of page 35.

Of the 56 letters, 23 are vowels, or 41.1 percent. In the first case, with 7 letters per row, we would expect about 2.8 vowels per row, and we never find fewer than 2 or more than 4. In the second case, with 8 letters per row, we expect 3.3 vowels and find variations from 0 to 6. We want numbers of vowels per row that cluster as tightly as possible around the expected value. The less variation we find the better.

For the block on the left, we expect (23/56) × 7, or 2.87 vowels per row and find the numbers clustering quite closely around this value.

EOTRU PSTAF FOTRS HCUIW IOUIH SNNOB CSOMD SNLHO NUOOT EANES ULOMS E

E	A	C	H	O	N	E	4		E	T	S	O	O	S	O	S	4
O	F	U	S	M	U	S	3		O	A	H	U	B	N	O	U	5
T	F	I	N	D	O	U	3		T	F	C	I	C	L	T	L	1
R	O	W	N	S	O	L	2		R	F	U	H	S	H	E	O	3
U	T	I	O	N	T	O	4		U	O	I	S	O	O	A	M	6
P	R	O	B	L	E	M	2		P	T	W	N	M	N	N	S	0
S	S	U	C	H	A	S	2		S	R	I	N	D	U	E	E	4
T	H	I	S	O	N	E	3										

For the block on the right, we expect (23/56) × 8, or 3.28 vowels per row and see that there is a substantial deviation from this value. All you have to do is consider the row with no vowels at all or the row with 6 vowels to conclude that this arrangement is wrong. (No shuffling of the order of the columns will change the number of vowels per row.) This time it is easy to choose between the two blocks, but usually the choice is not so clear-cut. Fortunately, a mathematical operation exists that can measure the dispersion of a set of numbers. It is called the *second moment,* or *variance,* and the formula is

$$M_2 = \frac{\sum_{i=1}^{n} (X_i - \overline{X})^2}{n}$$

where n = the number of numbers, $\overline{X}$ = the expected value, and X_i (i = 1, 2, . . . , n) are the numbers whose dispersion we want to measure. The parentheses represent the difference between each observation and the average value. If we just added these differences, the result would be zero, but if we square each difference, we make sure, first, that all contributions are positive and, second, that the larger differences are emphasized.

With a modest amount of algebra (see any introductory book on statistics), we can rearrange the equation for M_2 so that

$$M_2 = \frac{\sum_{i=1}^{n} X_i^2 - \overline{X}^2}{n}$$

We can compute this in BASIC, as follows:

```
S=0
T=0
FOR I=1 TO N
   S=S+X(I)*X(I)
   T=T+X(I)
NEXT I
   T=T/N
M2=S/N-T*T
```

For the sake of practice, we can also compute these by hand for the lefthand block, as follows:

$$\begin{aligned} \Sigma X_i^2 &= 4^2 + 3^2 + 3^2 + 2^2 + 4^2 + 2^2 + 2^2 + 3^2 \\ &= 16 + 9 + 9 + 4 + 16 + 4 + 4 + 9 \\ &= 71 \\ T &= 2.87 \\ T^2 &= 8.26 \\ M2 &= 71/8 - 8.26 \\ M2 &= .615 \end{aligned}$$

For the righthand block, we get

$$\begin{aligned} \Sigma X_i^2 &= 4^2 + 5^2 + 1^2 + 3^2 + 6^2 + 0^2 + 4^2 \\ &= 16 + 25 + 1 + 9 + 36 + 0 + 16 \\ &= 103 \\ T &= 3.28 \\ T^2 &= 10.79 \\ M2 &= 103/7 - 10.79 \\ &= 3.92 \end{aligned}$$

Doing this tells us what we knew already—that the lefthand block (the correct one) has low variance whereas the righthand block (the wrong one) has higher variance.

As a second example, let us look back at the 35-letter message on page 30. The two possible blocks are as follows:

```
L L U A Q    2     L Y I T E E B    4
E T T I A    3     E N P O A T L    3
A R O H B    2     A L O L I O E    5
W I L R L    1     W T I C H Q U    2
X P C E E    2     X R U T R A T    2
Y O T T U    3
N I E O T    3
```

We already know that the lefthand block is the correct one, but a mere look at the numbers offers no obvious choice. If, however, we compute M_2, we get 0.5 for the lefthand block and 1.16 for the right-hand block. This difference does not provide nearly as dramatic an example as the previous one, but it is at least in the right direction. Sometimes the fluctuations of chance will give us the wrong answer when we look for the block with the smaller variance, but it is always worthwhile to try the block with the smaller variance first.

It is easy to find the factors of numbers less than a hundred by eye, but to do so by computer is next to impossible if the language does not have a function that takes the integer part of a variable. With such a function, we can write

"IF (X−C*INT(X/C))=0 GOTO________"

and go off to the target of the jump if, and only if, C is a factor of X. At the target address we can compute M2 for a block with C columns and X/C rows and print out C, X/C, and M2. If we let C range from 2 to X/2 we will get all possible block arrangements. The user can then select the C that he wants to look at (not always the one with the smallest M2 when random fluctuations cause the variance test to fail), and the machine should print out or display the block for that C. If your machine doesn't give hard copy, you should make a note of the various possible C's and M2's so that you don't have to keep recomputing them.

Assume that we have read the ciphertext in, digitized it, and found a possible C. How do we now compute the number of vowels per row so that we can compute M2?

Once the letters are digitized (A = 1, B = 2, . . . , Z = 26), the six vowels AEIOUY are represented by the numbers 1, 5, 9, 15, 21, and 25. Any time a ciphertext character is equal to one of these digits, it represents a vowel, and we should increment the count for that row. To select the characters that make up row I, we select the characters with indices: I, I + 1*R, I + 2*R, and so on. For C columns and R rows, we can compute M2 as follows:

```
FOR I=1 TO R
   V=0
   FOR K=1 TO C
      L=T%(I+K*R)
      IF L=1 THEN V=V+1
      IF L=5 THEN V=V+1
      IF L=9 THEN V=V+1
      IF L=15 THEN V=V+1
      IF L=21 THEN V=V+1
      IF L=25 THEN V=V+1
   NEXT K
   S=S+V*V
   T=T+V
NEXT I
T=T/N
M2=S/N−T*T
```

To print out a block, we use the same indexing scheme, in which R is the number of rows and C is the number of columns.

```
L(1)=1
FOR I=1 TO R
   FOR K=0 TO C-1
      L(2)=T%(I+K*R)
      A$=CHR$(L(2)+64)
      PRINT A$; " ";
   NEXT K
   PRINT
NEXT I
```

A program for analyzing complete columnar tramps with unknown key for the proper block size is shown in Program 4.4; for finding the number of vowels per row in Program 4.5; for printing out a matrix of NC columns and NR rows in Program 4.6; and for calculating variance in Program 4.7.

Program 4.4 Analyzing Complete Columnar Tramps with Unknown Key for Proper Block Size

```
10   REM READ IN TEXT
20   GOSUB 10000
30   REM SQUEEZE OUT BLANKS
40   GOSUB 10200
50   REM TRY ALL POSSIBLE VALUES OF NC-NUMBER OF
     COLUMNS
60   FOR NC=2 TO J/2
70      IF (J-NC*INT(J/NC) <> GOTO 160
80      NR=J/NC
90      PRINT NC; NR,
100  REM GO FIND NUMBER OF VOWELS PER ROW
110     GOSUB 300
115     V(0)=NR
120  REM NOW COMPUTE THE VARIANCE
130     GOSUB 10700
140  REM PRINT VARIANCE
150     PRINT V2
160  NEXT NC
170  REM NOW PRINT OUT TRIAL MATRICES
180  PRINT "HOW MANY COLUMNS?";
190  INPUT NC
200  IF (J-NC*INT(J/NC)) <> THEN PRINT "NOT EVEN
     ROWS": GOTO 180
```

```
210   NR=J/NC
220   REM PRINT MATRIX
230   GOSUB 500
240   PRINT
250   GOTO 180
```

Program 4.4 (cont'd) Analyzing Complete Columnar Tramps Comments

This program is going to try to find the correct block size by looking for the arrangement with the most even distribution of vowels per line.

20 Read in the ciphertext.
40 Squeeze out the blanks.
60 - 160
NC is the number of columns we are trying. It will range from 2 to half the number of letters in the crypt.
70 We test to see if NC is a factor of J (see main text). If it isn't, we try the next value for NC.
80 The number of rows NR is NC/J.
90 Print NC and NR.
110 Go count the number of vowels on each row.
130 Go compute the variance of these numbers.
150 Print out the variance.
180 We have done the above for all factors of J; we therefore ask the user what block he wants us to construct.
200 We check to see that what he said was a factor of J.
230 We go print out the block.
250 Go back and try another block.

Program 4.5 Finding Vowels per Row for Complete Columnar

```
300   REM NC=NUMBER OF COLUMNS, NR = NUMBER OF ROWS
320   FOR R=1 TO NR
330      V(R)=0
340      FOR C=1 TO NC
350         X=T%(R+NR*C-NR)
360         IF X=1 GOTO 430
370         IF X=5 GOTO 430
380         IF X=9 GOTO 430
390         IF X=15 GOTO 430
400         IF X=21 GOTO 430
410         IF X=25 GOTO 430
```

```
420         GOTO 440
430         V(R)=V(R)+1
440       NEXT C
450    NEXT R
460    RETURN
```

Program 4.5 (cont'd) Finding Vowels Per Row Comments

This subroutine counts how many vowels there are per row of a tentative block with NC columns and NR rows.

320 - 450
R is the row of the block we are working on.

330 The count of vowels on this row is set to zero.

340 - 440
C is the column of the row we are looking at.

350 - 410
If the letter is the Cth column and R^{th} row is a vowel (AEIOUY), add 1 to the vowel count; otherwise, do not.

460 This routine returns with V(1), the number of vowels on row 1; V(2), the number of vowels on row 2; etc.

Program 4.6 Printing Out a Matrix of NC Columns and NR Rows

```
500  REM NC=NUMBER OF COLUMNS, NR=NUMBER OF ROWS
510  FOR R=1 TO NR
520     FOR C=1 TO NC
530        PRINT CHR$ (T% (R+NR*C-NR)+64);
540     NEXT C
550     PRINT
560  NEXT R
570  PRINT
580  RETURN
```

Program 4.6 (cont'd) Printing Out a Matrix Comments

510 - 560
NR is the number of rows and R is the one we are working on.

520 - 540
NC is the number of columns and C is the column we are working on.

530 Get the letter from T% that is in the Rth row and C^{th} column, translate it to an ASCII character, and print it out.

550 Carriage return at end of row.

Program 4.7 Variance

```
10700  REM COMPUTE VARIANCE OF VECTOR V. V(O)=NUMBER
       OF ELEMENTS. RETURN ANSWER IN V2
10710  S1=0
10720  T1=0
10730  FOR I1=1 TO V(0)
10740     S1=S1+V(I1)*V(I1)
10750     T1=T1+V(I1)
10760  NEXT I1
10770  T1=T1/V(0)
10780  V2=S1/V(0)-T1*T1
10790  RETURN
```

Program 4.7 (cont'd) Variance Comments

Compute the variance of the numbers in the vector V. V(0) tells how many numbers are involved.

10710 S1 is the sum of squares and is set to zero.
10720 T1 is the sum of entries.
10730 - 10760
I1 runs through all elements of the vector.
10740 Add the square of this element to S1.
10750 Add the element to T1.
10770 Change T1 to be the average of the elements.
10780 Compute the variance and put it in V2.

Using Digram Frequencies

Until now we have used the computer mostly for scut work, and it is not clear how we would employ a machine to match up columns so that we can tell which ones "look good" in comparison to the others. It is hard, if not impossible, to describe in language understandable to a computer how a human being intuitively recognizes word fragments and rejects improbable combinations. Fortunately, this is not necessary because a mechanical procedure already exists that systematizes a lot of our intuition. It involves something called *digram frequencies.*

A large body of English text is available in computer-readable form called the "Brown University Corpus." It consists of excerpts from newspapers, magazines, books, and many other sources. Raj Wall and Robert Gonter of our university were kind enough to write a program that went through the Brown tape and made a count of the number of times it found an A followed by A, A followed by B, A followed by C, etc., down through Z followed by A, Z followed by B, . . . , Z followed by Z. That is, their programs discovered how many times in four million letters the 26 × 26, or 676, different possible digrams or letter pairs occurred. Actually, they did this twice, once counting digrams across word divisions and the second time not counting two letters separated by a space as a pair. If, for example, the text read

THE PRESIDENT SAID . . . .

the first program, ignoring word divisions, would count a TH, an HE, an EP, a PR, and so on, whereas the second program, respecting word divisions, would not count the EP as a digram. Both counting methods are useful, and the results are reproduced in Appendices C and D of this book. Since the tapes contain many proper names, both American and foreign, together with initials and abbreviations, we find some quite unusual digrams having nonzero frequencies in the tables.

We are going to use these tables of digram frequency to make our computer decide which column should be put next to which other column. By putting two columns next to one another, we create a set of digrams automatically. If all, or most, of the digrams we create by juxtaposing columns I and J are of high frequency, then it is entirely possible, perhaps even likely, that these two columns stood next to each other in the original plaintext block before the columns were transposed. Assuming that the original plaintext was in English (in this book we will always make that assumption), the two adjacent columns must contain letter pairs that are common, or at least possible, in English.

Let's run through an example by hand to get a feeling for the method. Take the 35-letter message from the smuggler saying, "All quiet at harbor will expect you tonight." Assume that we have decided already that it breaks down into five columns of seven letters but that we have not yet begun to shuffle the columns around. Since the first seven letters of the ciphertext were LEAWXYN, we want to see if they will match up best with the second seven, the third seven, the fourth seven, or the last seven letters of the message. Moreover, since blanks between words are traditionally removed in transposition ciphers, we are going to look up digram frequencies in the table that ignore word divisions. The four possible pairings and their digram frequencies are shown at the top of the next page.

There are two things we should look at in each possible pairing. First, we should see which pair of columns has the largest total. Second, we should see which pair of columns has the most even distribution. We would rather see a pair of columns in which all the digrams are likely than a pair where one or two digrams are very frequent and the rest are rare. On this basis, we have to choose the pairing 1, 2 because its total is the highest and its distribution the most even. In the

1	2		1	3		1	4		1	5	
L	L	52	L	U	11	L	A	47	L	Q	0
E	T	81	E	T	81	E	I	40	E	A	98
A	R	87	A	O	1	A	H	3	A	B	20
W	I	33	W	L	2	W	R	3	W	L	2
X	P	5	X	C	2	X	E	1	X	E	1
Y	O	23	Y	T	19	Y	T	19	Y	U	1
N	I	40	N	E	64	N	O	51	N	T	121
		321			180			164			243

pairing 1, 5 almost all the contribution comes from two pairs (EA and NT), four of the remaining being very low, and the fifth (AB) being on the small side.

To measure the evenness of the distribution of numbers, we can use the variance we discussed earlier. We would then have to figure out, however, how to combine the values of variance and total contact frequency in order to come up with a single number for use in selecting a column. Fortunately, there is another way to select a column. It revolves about the fact that the rectangle of fixed perimeter that has the greatest area is a square.

We are going to take the product of the observed digram frequencies. This will be maximum for that column which has the most even distribution *and* the largest entries. Consider several columns, each with two digrams, that have the same total, and consider the products of the digram frequencies. For example, suppose that the total frequency is 6 and that for various column pairings A, B, . . . , it is divided as follows:

	Column pairings				
	A	B	C	D	E
First digram:	1	2	3	4	5
Second digram:	5	4	3	2	1
Sum:	6	6	6	6	6
Product:	5	8	9	8	5

Looking at the sums, there is no way to choose among the possible pairings. If we look at the products of the entries, however, we see that pairing C is to be preferred over the others. Thus, we can emphasize the smoothness of the distribution as well as the size of the entries if we take the product of the digraph frequencies instead of the sums.

Putting this matter another way, suppose that we divide the sums by the number of entries. This gives us the *arithmetic* average of the entries for each column pairing. Suppose on the other hand that we take the Nth root of the product of the entries, where N is the number of entries. This gives us the *geometric* average of the entries, which is just what we need.

Before we can use it, however, there is one small problem—namely, the number zero. If zero shows up in any column pairing, it will reduce the whole product to zero. If the zeros in the digram table were truly solid zeros, that would be the right thing to happen, but in actual fact they are not hard zeros. When we counted the four million odd character pairs in the Brown tape, we found almost every possible combination of letters. When we reduced the data to the number of occurrences per 10,000 digrams, we had to round off each number, and many small (but nonzero) numbers got rounded off to zero. Consider, just for a minute, the digram LQ, which is listed as having an occurrence rate of 0 per 10,000 digrams. In actual fact, we found the combination LQ one hundred times in 4,743,925 letter pairs, or .211 times per 10,000. Moreover, we know that in this message the phrase ALL QUIET does indeed occur and thus produces an LQ digram. (It isn't the one represented by column pairing 1, 5, but we couldn't be expected to know that.)

In order to allow for this kind of situation, we should replace all zeros in the digram frequency table by ones. This will distort the results slightly but not to any significant degree. Taking this approach, we get the following products:

Pair	*Product*	*Geometic average*	*Arithmetic average*
1, 2	5.5×10^{10}	34.3	45.8
1, 3	4.3×10^{6}	8.9	25.7
1, 4	1.6×10^{7}	10.7	23.4
1, 5	4.7×10^{5}	6.5	34.7

Obviously, we again have a clear win when we pair column 1 with column 2.

We should hasten to repeat that this method is not infallible either since a wrong pairing can show a higher geometric average than a correct pairing. Murphy's law requires it to do so. But as you can see, the arithmetic averages here are much closer to each other than the geometric ones and hence can be presumed to be more easily reversed by statistical fluctuation.

Loading the Digram Frequencies

In order to compute the geometric averages we have been talking about, we have to get the digram frequencies into the computer. I'm afraid there is no way to escape a lot of tedious typing at this point. In

BASIC, the most convenient way to load a lot of data is by using the DATA and READ statements.

In our list of subroutines for building the digram table, the following appear in lines 10800 onwards, as shown in Program 4.8:

```
FOR I=1 TO 26
   FOR K=1 TO 26
      READ D%(I,K)
      IF D%(I,K)=0 THEN D%(I,K)=1
   NEXT K
NEXT I
RETURN
DATA 2,20,41,37,1, . . . for 676 numbers
```

Since the inner loop is on K, K changes most rapidly; therefore, since we read in D%(I,K), the data runs across each row of the digram

Program 4.8 Subroutine to Read in Digram Frequencies

```
    4  DIM D%(26,26)
10800  REM GENERATE DIGRAM FREQUENCY TABLE
10810  FOR I=1 TO 26
10820     FOR K=1 TO 26
10830        READ D%(I,K)
10840        IF D%(I,K)=0 THEN D%(I,K)=1
10850     NEXT K
10860  NEXT I
10870  RETURN
10880  DATA 2,20,41,37,1, . . .
```

Program 4.8 (cont'd) Read In Comments

This routine will read in the digram frequencies from data statements and set up the array D%.

10810 - 10860
: I is the first letter of the pair.

10820 - 10850
: K is the second letter of the pair

10830 Read a frequency.

10840 This step replacea 0 frequency by 1 so that products will not be knocked down to 0, but if we want the real frequencies for some other purpose, we will have to remove this statement.

10880 - ?
: These frequencies are taken from the table of digram frequencies without regard to word boundaries in Appendix.

frequency table in turn. I chose to have the data statements contain the zeros where they occurred in the table and to replace the zeros with ones in statement 10830. As a result, the data statements will be an accurate reflection of the table in the Appendix (the one that ignores word boundaries) and, if at some later date I need the table with zeros in it, I can just eliminate statement 10830 and not have to reenter all those data statements again.

This subroutine should be called exactly once from the main program to read in the data statements and set up the matrix.

Testing Columns

To automate the column-matching process for a complete columnar tranposition, we need first to set up the digram table (GOSUB 10800), read in the ciphertext, and then squeeze out the blanks. Now we should ask the user how many columns he thinks there should be. Presumably he will have run the preceeding program, which tried various matrix sizes, and will therefore have a good idea of the number of columns. If he is mistaken, we should make it easy for him to change his mind. We should then check to see if the text breaks up into even-length columns that leave a full bottom row. The matching process will not work if a complete columnar does not come out even.

We print out an array of the possible matches: 1 with 1, 1 with 2, 1 with 3, . . . , 1 with the last column on a row, and then on the next row, 2 with 1, 2 with 2, 2 with 3, and so forth. If a column might match with itself, we merely print out a 1 as a place holder in the array. In a triply nested loop, the outer loop selects the column to be matched against (CA)—the lefthand member of the pair; the second loop selects the righthand member of the pair of columns (CB); and the inner loop steps down the columns to compute their product. Once the product has been calculated, we take its NRth root (NR = number of rows) to give the geometric average and then print that out. See Program 4.9.

Program 4.9 Complete Columnar Match, Column Against Column

```
 1  DIM T%(200)
 4  DIM D%(26,26)
10  GOSUB 10800
20  GOSUB 10000
30  GOSUB 10200
40  PRINT "INPUT NUMBER OF COLUMNS"
50  INPUT NC
60  NR = J/NC
```

```
70   IN NR <> INT (NR) THEN PRINT "UNEVEN LAST ROW":
     GOTO 40
80   PRINT "I(DOWN) MATCHED AGAINST J(ACROSS)"
90   FOR CA = 1 TO NC
100     PRINT CA
110     FOR CB = 1 TO NC
120        P = 1
130        IF CA = CB GOTO 190
140        FOR R = 0 TO NR-1
150        :TA = T%(CA+R*NC)
160        :TB = T%(CB+R*NC)
170        :P = P*D%(TA,TB)
180        NEXT R
190        PRINT INT(P ↑ (1/NR)*10)/10;
200     NEXT CB
210     PRINT
230  NEXT CA
240  GOTO 40
```

Program 4.9 (cont'd) Complete Columnar Match Comments

The user inputs the number of columns for the block for a complete columnar, and the computer tries all possible columns against one another, printing out the geometric average of the digram frequency found for each pair of columns.

10 Read the digram frequencies and set up the array D%. D%(I,J) will hold the number of times the letter I is followed by the letter J in ordinary English. Entries of 0 are changed to 1.

20 Get the ciphertext.

30 Squeeze out blanks.

40 - 50
Get the number of columns (= NC) for this block.

60 NR = number of rows.

70 Check to see if NC and NR are factors of J, the number of letters.

90 - 230
The two columns being matched are called CA and CB. This loop tries all possible CA's.

110 - 200
This inner loop tries all CB's against this CA.

120 The product P is set to 1.

130 There is no point in matching a column against itself.

140 We are going to go through all the rows, 1 through NR, but for convenience we offset row number R by 1.

150 TA is the character in column CA, row R.

160 TB is the character in column CB, row R.
170 P is multiplied by the number of times that letter CB followed letter CA in English.
190 We print the NRth root of P with only one figure after the decimal point, for that supplies sufficient accuracy and keeps the table neater.
210 Carriage return for the next CA.
240 The user may now try a different block size.

If your computer has sufficient space, you will probably want to combine this program with the last one and the one in the next section to save a retyping of the ciphertext each time. If not, well hobbies are supposed to be pastimes.

Expected Value of the Geometric Average

One of the useful functions of statistics is to tell us what to expect when we conduct an experiment. At the moment we would like to know how hard it will be to separate the correct column match from incorrect ones. There are two ways to go about doing this. The first would be to type in one thousand samples of English and determine the values for the correct alignments and the values for the incorrect ones. Although this might be the proper way to go about answering the question, it would involve rather more typing than we might feel up to at the present moment.

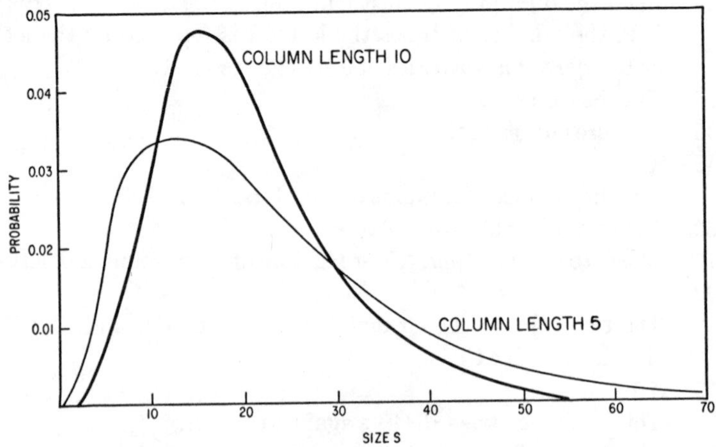

Fig. 4.1 Probability of finding a geometric average of size S versus S for "randomly" generated colums of a pseudo-digrams. The average value for column length 10 is 21.28 and for column length 5 is 23.27 (1,000 trials for each length).

The other method would be to select digrams at random to see what numbers come out. This is sometimes called the *Monte Carlo technique* in reference to the famous establishment of that name dedicated to the exploration of statistical fluctuations. We must be careful, however, about how we interpret the word *random.* Consider two incorrectly aligned columns. In each one the various letters appear with a frequency corresponding to their relative frequencies in English. In the first we would expect to find lots of E's, T's, O's and very few Z's, K's, and B's. Exactly the same distribution will be true of the second column. If the columns are indeed incorrectly aligned, however, the presence of a Q in the first column will have no influence at all on the presence or absence of a U in the corresponding position in the second column. To be more explicit, the letter frequencies will be those of English, but the putative digrams will not occur with their normal English frequencies. That difference is, after all, what we are relying on to separate the correct alignment from the incorrect ones. The former will have digrams exhibiting the normal English frequency; the latter will not.

Let us independently generate, therefore, two letters at random (with correct frequency distribution, of course) and combine them to make a "pseudo-digram." That's just what we want to represent the incorrectly aligned columns. We will then generate N such pseudo-digrams, take the geometric average of their occurrence rates, and repeat the whole thing one thousand times. Doing so will give us the average geometric average for pseudo-digrams as a function of N (the pseudo-column length) and, if we are clever, the distribution of these geometric averages as well. Figure 4.1 shows the probability of finding a geometric average of magnitude S as a function of S with two different pseudo-column lengths. As would be expected, longer columns smooth out some of the statistical noise, and the distribution for column length 10 peaks up more sharply than that for length 5. See Program 4.10.

Program 4.10 Pseudo-digram Column Match Experiment (Requires Read Digraph Subroutine)

```
5   DIM P(26),T%(500)
10  REM READ IN DIGRAPH FREQUENCIES
20  GOSUB 10800
30  T = RND(-TI)
40  REM CALCULATE LETTER FREQUENCIES
50  FOR I = 1 TO 26
60     P(I) = 0
70     FOR J = 1 TO 26
```

```
80        P(I)=P(I)+D%(I,J)
90      NEXT J
100   NEXT I
110   PRINT "HOW LONG A COLUMN"
120   INPUT LC
130   MG = 0
140   REM CLEAR TICK COUNTERS
150   FOR I = 1 TO 100 : T%(I)=0 : NEXT I
160   FOR I = 1 TO 1000
170     P = 1
180     PRINT I;     (Just for reassurance)
190     FOR J = 1 TO LC
200       GOSUB 1000
210       A = L
220       GOSUB 1000
230       B = L
240       P = P*D%(A,B)
250     NEXT J
260     P = P ↑ (1/LC)
270     MG = MG+P
280     P = INT(P)
290     IF P >100 THEN P=100
300     T%(P) = T%(P)+1
310   NEXT I
320   PRINT MG/1000
330   FOR I = 1 TO 100 STEP 5
340   PRINT I;"-";T%(I);T%(I+1);T%(I+2);T%(I+3);T%(I+4)
350   NEXT I
360   GOTO 110

1000  REM SUBROUTINE TO GENERATE A "RANDOM" LETTER
1010  T = INT(10000*RND(1)+1)
1020  T1 = 0
1030  FOR X = 1 TO 26
1040    T1 = T1+P(X)
1050    IF T1 > =T THEN L=X : X=26
1060  NEXT X
1070  RETURN
```

Program 4.10 (cont'd) Pseudo-digram Column Match Comments

We are going to generate columns of pseudo-digrams of length LC and compute their geometric average frequency, P. We will do this

1000 times and keep count in T%(I) of how many times we found a value of P of size 1, 2, . . . , 99, > 100. A pseudo-digram is a pair of letters, each chosen in accordance with English letter frequency but independently of each other.

20 Read in digram frequencies.

30 Initialize the random number generator.

50 - 100
For each letter I, calculate the frequency of occurrence of the letter by adding up the digram frequencies.

60 Set the frequency of this letter to zero.

70 - 90
For each possible successor to I, add the frequency of the digram I,J to the frequency of I.

110 - 120
Ask for the length of the column to be run.

150 Clear the tick counters T%(1) . . . T%(100). From now on we are going to keep count of how many times the geometric average P equals I.

160 - 310
Generate 1000 columns.

170 P is the product of the pseudo-digram frequencies for this column.

180 Since this is a very long-running program, I printed out the number of columns run so far just to be reassured that things were still proceeding.

190 - 250
A column consists of LC pseudo-digrams.

200 - 210
Generate a letter at random and put it in A.

220 - 230
Generate another letter and put it in B.

240 Multiply the product by the digram frequency of the pair AB.

260 Take the geometric average.

270 Since MG is the total of the geometric averages found so far, we can find the average of the averages.

280 Convert P to an integer.

290 If P is greater than 100, set it equal to 100.

300 Add 1 to the appropriate tick counter.

320 Print the average average.

330 - 350
Print out the tick counters five to a line.

Let me restate what we have done. We generate a column of N pseudo-digrams (N = 5 and N = 10). We find the geometric average of the digram occurence rates (taken from Appendix C). Call this geometric average P. If P lies between S and S+1, we make a tick in box S. After we have repeated this one thousand times, we count up the ticks in each box, print out the numbers, and plot the corresponding curve. From the curve for N = 10, you can see that there were roughly 47 ticks in boxes 12, 13, and 14 and that there were about 17 or 18 ticks in box 30.

Generating a Random Letter

We have not yet discussed how to generate a "random" letter with English frequency distribution. Since similar problems come up fairly often, the method is worth examining.

Suppose that we generate the following random number between 1 and 10,000,

X = INT(10000*RND(1)+1)

and suppose further that we have a Table L of letter frequencies in English. These can be taken from Appendix A or generated from the digram frequency table by summing the rows or columns.* In any event, we want L(1) to be *805* (the number of times A was found in 10,000 letters) and L(2) to be *153* (the number of times B was found in 10,000 letters), and so on.

When we want to generate a random letter, we work down the Table L, adding up the numbers one at a time until the sum exceeds the random number X generated above. If our random number generator is any good, X will have a uniform distribution; that is, any integer 1, 2, 3, . . . , 10000 will be equally likely. Suppose that there were only three letters in the alphabet and that their rates of occurrence per 10,000 were as follows:

A: 5000
B: 2000
C: 3000

In the first test, we see if X is less than 5000. If it is, we declare that the random letter is A. If not, we know that X is greater than 5000. We next test to see if X is less than 7000 (5000 + 2000). There is a probability of .2 (2000 chances out of 10,000) that it is. If it is, we call the random letter B. If not, we know it has to be C. By using this scheme, we generate an A with probability .5, a B with probability .2, and a C with probability .3. Extending the example to 26 letters and using real English letter frequencies accomplishes our aim.

A subroutine to generate a random letter is shown in Program 4.11.

---

*Because of roundoff errors, slightly different results will be obtained in the two directions.

A subroutine to generate a random letter is shown in Program 4.11.

Program 4.11 Subroutine to Generate a Random Letter

```
1010  T = INT(10000*RND(1)+1)
1020  T1 = 0
1030  FOR X = 1 TO 26
1040  T1 = T1+P%(X)
1050  IF T1 >=T THEN L=X:X=26
1060  NEXT X
1070  RETURN
```

True Digrams

We now have an idea of what to expect for misaligned columns. We still must generate a comparable measure for correctly aligned columns. The brute-force way of accomplishing this would be to provide Table L with 676 (26^2) entries and search down it to find a random true digram just as we found a random true letter. Since my own program to do incorrect column alignment took roughly an hour to run for column length 10 and since most of that time was apparently spent generating the letters, the idea of taking 26 hours per experiment was somewhat appalling. Perhaps there is a faster way (see Program 4.12).

Program 4.12 True Digram Column Match Experiment (Requires No Subroutines)

```
  5  DIM P%(300,V%(300)
 10  REM GENERATE PROBABILITY TABLE
 20  GOSUB 2000
 30  T = RND(-TI)
 40  PRINT "HOW LONG A COLUMN"
 50  INPUT LC
 60  MG =0
 70  REM CLEAR TICK COUNTERS
 80  FOR I = 1 TO 100 : T%(I)=0:NEXT I
 90  FOR I = 1 TO 1000
100     P = 1
110     PRINT I;
120     FOR J = 1 TO LC
130        X = INT(TF*RND(1)+1)
140        FOR K = 1 TO NE
150           IF X <P%(K)THEN D=V%(K) :K=NE
160        NEXT K
```

```
170         P = P*D
180       NEXT J
190       P =P ↑ (1/LC)
200       MG = MG+P
210       P = INT(P)
220       IF P >100 THEN P=100
230       T%(P) = T%(P)+1
240    NEXT I
250    FOR I = 1 TO 100 STEP 5
260       PRINT I;"-";T%(I);T%(I+1);T%(I+2);T%(I+3)
270    NEXT I
280    GOTO 40
```

Program 4.12 (cont'd) True Digram Column Match Comments

This program is going to generate 1000 columns of true digrams, but rather than generating a true digram at "random," it is going to find out (via the subroutine at 2000) the probability of finding a digram of size X and use this to select an X at random.

20 Generate the probability table. This routine will generate two vectors, P% and V%. P%(I) will be the cummulative "probability" that a digram has a value less than or equal to V%(I).

40 - 50
Find out the length (LC) of column to use.

60 Set the total of geometric averages equal to 0.

80 Clear the tick counters.

90 - 240
Do 1000 columns.

100 Start the product at value 1.

120 - 180
There will be LC terms in the product, one for each row of the column.

130 Generate a random number X between 1 and TF where TF, the total number of nonzero digrams, will be equal to 676 minus the number of digrams of zero frequency.

140 - 160
Step through the probability table until a P%(K) entry greater than X is found. Set D equal to the value V%(K) at which this entry is found, and exit from the loop by setting K equal to NE.

170 Multiply D, the new factor discovered, into the product.

190 Find the geometric average.

200 Add that average into MG.

210 - 220
  Convert P into an integer and limit it to 100.
230 Bump the appropriate tick counter.
250 - 270
  Print out the tick counters five to a line.

Look at the digram frequency table. There are 61 1's in it, 40 2's, 25 3's, and so forth. A digram of frequency F should be selected with probability F/10,000; then, if there are N digrams of this frequency, we should take out a term of magnitude F with a probability N*F/10,000. Since there are 89 different numbers appearing in the digram table, if we build two vectors called P and V of length 89, P(J) will contain the probability of selecting a vector of the Jth size and V(J) will contain the value of the digram frequency (see Program 4.13).

The first three entries in these vectors will have the following characteristics:

Number of times this value occurred	*Probability of selecting this value*	*Value to be selected*
66	66	1
40	80	2
25	75	3

The value vector V is needed because we squeeze out all numbers that never occurred in order to shorten up the vectors as much as pos-

Program 4.13 Subroutine to Generate the P and V Vectors

```
2000  FOR I = 0 TO 300 : P%(I)=0:NEXT I
2010  FOR I = 1 TO 676
2020     READ X
2030     P%(X)=P%(X)+1
2040  NEXT I
2050  J = O : P%(0)=0
2060  FOR I = 1 TO 300
2070     IF P%(I)=0 GOTO 2110
2080     J = J+1
2090     P%(J) = P%(J−1)+P%(I)*I
2100     V%(J) = I
2110  NEXT I
2120  TF = P%(J) : NE=J
2130  PRINT "TF,J=";TF;J
2104  RETURN
10880 DATA . . . digram frequencies
```

sible. There is another refinement we can add. Since we are going to be adding up these numbers continually to see if the sum exceeds our random number, why not do this addition once instead of 10,000 times? Then we can replace the probability with the cumulated total up to that point, as follows:

$$\begin{array}{rcr} 66 & \rightarrow & 66 \\ 80 & \rightarrow & 146 \\ 75 & \rightarrow & 221 \\ & \vdots & \end{array}$$

This method took about 75 minutes to run off the 1,000 trials for columns of length 10.

One further improvement could have been made. Before we did the cumulative addition, we might have sorted the pair of vectors so that the largest probabilities would have been at the beginning of the table. For the three entries above, we would have obtained the following:

Probability	*Value*
80	2
75	3
66	1

In this way we would have minimized the number of places that would have to be examined on the average and thus would have speeded up the search. Since this wasn't a production program to be run a million times—only a test vehicle to get out some numbers—I myself did not take this approach.

Suppose that we compute a geometric average for some possible column pairing. We would like to know what the probability is that this pairing is correct. Figures 4.2 and 4.3 show one way of answering this question, or at least of approaching an answer. Suppose that our computed average is G and that the column length is 10. If G = 40, we see by examining Figure 4.3 that only five times out of a hundred trials will an incorrect pairing give a G as *large* as 40 and that only 37 times out of 100 trials will a correct pairing give a G as *small* as 40. If G = 20, then the situation is reversed, and a correct pairing will produce so small a G only twice in 100 trials and an incorrect pairing will be this large 48 times. In the first case (G = 40), we would probably be right if we assumed that this was a correct pair, and in the second case (G = 20), that we had an incorrect pair. But if G = 31, then both probabilities are .15, and we can reach no conclusion at all.

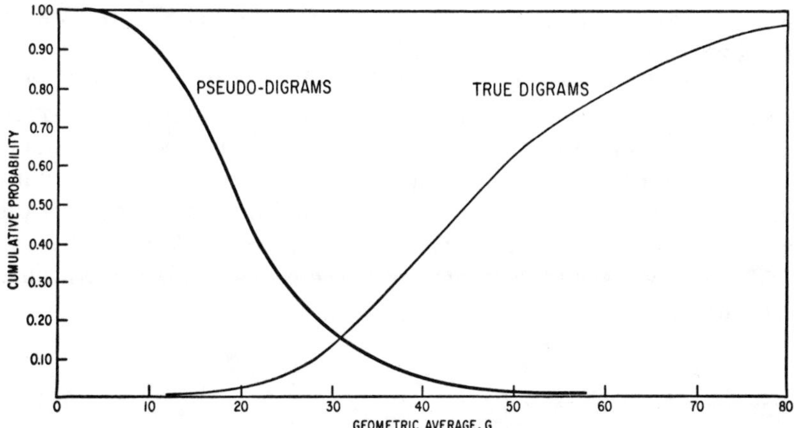

Fig. 4.2 Plot of the probability that a column of true digrams of length 10 has a geometric average as small as G and a similar column of pseudo-digrams has a geometric average as large as G.

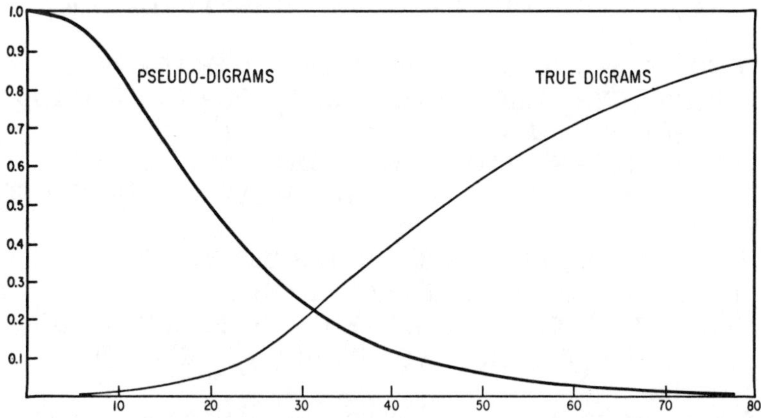

Fig. 4.3 Column length = 5.

Remember that the 5-percent chance of finding that G = 40 with an incorrect pairing is going to show up pretty often in actual fact. If we have six columns in our cryptogram and each column is matched against every other column, there will be 25 possible matches, only five of which will be correct. (Note that the figure is five rather than six since the last column has to match with the first after being shifted down by one, and we don't test for that possibility.) We will thus have 20 incorrect matches, and if one out of 20 gives a G of 40 or larger, we shouldn't be surprised to find such a false indication. The region where both eventualities have a probability of .05 or higher runs from a G of

24 to a G of 40. In this range we can try to make a choice, but we must be prepared to be wrong.

Figure 4.3 does the same job for columns of length 5. Here the "crossover" region, where both probabilities are above .05, extends from a G of 19 to a G of 53. This larger range proceeds from the fact that the G's of short columns are averaged over relatively few numbers and hence show considerable variation. You can still make a guess that if $G < 31$, it's an incorrect matchup, and that if $G > 31$, it indicates a good pairing. The shorter the columns are, however, the less certainty there will be about your guess.

Problems for Chapter 4

1. HLUTR IFNAT SHTBN AITTH ASOTE GNOIE AKEWU RSEFN ORSEY DTRTC IALOE SNHAH TCFLM N
   (*Mark Twain*)
2. TSNLB GIIWH MHDER ANETE AUNTT ITEEE OECTE VWSDA CLUUN OHNNM SROOA IHHOT TWTEO ALPNT EOICU TEWBH
3. HXONE OLHED ILRTB KNNAO OROGT ETARV ATSEH NTERN IICLT HOIOT MTAEF XREHI ODANE PWWSI LI
   (*Sir Joshua Reynolds*)
4. AEGAA OLLRE NLLOL ISRTL RIDIT AALTY UGIEA IIRDO USTTO AFTCS AHASF IESTE IYWNA NDBTD CNGES AE
5. STIAT SCCIS ESLLT YBSHX OIIRS EENHT ETEXL TADTE SBABE HYEET LCREV IEOOH MAN
6. ORECG UOYTN LYDEA OOEYE CWLIA NELED NLVOE LUNSI YCAOT SRTRL AYDHE OHURA EAELF TLCDF TOGNE
7. MWTYA LCOSA ENLTS ERETR EEEGI NUTME LMXVA ETREA EYAEN REEXS AAIIN SANHY VYNNN ATOOL TOCRD PRDIC HWYHU AESTL
8. ETAST AEHIH EUNLE SAEMT XTWTR AETUF ENLOE BERYW LXTHT OINTR LTMFD ILIEB OIXOI HAUSM
9. TESSS YSSTD TVISW EEEAC NXAEE MHAOI HWETE ANHII UMDUA YTCOA RODDY HHHKX
10. NHATA OYNTU IEELI OMWSE SEFAO OTHYB OSEHH LMNTN AMFRS PKRRC TWTTE DTCGA EETU

5

Incomplete Columnar Transpositions

The complete columnar transposition is easy to solve because only a limited number of matrix sizes will fit a given message length. Furthermore, once the number of columns has been determined—the columns being all of the same length—there will be a limited number of letters (those on the same row) against which each letter can be matched.

Let us suppose, however, that through carelessness or foresight, the encoder has picked a keyword whose length is not a factor of the message length. Our task suddenly becomes so much harder that this type of transposition has its own name—*incomplete columnar transposition*—and its own methods of attack.

The problems in analyzing incomplete columnar transpositions arise because of the different column lengths. Even if we know the length of the keyword, we will still have trouble lining up the letters.

Imagine that we want to send the message,

Now is the time for all good men to come

Using a keyword of length five, we set up the following encoding block:

```
N O W I S
T H E T I
M E F O R
A L L G O
O D M E N
T O C O M
E
```

Note that the first column has seven letters in it and that all the rest have six. Depending on the five-letter keyword chosen, we might first take out the long column and then the four short columns in some order or other; or first a short, then the long, and then the remaining shorts; or first two shorts, then the long, and two shorts; or first three shorts, then the long, and a short; or all the shorts followed by the long. Letting L stand for the long column and S for any of the short columns, we might have the following:

```
L S S S S
S L S S S
S S L S S
S S S L S
S S S S L
```

For a legitimate receiver of the message, this will present no problem because he has the keyword and can fill in the columns one after another from the ciphertext. Counting the number of letters in the ciphertext, he finds that there are 31. With a key length of five, that means there will be one column of length seven and four columns of length six. He lays this configuration out on a piece of paper with the long columns (only one this time) on the left and the short ones on the right, as shown in Fig. 5.1. He writes the keyword across the top and, starting with the first column to be filled in, enters as many letters from the ciphertext as there are places in the column. Everything works out automatically, and out pops the plaintext. The interceptor, on the other hand, will not know where to put the column breaks even if he knows that there are five columns.

The Classical Attack—Overlapping Word

In a real life situation, it would be likely that you will know something about the message contained in an intercepted cryptogram. You might know whom it was from or to, or you might have some clues about the subject matter. In amateur cryptanalysis, such a situation is simulated by giving the decipherer one or more "probable words" that might be found in the plaintext. The term "probable words" is a euphemism for "clue" since the "probable" words are almost invariably "certain" words; they are *always* there. If you aren't provided with any probable words, you will usually have enough information to allow you to guess at some (in this case they will be "possible" words).

For the incomplete columnar, the probable words are often quite long and will aid your solution. The ideal case is when you have a probable word known to be longer than the keyword. Let us see how this situation can help us. We receive the message,

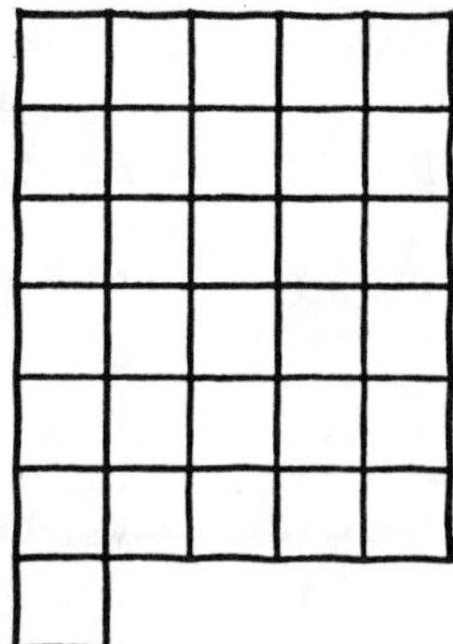

Fig. 5.1 Layout for an incomplete columnar transposition

PCRAY KNOII SAAEV OEELS EEULS NWMMR S

with the probable word SIRENS. Suppose that the keyword has three letters in it. Then there would be three columns in the plaintext block, and the word SIRENS would have to appear in one of the following patterns:

```
S I R      - S I      - - S
E N S      R E N      I R E
           S          N S
```

All three of these lead to the letter pairs SE, IN, and RS, which would have to appear some place in the ciphertext if there are indeed three columns in the block.

To simplify the search for possible pairs of letters we need to make a "contact chart." First, we write out the letters of the alphabet, A to Z. Taking the above message, we find P followed by C, C followed by R, and so forth. Thus, next to the P in our list we will put a C; next to the C we will put an R; and so on. This gives us the list shown at the top of the next page.

We find that S is indeed followed by E and that R is followed by S, but I is not followed by N so that if the word SIRENS really occurs in the plaintext, the latter cannot have been enciphered in a block of three columns.

With four columns we might have the following

```
S I R E    - S I R    - - S I      - - - S
N S        E N S      R E N S      I R E N
                                   S
```

A:	YAE	N:	OW
B:		O:	IE
C:	R	P:	C
D:		Q:	
E:	VELEU	R:	AS
F:		S:	AEN
G:		T:	
H:		U:	L
I:	IS	V:	O
J:		W:	M
K:	N	X:	
L:	SS	Y:	K
M:	MR	Z:	

each of which gives SN and IS. Since both these pairs occur in the ciphertext, we can conclude that four columns is a *possibility.*

With five columns we have, as one arrangement,

```
S I R E N
S
```

The other arrangements, of course, also give the pair SS. Since that pair doesn't occur in the ciphertext, five columns is not a possibility. Six or more columns might have been used, but in that case there wouldn't be any overlap of the probable word with itself.

There also might have been only two columns, giving

```
S I      S
R E    I R
N S    E N
       S
```

and we should look for the triples SRN and IES. Since there isn't even an IE pair, there is not much point in looking for an IES. A two-column format is therefore ruled out. That leaves four columns as the only candidate with overlap.

Let us again set up one of the four possible arrangements for SIRENS. Since there is only one SN and one IS in the ciphertext, we have a pretty simple situation. If there were a couple of possibilities for each pair, we would try them all. Since the message has 31 letters in four columns, they will be of length 8, 8, 8, and 7. Look at the ciphertext beginning at IS and running on to SN:

IS	A	A	E	V	O	E	E	L	S	E	E	U	L	SN
1	2	3	4	5	6	7	8	9	10	11	12	13	14	15

Starting at I and going on to S, we find 15 letters. We want to ask if it would be possible to get 15 letters between the two pairs if we had a four-column block. Set up a blank block and put the word SIRENS in it in all possible arrangements, as shown in Fig. 5.2.

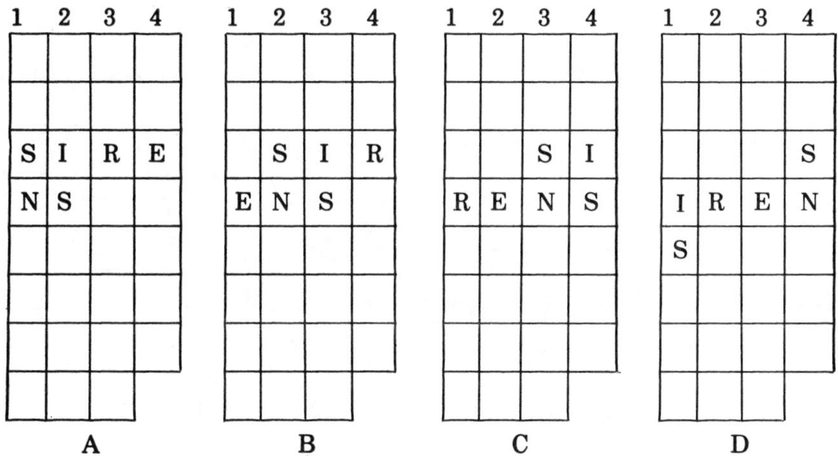

Fig. 5.2 Possible arrangements of SIRENS

Apparently the column containing IS was taken off before the column that contains the SN. We are trying to find out how many letters could lie between the I and the S of SN. It doesn't matter which row SIRENS appears on because if it were one row lower than where we have pictured it, there would be one less letter in the IS columm below IS and one more letter in the SN column before SN. Lay out the two columns for the four arrangements shown in Fig. 5.3 at the top of the next page.

For arrangement A we have a "gap" consisting of letters 6 through 12, for B we have the same, and for C and D we have a gap of letters 5 through 12. Depending on which arrangement actually exists, we need either seven or eight letters to fill the space between the end of the IS column and the beginning of the SN column. In arrangements A and B we do have a short column (4) of length 7 to fit into the gap, and in arrangements C and D we have a choice of one of two possible long columns (1,2) and (2,3) to fill the gap of length 8. From this we see that a block of four columns could have given rise to the spacing between the two pairs we observed. We will return to this discussion a little later.

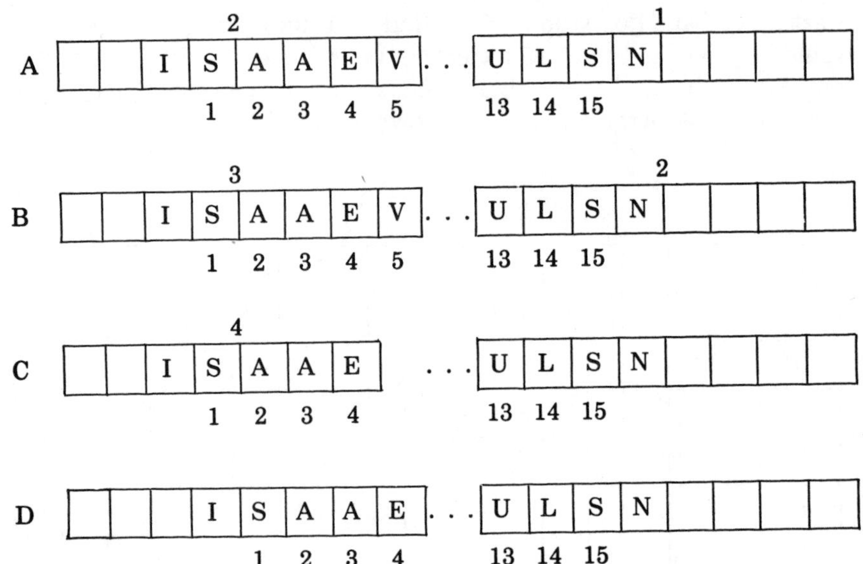

Fig. 5.3 Layout of the two columns for the four arrangements

Looking back at the ciphertext

PCRAY KNOI(I S)AAEV OEELS EEUL(S N)WMMR S

we note that there are only five letters following SN—not a large enough number to make up a column by themselves since these columns must have seven or eight letters in them. It must be remembered that when columns get read out of the block to form the ciphertext, they come out as units. Therefore, SNWMMRS has to come out of a single column. If this was an eight-letter column, the L came with them; otherwise it was at the bottom of some other column.

The beginning of the ciphertext has to represent a column taken from the block. It may have either seven or eight letters in it depending on whether it is a short or long column. Thus we have a column that begins PCRAYKN and may or may not have an O at the end.

Since we know that SN has exactly five letters following it, we can set up the possible blocks shown in Fig. 5.4.

For each of these arrangements we can circle out the letters we have used from the ciphertext:

A: PCRAY KNO [II SAAEV O] EELS EEU [LS NWMMR S]

B: PCRAY KNO [II SAAEV O] EELS EEU [LS NWMMR S]

C: PCRAY KNO II SAAEV OEELS EEU LS NWMMR S

D: PCRAY KNO II SAAEV O EELS EEUL S NWMMR S

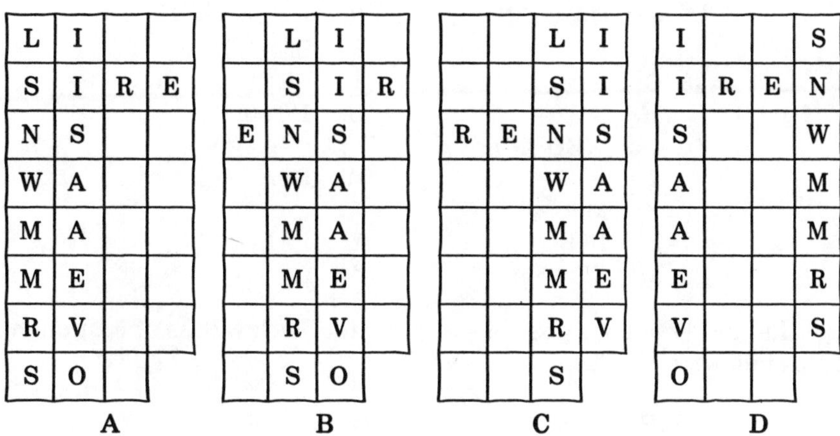

Fig. 5.4 Possible setup of blocks

Arrangement A leaves possible columns PCRAYKNO and EELSEEU. Since neither of these has an R in the second position to make the word SIRENS, arrangement A is out. Since arrangement B has exactly the same problem, it is out, too. Arrangement C leaves possible columns PCRAYKNO (as before) and OEELSEEU, giving us an R and an E in the third position. Substituting these into arrangement C gives the message

POLICE SIRENS ALWAYS MAKE ME NERVOUS

A reasonable sentiment, if scarcely one requiring secrecy.

Let us try a somewhat longer example,

EOHNT$_{5}$ YFLIW$_{10}$ RUIBI$_{15}$ OOATE$_{20}$ ARYAS$_{25}$ SNNIS$_{30}$
AANCF$_{35}$ PIOSW$_{40}$ SIUIP$_{45}$ RDUTC$_{50}$ THYEA$_{55}$ OAPKM$_{60}$
CWAEL$_{65}$ NLEOI$_{70}$ NCUMF$_{75}$ RRUEI$_{80}$ YOLUP$_{85}$ EDN

with the probable word/phrase, CAN BUY A LIFE.

Forming the contact chart first of all, we obtain the following:

A:	TRSANOPE	N:	TNICLC
B:	I	O:	HOASAIL
C:	FTWU	P:	IRKE
D:	UN	Q:	
E:	OAALOID	R:	UYDRU
F:	LPR	S:	SNAWI
G:		T:	YECH
H:	NY	U:	IITMEP
I:	WBOSOUPNY	V:	
J:		W:	RSA
K:	M	X:	
L:	INEU	Y:	FAEO
M:	CF	Z:	

Let us lay out the possible overlaps for block widths of 5 through 10, as follows:

Number of columns	*Pattern of overlap*	*Reject?*
5	CANBU YALIF E	No CY
6	CANBUY ALIFE	No CA
7	CANBUYA LIFE	No CL
8	CANBUYAL IFE	No CI
9	CANBUYALI FE	Possible
10	CANBUYALIF E	No CE

Of these, only the nine-column block is acceptable since CF is found in letters 34,35 and AE in letters 63,64. Taking 34 from 63 gives 29 intervening letters (counting the A of AE). Nine columns and 88 letters gives seven columns of ten letters and two columns of nine letters.

The nine-column block is laid out in Fig. 5.5 with the possible starting positions for the probable phrase shown by the numbers. Instead of trying to see how we could make up the gap of 29 in this particular case, let us examine the general problem.

The shortest gap we could have between the C of CF and the A of AE (counting the A) is if the two columns are taken off one right after the other. Taking off the CF column first, we would have one long column as the minimum distance for starting points 1 through 7. For

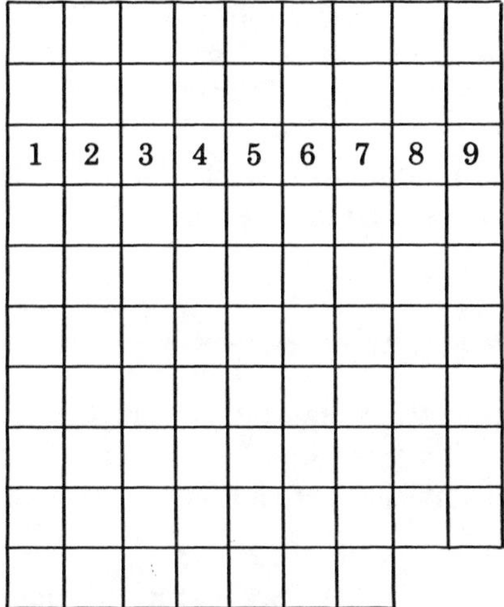

Fig. 5.5 Nine-column block with possible starting positions

starting point 8 we would have a short column and for starting point 9 a long column again. (Even though column 9 is short, the AE pair will be one row lower down and give a long column count.) So far we can account for separations of 9 or 10. The next smallest gap would occur when one other column is taken off after the CF column and before the AE column. From starting positions 1 through 7 we have a base of 10 because of the length of the CF column. To this we could add a short or a long column, generating possible gaps of 19 or 20. From starting position 8 we have a base of 9, but since the AE column uses up the only other short column, we can add only a long column, generating a 19. The problem is that we are taking off the CF column first and then the AE column, and if CF is short, then AE must be short also. If N_S is the number of short columns, then, when the lefthand column (the CF column) is taken off, we can first have at most N_S-1 short columns between the two pairs. If the righthand or AE column is taken off first and we are at starting position 7, we may have up to N_S short columns between the pairs. For example, if we take off the columns in the order 8, 9, 7, we will have a gap of 18.

When the lefthand column comes off first, we can have up to N_L long columns between the pairs. A starting point of 7 and a take-off order of 7, 1, 2, 3, 4, 5, 6, 8 will produce this as will a starting point of 8 and a take-off order of 8, 1, 2, 3, 4, 5, 6, 7, 9. Starting from position 9 might be imagined to give us an extra long column count, but the fact that the AE column uses up one of the long column precludes this possibility.

To summarize: When the column containing the lefthand pair is taken off first, we may have up to N_S-1 short columns and up to N_L long columns between the pairs. There must, of course, be at least one column count.

Letting S be the number of short columns between the pairs and L be the number of long columns, we can write:

$$\left.\begin{array}{l} S+L \geq 1 \\ 0 \leq S \leq N_S-1 \\ 0 \leq L \leq N_L \end{array}\right\} \text{Lefthand pair first}$$

When the righthand column is taken off first, we may have 0 to N_S short columns (starting positions 1 through 6) and 0 to N_L long columns (starting position 8 or 9) so that the constraints are:

$$\left.\begin{array}{r} N_S+N_L-1 \geq S+L \geq 1 \\ 0 \leq S \leq N_S \\ 0 \leq L \leq N_L \end{array}\right\} \text{Righthand pair first}$$

Now let's go back to our original problem, which was to find out if a gap of 29 was possible with a nine-column block. Our column lengths are 9 and 10, and the lefthand pair was taken off first. We see at once that 29 = 10 + 10 + 9 and that two longs and a short do the job nicely without violating any of the constraints.

We don't know what position the probable word began in, but we can make adjustment for that uncertainty later. Consequently, we will arbitrarily start it in column 1 and try to build around what we know.

```
I P
S K
A M
A C
N W
C A N B U Y A L I
F E
P L
I N
O L
S E
```

There is only one B in the ciphertext (letter 14) so that we can add a number of letters to the column in which it occurs, as shown at the top of the next page.

Since we know that the beginning of the ciphertext represents a column that must have had at least nine letters in it, we can stop the column we build on the B at the point at which room is left for nine let-

```
I P
S K   W
A M   R
A C   U
N W   I
C A N B U Y A L I
F E   I
P L   O
I N   O
O L   A
```

ters in the first column. If the column containing B begins with W, then B appears in row 5, but if it begins with R, then B appears in row 4. Look at the first ten letters of the crypt. They represent a column and in what will become rows 4 and 5 of this column, we find the letters N and C. One of these must occur somewhere in the probable word. Since N is the only possibility, we can now add the first column taken off from the beginning of the ciphertext to our reconstruction:

```
     I P
     S K   W
 1   A M E R
 2   A C O U
 3   N W H I
 4   C A N B U Y A L I
 5   F E T I
 6   P L Y O
 7   I N F O
 8   O L L A
 9       I
10       W
```

Since that column begins with E—the first letter of the ciphertext—we can lop off the tops of the other columns to be level with the E. Since doing so lops off the W (letter 10) from the column containing B, we must place it at the bottom of the N column, as shown. We should now extend all the other columns to this length.

We can similarly examine the end of the ciphertext because this too represents a column, although we don't know whether it is long or short. If long, we want to look at letter 82, which would come from row 4, and if short, at letter 83. Of these letters, O and L, the L will fit in but not the O. Now, lopping and extending columns and filling out the L column, we get:

	1	2	3	4	5	6	7	8	9
1	A	M	E	R				I	
2	A	C	O	U				Y	
3	N	W	H	I				O	
4	C	A	N	B	U	Y	A	L	I
5	F	E	T	I				U	
6	P	L	Y	O				P	
7	I	N	F	O				E	
8	O	L	L	A				D	
9	S	E	I	T				N	
10	W	O	W	E					

Column 8 is evidently a short column since we ran out of letters on reaching N. We now reproduce the ciphertext with the columns we have taken out circled:

```
       3                 4
[EOHNT  YFLIW] [RUIBI  OOATE] ARYAS  SNNI S
      5     10       15     20     25      30
       1
[AANCF  PIOSW]  SIUIP  RDUTC  THYEA  OAPK[M
      35    40       45     50     55      60
       2
 CWAEL  NLEOI]  NCUMF  RRUE[I  YOLUP  EDN]
      65    70       75     80     85
```

The remaining letters can now be fitted in. Since group 21–30 has an A in row 4, it becomes column 7. Since group 70–79 has a U in row 4, it becomes column 5. Since the group beginning with 41 has an I in row 4, it becomes column 9, and since the short columns have to be next to each other in the reconstructed block, column 9 must be a short column. The remaining letters drop into column 6, and we read that

> AMERICA IS A COUNTRY IN WHICH YOU CAN BUY A LIFETIME SUPPLY OF ASPIRIN FOR A DOLLAR AND USE IT UP IN TWO WEEKS.

Our big break came from the fact that there was only one B in the ciphertext, and it happened to be in our probable word. The second break was to discover that the leading and trailing sections of the ciphertext would only fit with the probable word in one way.

Let us try another cipher, this one with 68 letters and the probable word, EXAMPLE:

ILSSO$_{5}$ LRSNE$_{10}$ REIFP$_{15}$ EAARO$_{20}$ TETLA$_{25}$ IERTN$_{30}$
UUIOE$_{35}$ AAPEN$_{40}$ ELHDM$_{45}$ SSBOO$_{50}$ TSNRX$_{55}$ MKESS$_{60}$
YSWRE$_{65}$ MUC

Counting the occurrences of the letters in the probable word, we get:

E:	10
X:	1
A:	5
M:	3
P:	2
L:	4

Obviously, the one and only X at position 55 is the X in the probable word, EXAMPLE. Although this stroke of luck may strike you as being a bit artificial, in real life we may very well hope for a probable word with one or more uncommon letters in it. If the uncommon letter occurred twice or more, we would have to replicate all the work below for each occurrence. For the sake of brevity, we have chosen a probable word with a unique uncommon letter.

The next rarest letter, P, occurs in positions 15 and 38. We first make up a table of possible column lengths for block widths of 5 to 15, stopping when the columns become less than 5 in length. The table is as follows:

Block width or number of columns	*Number of long columns (length)*	*Number of short columns (length)*
5	3(14)	2(13)
6	2(12)	4(11)
7	5(10)	2(9)
8	4(9)	4(8)
9	5(8)	4(7)
10	8(7)	2(6)
11	2(7)	9(6)
12	8(6)	4(5)
13	3(6)	10(5)

For each of the possible P's, we can determine the distance between the P and X and then determine whether or not we could make up that distance from the limited number of short and long columns available for a given block width:

Block width	$P_{15}-X_{55}=40$	$P_{38}-X_{55}=17$
5	-	-
6	-	-
7	4×10	-
8	-	8+9
9	5×8	-
10	2×6+4×7	-
11	-	-
12	5×6+2×5	2×6+5
13	8×5	2×6+5

We can discard block lengths of 5, 6, and 11 because at least one of the P's has to be reachable from X by an integral number of columns.

Now let's do the same thing for the three available M's. Right away we can discard the M in position 56. In no way can we have a column length of 1, at least not within our rules. We are thus left with M_{45} and M_{66}, as follows:

Block width	$M_{45}-X_{55}=10$	$X_{55}-M_{66}=11$
7	1×10	-
8	-	-
9	-	-
10	-	-
12	2×5	5+6
13	2×5	5+6

Widths 8, 9, and 10 are thus eliminated since none of them will accommodate either M. Therefore, only one possible construction is left for block width 7 and four constructions for both block widths 12 and 13. We also have one more constraint we can apply. The distance between M and P must be commensurate with the available column lengths. This constraint will be strongest when both lie on the same side of X (both before X or both after it), but in any event we want to look for situations, that demand more long or short columns than we have available. We lay out the nine possibilities, as follows:

Block width	*Letters 1, 2, and 3*	*Needed for 1–2*	*Needed for 2–3*	*OK?*
7	$P_{15}\,M_{45}\,X_{55}$	30=3×10	10=1×10	Yes
12	$P_{15}\,M_{45}\,X_{55}$	30=5×6	10=2×5	Yes
12	$P_{15}\,X_{55}\,M_{66}$	40=5×6+2×5	11=5+6	Yes
12	$P_{38}\,M_{45}\,X_{55}$	7=No	10=2×5	No
12	$P_{38}\,X_{55}\,M_{66}$	17=2×6+5	11=5+6	Yes
13	$P_{15}\,M_{45}\,X_{55}$	30=6×5	10=2×5	Yes
13	$P_{15}\,X_{55}\,M_{66}$	40=8×5	11=5+6	Yes
13	$P_{38}\,M_{45}\,X_{55}$	7=—	10=2×5	No
13	$P_{38}\,X_{55}\,M_{66}$	17=2×6+5	11=6+5	Yes

For block width 7, of the four L's available in positions 2, 6, 24, and 42, only the one at 6 will fit with the X at 55. Since this limitation would pretty well tie down the reconstruction of the block—four partial columns being known out of seven—it seems worth throwing that block up just to see how it goes. Having only one possible reconstruction for a particular block length doesn't mean that the block length is correct. It merely means that it will be easy to test.

Writing out the probable word and building around it and also taking advantage of the fact that L_6 limits the possible row of the probable word, we get

	O		N	(E)	I	
	T		E	R	L	
	S		L	E	S	
	N		H	I	S	
	R		D	F	O	
E	X_{55}	A	M_{45}	P_{15}	L_6	E
	M		S	E	R	
	K		S	A	S	
	E		B	A	N	
	S		O	R	(E)	

Note that the E_{12} at the top of the P column eliminates the E_{12} at the bottom of the L column. Thus, the L column must be short. Circling the parts of the ciphertext we have used gives us

```
[ILSSO  LRSN] [E REIFP  EAAR]  O TETLA   IERT N
     5          10      15           20        25      30
UUIOE  AAPE   [N ELHDM  SSBO] [O TSNRX  MKES] S
     35         40      45          50         55      60
YSWRE  MUC
     65
```

This arrangement leaves us a group of 20 letters from 20 to 39, which obviously form two columns of ten each, and a group of nine letters from 60 to 68. The sixth letter in these three columns are A_{25}, E_{35}, and E_{65}, respectively. We will leave it to the reader to decide how to place these so that the resulting message may be read.

The Analytic Matrix

The process just discussed can, to some extent, be automated by constructing something called the *analytic matrix* or *combination block*. In order to do so we must know, or guess at, the block width. Suppose, due to a flash of psychic insight, we concluded without any examination that 7 was the proper block width. With 68 letters in the above ciphertext, we will have five long columns of ten letters and two short columns of nine letters but will not know the order in which they were taken off. Neither of the two methods of constructing an analytic matrix is terribly satisfactory. After you have made one for yourself a few times, the job gets easier, but, for me at least, it never becomes automatic.

Begin by assuming that all the long columns were taken off first and then the short columns:

```
I R T U E T S
L E E U L S Y
S I T I H N S
S F L O D R W
O P A E M X R
L E I A S M E
R A E A S K M
S A R P B E U
N R T E O S C
E O N N O
```

If the first column had been a short one, the E would have been lopped from its bottom, and since it can't be just thrown away, we will put it at the top of column 2. Working from the right-hand end, we note that the last column (7) might have been a long one, in which case it would steal the S from the bottom of column 6 to put above the S at its own top, as shown below:

```
  e         s
_____________
I R T U E T S
L E E U L S Y
S I T I H N S
S F L O D R W
O P A E M X R
L E I A S M E
R A E A S K M
S A R P B E U
N R T E O S C
E O N N O
```

We have written the letters above the top of the block in lower case to set them off from the body of the block, and we have drawn a line above the letters we may have to amputate at the bottom.

Now consider column 2. It might also be a short one. If both columns 1 and 2 were short, then the e would have to go at the top of column 2, and to make that column a short one, we would have to amputate two letters from its lower end and transfer them to column 3.

Working in from the right end, suppose that columns 6 and 7 were both long. Column 7 would steal one letter from column 6 in order to be long and column 6 would therefore have to steal two letters from column 5 to be long, as follows:

```
    r       o
  e o       o s
---------------
I R T U E T S
L E E U L S Y
S I T I H N S
S F L O D R W
O P A E M X R
L E I A S M E
R A E A S K M
S A R P B E U
N R T E O S C
E O N N O
```

When we look at column 4, only two of the three columns to its left can be short columns because there *are* only two short columns. Therefore, we will draw the bottom line above the T and N of column 3, and add T and N to the top of column 4. Column 5 has already donated the two O's at its bottom in order to extend the two short columns to its right. Column 5 can be, at most, 10 letters long. Counting upwards from B we need, at most, two letters from column 4 to make up the maximum of ten. We then have the complete analytic matrix:

```
    r t e o
  e o n n o s
---------------
I R T U E T S
L E E U L S Y
S I T I H N S
S F L O D R W
O P A E M X R
L E I A S M E
R A E A S K M
S A R P B E U
N R T E O S C
E O N N O
```

Writing out such a matrix on quadrille paper and cutting the columns apart into strips allows one to shuffle the strips and slide them up and down in a search for good column pairings. For instance (assuming we didn't have a probable word), one might begin by selecting the column with the X in it and looking for a column with an appropriately positioned E to place at its left (recall that the digram chart reveals that X is preceded by E 15 out of 20 times). Which letters could now stand to the right of the X on the same row? Examine first the column to the right of the X in the matrix. The X could be in either a short or long column. We count forward either nine or ten letters before arriving at R and E. Note that we don't count the lowercase letters because they are already being counted at the bottoms of the columns. To move to the left, we count upwards nine or ten letters from X, reaching the S and M of column 5.

Going yet another column over, we count either 18, 19, or 20 letters from X before reaching A, A, and E in column 4. Since there are only two short columns in this block, we now count a long column count from each of these positions to reach EIA in column 3. We continue in this way to the leftmost columns. Here we reproduce the analytic matrix with those letters compatible with X outlined:

```
      r  t  e  o
   e  o  n  n  o  s
--------------------
I  R  T  U  E  T  S
L  E  E  U  L  S  Y
S  I  T  I  H  N  S
S  F  L  O  D  R  W
O  P  A  E  M (X) R
L  E  I  A  S  M  E
R  A  E  A  S  K  M
S  A  R  P  B  E  U
N  R  T  E  O  S  C
E  O  N  N  O
```

If the probable word were EXAMPLE, we could select at once the only possible L, P, and M that could all on the same row as the X. If the probable word breaks and falls on two rows, on the other hand, the analysis has to be slightly different. As we know from solving the crypt, the phrase FOREXAMPLE comes out from the block as follows:

```
          F O R
    E X A M P L E
```

Taking FOREXA as a probable word, we must extend the boundaries up one when working out from E, X, or A, and down one when working out from F, O, or R.

To allow you to inspect another analytic matrix before we proceed to a method of computer solution, we will make up a block for the same crypt but this time use a block width of 9, as follows:

```
        t a
      e n p m
    p t u e s n
  s e l u n s r y
-----------------
I N A A I E B X S
L E A I O L O M W
S R R E E H O K R
S E O R A D T E E
O I T T A M S S M
L F E N P S N S U
R P T U E S R Y C
S E L U N
```

The first four columns might be short, throwing letters S, PE, ETL, and TNUU onto the tops of the following columns. Similarly, if the last five columns were long, they would need to borrow Y, NR, MSS, and APEN from their left-hand neighbors. Since we already know that this is not a valid matrix, we won't try to analyze it.

In order to get a bit more practice with this type of cipher, we will present another problem. All we know about it is that the block width is 11, but this is enough information to allow us to construct the analytic matrix, as follows:

```
            e  a  t  c
         w  r  n  d  t  f
      n  t  e  a  e  a  h  n
   c  r  m  f  i  m  e  w  t  e
---------------------------------
H  E  N  N  U  W  I  A  A  T  O
I  S  H  T  L  D  O  E  H  S  N
L  E  N  H  A  T  U  O  S  S  E
H  L  E  F  A  T  C  W  E  E  P
C  A  A  E  N  D  T  F  O  H  N
E  N  W  R  A  E  A  H  N  D  R
I  N  T  E  I  M  E  W  T  E  H
C  R  M  F

1  2  3  4  5  6  7  8  9  10 11
```

No obvious clue letters (such as EX or QU) jump out at us when we examine the matrix, but as Gaines (2) put it so succinctly: "It is better to do almost anything than to sit and stare at the ciphertext." In this spirit then, we will make up strips, label them 1 through 11, cut them out, and try shuffling them around.

Let us try to recreate the spirit, if not the exact details, of how one might go about solving this sort of crypt. Since there are lots of T's and H's and E's in it, we might reasonably expect the word THE to appear at some point. Start with the TH near the tops of columns 4 and 3. Trying column 2 doesn't seem too profitable, and neither does lining up the e of column 8 with the TH. Lining up the E of column 8, however, produces the arrangement shown in (b) below:

```
                  c
w          w      t
t  n       t  n  a
m  r       m  r  e
N  N       N  N  A
T  H       T  H  E
=====      ========
H  N       H  N  O
F  E       F  E  W
E  A       E  A  F
R  W       R  W  H
E  T       E  T  W
F  M       F  M

 (a)         (b)
```

To get columns of height 8 here, however, column boundaries must fall somewhere near the dotted lines, and although this is possible, it requires a lot of word breaks: m/re, N/NA, H/NO, R/WH, and ET/W. On second thought, this solution doesn't look very good at all. Abandon it and try something else. Since we have invested only about 15 seconds so far, there is no great loss. Eventually we might try columns 10 and 1, as shown in (a) at the top of the next page.

All the digrams here look reasonable. We find an E in columns 2, 5, 7, 8, and 11. Positioning these E's one by one, columns 2, 5, 8, and 11 all yield trigrams that need to be explained (SHL, SHF, ECW, and SLN and ECP, repectively). Column 7 seems the best possibility, as shown in (b). We can make words of all these trigrams—almost a sentence: "THE-TIME-SLIPS-SHOULD-HECK-DITTY-RECALL." (The U below SHO brought the word SHOULD to mind.)

Column 5 gives us the helpful U, and column 2 provides an L with nice word fragments showing up. Column 6 gives us a D, and things

```
                  t            t       a
n       n         d      n     d  e  c n
t H     t H e            t H   e  r  E a
===     =====
T I     T I m            T I   m  e  s i
S L     S L I            S L   I  f  e w
S H     S H O            S H   O  U  L D
E C     E C U            E C   U  L  A T
H E     H E C            H E   C  A  N T
D I     D I T            D I   T  A  N D
E C     E C A            E C   A  N  R E
            E                  E  A    M
                                  I

(a)      (b)                 (c)
```

look as they do in (c). Each row has a plausible interpretation. ECULAT seems to call for an E to follow it. Columns 4, 9, and 8 have E's in the right place, but otherwise they don't seem to fit very well. The E in column 3 does, however, and now the columns begin to fall into place as fast as we can move them: 3 followed by 8, by 4, by 9, and by 11. The message then reads

THERE ARE TWO TIMES IN A MAN'S LIFE WHEN HE SHOULD NOT SPECULATE: WHEN HE CAN'T AFFORD IT AND WHEN HE CAN.

This gem has been attributed to Mark Twain.

The method of solution just discussed requires lots of trials with lots of errors, but it doesn't take much time. For those who are interested in a more organized approach, we will examine a computerized method.

Computerized Attack on the Irregular Columnar

We are going to work under the premise that all we have been given is a ciphertext and the knowledge that it was enciphered as an irregular columnar transposition; we do not know the block width nor a probable word. We will read in the ciphertext and ask the user to suggest a column starting point and column length. The program will then try to match this putative column against all possible alignments. It will save the ten best alignments and print out the geometric averages of their digraph frequencies, plus all the block lengths that are commensurate with the starting point of the first column and the gap between the two columns. On command from the user, the program will then print out the alignment of any set of columns he wishes to see.

Since this program—Program 5.1—is intended to help the user solve a fairly complex problem and since there is a lot of information the user may want to look at, we should go out of our way to make it easy for him to review things.

Program 5.1 Irregular Columnar Tramp

```
1    DIM T%(200)
4    DIM D%(26,26)
6    DIM B(11),A(11)
7    B(11)=100000
10   REM LOAD DIGRAMS (ADD STATEMENT: 10845 IF
     D%(I,K)=0 THEN D%(I,K)=1)
20   GOSUB 10800
30   REM READ IN CIPHERTEXT AND SQUEEZE
40   GOSUB 10000
50   GOSUB 10200
60   REM GET COLUMN LENGTH
70   PRINT "ENTER COLUMN LENGTH"
80   INPUT CL
100  PRINT "TB=PRINT TEST BLOCK, SC=SCAN FOR COLUMN
     MATCH"
110  PRINT "CL=COLUMN LENGTH, CT=PRINT CIPHERTEXT,
     NT=NEW TEXT"
115  INPUT A$
120  IF A$="CL" GOTO 70
130  IF A$="CT" GOTO 1000
140  IF A$="TB" GOTO 2000
150  IF A$="SC" GOTO 3000
160  IF A$="NT" GOTO 40
170  PRINT "I BEG YOUR PARDON"
180  GOTO 100

1000 REM PRINT CIPHERTEXT (CHANGE: 10360 PRINT
     CHR$(T%(I)+64))
1010 GOSUB 10300
1020 PRINT
1030 PRINT
1040 GOTO 100

2000 PRINT "TRIAL BLOCK ALIGNMENT.ENTER COLUMN
     STARTING POINTS.END WITH 0."
2010 K=0
```

```
2020  K=K+1
2030  INPUT C(K)
2040  IF C(K) <>0 GOTO 2020
2050  FOR I=0 TO CL-1
2060     FOR L=1 TO K-1
2070        P=I+C(L)
2080        PRINT CHR$(T%(P)+64);
2090     NEXT L
2100     PRINT
2110  NEXT I
2120  GOTO 100

3000  PRINT "SCAN FOR MATCH.TEST COLUMN STARTING
      POINT="
3010  INPUT TS
3020  REM CLEAR BEST ARRAY
3030  FOR I=1 TO 10
3040     B(I)=0
3050  NEXT I
3060  REM TRY ALL MATCHING POINTS
3070  FOR I=1 TO J-CL+1
3080     P=1
3090     REM COMPUTE P
3100     GOSUB 3300
3110     REM INSERT IN BEST LIST
3120     GOSUB 3400
3130  NEXT I
3140  REM PRINT 10 BEST
3150  FOR I=10 TO 1 STEP-1
3160     PRINT
3170     PRINT A(I);B(I);
3180     REM TEST COMPATIBILITY
3190     GOSUB 3600
3200  NEXT I
3210  GOTO 100

3300  REM COMPUTE P
3310  FOR K=0 TO CL-1
3320     A1=TS+K
3330     A2=I+K
3340     P=P*D%(T%(A1),T%(A2))
3350  NEXT K
3360  P=P ↑ (1/CL)
3370  RETURN
```

```
3400 REM INSERT IN BEST LIST
3405 IF P <B(1) THEN RETURN
3410 FOR L=2 TO 11
3420    IF P <B(L) THEN B(L-1)=P: A(L-1)=I: L=11: GOTO 3450
3430       B(L-1)=B(L)
3440       A(L-1)=A(L)
3450 NEXT L
3460 RETURN

3600 REM TEST COMPATIBILITY
3610 FOR K=5 TO 20
3620    F=1
3630    D1=TS-1
3640    D2=A(I)-TS
3650    IF TS >A(I) THEN D1=A(I)-1: D2=TS-A(I)
3660       GOSUB 3800
3670    IF LS <5 THEN K=20: GOTO 3690
3680    IF F=1 THEN PRINT K;
3690 NEXT K
3700 RETURN

3800 REM TEST CONFORMITY
3810 REM LS=LENGTH OF SHORT,NS=NUMBER OF SHORT,NL=NUMBER OF LONG
3820 LS=INT(J/K)
3830 NL=J-K*LS
3840 NS=K-NL
3850 REM V=NUMBER OF COLUMNS
3860 V1=INT(D1/LS)
3870 V2=INT(D2/LS)
3880 REM S=NUMBER OF SHORTS,L=NUMBER OF LONGS
3890 L1=D1-LS*V1
3900 L2=D2-LS*V2
3910 IF L1 >V1 THEN F=0: RETURN
3920 IF L2 >V2 THEN F=0: RETURN
3930 S1=V1-L1
3940 S2=V2-L2
3950 REM WE NEED AT LEAST L1+L2 LONGS
3960 IF L1+L2 > NL THEN F=0: RETURN
3970 REM WE NEED AT MOST S1+S2 SHORTS
3980 IF S1+S2 <=NS THEN RETURN
3990 REM TRY TO CONVERT LS+1 SHORTS INTO LS LONGS
4000 IF S1 <LS+1 GOTO 4020
4010 L1=L1+LS: S1=S1-LS-1: GOTO 3960
```

```
4020  IF S2 <LS+1 THEN F=0: RETURN
4030  L2=L2+LS: S2=S2-LS-1: GOTO 3960
```

Program 5.1 (cont'd) Irregular Columnar Tramp Comments

10 - 20
: Load digram frequencies. Replace all 0's by 1's.

30 - 50
: Read in the ciphertext and squeeze out the blanks.

60 - 80
: Enter the column length.

100 - 180
: Ask user what he wants to do:

CL:	Change column length.
CT:	Print out the ciphertext.
TB:	Print out the test block.
SC:	Scan for a column match.
NT:	Enter new ciphertext.

1000 - 1040
: Print out the ciphertext. Note that line 10360 of the standard subroutine must be changed to print from T%.

2000 - 2120
: Print out a trial block alignment. Enter the column starting points. The list ends with 0.

2010 - 2040
: Load the starting addresses.

2050 - 2110
: Print out CL rows.

2060 - 2090
: Print K−1 letters, one for each column.

2070 I is the row you are working on, and C(L) is the starting point of the Lth column.

3000 - 3210
: See what group of letters best matches with the test column.

3010 TS is the starting point of the test column.

3020 - 3050
: Clear the vector B that is used to hold the best matches.

3060 - 3130
: Try all possible matching points.

3070 I points to the column you are going to test against the test column.

3100 Go to subroutine to compute P.

3120 Go to subroutine to insert in the "best matches so far" list.

3140 - 3200

Print out the best matches and their "compatibility."

3170 A(I) is starting address of a good match and B(I) is the "value" of the match, P.

3300 - 3370

Compute P.

3320 A1 is the address of the Kth letter of the test column.

3330 A2 is the address of the Kth letter of the other column.

3340 D% is the digram frequency and P = P*D% (of this pair of letters, the first is from the test column and the second from the other column).

3360 Take the CL^{th} root of P.

3400 - 3460

Insert this match into the best vector if it is better than the worst one there. Move down to leave a gap in which to put the new entry, thereby knocking off the worst one. Keep moving items down—2 →1, 3 →2, 4→3, and so forth—until this example is worse than the one above it. Then we insert this example.

3600 - 3700

Print out all block sizes from which these two columns could be drawn (see text for a complete discussion).

3610 For possible block sizes of 5 to 20.

3620 Set flag to 1.

3630 D1 is starting point of test column minus 1.

3640 D2 is difference between "other" column and test column.

3650 If "other" column comes first, reverse computation of D1 and D2.

3660 Go to subroutine to test compatibility.

3670 If there are fewer than five letters per column, quit.

3680 If the flag is still set, then the column starting points are compatible with the block size. Print out this block size.

3800 - 4030

Test to see if these two columns are OK, given block size K.

3820 Given K (the block size) and J (the number of letters), compute the length of the short columns, LS.

3830 NL is the number of long columns.

3840 NS is the number of short columns.

3860 V1 is the number of columns from the beginning of the text to the first of the two samples.

3870 V2 is the number of columns between the two samples.

3890 How many columns (L1) of V1 have to be long?

3900	How many columns (L2) of V2 have to be long?
3910	If too many columns have to be long, set flag to 0 and return.
3920	Same as 3910.
3930 - 3940	S1 and S2 are the number of short columns in V1 and V2.
3960	If the sum of L1 and L2 exceeds the number of long columns available, then we have failed.
3980	If the long columns are OK and S1+S2 is now less than the number of short columns, we have succeeded. Return with F=-1.
3990	Can we convert LS+1 short columns into LS long columns?
4000	If there are more short columns in S1 than LS+1, we can convert.
4010	Do the conversion and go back to see if things fit now.
4020	How about the space between the two samples? Can we do a conversion here? If not, then no conversions are possible and things will not fit; therefore, we have failed.
4030	Since conversion is possible, do it and try again.

The possible user options are as follows:

CT	Print the ciphertext for review
TB	Trial block
SC	Scan for a match

Under the trial block option, we need to specify the column length and the starting points of the various columns in the trial block. When scanning for a match, we need to know the starting point of the test column and its length. Let us make the setting of the column length be another command:

CL	Set column length

Perhaps the most straightforward way to decide what to do next is to input a command, compare it with each of the options, and jump off to a routine to accomplish the desired function, as follows:

```
100   PRINT "WHAT NEXT";
110   INPUT A$
120   IF A$="CT" GOTO 1000
130   IF A$="TB" GOTO 2000
140   IF A$="SC" GOTO 3000
150   IF A$="CL" GOTO 5000
160   IF A$="NT" GOTO 6000
170   PRINT "I BEG YOUR PARDON"
180   GOTO 100
```

Printing out the ciphertext at 1000 involves a simple subroutine call on the routine we have discussed before, followed by a jump back to statement 100 for another command. That routine must be modified to print out the "input buffer." The next simplest part of the program is getting the column length at statement 5000, as follows:

```
5000  PRINT "ENTER LENGTH OF COLUMN";
5010  INPUT CL
5020  GOTO 100
```

We should remember to execute this during the initial setup and before going to the first command so that the user doesn't try to run with zero-length columns and get confused.

At statement 2000, we want to set up a trial block and then print it out. A loop reading in column-starting numbers ended with 0 and followed by a printing loop for the column length will do the job, as follows:

```
   6  DIM C(25)
2000  PRINT "TRIAL BLOCK. ENTER STARTING NUMBERS OF
      COLUMNS. END WITH A 0."
2010  K=1
2030  INPUT C(K)
2040  IF C(K) <>0 THEN K=K+1: GOTO 2030
2050  FOR I=0 TO CL-1
2060     FOR L=1 TO K-1
2070        P=I+C(L)
2080        PRINT CHR$(T(P)+64);
2090     NEXT L
2100     PRINT
2110  NEXT I
2120  GOTO 100
```

The last section of code at 3000 has to find the ten best matches and print them out in order, along with the possible block lengths they conform to.

Most of the program is straightforward, and readers are invited to look at my solution if they have any trouble. Two points warrant a bit of discussion. The first of these is the "save ten best" subroutine. We are going to keep ten slots storing the ten largest geometric averages (P) we have found, and in a corresponding slot of a second vector we are going to keep the starting point where we found that average. We begin by comparing the new P with the smallest one in our table. If it is smaller than the latter, we can return at once, thus speeding up the program considerably. The ten best P's we have found will be stored in B(1)–B(10), smallest to largest. Their starting points will be stored in A(1)-A(10). Given that the new P is bigger than B(1), we know that we are going to want to keep it in the list. We therefore move B(2) to B(1) and A(2) to A(1). Now we check P against B(2). If it is still larger, we move B(3) to B(2) and A(3) to A(2). Eventually, we find a B(I) greater than P. At this point, we store P in B(I−1) and the starting point of this column in A(I−1), and we are done.

When we begin, we will clear B(1)-B(10) to zero and store a very large number in B(11). This will act as a "guard" or "fence" and force all the real P's to be placed below it—in B(1)-B(10)—just as we wanted.

The other routine that needs some elaboration is the place where we test to see what block widths are compatible with the two columns that we are trying to match. Let one column start at point A and the other at point B and assume that A <B. Let D_1=A−1 and D_2=B−A. There are J letters in the ciphertext and K columns in the block we are trying to build. The length of a short column will be

LS=INT(J/K)

and the long columns will obviously be one longer. The number of long columns in the block is the remainder from the division of J by K, and the number of short columns is K−NL. Next, we find out how many short and long columns we need to get from the beginning of the ciphertext to the point just to the left of A and from A to B. L_1 and L_2 are the numbers of long columns required and S_1 and S_2, the numbers of short columns. In the equations

V1 = INT(D1/LS)
L1 = D1−V1*LS

V1 is the number of columns required to make up the distance D1, and L1 is the number of those columns that must be long. Suppose that the distance is 10 and that LS = 7. Then V1 = 1 and L1 = 3. Obviously, this solution won't work, and we therefore test to see whether L1 is less than or equal to V1. If it isn't, we set the flag to zero and return, admitting failure.

Even if L1 ≤ V1 and L2 ≤ V2, it is possible that the two combined distances will require more long columns than we have in the block. Therefore, if L1+L2 > NL, we also fail to find conformity and must return. If we don't need too many long columns and we don't need too many short columns (S1+S2 ≤ NS), then we *can* start at these two points and thus return with F = 1.

If this doesn't work, we may be able to use long columns in place of some short ones. Suppose that D1 = 36 and that the length of a short column is 5 and of a long column, 6. We can construct a length of 36 by using seven columns, one long and six short, but we could also construct a length of 36 by using six long columns, each of length 6.

What we did was to take the length 30, which had been expressed as six columns of length 5, and convert it to five columns of length 6. If the original construction required too many short columns and had plenty of long columns left over, this tactic might help. Thus, for each of the distances D1 and D2 in turn, we see if we can do this conversion, changing LS+1 short columns into LS long ones. If we can do a conversion for either length, we do it and go back to see if $L1+L2 \leq NL$ and $S1+S2 \leq NS$. We will keep on converting as long as we can or until we either succeed or run out of long columns.

Allow me to recommend that you write down a little driver routine to check this subroutine before you accept the fact that it is working properly. Something like the following

```
10  INPUT J          (Length of ciphertext)
20  INPUT K          (Width of block)
30  INPUT D1         (Distance 1)
40  INPUT D2         (Distance 2)
50  F=1
60  GOSUB 3800
70  PRINT F
80  GOTO 10
```

will do the job nicely. Decide in advance on a set of numbers for testing, and compare your results with what you expect should happen.

Problems for Chapter 5

1. AEANT IRTHE TPSLF MDCDI LYIAR BEABT CLSMN ATPNC SYANU AASGI LOMCE EOAST SOANT EUIIO DEHEI IIIME MOES
2. SETLI KFTET AEEHE NWABN RGHOT UYICK LSNEH OOLAV IWOAT EOYWT WLTTC NOHOW ENGNT ORGNA NTTOV IUKIB EN (*Blaise Pascal*)
3. TEERG HTREU HCRSE HOOHH TOTEY SRWCS NAEIE IEUFE EWOIR UFTYR SWNTI BBUIW NUHOT SMCWH EHSRD ENAAI TNEEE ORODO REAOT YN
4. AACEN PRIOJ EOMYT IOEOK OMGGS PFNNH GSCSE FORTK YOOIN NNEEU DWITS RJGVC IDTYO NNUEU EI
5. SEESE AHATE EEITH RSWHE RAEOO IROCV HOWEH LNBYT YOOEC VURTU EDPMT ECEDM WPOEE RAMNR OASIH NITBE CRER
6. IKEGE ITITH UFIEH IZTSR TIGYA EEAIS ITNEU NSYNR MRTGI AIERO NARHH CENLH EHIDI WGTTV IATRN VNHER ADTNR NHONE GTODD

7. CAIAT TLATR YIWOH NEAUV SRTSS EATBF SEEKT NHGIO SYSCH NEAGY GEHYR SSHOA EERHA UHAON DITAB CLITU (*Ambrose Bierce*)
8. IOOWL MITOE GFTBH EOTOU OHLNT YPYNS IPUSE NONAE RNAEC EEDRC BSPOA UPETA SHEES NEAHS EELDE FNIEE EWL (*G. B. Shaw*)
9. NPTVS HSEEO TNSRR TAOEM ETIHO IAOVH TEFSR NEUOO EISOL DSGLI GSNOH OAAAA GSEDE ITEYT TGTLL LDLLG AWI
10. LTVST TXPGC TETME OOEAA OVISR SLPET TIEEO EDNRI ELOMM BBEIE EIOPV AEOLD ODPFI ADOIA HYALG CHNT

6

Other Forms of Transposition

There are many other forms of transposition cipher, and for each there are methods of hand solution. Some of these can be mechanized, and probably others that can take advantage of the computer's doggedness can be devised. In this chapter we will mention only three types of cipher and briefly discuss methods of attacking them.

The Double Transposition Cipher

The normal way analysts have advanced the history of cryptology has been by recognizing a regularity or pattern that remains after enciphering and exploiting that regularity to crack codes. In due course, the people desiring secrecy realize that their messages are being read freely, and, as a result they either abandon their present method of enciphering or, more usually, elaborate their method of removing any regularity the analysts might have noticed. This unending spiral leads to ever more difficult ciphers and, incidentally, to reasonable job security both for their creators and for those who attack that security.

Thus, we see that regular columnar transpositions give way to irregular columnar transpositions, and these in turn give way to double transpositions. As we have observed in the previous chapter, the way to attack an irregular columnar is to exploit the fact that the units taken out of plaintext comprise columns and that when two columns are juxtaposed in trying to reconstruct the original block, all, or almost all, of the digraphs these two columns form must be moderately common digraphs. The way to defeat this weakness is to break up the columns into parts so that the analyst cannot turn it to his advantage. A quite powerful method of breaking up columns is to perform an irregular transposition twice. For example, the message NOW IS THE TIME FOR ALL GOOD MEN TO COME TO THE AID OF THE PARTY can be enciphered using the keyword POLITICS, as follows:

6	5	4	2	8	3	1	7
P	O	L	I	T	I	C	S
N	O	W	I	S	T	H	E
T	I	M	E	F	O	R	A
L	L	G	O	O	D	M	E
N	T	O	C	O	M	E	T
O	T	H	E	A	I	D	O
F	T	H	E	P	A	R	T
Y							

giving

H R M E D R I E O C E E T O D M I A W M
I L T T T N T L N O F Y E A E T O T S F

G O H H O
O O A P

We now take another keyword, USUAL, write the singly transposed ciphertext under it in rows, as follows,

4	3	5	1	2
U	S	U	A	L
H	R	M	E	D
R	I	E	O	C
E	E	T	O	D
M	I	A	W	M
G	O	H	H	O
I	L	T	T	T
N	T	L	N	O
F	Y	E	A	E
T	O	T	S	F
O	O	A	P	

and then read these out in columns in the usual fashion, giving the doubly transposed ciphertext:

E O O W H T N A S P D C D M O T O E F R
T Y O O H R E M G I N F T O M E T A H T

I E I O L
L E T A

We have underlined the letters of two adjacent columns in each of their occurrences. As may readily be seen, it is no simple task to reassemble the columns so that the block may be put back together. In fact, this seemingly simple modification of a simple transposition provides a good deal of security, and, as a result, this method has been used as a military cipher on a number of occasions. It is sometimes called the "U.S. Army transposition" because it was used as a field cipher during part of World War I.

Our programs for enciphering and deciphering single-columnar transpositions (Chap. 4) can, with only trivial modifications, carry out enciphering and deciphering double-columnar transpositions, but the author is unaware of any method applicable to a home computer (or to hand operation either) that will help in cracking the kind of double transposition discussed here. The problem, of course, is that there are no clues to reveal when you have properly reassembled the columns. The only clues come when you try to put the supposedly reconstructed columns back into a block. This situation forces the would-be analyst into an exhaustive search of a very large space.

The professional cryptanalyst has to rely on the fact that in a real life situation many messages will be sent with the same keys. For example, keys are often changed once a day, and during a day many hundreds of messages may be sent. The professional analyst selects all the messages of the same length he can find and writes them down one under the other. With messages of 138 letters, for example, and a given pair of keys, the ith letter of each message will always be transposed to the jth position of the ciphertext. With this group of messages he can then form pseudo columns of letters, all coming from the same place in the plaintext. He then cuts those columns apart and shuffles them by hand, or better, he uses the program of Chap. 5, until he begins to get the plaintext. Having numbered his pseudo columns, he can then declare that plaintext letters i, i+l, . . . , go to ciphertext positions j, k, . . . , for messages of length N. Now he can begin to reconstruct the transpositions used, and the process begins to snowball. From these partial reconstructions he can assemble other pseudo columns in their supposed order, extend any islands of plaintext forward and backward, and thus improve and extend the decipherment.

Once the analyst has deciphered messages of length N, he will be in possession of transposition keys that can be applied to messages of other lengths as well.

It would be virtually impossible for a high-traffic operation such as those found in a military campaign to resist this kind of analysis. Keywords can be changed only so often, and there is no way messages of duplicate length can be prevented. Triple transposition will not help very much either. So, for professional use, the double transposition has become passē, but for a small, low-traffic, amateur clandestine operation, it is still quite acceptable.

May I remind my gentle readers that just because I don't know of a method of attack, that doesn't mean none exist; nor should it discourage you from trying to develop one; in fact, just the reverse.

The Turning Grill

People developed mechanical aids to enciphering long before computers became available. One of the earliest of these was the turning grill, invented by Cardano.

To make one of these grills, take a stiff piece of paper or cardboard and mark on it a square grid with an even number of cells per side: 4×4, 6×6, 8×8, etc. Divide the grid into quarters, and select a keyword or phrase with no repeats that will just fill one quarter of the grid. For a 6×6 grill, the keyword COLUMBIAN would be satisfactory; it is shown in Fig. 6.1 written into each quadrant. Arranging

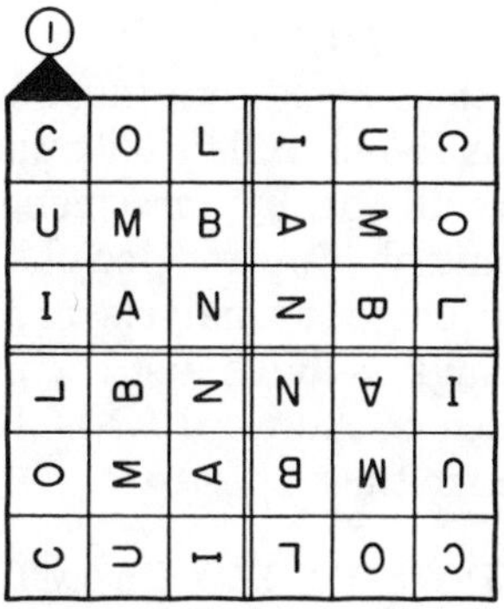

Fig. 6.1 A 6 × 6 turning grill.

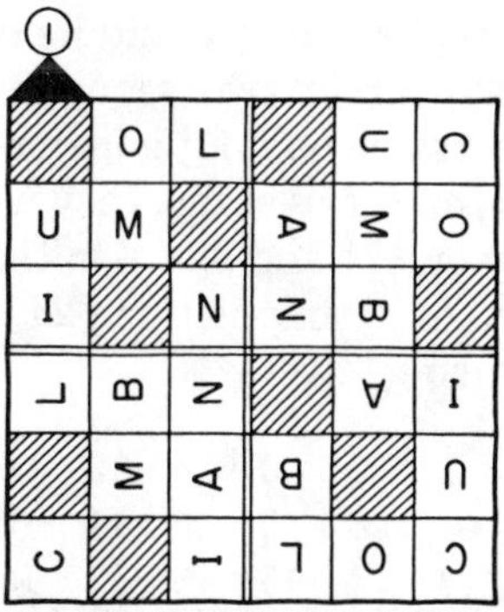

Fig. 6.2 Turning grill perforated and ready for use.

the letters of the keyword alphabetically we have ABCILMNOU. Nine letters divide into four groups of two with one left over. Consequently, we will punch or cut out ABC from the first quadrant, IL from the second, MN from the third, and OU from the fourth, as shown in Fig. 6.2. Note that you have removed exactly one of each of the letters of the key phrase and, note further, that if you rotate the grill 90, 180, or 270 deg clockwise, C's will tranpose into C's, O's into O's, etc.

Place the grill on a piece of paper, and write the first nine letters of your message in the holes you have cut out. Now rotate the grill 90 deg clockwise, and write the next nine letters. Repeat until you have written in letters in each of the four possible positions. Figure 6.3 shows the four steps required to enter the message,

Airport now in enemy hands X advise soonest.

The transmitter and receiver must agree on where to start the grill, which way to turn it, and which side is up. To decipher, one constructs an identical grill, writes the message in a square, lays the grill down in the first position, reads out the first group of letters, turns the grill to the second position, and so forth.

Messages longer than 36 letters must be sent in two or more blocks. As a rule, the last block will be only partly full. This last block may be filled out with nulls or, by agreement, the last row or last N rows can be ignored in enciphering and deciphering.

The standard approach to analysis requires a probable word. Look again at the message we have just enciphered. Suppose that we suspected the occurrence of the word ENEMY. The actual letters of this word are underlined in the ciphertext:

AWSIA INNRE EDSPS ONOXO ERAMT YNDNE SOVNT I

Notice that all the letters are present and that they have occurred in their proper order. With a longer probable word, it is possible that the grill will be turned somewhere in the middle of the word, and the letters might therefore appear in two sequences interlaced with each other. We note that there are no long gaps between the letters of the probable word and that, on the average, they will be four letters apart.

Since there is only one M and one Y in the message, those letters can be identified immediately in positions 24 and 26. Now look at the grid with numbers replacing letters:

	2	3	4	5	6
	8	9	10	11	12
13	14	15	16	17	18
19	20	21	22	23	(24)
25	(26)	27	28	29	30
31	32	33	34	35	36

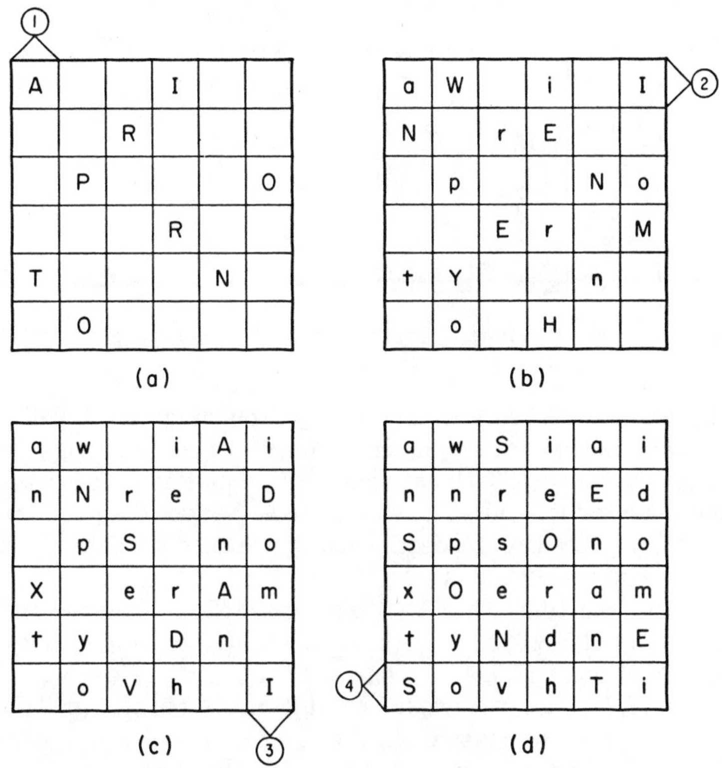

Fig. 6.3 Entering the ciphertext, AWSIA INNRE EDSPS ONOXO ERAMT YNDNE SOVHT I, in the grill of Fig. 6.2.

When the M and Y were written in, positions 24 and 26, corresponding to the C and M, respectively, of the keyword, were exposed. Since only one C was punched out, if position 24 was exposed, 13, 4, and 33 must have been covered. Writing the ciphertext in a block and circling known letters and crossing out impossible letters, we have:

A W S ~~I~~ A I
N ~~N~~ R E ~~E~~ D
~~S~~ P S O N O
X O E R A (M)
T (Y) N D ~~N~~ E
S O ~~V~~ H T I

Of the three E's left, one of them follows the Y, so that if this word was written in without turning the grill, it is "out" and the other two, in positions 10 and 21, are "in." Since there is only one N between the two E's (in position 17), it must be the letter needed to complete

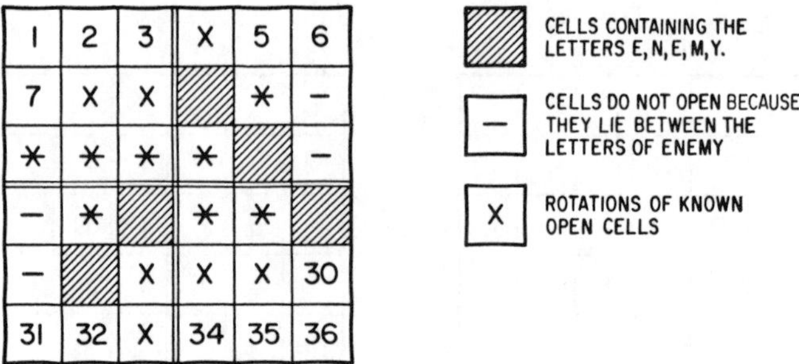

Fig. 6.4 Partial reconstruction of the turning grill.

the probable word. We now have 5 of the 9 openings in the grill and can be certain that there are no more openings in the range from 10 through 26 because if there were, they would expose a letter that would have to "fit" into the word ENEMY. More than this, we have five letters presently exposed, each of which will "inhibit" the exposure of three other positions.

Let us put together a 6×6 square (see Fig. 6.4), crossing out all the cells we know to be forbidden. Of the cells left, one of set [1,6,31,36], one of [7,5,30,32], one of [2,35], and one of [3,34] will be exposed. If, for instance, we have cell 2 exposed in this grill position, then cell 35 must be covered up. If cell 6 is exposed, cells 1, 31, and 36 will be covered, thereby presenting us with a baffling array of possibilities. ENEMY could be preceded by $A_1W_2S_3A_5I_6N_7$ and followed by $E_{30}S_{31}O_{32}H_{34}T_{35}I_{36}$, but if A_1 is chosen, we must eliminate I_6, I_{36}, S_{31}, and so forth.

Such complicated dependencies are too much for the unaided human mind. Fortunately, a mechanical procedure exists (due to Ohaver) that greatly simplifies our work. Remembering that there are nine cells in each quarter of our 6×6 grill, we prepare nine strips of paper. At the top of each strip we write (vertically) the four cells that would be exposed, in turn, by a perforation in this cell of the quarter. Since only one of these cells will be exposed at a time, we will automatically eliminate possibilities when we try to anagram a particular row. For convenience, we repeat the first three cell numbers, thus obtaining a column at the top of the first strip that consists of the numbers 1, 6, 36, 31, 1, 6, and 36. Below these numbers we write the letters that occur in these cells: A, I, I, S, A, I, and I. We proceed to construct a strip for each starting position, as shown in Fig. 6.5.

What we are going to try to do now is to build up the probable word by selecting strips, placing them adjacent to each other, and sliding them up and down as required. As before, we will select the solitary M and Y in the strips, beginning with numbers 13 and 8. Of the re-

1	2	3	7	8	9	13	14	15
6	12	18	5	11	17	4	10	16
36	35	34	30	29	28	24	23	22
31	25	19	32	26	20	33	27	21
1	2	3	7	8	9	13	14	15
6	12	18	5	11	17	4	10	16
36	35	34	30	29	28	24	23	22
A	W	S	N	N	R	S	P	S
I	D	O	A	E	N	I	E	O
I	T	H	E	N	D	M	A	R
S	T	X	O	Y	O	V	N	E
A	W	S	N	N	R	S	P	S
I	D	O	A	E	N	I	E	O
I	T	H	E	N	D	M	A	R

Fig. 6.5 The strips constructed for the turning grill.

maining strips 7, 14, and 15 contain E's and 7, 9, and 14 contain N's. Since we are going to need two E's and one N, we will take as a first guess the strip headed with 9 and lay it next to 13 and 8 with the letters NMY on one row. Lay the three strips containing E's to the right (see Fig. 6.6, where we have underlined the relevant letters and also the numbers of the cells in which they appear). Since plaintext letters on each grill are written into the openings left to right and top to bottom, then in any arrangement of strips, the cell numbers must increase monotonically. Cell numbers 17, 24, and 26 do just that. Of the three strips with E's, the E in 10 must precede the N, and the E in 21 must appear between N_{17} and M_{24}. This, of course, is just another way of saying what was said before when we were working directly with the block. Figure 6.7 shows our reconstruction at this stage. To be certain that this is the correct reconstruction, look at the other available N's in cells 7 and 23. If we had chosen N_{23}, we would have had the sequence,

$$N_{23} \quad M_{24} \quad Y_{26}$$

with no room for an E between the N and M. Had we chosen N_7, we would have had a gap of 24 − 7, or 17, cells with only one opening in the entire space. That would have had to be occupied by E_{10}, leaving a very long blank gap from 10 to 24, a most unlikely situation.

Returning to Fig. 6.7, we look two rows below the word ENEMY and, reading right to left, get the letters ESOON, which represent what would be exposed if the grill were rotated by 180 deg. Since the

9 17 28 20 9 17 28 R N D O R N D
13 4 24 33 13 4 24 S I M V S I M
8 11 29 26 8 11 29 N E N Y N E N
7 5 30 32 7 5 30 N A E O N A E
14 10 23 27 14 10 23 P E A N P E A
15 16 22 21 15 16 22 S O R E S O R

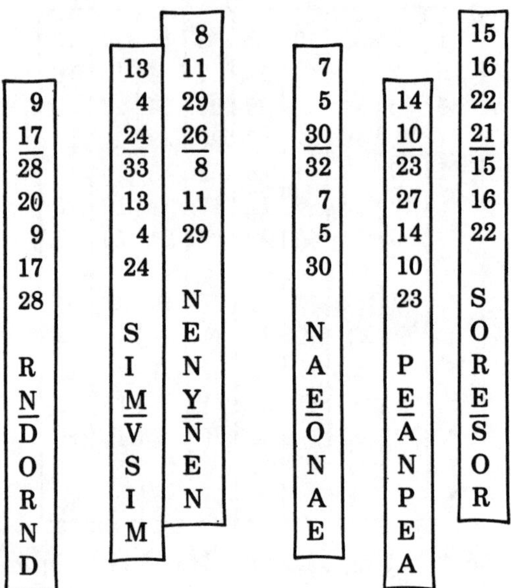

Fig. 6.6 Beginning to build the word ENEMY.

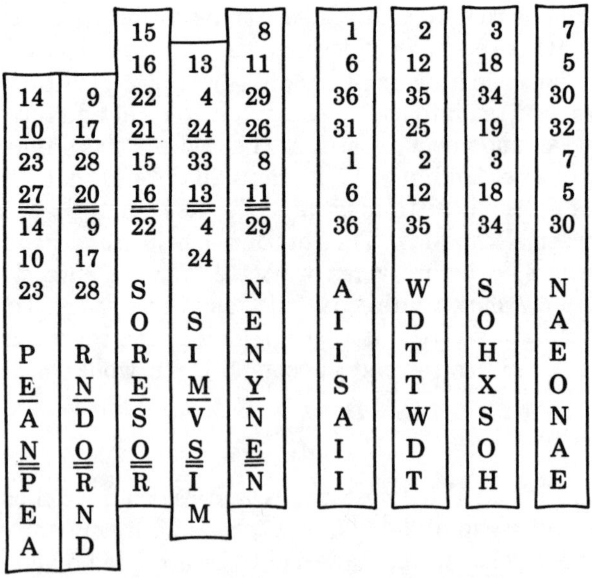

14 10 23 27 14 10 23 P E A N P E A
9 17 28 20 9 17 28 R N D O R N D
15 16 22 21 15 16 22 S O R E S O R
13 4 24 33 13 4 24 S I M V S I M
8 11 29 26 8 11 29 N E N Y N E N
1 6 36 31 1 6 36 A I I S A I I
2 12 35 25 2 12 35 W D T T W D T
3 18 34 19 3 18 34 S O H X S O H
7 5 30 32 7 5 30 N A E O N A E

Fig. 6.7 The probable word ENEMY has been found (unused strips are shown to the right).

English text, ___E SOON, is most plausible, the correctness of ENEMY as we have reconstructed it is confirmed. Unfortunately, however, neither ENEMY nor ESOON suggest good extensions in either direction.

Looking at the line above ENEMY, we find the letters,

$$P_{14} \quad R_9 \quad R_{22} \quad I_4 \quad N_{29}$$

Rearranging these to give monotonically increasing indices, we have

$$I_4 \quad R_9 \quad P_{14} \quad R_{22} \quad N_{29}$$

From the unused strips we find that between I_4 and R_9 we might put N_7 or A_5 but no other letters. Between R_9 and P_{14}, we might put D_{12}. Continuing, we find

$$\begin{Bmatrix} A_1 \\ W_2 \\ S_3 \end{Bmatrix} \quad I_4 \quad \begin{Bmatrix} N_7 \\ \\ A_5 \end{Bmatrix} \quad R_9 \quad \{D_{12}\} \quad P_{14} \quad \begin{Bmatrix} O_{18} \\ \\ X_{19} \end{Bmatrix} \quad R_{22} \quad \{T_{25}\} \quad N_{29} \quad \begin{Bmatrix} I_{36} \\ S_{31} \\ T_{35} \\ H_{34} \\ E_{30} \\ O_{32} \end{Bmatrix}$$

as possible letters inserted before, between, or after the ones we already have. Fortunately, we can narrow down these alternatives somewhat by remembering that on the row that contains ENEMY, we cannot have any numbers (except those already in ENEMY) in the range from 10 to 26. Examine O_{18} and X_{19} between P_{14} and R_{22}. If we line up the O_{18} with the IRPRN row, H_{34} falls on the row containing ENEMY. That placement is all right because 34 is outside the range 10 to 26. If we put X_{19} on the IRPRN row, S_3 would fall on the ENEMY row, and that is all right, too. Note that this is very much easier to do with the actual strips in front of you than to follow from a written text. Eliminating those letters that would cause a letter to fall in the forbidden range, we can reduce our possibilities to

$$\{A_1\} \quad I_4 \quad \begin{Bmatrix} N_7 \\ \\ A_5 \end{Bmatrix} \quad R_9 \quad \{D_{12}\} \quad P_{14} \quad \{O_{18}\} \quad R_{22} \quad \{T_{25}\} \quad N_{29} \quad \begin{Bmatrix} I_{36} \\ S_{31} \\ E_{30} \\ O_{32} \end{Bmatrix}$$

If the word AIRPORT doesn't pop out by now, then you can try the same approach on the row beneath the one containing ENEMY. Since that row will be two rows beneath the one we were working on, or 180 deg away, it should read, right to left,

$$\{I_{36}\} \quad V_{33} \quad \begin{Bmatrix} E_{30} \\ \\ O_{32} \end{Bmatrix} \quad D_{28} \quad \{T_{25}\} \quad A_{23} \quad \{X_{19}\} \quad S_{15} \quad \{D_{12}\} \quad N_8 \quad \begin{Bmatrix} A_1 \\ I_6 \\ N_7 \\ A_5 \end{Bmatrix}$$

If we include A_1 in AIRPORT, then we have to include I_{36} in the same row. Again, the strips do this automatically. They also automatically eliminate A_1 and I_6 on the right if we take A_1I_{36} into the two rows on the left. By now we should be able to construct the grill almost completely and extract the four message sections, which must appear in order. Our only problem is where the message starts, and that is usually obvious from the sense.

Suppose that we know our enemies are prone to use turning grills and we intercept a message of 64 letters. Not much chance that this is anything other than an 8×8 grill. A message of 72 letters would most likely consist of two blocks of 6×6. One of 144 letters would probably consist of four blocks of 36, and so on. We can check these assumptions by counting the number of vowels in each of the proposed blocks. The percentage of vowels (AEIOUY) should come very close to 40 percent in each block. If it does not, something is probably wrong. Either the suspected grill size is wrong, or perhaps a turning grill isn't being used after all.

With two or more blocks we make the strips long enough to include the index numbers and the selected letters of each block. Anagramming becomes easier because corresponding rows have to make sense in all the blocks. The turning grill is not often used professionally, but it has fascinating mathematical regularities and should be quite capable of a computer-aided solution.

The Skipping Tramp

The word *transposition* is too long to use as a regular thing, and the natural tendency would be to shorten it to "tranp," but somehow that abbreviation tends to come out with an "m" rather than an "n" sound. Since the idea of a 1930's type hobo tripping gaily down a country road was an image too strong to resist, I have named this form of transposition cipher the "skipping tramp."

We begin with a standard type of keyword such as

```
H O B O
2 3 1 4
```

to each letter of which we assign a digit: 1 to the alphabetically first letter, 2 to the alphabetically second, and so on. The plaintext is written out

NOWISTHETIMEFORALLGOODMEN

and the enciphering process begins by skipping and extracting letters. The number of letters to skip each time is dictated by the successive digits of the key. Thus, with a key sequence 2314, we should skip two letters, extract a letter, skip three letters, extract another, skip one, and so forth. When we reach the end of the key sequence, we repeat. This process continues to the end of the plaintext, the extracted letters forming the first part of the ciphertext,

NO IST E IMEF RA LGO D EN
W H T O L O M

and giving the initial ciphertext,

WHTOL OM

with the decimated plaintext,

NOISTEIMEFRALGOD EN

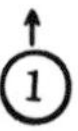

The arrow shows where the last ciphertext letter was extracted, and the circled digit below the arrow shows the number skipped to reach that letter.

The next number of letters to skip is 4. Since there are two letters left at the end of the message, we skip those, then go back to the beginning of the remaining plaintext and skip two more, bringing us to I. We continue from here with the key cycle, giving

NO ST IME R LGOD N
I E F A E

which produces

Ciphertext: IEFAE
Plaintext: NOSTIMERLGOD N

4

On the third pass, we begin by skipping two letters, the N at the end and the N at the beginning, as follows:

N STI E LGOD
O M R N

```
Ciphertext: OMRN
Plaintext:  NSTIELGOD^
                     (4)
```

The fourth pass produces

```
NS IEL  O
  T    G D
```

```
Ciphertext: TGD
Plaintext:  NSIELO^
                 (1)
```

The fifth pass produces

```
NSIE  O
    L
```

```
Ciphertext: L
Plaintext:  NSIE^O
                (4)
```

The sixth pass produces

```
N  IEO
 S
```

```
Ciphertext: S
Plaintext:  N^IEO
             (2)
```

The seventh pass produces (we skip 3, IEO, and take N)

```
 IEO
N
```

```
Ciphertext: N
Plaintext:  ^IEO
            (3)
```

The eighth pass produces

```
I O
 E
```

```
Ciphertext: E
Plaintext:  I^O
             (1)
```

The ninth pass produces (we skip 4, OIOI, and take O)

I
O

Ciphertext: O
Plaintext: I

The tenth pass produces

I

Ciphertext: I
Plaintext: all done

Collecting the ciphertext, we get

WHTOL OMIEF AEOMR NTGDL SNEOI

This is a tedious as well as an error-prone procedure. Clayton C. Pierce, known to the American Cryptogram Association as SiSi, has devised a much more accurate scheme. Using quadrille paper, lay out as many spaces as there are letters in the plaintext. Allow space for several rows. Count across from the left-hand end the number of skips required by the key, and encircle the square following the skip (see Fig. 6.8). The columns below these circled squares are crossed off as shown. Continue from column 23 with a count of four skips, wrapping back to the beginning of the row and not counting columns that have been crossed off. This second time through, encircle squares on the second row. Repeat as required, moving down to a new row each time you begin a new pass. Figure 6.9 shows the completed bar chart with the

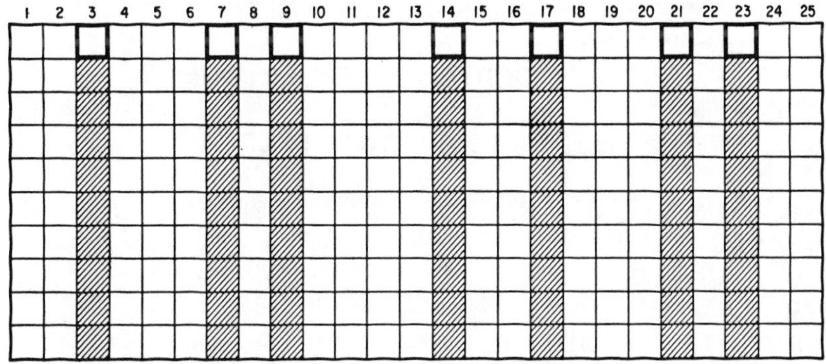

Fig. 6.8 First step in SiSi's method of encoding the skipping tramp.

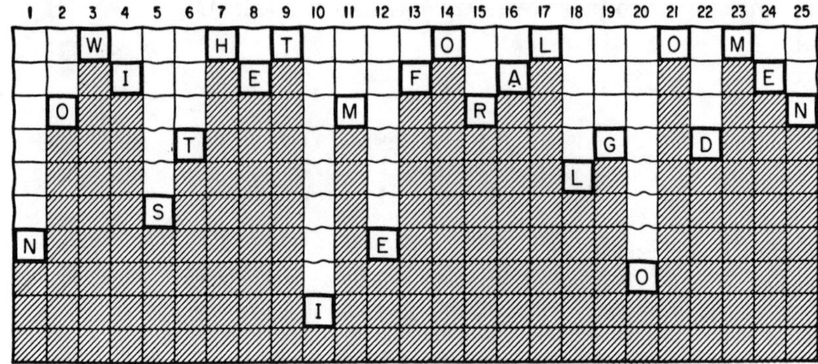

Fig. 6.9 The completed bar chart with plaintext entered.

plaintext entered left to right, one letter per column. The ciphertext is read off row by row starting with the top row.

Writing a computer program that will encipher a skipping tramp is a quite straightforward procedure. The trick is to zero out letters as they are removed and "skip" across only nonzero letters. Such a program is found in Program 6.1.

Program 6.1 Enciphering a Skipping Tramp

```
  5  DIM U(500),S(20)
 10  PRINT "ENTER SKIPS . END WITH 0."
 20  I=1
 30  INPUT S(I)
 40  I=I+1
 50  IF S(I) <> 0 GOTO 30
 60  REM GET PLAINTEXT
 70  GOSUB 10000
 80  REM SQUEEZE BLANKS LEAVES J LETTERS
 90  GOSUB 10200
100  REM L IS POINTER TO PLAINTEXT LETTER
110  L=0
120  REM I IS POINTER TO SKIP TO BE USED
130  I=1
140  REM K IS POINTER TO OUTPUT BUFFER U
150  FOR K=1 TO J
160     S1=S(I)+1
170     L=L+1
180     IF L > J THEN L=1
190     IF T(L) <> 0 THEN S1=S1-1
200     IF S1 <> 0 GOTO 170
```

```
210       I=I+1
220       IF S(I)=0 THEN I=1
230       U(K)=T(L)
240       T(L)=0
250    NEXT K
260    REM PRINT OUT U BUFFER
270    GOSUB 10300
280    STOP
```

Program 6.1 (cont'd) Skipping Tramp Comments

10–50
Put in the skips, and end the string with a zero.

30 Store the skips in a vector, S.

40 Increment the vector pointer.

50 If this is not a skip of zero, go back for more skips.

60–70
Go to the subroutine to read in the plaintext.

80–90
Go to the subroutine to squeeze out blanks and punctuation.

110 Set L to 0 (L is used as a pointer to a letter in the plaintext buffer).

130 Set I to 1 (I is a pointer to the skip vector telling what skip to use).

130–250
Skip through the plaintext, extracting letters and placing them in the output buffer (K is a pointer to the next slot in the output buffer U).

160 S1 is the skip plus 1.

170 Point to the next plaintext letter.

180 If you went off the end, start over.

190 If the letter is not zero, count down on S1.

200 Repeat until S1=0.

210 Increment the pointer to the skip vector.

220 If the skip is zero, reset the pointer.

230 Move the letter from the plaintext to the ciphertext.

240 Zero out the plaintext letter.

260–270
Print out the output buffer.

More interesting (but not yet done by computer), is the analysis of the skipping tramp.

Analysis with Known Key Length and Probable Word

Take the following ciphertext with a key length of 5 and the probable word HUMANITY:

HEOVT RSLHI YDEFK OWGAS EPULE
TDSME SOANP LNRNW YNLPE ITESM
THUNA LEATE LSSTA NTACT RYUSI
HBOEA AORYI DLTSE WAASI NRNIN
OI

There are 102 letters in the ciphertext. With a key length of 5, we know that there are going to be skips of 1, 2, 3, 4, and 5 in some order and that for each skip we will extract one letter. Each time we cycle through the key sequence, we extract five letters to put into the ciphertext and move across 20 letters of plaintext. Of these 20, we extract five and skip 15. Thus it will take five cycles through the key to pass once through the original 102-letter plaintext, generating 25 letters of ciphertext. On this first pass through the plaintext, we will pass through the probable word, assuming one is present, and extract some letters from it. Since these letters will come out in order, we should look among the first 25 letters of ciphertext for a subset of the letters of HUMANITY appearing adjacent to one another and in proper order. The only reasonable candidates are H I Y, which would be taken out as

$$\underline{H}\ U\ M\ A\ N\ \underline{I}\ T\ \underline{Y}$$

with skips of four spaces and then one.

At this point we could work with any of these three letters, but the I seems the easiest since it is the tenth ciphertext letter and exactly finishes up the second cycle through the key sequence. The I was the fortieth letter of the plaintext (because each cycle of five steps or over extracts exactly 20 letters), and on the first pass the I, the H, and eight other preceding letters were extracted. By the time we extract the I, we have taken out ten letters of the original 102, leaving 92 letters. If we go through four more cycles of the key sequence, we will step over a total of 80 letters, placing us twelve steps to the left of where the I was taken from, and we will extract 4 × 5, or 20 letters.

In pictorial form, we will be in this situation:

$$\boxed{E}\ X_{12}\ X_{11}\ X_{10}\ X_{9}\ X_{8}\ X_{7}\ X_{6}\ X_{5}\ \boxed{H}\ U_{4}\ M_{3}\ A_{2}\ N_{1}\ \underset{\uparrow}{\boxed{I}}\ T\ \boxed{Y}$$

The twentieth ciphertext letter following I_{10} is E_{30}, which will have been taken from the slot 13 places to the left of I. Remember that the H was taken out on the first pass and therefore isn't counted. Since I_{10} was extracted after a skip of four, E_{30} will also be taken out after a skip of four. Since we know a skip of four is followed by a skip of one, we know that the thirty-first ciphertext letter S_{31} corresponds to the letter labeled X_{11} in the above sequence. What we know about the key at present is the following:

$$1, K_a, K_b, K_c, 4$$

The sequence ends with 4 because I is the tenth ciphertext letter and the end of the second cycle; it was taken out on a skip of 4. It begins with 1 because Y came out on a skip of one following the I. K_a, K_b, and K_c then represent skips of two, three, and five, but not necessarily in that order. Working forward from $X_{11}=S_{31}$, we take out O, A, N, and P. If the order of skips had been two, three, and five, we would have skipped X_{10} and X_9, taken X_8 (ciphertext O_{32}), and then skipped X_7, X_6, and X_5 and taken U. But we didn't. Following the O, we got an A_{33}. The same argument rejects the ordering three, two, and five. Suppose that the order of K_a, K_b, and K_c was two, five, and three. Then, working from X_{11} (S_{31}), we would skip X_{10} and X_9 and take X_8 (corresponding to ciphertext O_{32}). Then we would skip X_7, X_6, X_5, U_4, and M_3 and take A, which is just what ciphertext letter 33 is equal to. Thus, both patterns two, five, and three and five, two, and three would work.

Pattern three, five, and two would skip X_{10}, X_9, and X_8 and take X_7; it would then skip X_6, X_5, U_4, M_3 and A_2 and take N_1. Indeed, there is an N in the ciphertext (N_{34}), but it is A_{33} that we have to account for. Therefore, patterns three, five, and two and five, three, and two are out, leaving only patterns two, five, and three and five, two, and three. At this point we have just taken out the A_{33} on a skip of K_b, and the key now looks as follows:

$$1, K_a, K_b, 3, 4$$

When A_{33} came out, 69 letters (102 − 33) were left, or three cycles of 20 plus an extra nine. Since three cycles generate 15 letters of plaintext, counting forward from A_{33} produces E_{48}, S_{49}, M_{50}, and T_{51}. The decimated plaintext now becomes

E	X	X	X	X	X	X	X	[H]	U	M	[A]	N	[I]	T	[Y]
48	9	8	7	6	5	4	3		2	1					
↑											↑				

with the E_{48} taken out nine to the left of the A on a skip of K_b. Now we need skips of three, four, and one, which will extract X_6, M_1, and T. Since X_6 corresponds to S_{49}, the M and T are correct. But we still don't know whether the key sequence is one, two, five, three, and four or one, five, two, three, and four. At this point we can try both to see which one generates English plaintext. Looking at the results, there is no great problem about selecting one in preference to the other. Clearly, the key sequence is one, two, five, three, and four, and the message reads

> The desire to solve mysteries is as old as humanity and the spell of an unknown writing has always been particularly potent.

Since doing this analysis by hand is extremely error prone, this would be an ideal time to apply a computer. One could search for fragments of the probable word, derive partial key sequences, and with them generate partial reconstructions of the plaintext based on the partial or possible key sequences.

Problems for Chapter 6

Double Transposition (four messages with common keys)

1. FASNC TENOE NRSNH ALACT NIVET POREE NRLEY NIAGI TTRPE CHOEA CMYAH ADHAU CSIOH NMCUW HNUY
2. TOLWK WSHGW TENDY RHOHE EXRCR FNCUW AYDEF RANON SIOEE SLAPO APTSW EAIUI TVSHA ADORD ACOE
3. SEBEC OESLA YOIOS CNCCN MEIDH EBIIT RWPTT OOLNI AOAUF TVHOW OTVRC AOHEA DOMCT RSNHY MYEL
4. EEFOE TELTH DRHFW BONTA SRSUH IMETS RBLTI TONTO ONDEY OLNET DTDNP DIUOG ASEPM ERBEI INCA

Turning Grills

1. (Probable word, DIPLOMAT)
   AEIAM BLDSA MIEPL AWAOM RYSNR SAWEA WHMOO TERDM SHRAA YBNES BUREI RRMET MAGEB TNEEX VH
2. (Probable word, OBSERVED)
   TSTAF SVRTI AECET ETRWN LYEID LASWW SHOBE BATTS NEICR EVHDT RHEHA OSDSG EBUO *(René Descartes)*

Skipping Tramps

1. (Probable word, INTELLIGENCE; key length, 6)
   ELEHH AWANY OAUAR EAUNL INLSS TWEOT TRNNE GLPET IHWYI TOOBT TRGST TIOOT HAHOE IGUHR CATOD NTENI DCE
2. (Probable word, VIRTUOUS; key length, 5)
   LSICT OHHSN UUNIL GNOAA HAERT IERSH BIMTN NAWNB OHNNF NIUII ESCBG HSTOO SAVER EEEEK LMYRU GWEI

3. (Probable word, MORALCRISIS; unknown key length)
   HTAEE EVFSW TGTRS STIUA HOPLE ETONR OCIAE
   IESNL RHMOL IITYE HROEA RTRTI EHFMN TCRIS ATARE
   NLOME DIRAL ESHNT ES
4. (Probable word, MECHANICAL)
   MRPTT OEGEA ITEEE WIEUT TAETI NDNLB SDHYP
   OGNET HHMHI RNTOU ORAAO IYEHH HRESW NLOEO
   KOMAA AWDEC PTLCI HDOSC GADIA RONWH ZSITE

7

Simple Substitution

Probably the most popular amateur cipher is the *simple substitution cipher.* Each plaintext letter is replaced in all its occurrences in the message by a unique ciphertext letter. For instance, plaintext a may be replaced by ciphertext Z, plaintext b by ciphertext Y, and so on. Each plaintext letter has a single substitute, and each ciphertext letter stands for exactly one plaintext letter.The technique is sometimes called *one-to-one mapping.* A typical substitution alphabet might look as follows:

Plaintext:	a	b	c	d	e	f	g	h	i	j	k	l	m
Ciphertext:	D	E	M	O	C	R	A	T	B	F	G	H	I

Plaintext:	n	o	p	q	r	s	t	u	v	w	x	y	z
Ciphertext:	J	K	L	N	P	Q	S	U	V	W	X	Y	Z

and the plaintext message

We need help come at once

would be enciphered as

WC JCCO TCHL MKIC DS KJMC

If word spacings and punctuation are preserved, this is commonly called an *aristocrat*; if blanks and punctuation are removed, it is called a *patristocrat.*

As you may have noticed in our example alphabet, the cipher alphabet was constructed using a keyword. The purpose of the keyword is to avoid "incriminating" evidence in the form of a translation key that just might fall into enemy hands or act as evidence against a spy. A keyword or phrase is chosen that can be easily remembered; when the need arises, the translation key can be readily constructed and destroyed after use. If the keyword contains duplicate letters, any occurrences of a letter after the first are simply deleted. Thus the phrase, "Mister Spock has pointed ears," would reduce to MISTERPOCK-

HAND. Following the keyword, the remaining unused letters of the alphabet are written out, and the entire set is then put into one-to-one correspondence with the regular alphabet. Sometimes the cipher alphabet is jumbled in this fashion, sometimes the plain alphabet, and sometimes both. After a jumbled alphabet has been generated, it is not necessary to make it immediately correspond with the other alphabet. As you can readily see, if we do so right away, the letters toward the end of the alphabet will tend to line up, if indeed they are changed at all, and become easy to identify. One way to suppress this tendency is to rotate one of the alphabets by a few positions. In place of the example given before, we might remember the key phrase 7 DEMOCRAT and obtain

Plaintext:	a	b	c	d	e	f	g	h	i	j	k	l	m
Ciphertext:	U	V	W	X	Y	Z	D	E	M	O	C	R	A

Plaintext:	n	o	p	q	r	s	t	u	v	w	x	y	z
Ciphertext:	T	B	F	G	H	I	J	K	L	N	P	Q	S

Even this trick still leaves considerable regularity. The fact that letters following the key phrase appear in ascending order can be exploited by a clever analyst. Another way to scramble the alphabet based on the same key, 7 DEMOCRAT, might be to write down the word *seven* and beneath it the jumbled alphabet, as follows:

4	1	5	2	3
S	E	V	E	N
D	E	M	O	C
R	A	T	B	F
G	H	I	J	K
L	N	P	Q	S
U	V	W	X	Y
Z				

and read them out like a columnar transposition cipher, giving

Plaintext:	a	b	c	d	e	f	g	h	i	j	k	l	m
Ciphertext:	E	A	H	N	V	O	B	J	Q	X	C	F	K

Plaintext:	n	o	p	q	r	s	t	u	v	w	x	y	z
Ciphertext:	S	Y	D	R	G	L	U	Z	M	T	I	P	W

Other, more elaborate, schemes can be used to approach the irregularity and unpredictability of random alphabets while retaining the ability to reconstruct the translation key from easily remembered key phrases and mechanical operations.

Our subroutine for generating a scrambled alphabet uses a shifted keyword for simplicity. We allow shifts of 0 (no shift) to 25 (almost back to where we started). If we specify a shift of seven for example, we move the scrambled cipher alphabet seven places to the right and take the last seven "overhanging" letters and put them in the empty spaces below the first seven letters of the plain alphabet. Using this scheme, a shift of 25 to the right is equivalent to a left shift of one.

The program to encipher a message in a simple substitution cipher is as simple as the name implies. Read in the shift and the keyword and generate the scrambled alphabet in CA(1) through CA(26). Now read in the plaintext and translate to numbers (A = 1, Z = 26). Punctuation and spaces are also translated to their ASCII equivalents minus 64. For each character in the input message, we test to see if it is in the range 1 through 26, that is, if it is a letter of the alphabet. If not, we leave it unchanged, but if it is a letter, we replace it with its ciphertext equivalent. For the ith letter of the input text, T%(I), we execute

```
T%(I)=CA(T%(I))
```

When we have done this for each letter of the input, we can print out the translated text by a loop on the instruction:

```
PRINT CHR$(T%(I)+64);
```

which converts the characters and the punctuation back to their ASCII representations and then prints them one at a time, one after the other. Enciphering a simple substitution is shown in Program 7.1. The subroutine to generate a keyword-shifted alphabet is shown in Program 7.2

Program 7.1 Enciphering a Simple Substitution

```
10   REM SIMPLE SUBSTITUTION ENCIPHERING
20   REM GET KEYWORD
30   GOSUB 12000
40   REM GET PLAINTEXT
50   GOSUB 10000
60   REM FOR PATRISTOCRATS CALL BLANK SQUEEZER AT
     10200
70   FOR I=1 TO J
80      IF T%(I) . 1 OR T%(I) □ 26 GOTO 100
90      T%(I)=CA(T%(I))
100  NEXT I
110  REM PRINT CIPHERTEXT, FOR PATS USE SUBROUTINE AT
     10300
```

```
120  PRINT
130  FOR I=1 TO J
140     PRINT CHR$(T%(I)+64);
150  NEXT I
160  GOTO 10
```

Program 7.1 (cont'd) Enciphering a Simple Substitution Comments

20 - 30
: Go get a keyword. Make a keyword alphabet and shift it.

40 - 50
: Get the plaintext but don't remove the punctuation.

70 - 100
: Do the substitution.

80 If the substitution isn't a letter, don't change it. Leave the punctuation alone.

90 Look up the letter in the cipher alphabet, and take the value stored there as the substitution.

110 - 150
: Print out the ciphertext, punctuation and all.

Program 7.2 Subroutine to Generate a Keyword-Shifted Alphabet

```
    7  DIM CA(52)
12000  REM GENERATE SCRAMBLED/SHIFTED ALPHABET
12010  FOR I=1 TO 52: CA(I)=0: NEXT I
12015  PRINT "ENTER SHIFT 0-25 POSITIONS"
12020  INPUT SH
12030  IF SH □25 OR SH .0 GOTO 12015
12040  PRINT "ENTER KEYWORD NO BLANKS ALLOWED"
12050  INPUT KW$
12060  FOR I=1 TO LEN(KW$)
12070     T%(I)=ASC(MID$(KW$,I,1))-64
12080  NEXT I
12090  L=1
12095  REM FOR EACH LETTER IN THE KEYWORD
12100  FOR I=1 TO LEN (KW$)
12110     F=0
12115     REM SEE IF IT HAS BEEN USED YET
12120     FOR K=1 TO I
12130        IF T%(I)=CA(K+SH) THEN F=1: K=I
12140     NEXT K
12150     IF F=0 THEN CA(L+SH)=T%(I): L=L+1
```

```
12160  NEXT I
12170  REM NOW DO REST OF ALPHABET
12180  M=L-1
12190  FOR I=1 TO 26
12200     F=0
12210     REM SEE IF USED YET
12220     FOR K=1 TO M
12230        IF I=CA(K+SH) THEN F=1: K=M
12240     NEXT K
12250     IF F=0 THEN CA(L+SH)=I: L=L+1
12260  NEXT I
12265  IF SH=0 GOTO 12300
12270  FOR I=1 TO SH
12280     CA(I)=CA(I+26)
12290  NEXT I
12300  RETURN
```

Program 7.2 (cont'd) Keyword-Shifted Alphabet Comments

12010 Clear CA, the cipher alphabet.

12020 Input the shift, SH.

12030 Check to see if SH □ 0 and 26.

12050 Get the keyword.

12060 - 12080
Convert the keyword to numbers in T%.

12090 L gets 1 (L is a pointer to the cipher alphabet).

12100 - 12160
Move letters from keyword to cipher alphabet, discarding any duplicates. Put them in order, beginning at SH+1, SH+2, etc.

12110 Clear the flag.

12120 - 12140
Search letters already in cipher alphabet to see if this letter has been used. If so, set the flag.

12150 If the flag is clear add the letters to the cipher alphabet.

12170 - 12260
For all letters of the alphabet, A through Z, add those to CA that aren't there already.

12265 If shift is 0, return.

12270 - 12290
Move the "overhanging" letters back to the beginning of the cipher alphabet.

Deciphering is approximately the same, except that we have to construct the reverse translation alphabet, sometimes called the *plain-*

text alphabet. We can do this conveniently by working from the ciphertext alphabet. A loop with I running from 1 to 26 on

PA(CA(I))=I

will accomplish our aim. Suppose that the first entry in the ciphertext alphabet, CA(1), is 13, standing for the letter M. Then, in the plaintext alphabet slot 13, PA(13)=PA(CA(1)), we enter the number 1, which stands for A since ciphertext M translates to A (see Program 7.3).

Program 7.3 Deciphering a Simple Substitution

```
  9  DIM PA(26)
 10  REM SIMPLE SUBSTITUTION DECIPHERING
 20  REM GET KEYWORD
 30  GOSUB 12000
 40  FOR I=1 TO 26
 50     PA(CA(I))=I
 60  NEXT I
 70  REM GET CIPHERTEXT
 80  GOSUB 10000
 90  FOR I=1 TO J
100     IF T%(I) . 1 OR T%(I) □ 26 GOTO 120
110     T%(I)=PA(T%(I))
120  NEXT I
130  PRINT
140  FOR I=1 TO J
150     PRINT CHR$(T%(I)+64);
160  NEXT I
170  GOTO 10
```

Program 7.3 (cont'd) Deciphering a Simple Substitution Comments

30 Get the keyword shifted alphabet in CA(1)-CA(26).

40 - 60
Make a plaintext alphabet from the ciphertext alphabet.

80 Get the ciphertext.

90 - 120
Convert from ciphertext to plaintext.

100 Leave the punctuation alone.

110 Substitute for the letters.

130 - 160
Print out the plaintext.

Now we have to face a problem that we have put off as long as possible. The BASIC compiler on the PET, and most other computers, gets confused by punctuation, particularly by commas. An aristocrat is supposed to carry all punctuation over to the ciphertext completely unchanged. If it were only commas that gave trouble, we could probably live with that, substituting some other character for commas (for instance, a minus sign) as we entered the plaintext. But worse than this difficulty, on the PET at least, the input routine seems to delete leading and trailing spaces from the input lines, thus making it impossible to have a word space at the end of a line.

Fortunately, there is a way around both these problems in the PET: the GET statement. Users of other variants of BASIC will have to either find their own way around the problem or else use minus signs for commas and perhaps plus signs in place of spaces.

For the PET, we can change the text input routine to look like the following:

```
10  GET A$: IF A$="" GOTO 10
20  PRINT A$;
30  B=ASC(A$)-64
40  IF B=-17 THEN RETURN
50  IF B=-44 THEN J=J-1: GOTO 10
60  J=J+1
70  T%(J)=B
80  GOTO 10
```

This routine is actually somewhat simpler than the one we had before and will accept any character the keyboard can generate. In statement 10, the GET A$ takes a character from the keyboard buffer; if that character is null (two quotes immediately adjacent, meaning that the user hasn't typed anything) the routine will loop on itself indefinitely. Once we get a character and the test for null fails, we print that character out so that the user can see what was entered and translate it to ASCII minus 64. In statement 40, if the character was a slash (since ASCII = 47, ASCII − 64 = − 17), we return. Otherwise, we add the character to the text buffer and go back to statement 10 again. Line 50 is present to take care of the "delete" key, which should act as an "erasing backspace." This does everything we want except display a cursor on the screen.

Analysis of the Simple Substitution Cipher

We have just received the following message from a seaborne confederate, but unfortunately we seem to have forgotten the keyword:

X DWXAZ RSOPLSNI WKR VSDDPA FXRP DS SBU STPUKDXSA. K TKDUSC LSKD XR QSCCSFXAV BR PEPUITCKMP FP VS.

There is nothing to be done except try to crack the cipher as any other analyst might do. First of all we should take a ciphertext letter frequency count, as follows:

A:	4	H:	0	O:	1	V:	3
B:	2	I:	2	P:	8	W:	2
C:	4	J:	0	Q:	1	X:	6
D:	7	K:	6	R:	5	Y:	0
E:	1	L:	2	S:	12	Z:	1
F:	3	M:	1	T:	3		
G:	0	N:	1	U:	4		

The most popular of these are the following:

S:	12
P:	8
D:	7
K:	6
X:	6
R:	5

Looking at Appendix A, we find that in the Brown sample of English, the most frequent letters are

E T A O I N

Our high-frequency ciphertext letters stand for several of these common letters, but it would be naive to expect that S stands for e, P for t, D for a, etc. We are dealing with a sample of only 76 letters, and normal statistical fluctuations will cause a letter to appear more or less frequently in such a small sample than we found in the much larger Brown corpus. Since it is better to do almost anything than just sit and stare at a crypt, let us try the assumption that the letters S, P, D, K, X, R do indeed stand for e, t, a, o, i, n, and in that order, and see what it shows us:

```
X DWXAZ RSOPLSNI WKR VSDDPA FXRP
i a i   ne t e    on  eaat   int

DS SBU STPUKDXSA. K TKDUSC LSKD
ae e   e t oaie   o   a e   eoa

XR QSCCSFXAV BR PEPUITCKMP FP VS.
in  e  e i    n t t      t  t  e
```

The first word has one letter as does the tenth. We have tentatively translated these as i and o. In ordinary English, there are only two one-letter words, i and a, since the exclamation is usually spelled "Oh." Although it is true that any letter can stand alone ("X is an uncommon letter," for an example), without the period that is associated with an initial or abbreviation, anything other than these two possibilities is too uncommon to be worthy of consideration. Thus, either X represents a and K stands for i, or the other way around. In either event, D can't represent a, which is all to the good since the fifth word seems to have three vowels in a row and the seventh word is a two-letter word apparently consisting of two vowels. We will guess that X is i, and if that doesn't work out, we can come back and change it to a. We now have

```
X DWXAZ RSOPLSNI WKR VSDDPA FXRP
i   i   ne t      an  e  t   int

DS SBU STPUKDXSA. K TKDUSC LSKD
 e e   e t a ie . a  a  e   ea

XR QSCCSFXAV BR PEPUITCKMP FP VS.
in  e  e i    n t t    a t  t  e.
```

Having seemingly extracted all the juice from the one-letter words, we will now examine the two-letter words to try to squeeze some blood from those stones. In particular, let us look at the next to last word, FP, which presently deciphers as –t. If P stands for t, then F must stand for a vowel. Since i and a are temporarily represented by X and K, the F must represent e, o, u, or y. But none of these make English words in this context. It is possible that there was an error in enciphering or in the transmission of the message, of course, but we will reject that hypothesis for now, coming back to it only as a last resort. Since it seems that P does *not* stand for *t*, we are left with

X = i
K = a

and possibly

S = e
R = n

with P and D to be assigned to t and o. If P can't be t, then maybe D can. Let's look at word seven, DS. If D stands for t, then S cannot stand for e. In fact, if D stands for t, then S must stand for o since no other assignment makes an English word. Substituting these letters, we get

```
X DWXAZ RSOPLSNI WKR VSDDPA FXRP
i t i   no        an  ott    in

DS SBU STPUKDXSA. K TKDUSC LSKD
to o   o   atio   a  at o   oat

XR QSCCSFXAV BR PEPUITCKMP FP VS.
in  o  o i    n        a       o.
```

Now let's look at the fourth from the last word, BR. If R is n, then B must be a vowel, and the only vowels left are e, u, and y, none of which make much sense in this context. Having to reject that hypothesis doesn't leave us many of our initial guesses still intact. But that's all right; at least it got us started. Now that n is available for representation by another letter than R, let's look at the third word in the second row that seems to end tio–. The two most common word endings in English are "tion" and "ing." Suppose, therefore, that A stands for n. As a result, the second word of the third line would end with in–. We now note that V occurs only three times. In the Brown sample, g occurs about twice per hundred letters; thus, V might very well stand for g–. Putting these assumptions under the message, we obtain

```
X DWXAZ RSOPLSNI WKR VSDDPA FXRP
i t in   o   o    a  gott n  i

DS SBU STPUKDXSA. K TKDUSC LSKD
to o   o   ation   a  at o   oat

XR QSCCSFXAV BR PEPUITCKMP FP VS.
i   o  o ing           a      go.
```

Since the fifth word of the first line is obviously "gotten," P must stand for e. The first word of the third line XR is assumed to be i–. Common two-letter words beginning with i are "it," "is," "in," and "if," of which "it" and "in" are not possible here (assuming that we are on the right track so far). Since R occurs five times in our message and in the Brown sample s occurs seven times per hundred and f occurs twice, the best bet is that R stands for s. Now the crypt becomes

```
X DWXAZ RSOPLSNI WKR VSDDPA FXRP
i t in  so e o    as gotten  ise

DS SBU STPUKDXSA. K TKDUSC LSKD
to o   o e ation. a  at o   oat

XR QSCCSFXAV BR PEPUITCKMP FP VS.
is  o  o ing  s e e    a e  e go.
```

In the last line, BR must be either "us" or "ys," giving us really only one choice. The other B in the message occurs in the second word of the second line, giving ou–, which might be "out," but isn't because t is already assigned; thus it has to be "our." That substitution makes the third word of this line "o–eration," which would translate nicely as "operation" if T is p. The last word of the first line, moreover, has to be either "vise" or "wise," and the next-to-last word of the last line enables us to choose between them. The message is now beginning to take shape:

```
X DWXAZ RSOPLSNI WKR VSDDPA FXRP
i t in  so e o    as gotten wise

DS SBU STPUKDXSA. K TKDUSC LSKD
to our operation. a patro   oat

XR QSCCSFXAV BR PEPUITCKMP FP VS.
is  o  owing us e er p a e we go.
```

The fourth word of the first line now seems to be "has," which makes the second word of the same line, "thin–," probably "think." In the second line, since we know that our friend is at sea, the words "patrol boat" more or less jump out at us. This substitution for C makes the second word of the third line "–ollowing," which with a bit of guessing produces

I think somebody has gotten wise to our operation.
A patrol boat is following us everyplace we go.

To summarize the methods (if that's not too strong a word) we have used:

1. Common letters will appear frequently in a message but don't expect an exact correspondence in popularity.
2. Start working with the shorter words first since there are fewer possibilities to explore.
3. Look for common endings such as "–tion," "–ing," "–ers," "–ent," "–ant," "–ted," "–ess," "–red," "–nce," and so on.
4. Guess a lot. Your brain has seen hundreds of thousands of words and your subconscious is a very powerful computer.
5. If you eliminate all except a few possibilities, try them in turn.
6. Every word has to have at least one vowel and usually has one or more consonants.
7. Keep trying to look for any coherent message. It is supposed to make sense in the end (certain advanced aristocrats to the contrary, notwithstanding).
8. Start some place—any place—and go forward.
9. Do lots of ciphers. That's the way to develop your intuition.

Using the following straightforward program (Program 7.4) will save you from wearing out innumerable erasers and making thin spots in your paper. In its present form, it offers three possible options: making an assignment, reviewing all assignments, and displaying the partial translation. The "pokes" are used to cause the PET to produce lower-case letters for plaintext and can easily be left out if that capability is not available.

Program 7.4 Substitution Helper Package

```
  9  DIM PA(26)
 10  REM SET PET TO PRINT LOWER CASE
 15  POKE 59468,14
 20  REM GET CIPHERTEXT
 25  GOSUB 10000
 30  FOR I=1 TO 26
 40     PA(I)=ASC("-")-64
 50  NEXT I
100  PRINT "ENTER COMMAND(1=DISPLAY MENU)"
110  INPUT A
120  ON A GOTO 150,200,300,400
150  PRINT "AVAILABLE COMMANDS ARE:"
160  PRINT "1-DISPLAY THIS MENU  2-SHOW ALPHABETS"
170  PRINT "3-ASSIGN LETTER      4-TRANSLATE TEXT"
197  PRINT
198  GOTO 100

200  PRINT "CIPHER=ABCDEFGHIJKLMNOPQRSTUVWXYZ"
220  PRINT "PLAIN = ";
230  FOR I=1 TO 26
235     IF PA(I) . 0 OR PA(I) □ 26 THEN PRINT CHR$ (PA(I)+64);:
        GOTO 250
240     PRINT CHR$ (PA(I)+192);
250  NEXT I
260  PRINT
270  GOTO 100

300  PRINT "ENTER CT LETTER FOLLOWED BY PT
     EQUIVALENT. SLASH ENDS THE LIST."
310  INPUT A$
320     A=ASC (MID$(A$,1,1))-64
330     IF A=-17 GOTO 100
335     IF LEN (A$) .□ 2 GOTO 300
340     B=ASC(MID$(A$,2,1))-64
350     IF A . 1 OR A □ 26 GOTO 300
```

```
360      PA(A)=B
370      GOTO 310

400   K=1
410   I=1
420   IF T%(I)=-51 THEN I=I+1: GOTO 500
430   PRINT CHR$(T%(I)+64);
440   I=I+1
450   IF I □ J GOTO 500
455   IF I-K □ 39 GOTO 500
460   GOTO 420
500   PRINT
520   FOR L=K TO I-1
530      IF T%(L) . 1 OR T%(L) □ 26 THEN PRINT CHR$(T%(L)+64);:
         GOTO 550
535      IF PA(T%(L))=-19 THEN PRINT "-";: GOTO 550
540      PRINT CHR$(PA(T%(L))+192);
550   NEXT L
570   PRINT
580   K=I
590   IF I □ =J GOTO 100
600   GOTO 420
```

Program 7.4 (cont'd) Substitution Helper Package Comments

15 Set up the PET so that it will print lower case.

30 - 50

Set the plaintext alphabet PA to all dashes "-".

100 - 198

Request command = 1, 2, 3, or 4.

(1) Display the menu.
(2) Show the alphabets.
(3) Assign a letter.
(4) Try a translation of the text.

200 - 270

Print out the cipher alphabet in order and below it (in lower case, yet) the plaintext alphabet as presently defined.

230 - 250

For any letter of PA that isn't a letter, print it in upper case. If it is a letter, print it in lower case.

300 - 370

Define a ciphertext letter. You may enter several pairs of CT followed by their PT equivalent. End list with a slash.

320 Set A equal to the numeric equivalent of the first letter of the pair.
330 If the equivalent is a slash "/", go look for another command. If not, it is the ciphertext letter the user is trying to define.
335 If there are more than two letters, there must be a mistake.
340 Set B to the numeric equivalent of the plaintext equivalent of this CT letter. This can be a dash or star or anything the user desires.
350 Check to make sure that A represents a letter.
360 Make the substitution in the plaintext alphabet PA.

400 - 600
Display the ciphertext and what is known about the plaintext on interlaced lines, with CT in upper case and PT in lower case.

400 K is a pointer to the beginning of the current pair of lines.
410 I points to the character in the input (CT) buffer.
420 If the character is a carriage return, then bump I and print the PT.
430 Print the next CT character just as it was entered.
440 Bump I.
450 If end of CT, go to the PT line.
455 If there are 39 characters on this line already, that's enough.
460 Print some more CT.
500 Carriage return. Now it is time to print the PT for the CT line just finished.
520 From K, the starting point of the line to I − 1 (I got bumped after the last character).
530 If character is not a letter, print it as it stands in upper case.
535 If the translation of the character is "–", print a dash.
540 Otherwise print the character in lower case.
570 New line.
580 Set K to the end of the current line (plus 1).
590 If finished, go back for a new command.

Discussion of Helper Package Program

In line 15 of Program 7.4, we set the PET to print lower-case letters in place of the graphics symbols when the shift key is depressed. Lower-case A can be printed by printing the character formed by adding 128 to the ASCII representation of A. That is,

```
ASC("A") = 65
ASC("a") = 193
```

To print A, use

```
PRINT CHR$ (65)
```

To print a, use

```
PRINT CHR$ (193)
```

We use the standard subroutine to load the ciphertext into buffer T%. J is set to the number of characters in the buffer. In lines 30–50, we initialize every letter of the plaintext alphabet to "-". Lines 100–110 look for a command. At present, only four commands are implemented, but room is left for adding new commands to the helper package as we develop them.

Starting at line 200, we print out the current values assigned to the translation alphabet. The underscoring that appears in statement 200 means that these characters are originally typed in with the shift key held down, which, combined with statement 15, will cause them to appear in lower case. If you aren't going to print plaintext in lower case, ignore the underscoring.

Lines 230–250 print out the plaintext alphabet. Again, if you are going to use just upper-case letters, eliminate statement 235 and replace statement 240 with

```
240  PRINT CHR$(PA(I)+64);
```

Statements 300–370 assign plaintext equivalents to ciphertext letters. If A=−17, it means that a slash has been typed. Lines 335 and 350 are there to guard against operator error. Line 360 does the actual assignment.

Lines 400–600 print out the ciphertext message interleaved with the plaintext equivalents presently known. K serves to mark the beginning of a line; I, the current position within the line; and −51, the offset equivalent of a carriage return that we have to look out for (line 420). Lines 450 and 455 are other conditions that can end a line.

Lines 500–600 print out the plaintext. If you are using just upper-case letters, then lines 535 and 540 can be replaced with

```
540  PRINT CHR$(PA(T%(L))+64);
```

Digram Information

To build up one's intuition about the behavior of letters in plaintext, it is useful to examine the digram frequency chart for digrams that respect word boundaries (Appendix D). The entire 26×26 matrix is too overwhelming to take in at once; let us therefore abstract information from it by looking only at those digrams that occur 100 or more times per ten thousand letter pairs. There are 24 such popular digrams, presented in diagramatic form in Fig. 7.1. A heavy arrow in this figure from letter α to letter β indicates that α is followed by β at least 200 times per ten thousand digrams. Arrows going in both directions between α and β indicate that both digram $\alpha\beta$ and its reverse, $\beta\alpha$, are common. Once you see these digrams pulled out for inspection in this manner it becomes obvious that they *are* the most popular ones. Most of the common short words of English can be made using only these pairs, which is not at all surprising because it is precisely this fact that makes these digrams so frequent. The four digrams—TH, HE, ER, and IN—each account for more than 2 percent of all digrams.

You might remember the popular digrams by the following foolish phrase, in which all the "within word" transitions are correct except for the T–T transition of the word *sitting*:

AND THERE IT IS AL! SITTING IN A TON OF ORE!

The two most frequent reversing digrams are ER–RE and IT–TI, but there are several others that are nearly as frequent although they don't show up on this chart. These second-rank reversals include ED–DE, AR–RA, EL–LE, and ES–SE.

Consider the case in which you have a cryptogram with a pair of letters that appear in both orders (AB—BA). If one of these letters has a frequency around 12 percent and the other around 6 percent, it is a good guess that you have identified ER, but only a guess: the T might have a higher than normal frequency in this crypt and the I slightly lower than normal. On the other hand, if the 12-percent letter also appears reversed with another letter in the frequency range of 3–6 percent, then it is pretty certain to be E.

With messages of only 100 characters, statistical variations are so large that digram reversals are often of relatively little help in identifying letters, although some people swear by them.

Consonant Line

Of much greater value are methods of identifying vowels and consonants. One of the better methods of doing so is called the *consonant line* and relies on the fact that there is a pattern in the way different letters contact one another. In particular, vowels tend to touch consonants and vice versa. Further, the letters that contact very few other letters are mostly consonants and the few letters they do contact tend to be vowels.

To find out which letters of a cryptogram pair with which other letters, one constructs a *letter contact chart* as shown below. Taking a second message from our sailor friends, we have

Q RHY EFSCN ZQE TSNV JA QDU LV ZQKV NQDQYVU FS VKQUV FZV TSQEFYJQCU. VMAVTF JE QF FZV CVYJWQC AWQTV FJVEUQO VKVDHDY.

We first write down the alphabet and as we pick off the letters of the crypt one by one, we write down the letters that precede and follow them against their place in the alphabet. Blanks are symbolized by * in this tabulation, and most people find it convenient to write the precursor and successor one above the other. Thus, for the message above: Next to Q we would write $\genfrac{}{}{0pt}{}{*}{*}$, next to R we write $\genfrac{}{}{0pt}{}{*}{\text{H}}$, next to H we put $\genfrac{}{}{0pt}{}{\text{R}}{\text{Y}}$, and next to Y we put $\genfrac{}{}{0pt}{}{\text{H}}{*}$. Going all the way through the message, we get the chart shown in Table 7.1. This chart gives us not only the contacts each letter makes, but it also gives us the letter frequency as a side benefit.

Table 7.1 Contacts and Frequency of Each Letter

A	J M * * V W	3	N	C S * * V Q	3
B		-	O	Q *	1
C	S Q * Q N U V *	4	P		-
D	Q Q V H U Q H Y	4	Q	* Z * Z N D K S J * W W U * E D K D Y U E C F C T O	13
E	* Q Q J V F * F * U	5	R	* H	1
F	E * * E T Q * * S S Z Y * * Z J	8	S	F T F T C N * Q	4
G		-	T	* * V Q S S F V	4
H	R D Y D	2	U	D V Q C E * * V * Q	5
I		-	V	N L K Y * U Z * A Z C T J * K * * * U K * * M T * Y * E K D	14
J	* Y * Y F A Q E W V	5	W	J A Q Q	2
K	Q V V V Q V	3	X		-
L	* V	1	Y	H Q F V D * V J J *	5
M	V A	1	Z	* * F F Q Q V V	3

Once again we need to extract information so that it can be made use of. For each letter of the alphabet, write down the letters which *fol-*

low it more than once. This exercise will extract the more frequent digrams for examination:

EF	TS
FS	VK
KV	WQ
QE	YJ
QD	ZQ
QC	ZV

One can use this information to draw a diagram, Fig. 7.2, that is similar to Fig. 7.1. Since letters with many contacts tend to be vowels, Q is quite likely to be a vowel. Since letters, moreover, tend to alternate—vowel-consonant-vowel-consonant—we can guess that E and S are consonants and F and T are vowels. Also, either K or V is a vowel and possibly either Y or J.

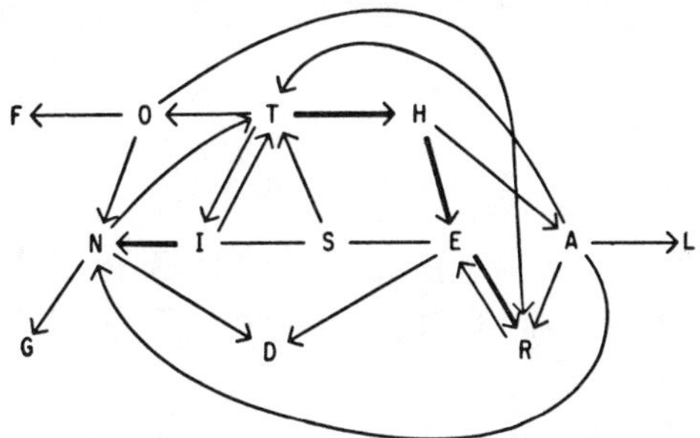

Fig. 7.1 Digrams that account for more than 1 percent of all pairs.

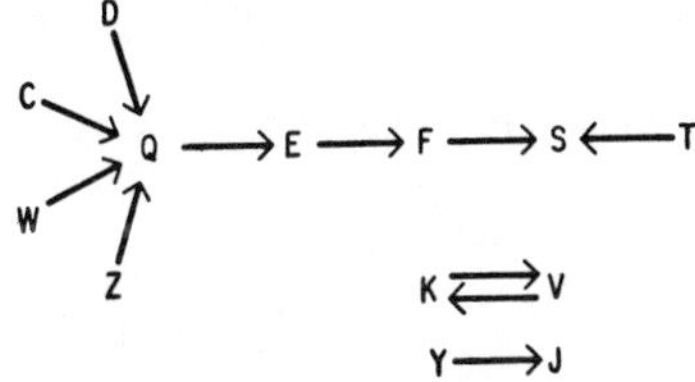

Fig. 7.2 Digrams of message.

To work the consonant line for identification of vowels, we first count up how many different letters each letter contacts. In our message, A was preceded by J and M was followed by V and W. Thus, it contacted four different letters. D was preceded by Q (twice), V, and H and followed by U, Q, H, and Y, for a total of six different letters. We repeat this counting for each letter, giving:

A:	4	J:	7	S:	5
B:	—	K:	2	T:	4
C:	5	L:	1	U:	5
D:	6	M:	2	V:	13
E:	5	N:	4	W:	3
F:	8	O:	1	X:	—
G:	—	P:	—	Y:	6
H:	3	Q:	14	Z:	3
I:	—	R:	1		

Since Q and V contact 14 and 13 different letters, respectively, they certainly look more and more like vowels. It's hard to tell about the others at this stage.

Now we draw a long line with a bar over the top of it and select one of the letters from this list with the fewest number of contacts. We pick L. Write L above the horizontal line and the letters that precede L (there aren't any in this case) to the left of the vertical line and those that follow it (V) to the right of the vertical line, giving:

L	
	V

Take the next lowest contact letter, O. Since it does not appear on our "T" diagram, we add it on the top and its contacts to the left and right of the vertical line:

LO	
	V
Q	

Since R, K, and M also do not appear, we add them also, putting all the same letters on a single line:

LORKM	
VVV	VVV
QQ	Q
	H
	A

The next lowest contact letters (appearing three times) are H, W, and Z. Since H already appears in the diagram, we skip it, uncertain whether it is a vowel or consonant at this point. But since neither W nor Z appear, we add them:

LORK	MWZ
VVVV	VVVV
QQQ	QQQ
H	H
A	A
J	JJ
F	
D	

The letters with four contacts are A, N, and T. A has appeared, but N and T have not. We thus have:

LORK	MWZNT
VVVVV	VVVVVV
QQQQ	QQQQ
H	H
A	A
J	JJ
F	F
D	
C	
S	SS

We proceed with letters of higher and higher numbers of contacts, omitting any letter already on the chart. This process eventually leads us to

LORKM	WZNTEY
VVVVVVV	VVVVVVV
QQQQQQQ	QQQQ
HH	H
A	A
JJ	JJJ
FF	FFF
DD	
C	
S	SS
	U

Omitted letters
H A C D S U J F V Q

In theory now, the letters across the top represent consonants whereas those that appear "frequently" on both sides of the vertical line are vowels. The word *frequently* is in quotes because it is interpreted differently depending on how the diagram looks. In this case, we can be pretty certain that Q and V are vowels; J and F are probably vowels; and H and S are possibly so. Likewise, L, O, R, K, M, W, Z, N, T, E, and Y are tentatively identified as consonants.

At this point we go back to the original message and argue that every word must have at least one vowel in it and that more than three or four consonants in a row are unlikely. Write out the message again, and underscore the letters that you are fairly certain represent vowels (Q and V):

Q RHY EFSCN ZQE TSNV JA QDU LV
ZQKV NQDQYVU FS VKQUV FZV TSQEFYJQCU.
VMAVTF JE QF FZV CVYJWQC AWQTV
FJVEUQO VKVDHDY.

We could have guessed that Q was a vowel (either I or A) because it appears as a one-letter word, but it is nice to see our hard work come out with the same answer. It gives one confidence. Look at the third word of the third line, QF. If Q is a vowel, then F isn't, and if F isn't, then in the third word of the second line, FS, we can be fairly certain that S is. Now look at the second word of line three, JE. Either J or E must be a vowel. According to our analysis, J is a vowel and E is a consonant. Filling in these deductions, we get

Q RHY EFSCN ZQE TSNV JA QDU LV
ZQKV NQDQYVU FS VKQUV FZV TSQEFYJQCU.
VMAVTF JE QF FZV CVYJWQC AWQTV
FJVEUQO VKVDHDY.

At this point we count up the number of occurrences of vowels that we have identified so far:

V: 14
Q: 13
J: 5
S: 4
36

or 36 probable vowels out of 93 letters. That's a percentage of 38.7 when we expected 40. Although this figure is as close as we are likely to get with the consonant line, we can come just a bit closer in this case. In the second word of line 1, RHY, we need a vowel. Of the three candidates, we have already assigned R and Y as consonants and H appears three times across the vertical line. Tentatively, therefore, we'll pick H for a vowel. Filling in these supposed vowels, we have:

Q RHY EFSCN ZQE TSNV JA QDU LV
ZQKV NQDQYVU FS VKQUV FZV TSQEFYJQCU.
VMAVTF JE QF FZV CVYJWQC AWQTV
FJVEUQO VKVDHDY.

As a result, we now have nicely spaced vowels in every word—a further clue that we are correct. Looking back at the diagram of Fig. 7.2, we tentatively identified Q, F, and T and either Y or J and either K or V. From our use of the consonant line method in conjunction with the need for a vowel in each word, we have identified Q, H, S, V, J—three hits out of five. Note that H wasn't on the diagram, and had we chosen S, we would have rejected F and T and been almost right.

Let us therefore assume that Q, H, S, V, J are correct and now try to identify the vowels if we can.

The first thing to look at is the frequencies of the vowels in the Brown sample. In order of their frequencies,

Letter	*Brown corpus*
E	12.5%
A	8.0%
O	7.6%
I	7.3%
U	2.7%
Y	1.7%

For our crypt:

Letter	*Our crypt*
V	14.5%
Q	13.5%
J	5.2%
S	4.2%
H	2.1%

We would, in general, be wrong to immediately conclude that V= *E*, *Q*=A, and so forth. The sample in our crypt is much too short to allow us to jump to that conclusion. Perhaps we can get some further information from examining the contacts that vowels make with one another and comparing these results with the contacts our supposed vowels make.

First, from the Brown corpus, we get the relationships shown in Fig. 7.3 where the numbers are percentages of all observed digrams. In our crypt there are 71 digrams (93 letters minus 22 because the last letter of each word doesn't start a digram). Thus, we might find an EA or an IO, perhaps, and possibly an EE, an AI, an IE, an OO, or an AY. Others would be unlikely, but of course they *do* occur *sometimes.* In

Second letter

First letter	A	E	I	O	U	Y
A	0	0	.4	0	.1	.3
E	.7	.4	.2	.1	0	.2
I	.2	.4	0	.7	0	0
O	.1	.1	.1	.3	1.0	0
U	.1	.1	.1	0	0	0
Y	0	.1	0	.2	0	0

Total nonpairs = 5.1%
pairs = 0.7%

Fig. 7.3 Relationships of first and second letters from Brown corpus.

our crypt, there are three vowel-vowel contacts, SQ, JQ, and JV. Three occurrences out of 71 is 4.2 percent, which compares favorably with the expected value of 5.1 percent for vowel-vowel contacts not of the EE or OO type. The vowel that serves most often as the second element of a vowel-vowel pair is O, followed in frequency by A or U. Since Q can't be O (since it serves as a one-letter word, it must be A or I), we can guess that it is A. It is, like A, the second most frequent vowel (although one more occurrence would have made it tie for first place). The letter U has such a low normal frequency that it is unlikely that it would occur more than 13 percent of the time, but if the message text has been deliberately distorted, such irregularities can, and do, occur. Furthermore, U doesn't occur as a one-letter word.

For the first elements of vowel-vowel pairs, E, O, and I, in that order, are the best guesses. If Q is really A, however, we can ask for the probability of finding XA, where X stands for one of the vowels. Here the likelihoods are E (much the highest), I, O, and U. But again, if this is undistorted text with reasonably normal probabilities, then J doesn't appear often enough to qualify as E. In fact, if we look at the letter frequencies, V is the only likely candidate to represent E, given that Q represents A. Can we find any other evidence to support this conjecture?

Initials and Terminals

Most letters have preferred positions in words. We will look more thoroughly at this in another chapter, but right now we are concerned merely with what letters tend to occur as initial and terminal letters in English words.

Perhaps you have already noted that in our chart for frequencies of digrams that do not span word gaps, the number of digrams with E as a first letter is one thousand thirty-nine while the number with E as a second letter is one thousand five hundred twenty-two. This difference is not due to sloppy counting. It is because E tends to occur very often as the last letter of words. And in that position, the E can't serve as the first letter of a digram.

From data on position preferences of letters, we can tabulate the letters which end or begin words. The popular endings, in order of frequency, are E, S, D, T, N, R, Y, and O. Appendix B contains the data. Approximately 20 percent of all words end in E. Another 13 percent end with S, and D accounts for over 10 percent. Plurals explain the high prevalence of S, and the past tense of verbs plus the word *and* are responsible for most of the D's. The letter O occurs mostly as a terminal in two-letter words: to, so, no, and the like.

Initial letters are not so easily explained. We must simply assume that "that's the way the language is written" and let it go at that. The popular beginnings are T, A, O, S, I, W, H, C, and B. Almost 16 percent of words (one in six) begins with a T. The next most common at 10 percent is A, and a great deal of its popularity can be traced to the word *and.*

Returning to our cryptogram, we have hypothesized that V represents the letter E. Of the 22 words in the crypt, seven end with V—about 32 percent. Next in popularity as terminals are U—three times—and Y, F, and E—each twice. Since we already suspect that V represents e because of its high frequency, its popularity as a terminal seems to put the cap on it, and we can declare V as good as identified.

As initial letters, we find:

F: 4
Q: 3
V: 3
J: 2
T: 2
Z: 2

From this, we might tend to guess that F is t and that either Q or V is a. Since we already believe Q to be a, we can take this as confirming evidence and make a tentative identification of F as t. Note that V shows up three times as an initial and that, while we believe V to be e, e is not a popular initial letter. We have two pieces of evidence that V is e (popularity of V and frequent occurrence of V as a terminal) against this indication that it is not. Here is where intuition, or if you prefer, higher, nonverbal mental processes, come into play. V "looks like" e if only because when you examine the crypt with V translated to e, it seems to fall in all the right places. In particular, we have the three-letter word FZV. We already suspect that F is t, and the most popular three-letter word of all is *the.* Surely that's enough evidence to warrant at least trying the substitution of e for V.

How about the other vowels? Well, we have this situation:

V: e
Q: a
J: } { o
S: } { i
H: } { u
{ y

Both o and i are popular initials, and we find that J has occurred twice as an initial. Perhaps J represents o or i. Back when we were looking at vowel-vowel contact pairs, we mentioned that both JQ and JV were found in our crypt. The vowel that most osten precedes a and e is i. IA occurs in 0.2 percent of all digrams and ie in 0.4 percent; oa and oe, ua and ue all occur only 0.1 percent of the time. As a first guess, then, we might equate J with i. If that fails, we can equate it with a or u. Since that seems to be about all we can do with the vowels at this point, we will turn to the consonants.

Identification of Consonants

The 17 letters in the crypt that we have identified as consonants are

F:	8	N:	3
E:	5	Z:	3
U:	5	H:	2
Y:	5	W:	2
C:	4	L:	1
D:	4	M:	1
T:	4	O:	1
A:	3	R:	1
K:	3		

In the Brown sample, the 20 consonants in order of frequency are as follows:

T:	925	P:	202
N:	710	G:	195
S:	655	W:	188
R:	613	B:	153
H:	542	V:	100
L:	414	K:	66
D:	397	X:	20
C:	310	J:	16
M:	257	Q:	11
F:	231	Z:	10

These are sometimes broken into three groups:

Popular (greater than 4 percent):	T N S R H
Medium (1–4 percent):	L D C M F P G W B V K
Rare (less than 1 percent):	X J Q Z

Sometimes L and D are put in the popular group and V and K in the rare group, but since the grouping is only approximate anyway, it really isn't too important. The popular group we can expect to find fairly often in a crypt. The rare letters may be absent in a short one.

Looking at initial letters in the crypt, we find, among the non-vowels,

F:	4	(18%)
T:	2	(9%)
Z:	2	(9%)

and as terminals,

U:	3	(14%)
Y:	2	(9%)
F:	2	(9%)
E:	2	(9%)

In the Brown sample, we find initial consonants

T:	16%
S:	7%
W:	6%
H:	5%
C:	5%
B:	5%

and terminal consonants

S:	13%
D:	11%
T:	9%
N:	9%
R:	6%

Looking at these numbers, it is hard to avoid identifying ciphertext F with plaintext t, as follows:

Letter	*Initial*	*Terminal*
F	18	9
t	16	9

Another good guess would be to equate U with d, or, less likely, with s.

About this point we should fill in what we have conjectured about the crypt and see how it looks now:

```
Q RHY EFSCN ZQE TSNV JA QDU LV
a            a     ei  a   e

ZQKV NQDQYVU FS VKQUV FZV TSQEFYJQCU.
 a e  a a e   t e a e t e   a t ia

VMAVTF JE QF FZV CVYJWQC AWQTV
e  e t i  at t e e i  a   a e

FJVEUQO VKVDHDY.
tie   a  e e
```

In the second row, fifth word, we can quite confidently identify Z as h in order to make "the." Since Z occurs as an initial letter 9 percent (twice) and h appears as an initial letter 5 percent of the time, the fluctuation is reasonable. One less initial Z would have been perfect, and you can't get a lot closer than that.

The first word of line two now becomes "ha–e," which might be interpreted as

hale	(as in "hale and hearty")
hame	(if our confederate is Scottish—he isn't)
hare	(a sea rabbit?)
have	(that looks good)
haze	(might be)

K occurs only three times, in word four of line two and in the last word of the crypt. Z doesn't seem to fit too well in either place, but v makes the last word "eve––––," where the first and third blanks are the same letter. It if wasn't already assigned, we might be tempted to say that the word was "evening." Hmm! Look at the other occurrence of K. The word is "eva–e," and "evade" pops to mind. If U is d, then the next to last word of the first line is "and," which makes D equal n and that substitution would be just right for "evening." Hmm again! Just for fun, let's try the whole thing again, with J unassigned and the terminal word equal to "evening":

```
Q RHY EFSCN ZQE TSNV JA QDU LV
a  ig  t     ha    e    and e

ZQKV NQDQYVU FS VKQUV FZV TSQEFYJQCU.
have  anaged  t evade the   a t  a d

VMAVTF JF QF FZV CVYJWQC AWQTV
e  e t  t at the eg  a    a e
```

```
FJVEUQO VKVDHDY.
t e da  even i ng.
```

The third word of line two has got to be "to," which gives the vowel assignments as

```
V: e
Q: a
S: o
H: i
J: ?
```

That leaves J as either u or y. It must be the former since J appears twice in two-letter words as the initial letter, and while "us" and "up" are fairly common, no two-letter words come to mind that begin with y. The second word of the second line is very probably "managed."

By this time, the phrase in the last line that looks like "tue-da-evening" must surely be "Tuesday evening." Inserting these new assumptions, we get

```
Q RHY EFSCN ZQE TSNV JA QDU LV
a  ig sto m has  ome u  and  e

ZQKV NQDQYVU FS VKQUV FZV TSQEFYJQCU.
have managed to evade the  oast ua d.

VMAVTF JE QF FZV CUYJWQC AWQTV
e   e t us at the  e gu a    a e

FJVEUQO VKVDHDY.
tues da y eve ni ng.
```

By now we can read the first sentence: "A big storm has come up and we have managed to evade the coastguard." Substituting the new letters into the last sentence, we get

```
VMAVTF JE QF FZV CUYJWQC AWQTV
e   e ct us at t he re gu ar   ace

FJVEUQO VKVDHDY
tues day eve ní ng
```

And that easily becomes "Expect us at the regular place Tuesday evening."

To summarize what we have learned this time around:

1. Separate vowels and consonants using the consonant line and remember that a vowel must appear in each word.

2. The sentence, "There it is, Al, sitting in a ton of ore," contains all the high-frequency digrams of English.
3. Compare vowel frequencies and vowel-vowel contacts to make initial guesses at the identities of the vowels.
4. Refine these guesses with data on the frequency of initial and terminal letters. E should be strongly identifiable by this time.
5. Where possible, identify (or guess at) consonant identities from frequency data and initial and terminal frequencies.
6. Keep trying to read for the sense of the message.

Problems for Chapter 7

1. RBY YUNLL QNHVSM TP MHSK VSMVKL H CHMY JHYULKLNHZ HSK YUL JHYULKLNHZ DVZZ IL ATNL JZTMLZF RHJXLK DVYU MHSK YUHS MRHJL VM DVYU MYHNM. (*Sir James Jeans*)
2. YB ABJ YB KAJB BJLZHI VI SBK PBKRY JLVJ JLZS ILBKRY YB KAJB SBK. JLZDH JVIJZI UVS ABJ WZ JLZ IVUZ. (*G. B. Shaw*)
3. BIV TQI'H CJUXV *MQXIVF'G BDVFQ *ABYVIXFZI QWHVF Q WZFGH YVQFZIX, QIU Z TVFHQZIAO UBI'H ZIHVIU YVQFZIX ZH Q GVTBIU HZSV. (*Gioacchino Rossini*)
4. ES T OJHYJO ES *RTKTST IRYGY TGY IMA HUJLLH AZ *WRGEHIABRYG *WALJOVJH, "ASY MRYS RY MTH T VAP TSX ASY MRYS RY MTH T OTS." (*Mark Twain*)
5. R NGPGMP PAG RNGZ HY EKHURFE HCN, LQP UAGF WHQ OHFMRNGK PAG ZCPGKFZPRTGM RP KGZCCW RMF'P MH LZN ZYPGK ZCC.
6. H AQP'Y SNE HPTQLB YNVBX KHJB BGBWEMQAE BKXB. H IZXY TNKK *ONXFHPDYQP NPA NXJ YFBL FQO LZTF YFBE PBBA.
7. DT DZW HWBCTU ISDZ N DTTDZNQZW, WGWU SX DZW ITBEV SC DTDDWBSUY, DZWBW SC UTDZSUY MTBW SMHTBDNUD DZNU N GSCSD DT DZW VWUDSCD. (*G. B. Shaw*)
8. XZJQIFPDJ PN EMJ FPNTPSJ OWI KJJT KWZ NWUJWVJ CJKWZJ OWI SVWH MPU HJTT JVWILM EW MAEJ MPU.
9. N LNM DEKE YBB RYW MKWNFI MG HEKLOYRE HEGHBE MG RG MDNFIL MDEW GOIDM MG DYQE LEFLE EFGOID MG RG UNMDGOM CW DYQNFI MG HEKLOYRE MDEC. (*H. S. Truman*)
10. BXDBEX HSQ JASJ JAXGX TKHJ UX XNJAXG BGDZGXHH DG GXZGXHHNDL. VDLHNWXG JASJ JAX *XZQBJNSLH TSLSZXW JD WD ONJADKJ XNJAXG YDG JAGXX JADKHSLW QXSGH.

8

Other Aids for the Aristocrat

Knowing where word divisions occur is a great aid in solving a cipher. Two of the major ways it helps is in identifying vowels, at least one of which must occur in every word, and in identifying letters on the basis of where they fall within words. We have already looked briefly at the identification of initial and terminal letters. In this next section we will explore further the preferences of letters for certain positions in words.

Position Preferences

My first exposure to position preferences was in the book, *Cryptanalysis of the Simple Substitution Cipher with Word Divisions* by Wayne G. Barker,* in which he devotes a chapter to the separation of vowels and consonants in accordance with the position of the letters within words. His argument is roughly illustrated in Fig. 8.1. The idea here is that, for example, in a four-letter word, the first and last letters tend to be consonants, the second letter tends to be a vowel, and the third letter could be either one or the other with approximately equal likelihood. The analyst takes each occurrence of each letter of the crypt and makes a table of whether letters in that position of a word are more likely to be vowels (V) or consonants (C). Suppose that the ciphertext letter A appears in the crypt as the first letter of a five-letter word (C), as the third letter of a three-letter word (–), as the last letter of an eight-letter word (C), and as the third letter of a five-letter word (V). We tabulate each appearance, getting for A:

A: C–CV

We repeat this tabulation for every letter of the crypt, a mechanical operation that could readily be adapted to a computer. Now comes the interpretive part, which might be harder to computerize. Barker suggests as an example that if a letter has four C's marked against it, we should consider it a consonant, and if it has two or more V's, we

*Aegean Park Press, P.O. Box 2837. Laguna Hills, CA 92653, published 1975.

One-letter word:	1 V							
Two-letter word:	1 V	2 C						
Three-letter word:	1 C	2 C	3 -					
Four-letter word:	1 C	2 V	3 -	4 C				
Five-letter word:	1 C	2 C	3 V	4 C	5 C			
Six-letter word:	1 C	2 V	3 C	4 -	5 -	6 C		
Seven-letter word:	1 C	2 V	3 C	4 C	5 -	6 -	7 C	
Eight-letter and longer words:	1 C	2 C	3 -	4 -	5 -	• -	• -	Final C

Fig. 8.1 Position preferences.

should take it to be a vowel. What one is to do with a letter that has two V's and four C's or various other patterns is not discussed nor is the origin of Fig. 8.1 nor how strong the position preferences may be. The idea, however, is brilliant, and the success Barker reports for it is tantalizing. The limited personal success I had with the method as Barker presented it was exciting enough for me to look into the matter more deeply.

My noble, patient assistant, Raj Wall, and the Cyber 74 of the University Computing Center at the University of Massachusetts, Amherst, combined their talents to reanalyze the Brown corpus for the position preferences of letters in everyday English. Figure 8.2 shows one of the 26 tables of position preference. Pick a four-letter word at random that appears in the Brown corpus. Make this random choice with due regard for the popularity of different words, that is, by considering the following. Four-letter words appeared 161,485 times among the million-odd words of the corpus. Of those appearances, 10,597 were the word *that,* or about one time in 16. Figure 8.2 shows that the probability that A will be the first letter of such a randomly chosen four-letter word is 0.0216; expressed as a percentage, 2.16 percent of all four-letter words will begin with A. Moreover, 17.54 percent will have A as their second letter and 12.88 percent will have A as their third letter.

To be able to identify individual letters just on the basis of their position preferences would be too much to hope for, particularly as several letters may display the same general kinds of preferences. Thus

Word length	N (position within the word) 1	2	3	4	5	6	7	8	9	10
1	72									
2	10	0								
3	19	13	0							
4	2	18	13	1						
5	7	11	12	5	1					
6	7	15	8	5	5	1				
7	7	11	10	7	8	7	1			
8	9	10	8	7	7	8	8	1		
9	8	8	7	5	8	9	9	6	1	
10	9	7	5	6	5	10	10	5	7	1

Fig. 8.2 Position preference for the letter A (percent of all words of given length that have A as the Nth letter).

we are faced with the task of trying to group letters to maximize their identifiability, that is, by grouping those that behave the same way. The first approach is to compute something called the *cross-correlation coefficient* of each letter with every other letter.

Because of computer memory limitations, we have confined our attention to words of one to ten letters. This gives 55 possible letter positions, one in one-letter words, plus two in two-letter words . . . , plus ten positions in ten-letter words. Let there be two letters, A and B, and let A_i be the probability that letter A appears in position i where i ranges over 55 possible positions. Then the *cross correlation* of A with B is given by the equation

$$\phi_{AB} = \frac{\sum_{i=1}^{55} \left(A_i\right)\left(B_i\right)}{\left(\sum_{i=1}^{55} A_i\right)\left(\sum_{i=1}^{55} B_i\right)}$$

After this calculation had been repeated for all 676 letter pairs, groups of letters that correlated with each other were extracted:

Group I: A I O U H X Z
Group II: D G S Y
Group III: E L N R
Group IV: B C F J K M P Q V W

The first group contains the vowels, except for E and Y, with H, X, and Z added in. Since Y tends to appear as a terminal, which A, I, O, U, H, and X do not, better discrimination will be obtained if Y is placed in

Word length	*N (position within the word)* 1	2	3	4	5	6	7	8	9	10
1	90									
2	71	19								
3	34	70	4							
4	14	72	28	11						
5	16	59	46	20	9					
6	15	54	28	36	19	4				
7	17	47	29	26	45	18	3			
8	20	46	26	32	34	40	21	3		
9	21	44	21	26	34	29	49	19	2	
10	24	44	17	31	29	32	33	46	27	2

Percentage of all letters within this group = 30.1%

Fig. 8.3 Position preference for Group I: A I O U H X Z (percentage of all words of a given length that have a letter of the group as the Nth letter).

Word length	*N (position within the word)* 1	2	3	4	5	6	7	8	9	10
1	2									
2	2	15								
3	7	0	31							
4	13	2	10	22						
5	20	3	10	13	34					
6	22	2	11	12	10	45				
7	19	4	11	12	6	12	50			
8	20	3	14	13	11	8	10	55		
9	21	3	11	11	9	13	8	7	54	
10	19	4	15	10	12	13	14	4	4	49

Percentage of all letters within this group = 14.8%

Fig. 8.4 Position perference for Group II: D G S Y (percentage of all words of given length that have a letter of the group as the Nth letter).

Group II rather than Group I. The position preferences of Group I are shown in Fig. 8.3.

Group II consists of the letters that are predominately terminals. Although S is often an initial letter, it is frequently a terminal as well. By putting it into this group, along with D, G, and Y, we are better able to distinguish this group from the others. Figure 8.4 shows the position preferences.

Word length	1	2	3	4	5	6	7	8	9	10
	N (position within the word)									
1	2									
2	1	34								
3	5	26	52							
4	10	24	37	39						
5	11	26	29	47	41					
6	17	33	29	26	59	37				
7	14	40	32	28	32	56	32			
8	17	38	31	30	31	30	54	33		
9	17	38	31	35	35	28	24	61	31	
10	17	38	29	30	40	29	23	30	53	37

Percentage of all letters within this group = 31.1%

Fig. 8.5 Position preference for Group III: E L N R (percentage of all words of given length that have a letter of the group as the Nth letter).

Word length	1	2	3	4	5	6	7	8	9	10
	N (position within the word)									
1	4									
2	11	24								
3	19	1	4							
4	40	3	15	8						
5	39	8	9	13	2					
6	39	6	21	13	7	4				
7	45	7	19	18	9	7	4			
8	38	11	22	18	13	14	6	3		
9	35	11	28	19	13	15	10	5	2	
10	37	10	32	22	13	14	11	10	8	4

Percentage of all letters within this group = 15.0%

Fig. 8.6 Position preference for Group IV: B C F J M P Q V W (percentage of all words of given length that have a letter of the group as the Nth letter).

Group III—E, L, N, and R—appear predominately as the last or next to last letters of longer words. Position preferences are shown in Fig. 8.5.

The last group, Group IV, is rather a mixed bag. These letters (B, C, F, J, K, M, P, Q, V, and W) tend to appear frequently as the first letter of words and comparatively seldom (except for two-letter words) as the terminal letter. Position preferences are shown in Fig. 8.6.

The letter T has been omitted from all groups because it was found that adding it to either Group III or IV (the two groups it best correlates with) degraded the recognition process rather than enhancing it. When it comes to analyzing cryptograms, we will "pretend" that the letter T belongs to Group IV, since that is the one it seems to fit best with.

Perhaps a word or two about the correlation process would be in order. Assume that the language consists only of five-letter words and that we have three letters—A, B, and C—that appear in the following percentages:

Position	*1*	*2*	*3*	*4*	*5*
A	20	10	0	0	0
B	10	5	5	5	5
C	0	0	0	0	30

The correlation of A with B will be:

$$\phi_{AB} = \frac{(20 \bullet 10) + (10 \bullet 5) + (0 \bullet 5) + (0 \bullet 5) + (0 \bullet 5)}{(20 + 10 + 0 + 0 + 0)\ (10 + 5 + 5 + 5 + 5)}$$

or

$$\phi_{AB} = \frac{200 + 50 + 0 + 0 + 0}{(30)(30)} = \frac{250}{900} = 0.278$$

The correlation of B with C is

$$\phi_{BC} = \frac{(10 \bullet 0) + (5 \bullet 0) + (5 \bullet 0) + (5 \bullet 0) + (5 \bullet 30)}{(10 + 5 + 5 + 5 + 5)\ (0 + 0 + 0 + 0 + 30)} = 0.167$$

and of A with C

$$\phi_{AC} = \frac{(20 \bullet 0) + (10 \bullet 0) + (0 \bullet 0) + (0 \bullet 0) + (0 \bullet 30)}{(20 + 10 + 0 + 0 + 0)\ (0 + 0 + 0 + 0 + 30)} = 0$$

We can also correlate each letter with itself, if we want, giving "autocorrelation" coefficients:

$$\phi_{AA} = 0.556$$
$$\phi_{BB} = 0.222$$
$$\phi_{CC} = 1.000$$

The higher the autocorrelation coefficients, the more the distributions of the letter tend to "lump up" in one place. As may be seen, C appears only as the fifth letter, A appears in only two places, whereas B can be found anywhere.

Looking at the distributions of A, B, and C, we find that since A and B tend to occur as initial letters, their cross correlation is relatively high. Since C occurs only as a terminal (which A never does), ϕ_{AC} is zero. Since B does occur occasionally as a terminal, its correlation with

C is nonzero, but because it doesn't "lump up" where C does, their correlation is small.

Now suppose that we examine a crypt and find a letter D that appears five times as an initial, once as a third letter, and twice as a terminal:

$$D = 5\ 0\ 1\ 0\ 2$$

Since we "know" that D is really an A, B, or C in disguise, we correlate D with all of them to see which one it is most like, as follows:

$$\phi_{AD} = \frac{(20 \bullet 5) + (10 \bullet 0) + (1 \bullet 0) + (0 \bullet 0) + (0 \bullet 2)}{(30)\ (5+1+2)} = 0.417$$

$$\phi_{BD} = \frac{(10 \bullet 5) + (5 \bullet 0) + (5 \bullet 1) + (5 \bullet 0) + (5 \bullet 2)}{(30)\ (8)} = 0.271$$

$$\phi_{CD} = \frac{(0 \bullet 5) + (0 \bullet 0) + (0 \bullet 1) + (0 \bullet 0) + (30 \bullet 2)}{(30)\ (8)} = 0.25$$

From these coefficients, we would conclude that D was "most like" A, but if the distributions are really as stated above, the only possibility is that D is actually B because A "never" appears as a terminal, which D does, and C "never" appears as an initial, which D also does. It's the word *never* that makes the problem. The correlation coefficients assume that 0 means *hardly ever* rather than *never.*

For relatively flat distributions such as displayed by E and T, the correlation approach does not work as well as a related method based on variance. But on the basis of an admittedly limited sample, we have found that the correlation method identifies more letters correctly than the variance method and that the program runs considerably faster. Consequently, we have decided to use the former rather than the latter. This is an area where more research is clearly called for and one where the amateur can make major contributions.

Table 8.1 shows the results of ten trials of this algorithm. Out of 192 letters, 120 were correctly grouped, or just over 62 percent. If we look only at Group I versus the rest of the letters, we find 168 correct, or 87 percent.

Table 8.1 Results of ten trials of the grouping algorithm

Group the letter belonged in (i)	*Group the letter was assigned to (j)* *I*	*II*	*III*	*IV*
1	42	1	2	5
2	2	19	3	14
3	7	10	13	8
4	7	10	3	46

Table 8.2 Assignment of ten samples

Number of letters	*Group I*	*Group II*	*Group III*	*Group IV*
70	AGINOU	DETY	LR	BCHMPS
82	ABHINUVW	GT	LY	CEFKORS
102	AGHIO	DERT	SU	BCFMNWY
72	AEIOR	GMSTU	NR	CDFHJKVWY
73	HIOU	DRSY	ELMN	ABCPTW
84	AHIKO	EGMSY	NU	CDLRTVWZ
80	AHILU	CDKNRY	E	BFGOSTVW
83	ABHIOU	SY	EGN	CDFLMPRTW
70	AHIORTUV	ERY	N	DFGLSW
68	AHINOX	DEMRY	CL	BFGPSTV

Letters assigned correctly most of the time were A, B, C, F, H, I, J, O, P, and W. Letters which did very badly—that is, that were assigned correctly less than half the time—were E, G, L, M, R, and S. In fact, R was assigned correctly only once in the ten trials. If we had just flipped a coin, we would have been right one time in four, for a 25-percent correct assignment, but R, which belonged in Group III, was assigned more frequently to each of the other groups. These ten samples yielded the assignments shown in Table 8.2.

For the benefit of anyone who might be interested in pursuing this approach, we present in Table 8.3, the correlations of each of the letters with the groups as we identified them. It is not the magnitudes of the numbers in this table that are significant but rather their relative magnitudes within a row or a column. As may be seen from this table, there is only a small difference between the way letters E, L, R, and T correlate with the different groups. Consequently, we would expect these letters to be hard to identify and to join groups more or less at random. Since we would have expected better of G, M, and S, perhaps we were the victims of simple statistical fluctuation.

Given that we have tentatively identified a group of letters, we can often use letter frequency and digraph frequency to separate the letters from one another. For example, in Group I, AIO will have high frequency, H middle frequency, and U, X, and Z low frequency. H will tend to combine most often with other letters of this group. Both X and H will combine with E, which is hopefully to be found in Group III. Group IV consists predominately of low-frequency letters. Any high- or even middle-frequency letter found in this group is likely to be an interloper unless it is the letter T.

One further way this approach can be applied is to divide the cryptogram in half and examine the position preferences of the two halves. Letters that appear in the same group in each half as well as in the total crypt can be considered pretty well pinned down to that

Table 8.3 Correlation of the position preferences of the individual letters with the four groups of letters (magnitudes are relative)

	AHIOUXZ *Group I*	*DGSY* *Group II*	*ELNR* *Group III*	*BCFJKMPQVW* *Group IV*
A	27	11	15	16
B	20	15	12	29
C	16	18	17	26
D	10	34	19	16
E	16	19	22	14
F	14	18	15	31
G	11	32	18	17
H	26	12	16	14
I	25	10	16	16
J	10	21	10	45
K	15	19	19	22
L	16	19	21	17
M	16	18	16	26
N	17	18	21	15
O	24	10	18	16
P	16	18	15	31
Q	15	19	13	36
R	17	18	20	18
S	11	30	18	20
T	16	19	17	20
U	23	11	19	17
V	19	13	19	22
W	14	18	11	33
X	27	4	22	11
Y	8	42	20	10
Z	28	5	18	13

group and to be among those in Table 8.3 with large differences between groups. Letters that jump from group to group are less well identified and may very well be those with small differences in their correlation coefficients. Of course, with crypts of the order of 100 letters, half a crypt is hardly sufficient for statistical reliability, but for longer crypts this technique might be useful.

The Correlation Program

The program to discover letter position preferences is built around the fact that 10 + 10 + 10 = 3*10. We set up four sets of "bins" or "buckets"—one set for each group. Every time we find a letter α, we note the length of the word it is in and the position it occupies. Then to the αth bucket of each set we *add* the number of times a letter of that group appeared in that position of that word length. For example, suppose that the letter M occurs as the third letter of a four-letter word. Then to the thirteenth bucket of set 1, we add 28 (see Fig. 8.3); to the thirteenth bucket of set 2, we add ten (see Fig. 8.4); to the thirteenth bucket of set 3, we add 37 (see Fig. 8.5); and to the thirteenth bucket of set 4, we add 15 (see Fig. 8.6). We add to the thirteenth bucket of each set because M is the thirteenth letter of the alphabet. If M occurs again in this position, we will add the same numbers again. This double addition is equivalent to multiplying the entries in Figs. 8.3 through 8.6 by two and then adding them to the total correlation coefficients of the letter M. It is a great deal faster and uses much less space than developing the distributions for each of the 26 letters and forming the sums of the products (see Program 8.1).

Program 8.1 New Position Preference

```
1    DIM T%(200)
2    DIM C1(26),C2(26),C3(26),C4(26)
3    DIM G1(55),G2(55),G3(55),G4(55)
4    DIM NL(26)
20   FOR I=0 TO 55: READ G1(I): NEXT I
30   FOR I=0 TO 55: READ G2(I): NEXT I
40   FOR I=0 TO 55: READ G3(I): NEXT I
50   FOR I=0 TO 55: READ G4(I): NEXT I
60   FOR I=1 TO 26
70      NL(I)=0: C1(I)=0: C2(I)=0: C3(I)=0: C4(I)=0
80   NEXT I
90   GOSUB 10000
110  I=0
120  GOSUB 1000
122  IF L=0 GOTO 195
130  TP=W*(W-1)/2+N
140  NL(L)=NL(L)+1
150  C1(L)=C1(L)+G1(TP)
160  C2(L)=C2(L)+G2(TP)
170  C3(L)=C3(L)+G3(TP)
180  C4(L)=C4(L)+G4(TP)
190  GOTO 120
195  PRINT: PRINT
200  G$(1)="": G$(2)="": G$(3)="": G$(4)=""
210  FOR I=1 TO 26
215     IF NL(I)=0 GOTO 270
220     M=C1(I)/(NL(I)*G1(0)): PRINT CHR$(I+64);INT(100*M),
225  MM=1
227  T=C2(I)/(NL(I)*G2(0)): PRINT INT(T*100),
230     IF T> M THEN M=T: MM=2
```

```
235      T=C3(I)/(NL(I)*G3(0)): PRINT INT(100*T)
240      IF T > M THEN M=T: MM=3
245      T=C4(I)/(NL(I)*G4(0)): PRINT INT(100*T)
250      IF T > M THEN MM=4
260      G$(MM)=G$(MM)+CHR$(I+64)
270   NEXT I
280   PRINT "G1(AIOUHX)="; G$(1)
290   PRINT "G2(DGSY)="; G$(2)
300   PRINT "G3(ELNR)="; G$(3)
310   PRINT "G4(BCFJKMPQTVWZ)="; G$(4)
320   GOTO 60

1000  IF I=0 GOTO 1050
1002  I=I+1
1005  IF I > J THEN L=0: RETURN
1010  IF T%(I) > 26 OR T%(I) < 1 GOTO 1050
1020  N=N+1
1030  L=T%(I)
1040  RETURN
1050  N=0
1080  P=I
1090  P=P+1
1095  IF P > J GOTO 1110
1100  IF T%(P) < 27 AND T%(P) > 0 GOTO 1090
1110  W=P-I-1
1120  IF W > 10 THEN I=P: GOTO 1050
1130  GOTO 1002
```

Program 8.1 (cont'd) New Position Preference Comments

20-50

Read in the distributions of the groups from data statements that must follow the program. G1(0) will contain the average value of an entry in vector G1, and the same will hold true for the other 0th entries.

60-80

Zero the number of letters found and the 4×26 correlation coefficients.

90 Read in the ciphertext.

110 I is now a pointer to a letter in the ciphertext.

120 Call a subroutine that will identify W, the word length; N, the position within the word; and L, the letter in the Ith element of the ciphertext. This routine skips over spaces and punctuation and returns with an L equal to 0 when the ciphertext is completely scanned.

122 Check to see if all the ciphertext is processed.

130 Compute TP, the index into vectors G1, G2, G3, and G4, which corresponds to this position, N, in this length of word, W.

140 Add 1 to the count of occurrences of this letter.

150-180

Add in the numbers from vectors G1 through G4 to the correlation coefficients, C1 through C4, for this letter.

190 Repeat from 120.

200 Clear strings G$(1) through G$(4).

210-270

For each letter of the alphabet.

215 If it didn't occur, then forget it.

220 Compute the correlation coefficient for this letter (I) against Group I by dividing the sum, (C1(I)), by the number of times the letter appeared and by the average entry in G1. Put it in M. If you want to see this matrix of 4×26 correlation coefficients, include the print statement; otherwise, leave it out.

225 Set pointer MM to Group 1 since that's the largest (and only) correlation coefficient we have found so far.

227 Compute the correlation coefficient for this letter versus Group II. The same comment applies to the print statement as to line 220.

230 Test to see which is larger and keep it, updating the pointer MM if the second is larger than the first.

235-250

Repeat the calculation and comparison for Groups III and IV.

260 By now, MM points to the group this letter correlates best with; therefore, add this letter to string G$(MM).

280-310

Print out the four strings.

320 Get a new crypt.

1000-1130

This subroutine identifies letters, the length of the word they occur in, and their position within the word.

1000 Since this is the first time I = 0, we go to "start a new word" at 1050.

1002 Point I at the next character of the ciphertext.

1005 If we run out of ciphertext, set L equal to 0 and return. J is the number of characters in the ciphertext set in the "read in" subroutine.

1010 If this character, T%(I), is not a letter, start a new word.

1020 Increment the position number, N.

1030 Set L to be this character.

1040 Return.

1050 Start a new word, and set N to 0.

1080 We are going (temporarily) to leave I pointing at the space just to the left of this new word and use P to step across the word until we get to another space or punctuation mark.

1090 Increment P.

1095 If this is the end of the text, it also ends the current word.

1100 If this is a letter (A–Z), keep counting.

1110 We are at the end of a word; compute its length, W.

1120 If W is greater than 10, discard this word and look for another.

1130 Get a letter from this word.

An Example

As an example of the use of position preferences, we will look at an aristocrat by SWISS that appeared in the March–April, 1979 issue of *The Cryptogram*:

AH WLNK AD UAPPBKDNE FYNE YBLN RSBIR WH GPBKDNE,
BKN FYNAK OWPAFASABDR PAUN *AGNKAB'R
"WKBFWKNBIWKR" FYKWTNKR WH FYN GVPP?

When we run the position-preference program, we get

Group I:	A B D L S T V W Y
Group II:	E R
Group III:	I K N
Group IV:	F G H P O U

and when we count letter frequencies, we find

A:	10	H:	3	O:	1	V:	1
B:	9	I:	2	P:	7	W:	8
C:		J:		Q:		X:	
D:	4	K:	11	R:	6	Y:	5
E:	3	L:	2	S:	2	Z:	
F:	6	M:		T:	1		
G:	3	N:	12	U:	2		

It is often useful to make out a chart combining this information as shown at the top of the next page. On the left is what we found in this crypt, and on the right, the expected Brown grouping and letter frequencies per one hundred letters.

As an opening guess, we can identify R with s since R ends several words, appears in the proper group, has the right frequency, and comes after an apostrophe. For similar reasons, we can identify K with e and E with y. After a considerable amount of pondering, we decide to erase these assumptions and start over.

This crypt	*Brown corpus*
A B D L S T V W Y	A H I O U X Z
10 9 4 2 2 1 1 8 5	8 5 7 8 3 0 0
E R	D G S Y
3 6	4 2 7 2
I K N	E L N R
2 11 12	13 4 7 6
F G H P O U	B C F J K M P Q T V W
6 3 3 7 1 2	2 3 2 0 1 3 2 0 9 1 2

Since K didn't work too well for e, let us allow N to represent e. Since we find terminal NE three times in the ciphertext, it would be reasonable to have E represent d, being of the right group and right frequency. Since R still looks as if it might be s, let us insert it again, and now the word after the quote ends "e–s." The letter in the "something" slot is K, which is in the right group to represent r although its frequency is rather high. The word after the comma, BKN, would then become "–re," and B is doing all the right things to stand for a. Making these substitutions, we get:

```
AH WLNK AD *UAPPBKDNE FYNE
     er          ar e d   ed

YBLN RSBIR WH GPBKDNE, BKN
 a e  s a s        ar  ed  are

FYNAK OWPAFASABDR PAUN
  e r          a s

*AGNKAB'R "WKBFWKNBIWKR,"
    er a's    ra   rea   rs

FYKWTNKR WH FYN GVPP?
  r   e s      e
```

The next thing to look for is t. If it ended up in Group IV, which it well may not have, then on a frequency basis, it should be either F or P. A double t at the end of a question (GVPP?) seems odd, and FY starts four words. Y may very well be h since it has just the right frequency and appears in Group I. Thus if we take Y as h and F as t, the word FYNE come out "thed," which is probably not quite right. It might be "then" or "they." Since E looks more like y than n, we will make that assignment. Now the following word would appear to be "have," producing "they have." We therefore let L represent v despite the fact that it appears in Group I.

With this assignment, the second word of the crypt, "-ver," must be "over," which gives W as o. That assignment is reinforced by both the frequency and the group of W. Suddenly the last four words of the crypt become "throwers of the bull," and our search is just about over. H as f, G as b, and V as u are all correct in terms of group and about right for frequency, whereas T as w and P as l are not in the proper groups. With the first word "if" (A is in the right group for i), the third word "in," we get

> If over in Killarney they have scads of blarney, are their politicians like Iberia's "oratoreadors," throwers of the bull?

Pattern Words

Another powerful tool for the solution of aristocrats is the use of *pattern words.* A pattern word is a word in which one or more letters are repeated. Examples are "pattern," "ever," "banana," and "bookkeeper." Even if we have not identified any letters in a crypt, the existence of pattern words often offer us a start. Surely there can't be many English words with the repeats appearing in "banana" or "bookkeeper." These patterns, of course, make themselves evident no matter how the text is encrypted. PXMXMX has the pattern of "banana" and cannot be disguised by simple substitution with word divisions.

Several tables of pattern words have been published over the years. Most of them suffer from one drawback or another. Either they are extremely cumbersome or are cluttered with thousands upon thousands of compound words that hardly, if ever, appear in normal prose.

Having access to the redoubtable Brown corpus in machine-readable form, it is relatively easy to extract those words having repeated letters. First, we separate the words into "dictionaries" of length N, with N ranging from 1 to 22. Then each word, in effect, is enciphered, using the word itself as a keyword with a shift of zero. Thus "banana" becomes ABCBCB, "bookkeeper" becomes ABBCCDDEDF, and "pattern" becomes ABCCDEF. Using this encipherment as a key, each dictionary is sorted alphabetically so that key AAAA comes first, then AAAB, AABA, AABB, and AABC, in that order. The words from the Brown corpus with that pattern are listed under each key. These lists are reproduced in Appendix G of this book.

If your crypt has a pattern word in it and you don't find any acceptable words listed in the Appendix, don't give up hope. Remember that Appendix G is based on a total dictionary of about 36 thousand words and Webster's Unabridged has perhaps ten times that many.

Using a Pattern Word List

If your crypt has one or more pattern words, you can try the pattern word list to see if it will help your solution. First you look to see how many words in the list have the pattern you are looking for. If there is only one, then you are probably justified in plugging that word into your crypt immediately, remembering that not all English words are in our lists. If there are several pattern words, say less than ten, you can test them one at a time against letter frequencies, vowel-consonant separations, digrams, and position preferences. Sometimes this will be sufficient to narrow the list down to only one or two candidates which you can try in turn. If you already have surmises about the identities of one or more letters, you can use this to narrow down a long list very dramatically. In most cases you can do this by hand winnowing in a few moments. If your computer has a disk on line, you can put the pattern word lists on a disk, call in the desired list, and search it by brute force in a few seconds. (Does this word match the constraints? Does this one? The next? and so forth.)

Much more elegant would be a content-addressable memory,* or CAM. With a CAM, each memory cell has intelligence and can compare the word it is storing with a pattern broadcast simultaneously to all cells. Thus, when you ask every cell of memory to "hold up your hand if the word you are storing matches this pattern," each cell does its own comparison in only a few microseconds and holds up or holds down its hand. You can then read out the contents of those cells with their hands up. Unfortunately, since CAMs are still relatively expensive and have to be programmed in assembly language, they are well beyond the scope of this book.

Suppose now that your crypt has two pattern words and that they share one or more letters. For example, "banana" and "pattern" have a common a, but when enciphered and their pattern lists are relatively long, you have a problem. If there are N words that share the pattern of "banana" and M words that share the pattern of "pattern," then you have to do N times M comparisons when working by hand or with an ordinary home computer. After you take the first word from list 1 and see what values it gives to the shared letter or letters, you then use these as constraints while searching list 2 to see if any words with pattern 2 meet the constraints. Then you take the next word from list 1 and do the same thing. If the values of N and M approximate ten, this a feasible process by machine or even by hand if your perseverance level is high enough. But if the values of N and M approximate 50, then there will be around 2500 comparisons to do, and your average

---

*C. Foster, *Content Addressable Parallel Processors,* Van Nostrand, Reinhold, New York, 1976.

home computer is going to eat up a lot of time. With a CAM, of course, you could put the larger list in the CAM, run the shorter one by it, and be finished in N operations instead of N×M, but we have already dismissed the CAM as a likely tool.

The frustrating part of it is that just two overlapping pattern words would probably provide enough information to crack the crypt right there. If you have a disk and a lot of time, therefore, go to it on your own; if you have a disk and a rich uncle as well, please give us a call and we'll be delighted to steer you to manufacturers and the like.

Summary of Letter Behavior

Herewith we present a summary of the behavior of each of the 26 letters of the alphabet, in order. Remember when you read these summaries that they are based on statistical data only. The words *Never* and *always* don't exist in this realm; anything can and will happen sooner or later.

A occurs eight times per hundred. As a vowel, it contacts the low frequency letters a lot. It tends to follow h and precede n and reverses with r and t. It is seldom doubled. It sometimes follows e and precedes i and o. It belongs to Group I with good reliability. The most frequent one-letter word, it often appears as the first letter of two-letter words but seldom as the second letter and very seldom as a terminal. It appears frequently as the fifth letter from the end of longer words (–ation) and also as the fourth from the end (–able).

B occurs two times per hundred. It precedes a, e, o, u, l, and y, follows a, and sometimes follows o and u. It is seldom doubled. Although it belongs in Group IV, it often appears elsewhere, particularly in Group I. It occurs as an initial letter and as third from the end of longer words (–able).

C occurs three times per hundred. It precedes a, e, i, o, h, and t, and follows a, e, i, and m and sometimes o, u, and s. It is seldom doubled. It belongs to Group IV and usually stays there. Frequently it serves as an initial and as a fifth and sixth letter from the end of longer words.

D occurs four times per hundred. It precedes a, e, i, and sometimes o. It follows e very frequently (–ed), n frequently, and r less often. It also follows a and i. It is seldom doubled. Frequently a terminal, it is also a common initial letter. For what it's worth, it appeared 14 percent of the time as the second letter of 14-letter words. Not 13- or 15-letter words, just 14. Probably some one 14-

letter word accounts for the better part of this percentage. D belongs to Group II; if not there, it usually appears in Group IV.

E occurs 13 times per hundred. The most frequent letter in English, it is often doubled. It precedes r, n, d, and s frequently and l, t, c, m, and v less frequently. It also precedes a and is almost the only letter to precede x. It follows h, with which it forms the second most frequent digram in English, follows r and t very frequently, and also follows s, l, v, m, d, n, c, and b. Although it belongs to Group III, it wanders a lot. It is common as a terminal, as a next-to-last letter (–ed), and also as third letter from the end. It is seldom the first letter of two- and three-letter words.

F occurs two times per hundred. It doubles at times and precedes a, e, i, o, r, and sometimes u. It follows o frequently and also e and i. A member of Group IV, it is usually found there. It tends to occur as the initial letter in words between three and twelve letters in length, as the terminal of two-letter words (of, if), and as the third or fourth letter of longer words.

G occurs two times per hundred. It rarely doubles. It precedes a, e, i, o, h, and r. It follows a, e, i, and u, and often follows n (–ing). Frequently a terminal, it is almost never in the second position or next to last. Although it belongs to Group II, it wanders a lot.

H occurs five times per hundred. It never doubles. It precedes a, e, i, and less frequently o. It follows c, g, s, w, and of course t but rarely follows vowels. With t, it forms the commonest digram in English—th. Not only does it belong to Group I, it is found there most of the time. It occurs as the second letter of three-, four-, and five-letter words and as the initial of two-, three-, and four-letter words. Seldom a terminal, it appears even less frequently as the next to last letter.

I occurs seven times per hundred. It never doubles, precedes o, e, and a, and follows a and e. It precedes n very frequently, s and t often, and then c, l, d, m, r, v, and g in that order. Again in order of frequency, it follows t, then h, r, l, s, d, and w. A member of Group I, it seldom wanders. Often found as a single letter, it also appears as the first letter of two-letter words, as the third letter from the end of words of most lengths, and also near the middle of longer words.

J occurs only twice per thousand, usually preceding a vowel. It belongs to Group IV and usually occurs as an initial letter, often in four-letter words.

K occurs one time per hundred. It precedes e and i, also n and sometimes s. It follows a, o, c, and r and occasionally n and s. Although it belongs to Group IV, it is likely to desert that group. It terminates four- and five-letter words and occurs toward the middle of words that are four to eight letters long.

L occurs four times per hundred. It precedes a, e, i, and o, also d and y, and occasionally u. It follows a, e, i, o, and u, and also p and b. Frequently doubled, it belongs to Group III but appears in other groups about half the time. It tends to appear as the next-to-last letter (–le, –ly) and also as a terminal.

M occurs three times per hundred. It precedes and follows a, e, i, o, and sometimes u. Among the consonants, it precedes p and follows r. It is doubled but not often. Although belonging to Group IV, it is absent as often as present. It appears mostly as an initial letter.

N occurs seven times per hundred. It precedes a, e, i, and o occasionally, but is more likely to follow them and u. It also precedes d (and), g (–ing), t (–nt), s, and c. It is usually found in the form, "vowel-n-consonant." There is some doubling. It belongs to Group III but is there only half the time. Common as the next-to-last letter, it also appears as the last and the third from the last. Moreover, it is common as the second or third letter of longer words.

O occurs eight times per hundred. Commonly doubled, it precedes u and also precedes f, n, m, l, w, and s. It follows t, c, r, h, f, l, s, m, and p. It belongs to Group I and is usually found there. Although it appears in either position of two-letters words, it is otherwise very rare as a terminal. It very frequently appears as the second letter of a word and as the next to last one (–tion).

P occurs two times per hundred. Frequently doubled, it precedes a, e, i, and o and also follows them. Among the consonants, it precedes r and l and follows m and s. Not only does it belong to Group IV, it seems to like it there. Common as an initial letter, it is rare as a terminal.

Q occurs one time per hundred. Never doubled, it precedes only u (in English, of course). It follows e and occasionally i, n, and s. It belongs to Group IV and almost always appears there. Never a terminal, it occasionally appears as the third letter from the end but is most common near the beginning of words (among the first three or four letters).

R occurs six times per hundred. Doubled occasionally, it precedes a, e, i, and o and follows a, e, o, and u. Among the consonants, it precedes s and t and follows t. Belonging to Group III, it nevertheless prefers other groups. Although it appears in all positions, it is more common as the second, third, fifth, or sixth letter. The commonest reversal in English is er/re.

S occurs seven times per hundred. Doubled frequently, it reverses with a, e, i, o, and u; precedes t and h; and follows n, r, t, and w. Although it belongs to Group II, it appears as often in Group IV. Common as both an initial and a terminal, in two-letter words it is most often terminal (is, as) but can be initial (so).

T occurs nine times per hundred. It doubles occasionally and reverses with all the vowels. It precedes h to form the commonest digram in English and also precedes r and s. It follows s, n, c, and r. Assigned to Group IV, it appears either there or in Group II most of the time. It is frequently the initial letter in words of five or fewer letters and the terminal in four-letter words. Although less common as a second letter, it may appear anywhere.

U occurs three times per hundred. It very rarely doubles. It follows o but only rarely adjoins the other vowels. It precedes r, s, t, n, and l and follows s, t, and b. Although it belongs to Group I, it appears in Groups II or III about a third of the time. It appears most often as the second letter of a word but very rarely as a terminal.

V occurs one time per hundred. It never doubles and tends to precede and follow vowels only, e being the most frequent. A member of Group IV, it also appears in Groups I and III. Very rare as a terminal, it is commonest as the third letter of longer words.

W occurs two times per hundred. It never doubles and, among the vowels, precedes a, e, i, and o and follows o. It also precedes h and s. It belongs to Group IV and is usually found there. It appears as the initial letter of three-, four-, and five-letter words (who, what, where) and also six- and seven-letter words.

X occurs two times per thousand. It never doubles, precedes a, e, and i, and almost always follows e. It also precedes p and t. A member of Group I, it appears there most of the time. It tends to appear as the second letter of longer words.

Y occurs two times per hundred. It never doubles. Among vowels, it precedes o and e (you, yes) and follows a and e. It also follows l, r, t, and b. It belongs to Group II and appears there most of the time. If not there, it is likely to be in Group III or IV. It frequently appears as a terminal.

Z occurs one time per thousand. It rarely doubles, precedes e, and follows i (-ize). It belongs to Group I but may wander. It tends to appear as the third or fourth letter from the end.

Problems for Chapter 8

1. M AU DMIIFHFVR IHXU *SAEKMVJRXV; M KAYF A KMJKFH, JHAVDFH ERAVDAHD XI ZHMVBMZQF. KF BXYQD VXR QMF. M BAV QMF, LYR M SXV'R. (*Mark Twain*)
2. P LXRN CNJMXPDTV EDFSD BFJN BND YNKMJFVNY ZV MLN YNKPJN MF LXRN X SPIN XDY CLPTY XDY MF ENNG MLNB PD CFBIFJM MLXD P LXRN KNND YNKMJFVNY ZV YJPDE XDY LXJTFMK. (*William Butler Yeats*)
3. BFX BUXX SY ORTXUBL MGAB TX UXYUXAFXW YUSM BRMX BS BRMX JRBF BFX TOSSW SY PQBURSBA QIW BLUQIBA. (*Thomas Jefferson*)
4. REDG MED FSGSLMDK ZLBDY MED ZNDY *GDR *DGNCZGYDK, "EZQD VHP FZYD VHPK IDZAD RSME *NHY?" MED AKPLMV *VZGBDD KDICSDY," RD ZSG'M JPZKKDCCDY CZMDCV."
5. GXKB MKT LQ KPPQP BU BXQ XKNNYTQSS UV K RKT GXU YS YT XQKOBX, UCB UV PQLB, KTP XKS K MOQKE MUTSMYQTMQ? (*Adam Smith*)
6. DTK YEPJKL TK DFYXKJ EM TUA TENEL, DTK MFADKL SK IEPNDKJ EPL AWEENA. (*Ralph Waldo Emerson*)
7. MZ YHYBKSRY MR DOY ISBTX XYWMXYX DS VY FWMYRDMFDF, M DOMRU M ISGTX DQUY GA ATGEVMRC QRX CYD BMWO WOQBCMRC IOQD M ATYQFYX.
8. FETATOY CEWYEPKL TL P SWKQTOPATWO WX QEPTOL POU ZPEU FWEI. AZV KWEV JWR CRA TO WX AZV XWEKVE AZV NVLL JWR FTNN OVVU WX AZV NPAAVE.
9. Q FZX'O NAXO A VANYGC OZ OGVV WG NLAO Q DAXXZO FZ; Q LQCG LQW OZ OGVV WG LZN OZ FZ NLAO Q NAXO OZ FZ. (*J. P. Morgan*)
10. *OMEXRTWSXMSB PT STC HTWWK MNTFC QMWCVDFMZQB. CVQK NQEXQGQ CVMC HVQS CVQ NXU TSQ OTAQB XC HXEE NQ CVQ QMBCQWS IMWC TR CVQ OTFSCWK CVMC UTQB FSPQW.
11. *LESTXPL XI OWS NGDJ GLOXNG XG WXIONTJ FWXPW EXTLPBDNBIDJ WLI VNGS QXTSPODJ UTNE MLTMLTXIE

ON QSVSGSTLOXNG FXOWNBO OWS BIBLD XGOSTCLD NU PXCXDXKLOXNG. (*George Clemenceau*)

12. KCT BDDITJJTZ WIT WRRBOTZ BGYT TNTIQ HTO QTWIJ KB ZTYLZT OCLYC DWIKLYMRWI UTUXTIJ BH KCT BDDITJJLGE YRWJJ WIT KB ITDITJTGK WGZ ITDITJJ KCTU. (*Karl Marx*)
13. MXRMIX AT ZXTXDSI SDX XBHSIIO PRDDAYAXW SG PXSDATZ GPX *VPDAFGAST DXIAZART WRHUG XW, STW SG FXXATZ AG MDSVGAVXW. (*Samuel Butler*)
14 ZW J RJI ZL XVISZIVEG SIYJNNG DZTY YZL XCBVOIRVIT ZI J UVRCQOJQG, TYVOV DZEE KV IC IVVU TC SOXV YZR TC XC CST TC BCTV. YV'EE KV WZOLT ZI EZIV DYVI TYV NCEEL CNVI.
15. *DSFSO ZSDO'F S DLOYGW DSGSCLWV ZWGEWC, FZW *REERDLFLRO WHEGRPD S HLGGLRO. (*Mark Twain*)
16. TGPLRB'N EN ZU NUKKEZLU ES E JPGNUR MGIU KULEYZLU MNYNEMNECM TDECD HKGQU NDYN IGKU HUGHLU YKU RKEQUB EBMYBU NDKGPAD KULEAEGPM DWMNUKEY NDYB ZW RKEBOEBA YLCGDGL? (*W. C. Fields*)
17. FAX CRE SY FAX BVASMQN CB ISNX BQVNXW FAQR FAX TMSSW SY FAX IQNFON—ISAQIIXW.
18. EK RFNDRXXW JH UBHLPN LBHY KTUKBPKZFK. ORBJXW RZWCHJW ERVKA DU NOKPB AKFHZJ CRCW QDAN NH AKK PN AYPXK.
19. MF IUEF QSZ NSYZ GUJZI, BTZ MF IUEF ZXUQYGFXXFD JZ GXSO *HSD ZS ZIF OFDJCUN VXSGFYYJSQ. (*G. B. Shaw*)
20. BUM IVVR DBU GHRR GKH GYEGK, CEG OG YHXEOYHZ B SBU VI ZVSH ZHUZH GV QUVT KVT GV ROH THRR. (*Samuel Butler*)

9

Polyalphabetic Substitution

One type of substitution cipher was considered to be unbreakable for well over four centuries. Called the *Vigenère Polyalphabetic Cipher,* it has close relatives, the Porta and the Beaufort. The general scheme, invented by Leon Battista Alberti around 1466, has been modified and improved since then. It was not until the late nineteenth century that a man by the name of Kasiski developed an attack that was capable of cracking the system regularly. Although there had been occasional solutions during the intervening years, no organized approach was ever developed. During the present century a number of refined methods have made possible an almost completely mechanical solution of the polyalphabetic, but it is still interesting because of its long history.

The cipher is generally described in reference to a "tableau" similar to that shown in Fig. 9.1. We choose a keyword and write it repeatedly over the plaintext. Supposing that the plaintext is "Now is the time for all good men" and that the keyword is TABLE, we write:

```
T A B L E T A B L E T A B L E T A B L E T A B L E
n o w i s t h e t i m e f o r a l l g o o d m e n
```

To encipher, we find the intersection of the key letter column and the plaintext letter row. Since the intersection of column T and row n in Fig. 9.1 is G, the first ciphertext letter is G, and since the intersection of column A and row o is O, that is the second ciphertext letter. Enciphering the whole message, we get:

```
T A B L E T A B L E T A B L E T A B L E T A B L E
n o w i s t h e t i m e f o r a l l g o o d m e n
G O X T W M H F E M F E G Z V T L M R S H D N P R
```

which we are to read off in five-letter groups (always five regardless of the length of the keyword).

We should notice several things about this system. The two l's of the word "all" get translated as LM. The t's of "the" and "time" get translated as M and E. The three M's of the ciphertext stand for t, i,

Key letter

Plaintext letter	*A*	*B*	*C*	*D*	*E*	*F*	*G*	*H*	*I*	*J*	*K*	*L*	*M*	*N*	*O*	*P*	*Q*	*R*	*S*	*T*	*U*	*V*	*W*	*X*	*Y*	*Z*
A	A	B	C	D	E	F	G	H	I	J	K	L	M	N	O	P	Q	R	S	T	U	V	W	X	Y	Z
B	B	C	D	E	F	G	H	I	J	K	L	M	N	O	P	Q	R	S	T	U	V	W	X	Y	Z	A
C	C	D	E	F	G	H	I	J	K	L	M	N	O	P	Q	R	S	T	U	V	W	X	Y	Z	A	B
D	D	E	F	G	H	I	J	K	L	M	N	O	P	Q	R	S	T	U	V	W	X	Y	Z	A	B	C
E	E	F	G	H	I	J	K	L	M	N	O	P	Q	R	S	T	U	V	W	X	Y	Z	A	B	C	D
F	F	G	H	I	J	K	L	M	N	O	P	Q	R	S	T	U	V	W	X	Y	Z	A	B	C	D	E
G	G	H	I	J	K	L	M	N	O	P	Q	R	S	T	U	V	W	X	Y	Z	A	B	C	D	E	F
H	H	I	J	K	L	M	N	O	P	Q	R	S	T	U	V	W	X	Y	Z	A	B	C	D	E	F	G
I	I	J	K	L	M	N	O	P	Q	R	S	T	U	V	W	X	Y	Z	A	B	C	D	E	F	G	H
J	J	K	L	M	N	O	P	Q	R	S	T	U	V	W	X	Y	Z	A	B	C	D	E	F	G	H	I
K	K	L	M	N	O	P	Q	R	S	T	U	V	W	X	Y	Z	A	B	C	D	E	F	G	H	I	J
L	L	M	N	O	P	Q	R	S	T	U	V	W	X	Y	Z	A	B	C	D	E	F	G	H	I	J	K
M	M	N	O	P	Q	R	S	T	U	V	W	X	Y	Z	A	B	C	D	E	F	G	H	I	J	K	L
N	N	O	P	Q	R	S	T	U	V	W	X	Y	Z	A	B	C	D	E	F	G	H	I	J	K	L	M
O	O	P	Q	R	S	T	U	V	W	X	Y	Z	A	B	C	D	E	F	G	H	I	J	K	L	M	N
P	P	Q	R	S	T	U	V	W	X	Y	Z	A	B	C	D	E	F	G	H	I	J	K	L	M	N	O
Q	Q	R	S	T	U	V	W	X	Y	Z	A	B	C	D	E	F	G	H	I	J	K	L	M	N	O	P
R	R	S	T	U	V	W	X	Y	Z	A	B	C	D	E	F	G	H	I	J	K	L	M	N	O	P	Q
S	S	T	U	V	W	X	Y	Z	A	B	C	D	E	F	G	H	I	J	K	L	M	N	O	P	Q	R
T	T	U	V	W	X	Y	Z	A	B	C	D	E	F	G	H	I	J	K	L	M	N	O	P	Q	R	S
U	U	V	W	X	Y	Z	A	B	C	D	E	F	G	H	I	J	K	L	M	N	O	P	Q	R	S	T
V	V	W	X	Y	Z	A	B	C	D	E	F	G	H	I	J	K	L	M	N	O	P	Q	R	S	T	U
W	W	X	Y	Z	A	B	C	D	E	F	G	H	I	J	K	L	M	N	O	P	Q	R	S	T	U	V
X	X	Y	Z	A	B	C	D	E	F	G	H	I	J	K	L	M	N	O	P	Q	R	S	T	U	V	W
Y	Y	Z	A	B	C	D	E	F	G	H	I	J	K	L	M	N	O	P	Q	R	S	T	U	V	W	X
Z	Z	A	B	C	D	E	F	G	H	I	J	K	L	M	N	O	P	Q	R	S	T	U	V	W	X	Y

Fig. 9.1 A polyalphabetic tableau.

and l in the plaintext, and the two F's of the ciphertext stand for e and m. Thus, the same plaintext letters may get translated to different ciphertext letters, and the same ciphertext letters may stand for different plaintext letters.

Deciphering is the opposite of enciphering. We write down the ciphertext with the keyword repeated over it as required, look down the key letter column until we come to the entry equal to the ciphertext letter, and then write down the row that entry is found in as the plaintext letter. Thus the entry G in column T is in row N, the entry O in column A is in row O, and so forth.

What we are doing with this system is to use a number of Caesar ciphers in rotation. Each column represents a simple Caesar cipher with a shift equal to the cardinality of the letter at the head of the column. At one blow this takes away two of the analyst's most powerful tools: letter frequencies and digram frequencies. Because the letters are enciphered by many different alphabets, letter frequencies are blurred between these different alphabets. Because the way a digram is enciphered depends on where it occurs in the message relative to the keyword, digram statistics are also obscured.

Look at the following message:

> Our latest shipment of one hundred bales is now loaded. Local harbor police will not interfere. We can sail anytime this week. Please advise conditions at your end.

The encipherment, with the keyword CONVERT, becomes

```
QIEGE  KXUHF  CMGFG  BGJJF  GGVHI  HIXFP
NGIJB  UBBRP  FTFSQ  GSTTN  VNMFF  KRCYD
GVPKZ  YISKB  PHRMJ  VKGKR  XEELC  WYVRP
MKARO  LZLYS  RFTCX  CGRVH  MBUSP  JRUBV
WBIWR  MACHM  IEW
```

From this, we get the following letter frequencies for plaintext and ciphertext, which have been ranked from the most frequent to the least frequent letters:

Plaintext				*Ciphertext*			
E:	18	H:	4	G:	11	S:	5
N:	12	W:	4	R:	10	T:	4
A:	11	P:	3	F:	9	U:	4
I:	11	U:	3	B:	8	W:	4
O:	11	B:	2	I:	7	X:	4
L:	10	F:	2	K:	7	Y:	4
S:	9	M:	2	M:	7	L:	3
T:	9	Y:	2	V:	7	N:	3
D:	7	K:	1	C:	6	A:	2
R:	7	V:	1	H:	6	Z:	2
C:	4			P:	6	Q:	2
(No G, J, Q, X, or Z)				E:	5	D:	1
				J:	5	O:	1

Observe that both distributions have the same number of occurrences per letter on the average (5.1), which is only as it should be since letters are neither created nor destroyed by this method of enciphering. In the polyalphabetic cipher, however, every letter appears at least once. In the plaintext, E appears as 13.5 percent of the letters, or just what we would expect. In the ciphertext, the most frequent letter appears only 8.3 percent of the time. In a simple substitution cipher, whatever letter disguise E was wearing would still appear exactly the same number of times that E appeared, and we could make a good guess as to which letter stood for E just on the basis of frequency. But now E is represented by G, S, R, Z, I, V, and X, and at various times G stands for E, S, T, L, C, P, and N. Thus, even if by some strange chance the G in the ciphertext had the same frequency as the E in the plaintext, we wouldn't be any further ahead in solving the cipher.

Enciphering Program

To encipher and decipher a polyalphabetic, we are going to take advantage of a mathematical scheme to represent the encipherment.

Look at the top row of the tableau in Fig. 9.1. In each column, A is going to be represented by the key letter. B will be represented by the key letter plus one, except in the last column where it will be represented by A. C will be represented by the key letter plus 2, except for the last two columns, which we will deal with shortly. Let 1 stand for A, 2 for B, . . . , and 26 for Z, as usual. Then the ciphertext representation of plaintext letter P under key letter K will be given as

$$C = [P+K-1]_{\text{mod } 26}$$

where the sum is taken "modulo 26." That means that if we get a number larger than 26, we are to subtract 26 from it. Thus, for P=13(M), K=20(T), we have

$$C = [13+20-1]_{\text{mod } 26} = [32]_{\text{mod } 26} = 6$$

where 6 stands for F, and that is just the letter we find at the intersection of column T, row M.

Then if the plaintext is in vector T% and the translated keyword in vector K%, we can generate a ciphertext character with the following:

```
C%(X)=T%(I)+K%(KP)-1
IF C%(X) > 26 THEN C%(X)=C%(X)-26
```

The rest of the program (Program 9.1) is straightforward.

Deciphering is the inverse of enciphering so that the program is identical to Program 9.1 except for lines 120 and 130, which will read as follows:

```
120  C%(I) = T%(K)-K%(L)+1
130  IF C%(I) < O THEN C%(I)=C%(I)+26
```

Program 9.1 Enciphering a Polyalphabetic

```
  1  DIM K%(50),C%(250)
 10  REM READ PLAINTEXT AND SQUEEZE OUT BLANKS
 20  GOSUB 10000
 30  GOSUB 10200
 40  PRINT "ENTER KEYWORD (NO BLANKS)"
 50  INPUT A$
 60  FOR I=1 TO LEN(A$)
 70     K%(I)=ASC(MID$(A$,I,1))-64
 80  NEXT I
 90  L=0
100  FOR I=1 TO J
110     L=L+1: IF L > LEN(A$) THEN L=1
120     C%(I) = T%(I)+K%(L)-1
130     IF C%(I) > 26 THEN C%(I)=C%(I)-26
140  NEXT I
150  GOSUB 10300
160  GOTO 20
```

Program 9.1 (cont'd) Enciphering a Polyalphabetic Comments

10–30
: Read in the plaintext and remove blanks and punctuation.

40–80
: Get the keyword and set it up.

70 Translate the ith character of the keyword to a digit between 1 and 26.

90 L is a pointer to the letter of the keyword whose turn it is to be used.

100–140
: Encipher each letter of the plaintext (J is the number of plaintext letters).

110 Use the next keyword letter. If you have run off the end of the keyword, go back to the beginning.

120 Encipher a letter.

130 If the result is bigger than 26, correct it.

150 Print out the ciphertext in five-letter blocks.

160 Ask for another plaintext.

Analysis Without a Keyword

To illustrate Kasiski's method of cracking the polyalphabetic cipher, let us suppose that among your grandfather's old and dusty records you found a slip of paper bearing the following puzzling message:

```
G F V T Z   Q V W M F   J T G Q E   S G K L E   K N R X X
        5           10          15          20          25
I S A V N   Y I K V M   S S M D E   E C J A J   G Y S N J
       30           35          40          45          50
I T Z Y Y   S N J I I   K J R M G   K I D O B   Z X X Z R
       55           60          65          70          75
B S W B S   Y K L E Z   I L W X K   L E J Y Z   W T I I D
       80           85          90          95         100
T U I R P   Z X H S F   R V Z V I   L E N I I   X R X T Z
      105          110         115         120         125
Y J M W V   X H J Y V   L N E H R   W X W I X   K A E K N
      130          135         140         145         150
F J M Y I   E D G K V   X V X H W   L V E K V   X H W L V
      155          160         165         170         175
Q T Z R S   G Z R R H   C H W W F   C H B X J   I X N V I
      180          185         190         195         200
G W I E L   M F Y M Y   A E K N F   J M Y I W   W F C
      205          210         215         220
```

A count of letter frequencies reveals at once that this is neither a transposition nor a simple substitution. Your quick mind jumps to the idea of a polyalphabetic substitution. If you are correct in your assumption, then the first thing to do is to discover, if you can, the length of the keyword.

When Kasiski noted was that a plaintext word or sequence of letters would be occasionally repeated and furthermore that it would sometimes fall by chance at the same position under the keyword. Whenever this happened, there would be repeated blocks of identical ciphertext that would be separated by an integral multiple of the keyword length. Of course, some repeats will be accidental and not caused by repeated plaintext; these will appear with random separations not related to the keyword length.

To find all the repeats in a message, we can make a regular trigram tabulation since we really should not bother looking at repeated digrams. From such a tabulation we can select repeated trigrams and, referring back to the original message, extend these adjacent trigrams to form longer repeats. Doing this, we get the tabulation shown at the top of the next page.

Here we have taken the difference between the locations of the two occurrences and listed the factors of these differences. From this multitude of factors we must now try to pick out the one factor that represents the length of the keyword. The longer the repeated sequence, the less likely that it is accidental and hence the more attention we should pay to it. On this basis, the long repeat AEKNFJMYI has factors of 2, 4, 8, 16, 32, and 64. Now, 64 and 32 are probably too long, and 2 is certainly too short. If the real keyword length is 4 and we choose 8, then the effect will be to cause the keyword to appear to be repeated. On the other hand, if the real key length is 8 and we choose 4, we will be confusing one alphabet with another by mapping alphabet 5 onto alphabet 1, alphabet 6 onto alphabet 2, etc. When in doubt, take

	N-gram	*First*	*Second*	*Difference*	*Factors*
1	EKN	20	150	130	2 5 10 13 26 65 130
2	EKN	20	212	192	2 3 4 6 8 12 16 24 32 48 64
3	AEKNFJMYI	147	211	64	2 4 8 16 32 64
4	WWFC	188	220	32	2 4 8 16 32
5	VXHWLV	162	170	8	2 4 8
6	KLE	18	82	64	2 4 8 16 32 64
7	KLE	18	90	72	2 3 4 6 8 9 12 18 24 36 72
8	KLE	82	90	8	2 4 8
9	KVX	159	169	10	2 5 10
10	YSNJI	47	55	8	2 4 8
11	TZY	52	124	72	2 3 4 6 8 9 12 18 24 36 72

the larger choice. If two popular factors are 4 and 6, choose 12 if that is also a factor for each repeat.

If we choose 8 as the tentative key length that will "explain" repeats 2, 3, 4, 5, 6, 7, 8, 10, and 11, then 1 and 9, both trigrams, can be explained as accidentals. How many three-letter accidentals should we expect in a message of 223 letters? The chances that two blocks of three letters will agree with each other is $(1/26)^3$. From 223 letters we can choose the first block of three contiguous letters 221 ways (we can't start a triple in either of the last two letters). Since the second block should not overlap the first block, there are 218 such second blocks. Now, however, we have chosen each block twice, once as a first block and then again as a second block; we should therefore divide the number of pairs by two to correct this situation. Then we have (221×218)/2, or 24,089 possible pairs of triples and one chance in 26^3, or 17,576, that a triple chosen at random will agree with another triple chosen at random. We can therefore say that in a message of 223 letters we should expect 24,089/17,576, or 1.37 accidental triples. Then two such accidentals are not unreasonable.

Suppose, on the other hand, we had decided that 6 was the key length. Then we would have 8 supposed accidentals to explain away, and that is more than chance would allow.

Now that we have a tentative key length, we should write out the message in eight columns (see Fig. 9.2). From this we can conveniently count letter frequencies in each column to see if the frequencies look

G	F	V	T	Z	Q	V	W
M	F	J	T	G	Q	E	S
G	K	L	E	K	N	R	X
X	I	S	A	V	N	Y	I
K	V	M	S	S	M	D	E
E	C	J	A	J	G	Y	S
N	J	I	T	Z	Y	Y	S
N	J	I	I	K	J	R	M
G	K	I	D	O	B	Z	X
X	Z	R	B	S	W	B	S
Y	K	L	E	Z	I	L	W
X	K	L	E	J	Y	Z	W
T	I	I	D	T	U	I	R
P	Z	X	H	S	F	R	V
Z	V	I	L	E	N	I	I
X	R	X	T	Z	Y	J	M
W	V	X	H	J	Y	V	L
N	E	H	R	W	X	W	I
X	K	A	E	K	N	F	J
M	Y	I	E	D	G	K	V
X	V	X	H	W	L	V	E
K	V	X	H	W	L	V	Q
T	Z	R	S	G	Z	R	R
H	C	H	W	W	F	C	H
B	X	J	I	X	N	V	I
G	W	I	E	L	M	F	Y
M	Y	A	E	K	N	F	J
M	Y	I	W	W	F	C	

Fig. 9.2 The message written in eight columns.

like those of ordinary English. In Fig. 9.3 this has been done, and in each column we see a typical pattern of some very frequent letters and many other letters not used at all. In each column of Fig. 9.3 we see exactly this pattern but with different popular letters so that if we add across columns as has been done in the column marked "Sum," we see every letter appearing, most of them a number of times, and no single letter or letters being outstandingly popular like E or T.

Hoping that this message was enciphered with a Vigenere, that is, with rotated-normal-order alphabets as shown in Fig. 9.1, we can attempt to recover the keyword by taking the normal English frequencies and plotting them on the same scale as that used to construct Fig. 9.3 and sliding it down until frequent English letters fall next to frequent letters in the column and rare English letters fall next to rare letters in the column.

We can do this in a crude way as follows. ETOAN are popular letters, ISHRDLU are medium-frequency letters, and the remaining letters are of low frequency. Make up a chart like that of Fig. 9.4, and

	Column 1	2	3	4	5	6	7	8	Sum
A			//	//					////
B	/			/		/	/		////
C		//					//		////
D				//	/		/		////
E	/	/		卌 //	/		/	//	卌 卌 ///
F		//				///	///		卌 ///
G	////				//	//			卌 ///
H	/		//	////				/	卌 ///
I		//	卌 ///	//		/	//	////	卌 卌 卌 ////
J		//	///		///	/	/	//	卌 卌 //
K	//	卌			////		/		卌 卌 //
L			///	/	/	//	/	/	卌 ////
M	////		/			//		//	卌 ////
N	///					卌 /			卌 ////
O					/				/
P	/								/
Q						//		/	///
R		/	//	/			////	//	卌 卌
S			/	//	///			////	卌 卌
T	//			////	/				卌 //
U						/			/
V		卌	/		/		卌	//	卌 卌 ////
W	/	/		//	卌	/	/	///	卌 卌 ////
X	卌 /	/	卌		/	/		//	卌 卌 卌 /
Y	/	///				////	///	/	卌 卌 //
Z	/	///			////	/	//		卌 卌 /

Fig. 9.3 Occurrence of letters in each column.

slide it against the first column of Fig. 9.3. It is convenient if you double the length of the chart of Fig. 9.4 so that it goes through the alphabet twice and you don't have to worry about "folding it around" to get back to the beginning of the column.

Using Fig. 9.4, we should search out a sliding position such that all, or almost all, of the letter occurrences in a column fall next to letters with bars drawn, and if possible, with the more frequent column letters next to the longer bars.

For column 1, this condition is met if we place the plaintext A of Fig. 9.4 next to the ciphertext T of column 1 in Fig. 9.3, giving T as the first letter of the keyword. Since the remaining columns yield the key letters R, E, A, S, U, R, and E, the keyword is TREASURE. We will leave the content of the message for the reader to puzzle out.

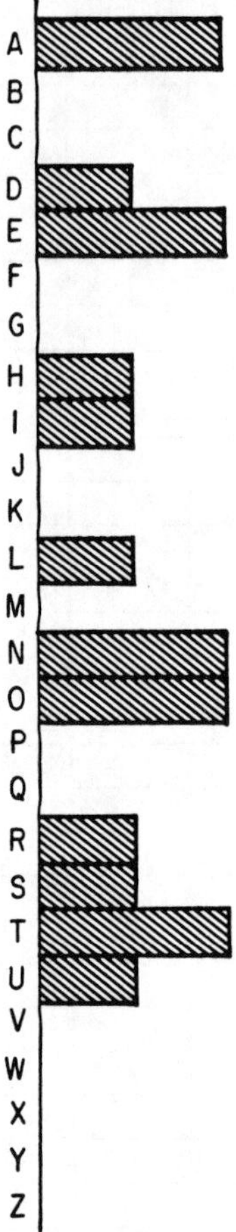

Fig. 9.4 Crude approximation to English letter frequencies.

We can continue with column 2, and so on, using Fig. 9.4 to discover the keyword, or we can turn to the computer and do the same thing more formally. What we are doing when we slide Fig. 9.4 against a column is a form of cross correlation. We are trying to put large numbers against large numbers and small against small. Mathematically, we want to find for each column the value of i that maximizes the formula

$$X_i = \sum_{j=1}^{26} C_j * A_{i+j}$$

where

C_j = the number of times the jth letter appears in the column count

A_{i+j} = the number of times per 1000 that the i+jth letter appears in English

and the sum, i+j, is taken modulo 26. To be a true cross correlation, we would have to divide X by the number of letters in the column $(\sum_j C_j)$ and by 1000 $(\sum_j A_j)$, but since these will be the same for each i and we are searching for the maximum X we can leave this step out.

A program to accomplish our purpose should do the following:

1. Read in the ciphertext.
2. Read in the proposed keyword length.
3. Perform the "slide" or cross correlation for each column.
4. Print out the letters that correspond to the i's that maximize X for each column (these will constitute the reconstructed keyword).
5. Allow the user to choose a keyword.
6. Print out the supposed plaintext using this keyword.

We can improve this program even before we write it by using a twentieth-century method of identifying the keyword length. This method was devised by William Friedman, who was perhaps the greatest cryptanalyst of this or any other century.

His method as applied to our present problem would be to find how well a tentative column matches the distribution of frequencies found in English. Friedman called this the "index of coincidence," but today we would be more likely to call it the "auto correlation coefficient." To state it another way, we take the cross correlation of a column's frequency distribution with itself. Mathematically this is expressed as

$$\phi = \frac{\sum_{i=1}^{26} C_i^2}{\left(\sum_{i=1}^{26} C_i\right)^2}$$

This time we have to include the denominator because we are going to be comparing distributions with different numbers of letters in them.

Let us look at function ϕ. Suppose we have a distribution in which each letter appears exactly three times. Then we have:

$$\phi = \frac{(9 + 9 + 9 + \ldots + 9)}{(3 + 3 + 3 + \ldots + 3) * (3 + 3 + 3 + \ldots + 3)}$$

which is equal to 1/26, or 0.0385.

Suppose instead that only one letter appears 3 × 26, or 78 times, which is as "peaked up" as a distribution can get. Then

$$\phi = \frac{(0 + 0 + 0 + \ldots + 78^2 + \ldots + 0)}{(0 + 0 + 0 + \ldots + 78 + \ldots + 0) * (0 + 0 + 0 + \ldots + 78 + \ldots + 0)}$$

$$= 1$$

Any distribution between these two extremes will generate a ϕ intermediate between 1/26 and 1, and the more "peaked up" it is, the nearer ϕ will be to 1.

When we come to the actual calculaton of ϕ, we use a formula slightly different from the one given above. Instead of computing the sum of C_i^2, we compute the sum of $C_i\ (C_i - 1)$. By statistical arguments beyond the scope of this book, it may be shown that this gives a better estimate of ϕ than the formula given above. Sinkov has an admirably clear discussion of the reasons why this is so. Here we can just take it on faith. Suffice it to observe that as the number of occurrences of a letter gets large, C_i^2 and $C_i(C_i - 1)$ approach each other arbitrarily closely and that there is no difference between the two formulae.

For ordinary English, ϕ comes out to be 0.067. If two or more alphabets shifted with respect to one another are added together, the ϕ of the resultant alphabet will approach 0.0385. Knowing these facts, we can try various key lengths, and for each one we can compute the average ϕ for the N columns generated by this key length and then select that key length which gives the highest average ϕ.

Let me suggest that you check out Program 9.2 against the two ciphertexts given above. In both cases, the correct keyword pops out on the screen as if by magic.

If any of you should fall into a "time warp" and reappear at any time between the years 1400 and 1850, the obvious thing to do would be to hire out to some count or duke or king as a cipher clerk. But remember: Don't publish! Keep the method a secret! Otherwise you might change history!

Program 9.2 Polyalphabetic Analysis

```
1   DIM X%(20,26),E(26),T%(500),U%(500)
5   GOSUB 4000
10  GOSUB 10000
20  GOSUB 10200
50  PRINT "ENTER MINIMUM KEY LENGTH =";
60  INPUT SK
70  PRINT "ENTER MAXIMUM KEY LENGTH =";
80  INPUT LK
90  M=0
100 FOR K=SK TO LK
```

```
110      GOSUB 1000
120      T=0
130      FOR C=1 TO K
140         GOSUB 2000
150         T=T+PH
160      NEXT C
170      T=T/K
180      IF T > M THEN M=T: KK=K
190   NEXT K
200   PRINT “BEST KEY LENGTH =”; KK, “PHI-BAR=”; M
210   PRINT “USE WHAT KEY LENGTH?”
220   INPUT K
230   GOSUB 1000
240   FOR C=1 TO K
250      GOSUB 3000
260      SH(C)=D
270      PRINT CHR$(D+64);
280   NEXT C
290   PRINT: PRINT
300   PRINT “SELECT KEYWORD=”;
310   FOR C=1 TO K
320      GET A$: IF A$=“ ” GOTO 320
325      PRINT A$;
330      SH(C)=ASC(A$)-64
340   NEXT C
350   REM SHIFT OUTPUT
360   C=0
370   FOR I=1 TO J
380      C=C+1: IF C > K THEN C=1
390      U%(I)=T%(I)-SH(C)+1
395      IF U%(I)<1 THEN U%(I)=U%(I)+26
400   NEXT I
410   GOSUB 10300
420   PRINT: PRINT
430   PRINT “K=NEW KEYWORD,L=NEW KEY LENGTH,C=NEW
      CIPHERTEXT,R=NEW KEY RANGE”
440   GET A$: IF A$=“ ” GOTO 440
450   IF A$=“K” GOTO 300
460   IF A$=“L” GOTO 210
470   IF A$=“C” GOTO 10
480   IF A$=“R” GOTO 50
480   GOTO 430


1000  REM LETTER DISTRIBUTION PER COLUMN
1010  FOR I=1 TO K
```

```
1020      FOR L=1 TO 26
1030         X%(I,L)=0
1040      NEXT L
1050   NEXT I
1060   C=0
1070   FOR I=1 TO J
1080      C=C+1: IF C > K THEN C=1
1090      L=T%(I)
1100      X%(C,L)=X%(C,L)+1
1110   NEXT I
1120   RETURN
2000   REM INDEX OF COINCIDENCE
2010   N=0
2020   D=0
2030   FOR L=1 TO 26
2040      N=N+X%(C,L)*(X%(C,L)-1)
2050      D=D+X%(C,L)
2060   NEXT L
2070   PH=N/(D*D)
2080   RETURN

3000   REM CROSS CORRELATION TO NORMAL ENGLISH FREQS
3010   M=0
3020   FOR S=1 TO 26
3030      P=0
3040      FOR I=1 TO 26
3050         F=I-S+1
3060         IF F < 1 THEN F=F+26
3070         P=P+E(F)*X%(C,I)
3080      NEXT I
3090      IF P > M THEN M=P: D=S
3100   NEXT S
3110   RETURN

4000   REM SETUP ENGLISH FREQS
4010   FOR I=1 TO 26
4020      READ E(I)
4030   NEXT I
4040   RETURN
4050   DATA
```

Program 9.2 (cont'd) Polyalphabetic Comments

10-20
Input the ciphertext and squeeze out blanks.

40 A subroutine to set up a vector of the English letter frequencies.

50–80
Input the minimum and maximum range of key lengths to be investigated. One can use this to screen out a key length that gives false results.

90–120
This section is going to search for the key length that gives the maximum average auto correlation.

90 Maximum M is set to zero.

100 For range entered above.

110 Call subroutine to compute the letter frequencies for this value of K.

120 Sum T of auto correlation is set to zero.

130–160
Compute the sum of the auto correlations for all K columns.

140 Call subroutine to actually compute auto correlation for this column.

150 Add to total.

170 Compute average.

180 If this average is larger than M, the maximum found up to now, keep it, and set KK to equal the present value of K.

200 Print KK and its auto correlation coefficient.

210–220
What key length should we try? (Most probably KK, but maybe not.)

230 Go to subroutine to lay out letter frequencies again.

240–280
Calculate the best "shift" for each column and print it out as a keyword. If all has gone properly, this should be the original keyword reconstructed.

240 For each column of the message.

250 Subroutine to do the cross correlation at each possible slide.

260 Set shift for this column.

270 Print the letter.

290 Space the display.

300–340
Input a keyword (probably the one just printed out).

350–400
Shift the ciphertext in each column according to the keyword.

370 For each letter of the ciphertext.

380 Cycle through the k columns, one after another.

390 Shift the ciphertext letter back by the amount called for by the Cth letter of the keyword.

410 Print out the reconstructed plaintext.

430–480
See what the user wants to do next.

1000 Count the number of A's, B's, etc., in each column.
1010-1050
Zero the array.
1070 For each letter of the ciphertext.
1080 Cycle through the columns.
1090 Get the letter to L.
1100 Add one to the count in the Lth letter of column C.
1120 Return.

2000 Index of coincidence of the frequencies of a column with themselves.
2010-2020
Numerator and denominator are cleared to zero.
2030 For each letter L:
2040 Add (frequency of L) times (frequency−1) to numerator.
2050 Add frequency of L to denominator.
2070 Compute phi.
2080 Return.

Problems for Chapter 9

1. EQVWG GVRWP LBSEY CIAXW FRHRF
LLFIH UWTRK EHNCB RXAJR JMLVI
CEDWM FZZLZ HTVFV NLBJK TWFZT
TGQBF LAIPI WYDKI DQAOW KLFIY
VFWAV ISEWM SKMYR LAIDA BNDES
LDDVU GMTE

2. IFIIL JSRNE BQWBV NTFIM KMOEE
FIZXM HUIZH AMPOG MAOMR ECATN
VGMPS LADFB AMGZI XFWYI PNBKU
PXEOT ORBLH OGGAU MIGLH UEXPD
XWTNG APLPW ANN

3. BBRPB IAJOC SAZLI ACIZC OLPUA
ZJPRT MPWAK LJGGY VRCNB MVTSQ
FWTHY AAWKG ODWDH JNUGI ZCOLP
UTGYQ UGGQV NVPNA ZNMUG WQTGH
PAGXZ NVQGQ GAOEJ WMZNV HNTWX
NZEAF NMJTH VU (*Buckminster Fuller*)

4. YVYET NIQCJ EIMTA SIHIL QKHRN
JASMS YHBVL OSBNS OSLXO HEFYZ
CBXVD ORHIL JSWRG KAWNZ UWRIO

GVWHY NWIES KZSLQ DCXPW GWWGH
TSMJE JAWNZ JWMSR GZSLQ GLWVP
ZXVYK EVIFL HYGXJ KJYI

5. LCKFH IFXGA IWLWK SLHST TLASD
VFNGC SUDLT RWLHK IMAHF FZAKZ
SCYDE GLWTF DRXLS LUMON LDCOH
TAKSC EOYLL SYSQH BGUDP FALMV
CZROH NHMGD LTRWL HKIMA HFFPO
QBHAB AEBG

6. GGTZX IIYWZ YWGHI HUIKJ YQVDQ
LSLGH UFLHG IKWAI LVVBA TXAIM
ZVRRE SNXER HCVUH NKMLJ VXEEZ
IBQGG WODXB AHFRM YEFIQ LAHQG
XTABC SBJYP BOAWZ LPKWL BADBB
RKQXU UHF

7. YYHHD BVAFE UAWEC SNOWA KBQHG
TGYQM IVFRC UAYEL UOPPV ISDHE
UAPRI FSLKZ PEYKE ICUMA KDUSJ
AZNRK XAVPW ASXMP CWMES FOIXP
TRRYU NGLZV RYIHG YMGLW FETTP
LHJML KJZNQ UMMGI IPOSE WCAME
KGMT

8. KLWLP TIILQ ZMYMF ADRFY KBZNC
HDYLK EMXSZ NVBHY NMKSK JPGUC
GOCEZ JWXZB EKJYD XRVUB QBIWL
SZNJL GOWWC ISLYA FALID HCZWJ
CHSPW GDULX EICXZ QHICM RRLSZ
NJLGO WWCIS LYAFA LIDXC IUNAK
FFDYX LKLSN STMIK IWNKM GHD

9. DUQLG EAWGR RQKUK LAVSJ SQOTA
SLWCJ TMSTA FGDKR RMTSG DDLSI
SMSEL GFLBZ STJNY ATBCL TMLEV
APOCD AOZOM LOIKR RMODL ZEWVZ
NSXOM DDIOC LRMAL ANDKV EWXID
DDRUV RE

10. MKZGY JDOAX SDRYV BZGGE OVJHY
PKWFA LPKVV NGIGI VRJSI HFBGL
IVERJ DWDRR GZCGS JKPRJ SIVMF
JSXGX SFTOI GZSQE ARPMF JJVBY
PUTCE HZRRV XYVFV ARHVZ ICVBX
IYGBJ XYVZV PUOAH XYVFL QSSE

10

Variations on a Theme

A number of systems similar to the Vigenère are no more secure and often less secure than the original. For historical interest, and to allow you to do more of the problems in *The Cryptogram,* we will mention some of them in this chapter. The order of presentation will be more or less at random.

Gronsfeld

This system, invented by the Count of Gronsfeld in the seventeenth century, is a shortened variation on the Vigenère. The key is the sequence of digits 0 through 9. These digits correspond to columns A through J of the Vigenere, being, in fact, the shifts introduced by these columns. Because only ten alphabets are used instead of a possible 26, the system is somewhat more vulnerable than the original and has seldom been used for security purposes.

Porta

In 1563, Giovanni Battista della Porta* published a book on cryptography at the age of 28. Aside from being the first to suggest the use of probable words to crack and *almost* inventing Kasiski's method (he failed to recognize what he had done), he described a variety of polyalphabetic that bears his name. This method is best described by Table 10.1.

To encipher the letter E with key letter Q or R, we find the intersection of column E with row QR, which is Z. Since the encipherment is reciprocal, E will be the ciphertext for plaintext Z with key Q or R. We can develop these 13 cipher alphabets into normal form by "unfolding" this table. For example, the EF alphabet (for either enciphering or deciphering) is

a b c d e f g h i j k l m n o p q r s t u v w x y z
P Q R S T U V W X Y Z N O L M A B C D E F G H I J K

*In Renaissance Italy, it certainly would have been a good idea to have been named after John the Baptist if you wanted to go into cryptography.

Table 10.1 della Porta's method

	A	*B*	*C*	*D*	*E*	*F*	*G*	*H*	*I*	*J*	*K*	*L*	*M*
AB	N	O	P	Q	R	S	T	U	V	W	X	Y	Z
CD	O	P	Q	R	S	T	U	V	W	X	Y	Z	N
EF	P	Q	R	S	T	U	V	W	X	Y	Z	N	O
GH	Q	R	S	T	U	V	W	X	Y	Z	N	O	P
IJ	R	S	T	U	V	W	X	Y	Z	N	O	P	Q
KL	S	T	U	V	W	X	Y	Z	N	O	P	Q	R
MN	T	U	V	W	X	Y	Z	N	O	P	Q	R	S
OP	U	V	W	X	Y	Z	N	O	P	Q	R	S	T
QR	V	W	X	Y	Z	N	O	P	Q	R	S	T	U
ST	W	X	Y	Z	N	O	P	Q	R	S	T	U	V
UV	X	Y	Z	N	O	P	Q	R	S	T	U	V	W
WX	Y	Z	N	O	P	Q	R	S	T	U	V	W	X
YZ	Z	N	O	P	Q	R	S	T	U	V	W	X	Y

The program presented in Chap. 9 works up to the point of discovering the keyword. At that point it should be changed to attempt to match English letter frequencies in the order shown for the ciphertext alphabets against the observed column frequencies. My own first approach would probably be to store the 13 different frequency tables and try for the best possible match, but there might very well be a simple way to generate a frequency table when needed from the normal English letter frequencies although I haven't tried to do so.

Beaufort

In 1857, Admiral Sir Francis Beaufort, R.N., inventor of the scale of wind velocities, published yet another variation on the Vigenere. In fact, he published two variations. Using Fig. 9.1 for the original Beaufort scheme, we begin with the row headed by plaintext letters. Trace across that row until you find the key letter. The column containing that key letter is the ciphertext letter. Thus, to encipher plaintext J by key letter M, we enter row J and find M in column D, which will be the ciphertext letter standing for J. To decipher, we follow the same procedure. We enter the ciphertext letter row (row D) and trace across it to find the key letter M in column J, which becomes the plaintext equivalent of D under key M.

Beaufort's second system, called the *variant Beaufort,* begins with the key letter (M) and traces across that row to find the plaintext letter J in column H. Thus H will be the ciphertext equivalent of J under key M for the variant Beaufort. To decipher the variant Beaufort, we find the plaintext letter at the intersection of the key letter row with the ciphertext column.

Notice that the variant Beaufort and the Vigenere are in some fashion reciprocals of one another. Enciphering in one is the same as deciphering in the other. The true Beaufort is "self-reciprocal" since enciphering and deciphering are identical.

The reader may enjoy working out ways of adapting these variations to a computer based on the methods we have used previously.

Autokey

Blaise de Vigenère, as we have noticed, did not invent the Vigenère polyalphabetic cipher—Alberti did—but he somehow got his name attached to it and so it is called to this day. What he did invent was a method of producing a very long key for a polyalphabetic—a nonperiodic key, in fact. Now if the key doesn't have a period, our program in Chap. 9 will not be able to find a period and we will be stymied if we use that approach.

In 1585, Vigenère was very close to inventing the most modern form of polyalphabetic, called the *one-time pad*. We will describe it in the next section, but first let us look at what Vigenère actually did invent.

To be nonperiodic, a key must be as long as the message. What has the same length as an arbitrary message with more exactness than the message itself? Let us use the message itself as a key. Vigenère used a single letter "priming" key, but we will generalize his method to use a typical keyword of several letters known to both the transmitter and the receiver of the message. Taking the priming key TYPE and using our favorite message, we get the following:

Key:	T	Y	P	E	N	O	W	I	S	T	H	E	T	I	M	E	F	O
Plaintext:	n	o	w	i	s	t	h	e	t	i	m	e	f	o	r	a	l	l
Ciphertext:	G	M	L	M	F	H	D	M	L	B	U	I	Y	W	D	E	Q	Z

Deciphering is a matter of subtraction of the plaintext, as it is developed, from the ciphertext. One begins with the known priming key and works forward. If the priming key is unknown, it is possible by a very clever trick invented by Basseries to reduce an autokey to a periodic cipher that can then be attacked by the methods of the previous chapter.

To show how to do so, consider the plaintext message *a* b c d e . . . and the priming key A B C D. Enciphering by Vigenère's method, we get

A	B	C	D	*a*	b	c	d	e	f	g	h	i	j
a	b	c	d	e	f	g	h	i	j	k	l	m	n
X_1	X_2	X_3	X_4	X_5	X_6	X_7	X_8	X_9	X_{10}	X_{11}	X_{12}	X_{13}	X_{14}

in which we let X_i stand for the ith ciphertext letter. We assume a priming key a a a . . . of whatever length seems reasonable. In this case, we choose a length of 4, but notice the case below in which we don't know the correct length. We now decipher the ciphertext message to get a string of intermediate text letters Y_1, Y_2, . . . , as follows:

Key:	a	a	a	a	Y_1	Y_2	Y_3	Y_4	Y_5	Y_6	Y_7	Y_8	Y_9
Ciphertext:	X_1	X_2	X_3	X_4	X_5	X_6	X_7	X_8	X_9	X_{10}	X_{11}	X_{12}	X_{13}
Intermediate:	Y_1	Y_2	Y_3	Y_4	Y_5	Y_6	Y_7	Y_8	Y_9	Y_{10}	Y_{11}	Y_{12}	Y_{13}

Look at X_1, X_5, X_9, and X_{13} and the corresponding Y's. Since the X's were formed by *enciphering,* we can write equations:

$$\begin{aligned} X_1 &= A + \alpha \\ X_5 &= \alpha + e \\ X_9 &= e + i \\ X_{13} &= i + m \end{aligned}$$

Since the Y's were formed by *deciphering,* we have

$$\begin{aligned} Y_1 &= X_1 - a \\ Y_5 &= X_5 - Y_1 \\ Y_9 &= X_9 - Y_5 \\ Y_{13} &= X_{13} - Y_9 \end{aligned}$$

The pseudo priming key of a a a results in no change whatsoever, and therefore

$$Y_1 = X_1 = A + \alpha$$

Substituting for X_5 and Y_1, we get

$$Y_5 = X_5 - Y_1 = \alpha + e - A - \alpha = e - A$$

Similarly,

$$\begin{aligned} Y\text{-} &= X_9 - Y_1 = e + i - e + A = i + A \\ Y_{14} &= X_{13} - Y_9 = i + m - i - A = m - A \end{aligned}$$

By the same logic, we can chase down the chain for B as follows:

$$\begin{aligned} Y_2 &= B + b \\ Y_6 &= f - B \\ Y_{10} &= j + B \\ Y_{14} &= m - B \end{aligned}$$

Dividing the intermediate text up into blocks of length k—the length of the assumed priming key—we find that successive blocks of intermediate text are enciphered alternately by Vigenère and by variant Beaufort:

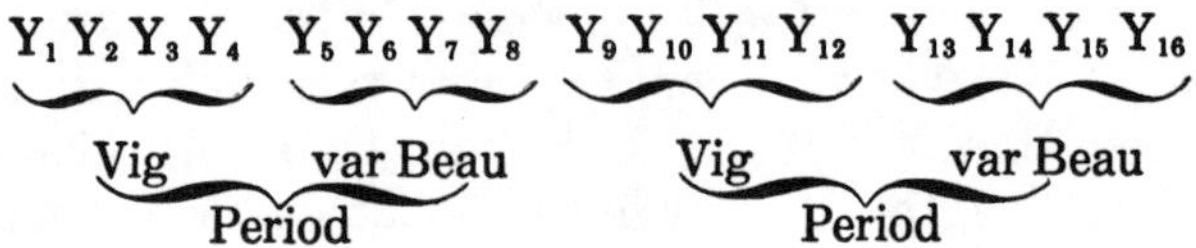

Looked at in this way, the nonperiodic autokey has been converted to a periodic polyalphabetic with period 2*k, and we can attack that with a modification of the program of Chap. 9. Then, even if we don't know the length of the priming key, we can search for it, as follows:

1. Assume a length k for the priming key
2. "Decipher" the ciphertext generating the intermediate text.
3. Assume that the intermediate text has a period of 2·k, and take the autocorelation of the 2·k frequency distributions.
4. Select the key length k that gives the largest autocorelation value.

Once you have the correct period, you can do a cross-correlation on the first k columns to discover the original keyword, or you can work out a way to combine the information from columns i and i+k to get better statistical accuracy. Doing so will be left as an exercise for the reader.

After the keyword has been uncovered, it should be reasonably straightforward to combine a block of Vigenère deciphering followed by a block of variant Beaufort deciphering (or Vigenère *enciphering,* which is the same thing) and print out the original plaintext.

The One-Time Pad

The basic idea of Vigenère's autokey was excellent. The method of attack found by Bassières relied on the fact that there was a perfect correlation between the message and a key displaced by the length of the priming key. Suppose that we could find a key as long as the message that was uncorrelated with it. Suppose also that we use a string of randomly selected letters, and suppose further that after using a key once we agree to destroy it so that it can never be used again. Let us make up a number of sheets of random letters into a "pad" and make a copy of the pad so that the transmitter and receiver each has a copy. The transmitter approaches his pad with a message to encipher. Using the letters on the topmost page (say page 12), he enciphers his message and puts a label "12" on it so that the receiver is properly oriented. The transmitter sends his message, rips off the top sheet, and destroys it.

An interceptor looking at the ciphertext sees a string of letters that appear to be random; in fact, no matter what test he may care to apply, he will find that they are indeed random. As a matter of fact, it may be shown that there is no way for the interceptor to discover the message. To simplify the proof of this, think about the following: Suppose that A needs to send a single digit (0 through 9) to B. They have previously agreed to encipher it by adding 3 to the digit and taking the sum modulo 10 (throw away the ten's place, if any). C intercepts the message (say "5") and argues thusly about the putative additive key and the corresponding plaintext:

Additive key	*Plaintext*
1	4
2	3
3	2
4	1
5	0
6	9
7	8
8	7
9	6

But which additive key did they actually choose? The interceptor hasn't a clue, provided the key has not been compromised!

The reason why each key is used only once is to defeat what is called "analysis in depth." If the same key had been used repeatedly, the analyst could collect the messages, and taking the ith letter of each message for a frequency distribution, cross-correlate it with normal English frequencies to recover the ith key letter.

It is the one-timeness of the one-time pad that prevents its being used more widely. After all, it is quite simple to implement and is known to be unbreakable, but as soon as traffic gets heavy, it becomes impractical. The sheer volume of keys that have to be distributed, and distributed *securely*, becomes overwhelming. For a spy in the field the possession of a supply of one-time pads is a problem because there is no plausible excuse for possessing them. Moreover, he can't "construct" one when he needs it. If he could, there would have to be some rule or method of construction, and if that were the case, the system wouldn't be random.

Pseudo-Random Sequences

It is possible to generate very long keys using rather complex rules on a computer. Although these do not have the absolute security of a true one-time pad, the generating rules can be made complex enough to defy amateur analysis. Almost every microcomputer accepts BASIC, and almost every version of BASIC has a random-number generator. Donald Knuth's classic work, *The Art of Computer Programming*, has a long chapter devoted to a discussion of random-number generators that is far beyond the scope of this book.

Using the random-number generator provided by BASIC is perhaps the simplest approach to generating pseudo-random sequences. You had better be careful to make sure that the transmitter and receiver have identical machines because generators are usually different for different BASICs and are probably sensitive to subtleties of the hardware that could produce a different sequence in two otherwise compatible versions of BASIC running on different machines.

To seed the random-number generator, you usually call the routine with a negative number. One way to do this is to input a keyword, convert each letter to a number between 1 and 26, and generate a key number by some algorithm such as the following:

```
SM=0
FOR I=1 TO KK
  SM=26*SM+K(I)
NEXT I
```

where KK is the length of the keyword and K is the vector of letters. If the keyword is ABCDE, this will produce a sum equal to

$$SM = 26^6 \bullet A + 26^3 \bullet B + 26^2 \bullet C + 26 \bullet D + E$$

Then the seeding is done by

```
T=RND(-SM)
```

where T is a dummy variable used only to perform the seeding operation.

Once the generator has been seeded, it can be used as follows:

```
TT=T%(I)+INT(26*RND(1))
IF TT> 26 THEN TT=TT-26
U%(I)=TT
```

The first line adds a "random" number between 0 and 25 to the plaintext letter in T%. The second line corrects the sum to a value between 1 and 26, and the third line assigns it to the output buffer.

An analysis in depth of traffic sent with the same key should lead to the recovery of parts of the sequence of random numbers. From a block of numbers, it should be possible to recover the original seed, but I confess to being intimidated by the task and have never really looked into it.

Randomized Alphabets

One of the first improvements every amateur thinks of when meeting the Vigenère for the first time is to scramble the alphabets in the tableau. In actuality, this ploy adds little to the security. Assuming that the system does not use 27 key words (a rather large number to remember)—26 of them for scrambling the 26 alphabets independently and the last one to act as the enciphering key—the most likely possibility is to use one key to scramble all the alphabets, which are then rotated or shifted as in a standard Vigenère, and a second key for enciphering. In this case, we cross-correlate the various column alphabets with one another rather than with standard English order and frequencies. At each stage, we take the highest cross-correlation coefficient or else the one that shows the largest gap between the best and the next-best coefficients and merge those two alphabets. In a short time, we will have the relative offsets of each column, one from the other. We can apply these offsets to the ciphertext as if they were a keyword and the intermediate text thus produced will be a simple substitution cipher without word divisions that may be solved by appropriate means with no great difficulty: letter frequency, contacts, digrams, and so forth.

St. Cyr Slide

A number of mechanical devices have been developed over the years to aid in performing polyalphabetic encipherment and decipherment. The most widely used of these is the St. Cyr Slide, named after the French military academy where the device was first used. In its simplest form, it consists of a device with a stationary piece and a movable piece that slides along the stationary one, much as in a slide rule. On each piece there is an alphabet in normal order that is repeated twice. Taking the stationary piece as containing both the key and the plaintext letter, one places the A of the movable piece next to the key letters. If the key letter we wish to work with is P, we would adjust the slide so that the device will appear as follows (stationary pieces on top line):

A B C D E F G H I J K L M N O P Q R S T U V W X Y Z

L M N O P Q R S T U V W X Y Z A B C D E F G H I J K
↑

To encipher E with this key, we would then look along the stationary piece for E and read out the ciphertext P; likewise, plaintext L would give W, and so on. Deciphering is accomplished in a similar manner, the ciphertext letter being found on the movable slide and the plaintext equivalent being read off above it. Such a slide will work equally well for Vigenere and variant Beaufort, but for true Beaufort the movable alphabet must be reversed, reading right to left. A version of the once, no doubt, highly secret St. Cyr slide is now available as "Hokey's Secret Decoder" for $1.50.

One variation on the slide consists of a pair of concentric disks with the alphabets written around the perimeters. If you cannot find one made of plastic (for a couple of dollars), you can construct one of cardboard. With disks each alphabet needs to appear only once. Both disks and slides are equivalent to the tableau but are somewhat easier to use and less subject to errors.

Wheatstone Disk

Charles Wheatstone is well known to electrical engineers for his invention of the Wheatstone bridge for the measurement of resistance. He also invented two cryptographic systems. One of these, which we will devote some time to later on, is called the "Playfair" system. The other he called a "cryptograph." Although it appears to be very ingenious, it turns out to be a very weak system. It is constructed with two concentric alphabets, the outer having 27 letters (A through Z and a blank) and the inner having 26 letters in scrambled order. There are two hands, one long and one short. These hands are geared together in such a way that if the inner hand makes one complete revolution, the outer has gone only twenty-six twenty-sevenths of the way around. The outer alphabet serves as plaintext; the inner, as ciphertext. To begin, the outer hand is brought around to point at the blank, and the inner hand (which had a slip clutch) is moved to point at the key letter. Now, moving clockwise, the outer hand is made to point at successive letters (and spaces) of the plaintext. As each plaintext letter is pointed at by the long hand, the short hand points to a ciphertext letter. Deciphering works approximately the same way. The key letter is set up and the gears are then turned so that the short hand points to successive ciphertext letters and the long hand points to successive plaintext letters. All that is necessary is to remember always to turn the hands clockwise, never backing up.

This system has the apparent advantage of using a new enciphering alphabet on every revolution, but the rigidity of the gears defeats most of this apparent complexity. Let us suppose that as an interceptor you have a copy of the device together with its scrambled inner alphabet. This is not an unreasonable assumption since these devices have been on sale on the open market, and since the face of the disk is brass with the alphabets engraved on the metal, it would not be a trivial matter to change the inner sequence of letters. As Kerchoff once warned, this is exactly the sort of attack that any respectable cipher system must be able to stand up against.

With the intercepted message in front of you, set the short hand to point at the first ciphertext letter. Let the long hand point at some convenient letter, say J. Proceed to "decipher" the message just as if you were the legitimate receiver. Decipher 10 or 15 letters and then "run down the alphabet" under this deciphered intermediate text, as follows:

Intermediate text:	J	K	S	E	O	P	D	A	P	E	I	A	B	K	N	X	H	H
	K	L	T	F	P	Q	E	B	Q	F	J	B	C	L	O	Y	I	I
	L	M	U	G	Q	R	F	C	R	G	K	C	D	M	P	Z	J	J
	M	N	V	H	R	S	G	D	S	H	L	D	E	N	Q	ƀ	K	K
Plaintext:	N	O	W	I	S	T	H	E	T	I	M	E	F	O	R	A	L	L

where ƀ stands for a blank. Now you can see that at the initial point when the short hand was pointing at the first ciphertext letter, the long hand should have been pointing at N rather than at J. You could program all of this with two indices P and C, one of which runs from 1 to 27 and the other from 1 to 26, and a vector of the letters plus a blank. You could even "run down" the alphabet by doing a cross-correlation of the letters of the intermediate text with English frequencies.

If you do not possess a copy of the scrambled alphabet, the task becomes somewhat harder but not impossible. For example, a pair of identical letters in the ciphertext will indicate a reversed plaintext pair like ON or TS, which might well serve as an entry. Because of this system's mechanical regularities, it would seem to be an ideal one to play with on a home computer.

Jefferson Wheel Cipher

A much more robust cryptographic system was invented by none other than our third president, Thomas Jefferson. Jefferson's invention was filed and forgotten, and it wasn't until it had been reinvented by another and adopted by the U.S. Navy that his work was uncovered.

He constructed a set of short cylinders each about two inches in diameter and a quarter of an inch high. The cylinders were numbered 1 through 36 and pierced in the center so that they could be mounted on an axle. Around the outside of each cylinder was written a mixed alphabet, and each cylinder had a different mixing scheme. A key would consist of an ordering of the cylinders—say, 10-22-1-17-5, etc.—in which they should be slid onto the common axle and read from left to right.

To send our favorite message, you line up the N of the first cylinder, the O of the second, the W of the third, and so on, until you spell out the first 36 letters of the message. At this point, you tighten the clamp on the axle to prevent the cylinders from slipping with respect to one another. You now have the message on one row running along the cylinders and 25 other sets of meaningless strings of characters above and below it. Select one of these sets at random and send it as the first 36 letters of ciphertext. For long messages, you must repeat the process enciphering 36 letters at a time.

The receiver sets up his disks in the key order, lines up the first 36 letters of ciphertext in a row, and looks around the cylinder for a row that makes sense as plaintext. The odds of there being two such rows, while not zero, are much too small to worry about.

An attack on this system is based on the possession of a set of cylinders and a probable word. One assumes that the probable word was enciphered within a single block of 36 letters. When the encipherer had set up the probable word, he had "spun" the cylinder to select a ciphertext row i rows below the plaintext, where i might be any number from 1 to 25. Suppose for a moment that i is equal to 1. Take the first letter of the probable word, say P. One row below the P on each cylinder there is some other letter. Collect all these letters and call them $S_1(p)$, that is, "the set of letters one around from p." Usually, not all the letters of the alphabet will be present in this set. Do the same thing for the other letters of the probable word: $S_1(r)$, $S_1(o)$, $S_1(b)$, etc. Search through the ciphertext for a sequence of letters such that the first one is a member of $S_1(p)$, the second of $S_1(r)$, and so on. If you don't find such a sequence, then generate the set of letters two around from "p," $S_2(p)$, two around from "o," $S_2(o)$, etc., and make the same search as before.

When you find such a sequence, there are still further constraints to apply. For example, you may find that the letter needed to stand for p occurs on several cylinders. On the other hand, it may turn out that the cylinder needed to provide the letter standing for p is the only cylinder that, for this value of i, can supply the letter needed to stand for r. In that event, you have made a false identification and must renew searching. Sooner or later, given enough patience, you will come upon a sequence that might be a rotation of the probable word. At this point you have one or more tentative clusterings of cylinders in the order that would have generated the ciphertext that you observed from the probable word. More than one cluster, if more than one cylinder, could have supplied a certain letter. Take each cluster in turn and apply it to the ciphertext to see if it produces recognizable English at other locations in the crypt. Remember that while the enemy probably used the same cylinder setup for the entire message, it was not mandatory for him to use all 36 cylinders in each key. Thus, the interval between the proper applications of your tentative cluster may not be exactly 36 letters.

Once you have a cluster that brings out the plaintext at several points in the message, you are a long ways toward the solution. By inspired guessing you can extend a fragment of plaintext a few letters, and by using the same process as above, you can verify that it produces intelligible plaintext at other points. Diligence, perseverance, and lots of luck will eventually crack the message, and tomorrow when they change the key you will have the opportunity to do it all over again.

This is obviously a job for a computer and quite probably for a large and fast one at that. If carried out by hand, the cryptanalysis of a Jefferson wheel cipher would probably consume several days, thus providing considerable security for a field cipher.

Ultra and Purple

The story of how the British cracked the German's top secret code, Ultra, and the Americans cracked the Japanese code, Purple, has been told in detail elsewhere [see Kahn (1), Winterbotham (7), and Clark (8)]. Both of these codes were based on a mechanical cipher machine invented in Sweden and developed in Germany during the thirties. This was a very complicated electromechanical device with turning disks, ratchets, pawls, gears, keys, and lights. Rather than describe it in all its original glory, we will present here a computer algorithm to give the flavor of the beast, if not an exact analogue.

We will model a "five-rotor" machine as follows. (Take note that all index arithmetic is assumed to be carried out modulo 26 so that we do not have to keep repeating that fact.)

There are five pointers, called P1, P2, . . . , P5. A five-column by 26-row matrix is called the *scrambling matrix,* S. Each column of this matrix consists of the integers 1 through 26 in some random order, each column being different. To encipher a plaintext letter, L, we first convert L to an integer between 1 and 26 in the usual fashion. We add L to P1 and use that as an index I1 to retrieve an entry from the first column of S(1,I1). Call this entry V1. We add V1 and P2 to form an index, I2, to retrieve an entry from column 2 of S = S(2,I2). Call this V2. V2 + P3 is used to access column 3, and so forth. The entry retrieved from column 5 (V5) is the numerical form of the ciphertext letter C corresponding to L. C is then sent off to a printer or copied down carefully. This whole operation can be expressed in a single line of BASIC code as

$$C=S(5,P_5+S(4,P_4+S(3,P3+S(2,P2+S(1,L+P1)))))$$

Deciphering can take place by searching column 5 of S for entry C, subtracting P5 from the location at which it is found and then searching column 4 for that difference, and so forth until you are back to L. Much faster would be to store a "descrambling" matrix in which you look up the entry by indexing and read out as a value the location at which it was originally stored in the scrambling matrix. For example, restricting ourselves to a five-letter alphabet, one column of the scrambling matrix and the corresponding column of the descrambling matrix might look like those shown in Fig. 10.1.

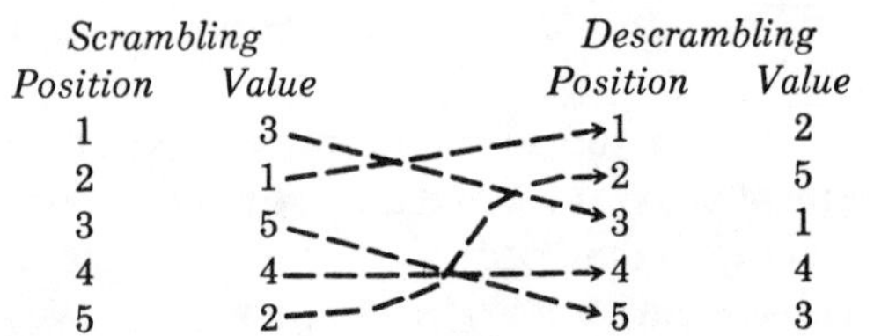

Fig. 10.1 Scrambling and descrambling column matrices.

If this were all the machine did, it would provide no more than a very cumbersome way of generating a monoalphabetic simple substitution cipher since each column represents a one-to-one mapping of letters onto letters and for any set of five columns there exists a single column that would do the whole job.

Therefore, a modification stage was added after each letter was enciphered so that the operation went: encipher, modify, encipher, modify, and so forth. To accomplish this, we need a second matrix of four columns and 26 rows called M. Each entry in this matrix is either 0 or 1 in our simplified version of the machine.

The modify operation is going to change the values of pointers P1 to P5. In each "modify," we begin by adding 1 to P1. Next we retrieve the entry in the first column of M that P1 is pointing to: M(1,P1). If this entry is zero, we terminate, and otherwise we add 1 to P2 and repeat—terminating with the first zero entry.

Being freed of any mechanical restrictions such as the strength of gear teeth, we should probably make each entry in M be equally likely to be zero or one. This will maximize the uncertainty of when a substitution alphabet (column) is going to advance and hence maximize the interceptor's task. The "key" for a particular day would consist of the initial values of the five pointers P1 to P5 plus the scrambling matrix, S, and the modifying matrix, M.

There are any number of ways to elaborate on this design. I can't resist suggesting a couple although I really have no idea if they would add to the security of the device or not. The first and most obvious would be to increase the number of columns in the matrices, which would probably be of some help. A second might be to have M store numbers between 0 and 25 that would be used as the modifiers for successive pointers. (Some of the actual mechanical machines did allow changes of 0, 1, or 2.) The most promising, but completely unstudied, possibility would be to have M consist of a matrix of integers in the range 0 to 5. If the retrieved M was 0, no change would take place, but if it were i, we would add 1 to P_i. You might want to worry about infinite or even very large loops of changes by limiting yourself to no more than, say, five changes per modify step, but surely this measure would allow you increased complexity in the sense of which alphabets were to advance at which time.

The analysis of machines of this kind are *way* beyond the scope of this book.

11

The Playfair Cipher

Wheatstone, you will remember, invented two cipher systems—a rather trivial one that bears his name and another quite sophisticated one that bears the name of his close friend, Lyon Playfair. This is not your standard case of the theft of an invention. On the contrary, Playfair spent so much energy and time promoting what he called "Wheatstone's symmetrical cipher" that it became identified with Playfair rather than its originator.

This cipher was the first one to treat pairs of letters as a unit for enciphering. By so doing, it disguises individual letter frequencies and also inhibits the identification of digrams.

As currently used, the system involves a 5×5 square in which the letters of the alphabet are entered, with i and j occupying the same cell. The assignment of letters is done with a keyword. For instance, if the keyword is MAGNETIC, one might write:

```
M A G N E T I C
B D F H K L O P
Q R S U V W X Y
Z
```

and then read out these columns left to right to fill in the 5×5 square:

```
M B Q Z A
D R G F S
N H U E K
V T L W I
O X C P Y
```

Any other scheme that results in good mixing and is easily remembered may be used instead.

The plaintext is divided into pairs of letters. Any time a pair contains identical letters, one of the pair may be suppressed or else a null character such as Q or X or Z may be inserted between them. For example, no wi st he ti me fo ra lq lg oq od me nx

The two letters of a pair are located in the square, and one of three following rules is applied to translate them to ciphertext:

1. If the two letters are in the same row, take the pair of letters that stand to the right of the plaintext letters. The row is considered to be circular, with the first letter following the last.
2. If the two letters are in the same column, take the pair of letters that stand below the plaintext letters. Again, the column's last letter is followed by its first letter.
3. If the two letters are in different rows and columns, they are considered as forming two corners of a rectangle. Take the two letters at the other corners of that rectangle as the ciphertext. The letter in the same row as the first plaintext letter is taken as the first cipher letter.

Applying these rules and using the square already established, we find that n and o are in the same column and therefore take the letters below them: VM. Since we find w and i in the same row, we take the letters to their right: IV. Since s and t are not in the same row or column, we take the letters at the other corners of the rectangle they form: RI. Completing the enciphering of the above message, we get:

no	wi	st	he	ti	me	fo	ra	lq	lg	oq	od	me	nx
VM	IV	RI	UK	LV	ZN	DP	SB	CG	CU	CM	MN	ZN	HO

Deciphering is much the same as enciphering except that one moves *left* in a single row or *up* in a single column.

Programming

Programs for enciphering and deciphering the Playfair system present something of a challenge, most of it in the set-up of information about the matrix. We will need to know where a particular letter is, that is, its row and column, and we will also want to know what letter is stored in row i, column j. We'll begin by reading in a keyword, converting it letter by letter to numbers, and removing the j's if any occur. Let there be K distinct letters in the keyword. As part of the process of making sure that these letters are distinct, we can cross out "used" letters in a 26-slot vector, thereby leaving the nonkeyword letters "uncrossed out." We will move the remaining "uncrossed out" letters down to form a single 26-letter array. Then we will take the letters in positions 1, K+1, 2K+1 until we reach the twenty-fifth letter (no J, remember), back up, and take letters 2, K+2, 2K+2, and so forth, placing each letter into a 5×5 grid as we pick them up. A program for enciphering a Playfair is given in Program 11.1 and for deciphering in Program 11.2. A subroutine to make a scrambled and transposed alphabet is shown in Program 11.3.

Program 11.1 Enciphering a Playfair

```
10   REM READ IN KEYWORD
15   U=-1
20   GOSUB 12000
30   GOSUB 10000
40   GOSUB 10200
50   T%(J+1)=24
60   FOR I=1 TO J STEP 2
70      L1=T%(I)
80      L2=T%(I+1)
90      IF L1 <> L2 GOTO 120
100     I=I-1
110     L2=17
120     I1=LI%(L1): J1=LJ%(L1)
130     I2=LI%(L2): J2=LJ%(L2)
140     GOSUB 1000
145     U=U+2
150     S%(U)=C1
160     S%(U+1)=C2
180  NEXT I
190  GOSUB 10300
200  GOTO 10

1000 REM ENCIPHER TWO LETTERS
1010 IF I1=I2 GOTO 1060
1020 IF J1=J2 GOTO 1110
1030 C1=PA%(I1,J2)
1040 C2=PA%(I2,J1)
1050 RETURN
1060 K1=J1+1: IF K1=6 THEN K1=1
1070 K2=J2+1: IF K2=6 THEN K2=1
1080 C1=PA%(I1,K1)
1090 C2=PA%(I2,K2)
1100 RETURN
1110 K1=I1+1: IF K1=6 THEN K1=1
1120 K2=I2+1: IF K2=6 THEN K2=1
1130 C1=PA%(K1,J1)
1140 C2=PA%(K2,J2)
1150 RETURN
```

Program 11.1 (cont'd) Enciphering a Playfair Comments

15 U is a pointer to the output buffer. Since it will be incremented by 2 before it is used, we start it at −1.

20 Read in the keyword scramble and transpose the alphabet. If you want a key square similar to the ones used in the Cryptogram (that is, scrambled but not transposed), use Program 7.2 here; otherwise, use Program 11.3.

30-40
Input the plaintext and deblank it.

50 Add an X to the end of the text in case there are an odd number of letters.

60-180
Translate the letters pair by pair.

70-80
L1 and L2 are the two plaintext letters of this pair.

90 If they differ, there is no problem; go to 120 to encipher them.

100 If they are the same, back up I by one because we are going to take only the first letter of the pair.

110 Set L2 equal to Q.

120 I1 and J1 are the row and column of L1 in the key square.

130 I2 and J2 are the same for L2.

140 Go to the subroutine to do the enciphering.

145 Bump the output pointer by 2.

150-160
Put the enciphered letters in the output buffer.

190 Print the output buffer. You can use the standard five letters per block or modify to print 13 pairs of letters per line.

1000-1150
Encipher a pair of letters.

1010 If they are on the same row, go to 1060.

1020 If they are in the same column, go to 1110.

1030-1050
Otherwise, take the letters at the opposite corners of the rectangle and return.

1060-1070
If they are on the same row, move right one column and watch out for a wrap around.

1080-1100
Take the letters one to the right and return.

1110-1120
If they are in the same column, move down one row and watch out for a wrap around.

1130-1140
Take the letters one below and return.

Program 11.2 Deciphering a Playfair

This program is the same as the enciphering program with the following changes:

```
1060   K1=J1-1: IF K1=0 THEN K1=5
1070   K2=J2-1: IF K2=0 THEN K2=5

1110   K1=I1-1: IF K1=0 THEN K1=5
1120   K2=I2-1: IF K2=0 THEN K2=5
```

Program 11.2 (cont'd) Deciphering a Playfair Comments

1060–1070
When on the same row, move left.

1110–1120
When in the same column, move up. In both cases, watch out for a wrap around.

Program 11.3 Subroutine to Make a Scrambled and Transposed Alphabet

```
12000  REM GENERATE SCRAMBLED ALPHABET
12010  I1=0
12020  FOR I=1 TO 26: L%(I)=1: NEXT I
12025  FOR I=1 TO 15: GET A$: NEXT I
12030  L%(10)=0
12040  PRINT "ENTER KEYWORD-NO BLANKS"
12050  INPUT KW$
12060  FOR I=1 TO LEN (KW$)
12070     T=ASC(MID$(KW$,I,1))-64
12080     IF L%(T)=0 GOTO 12120
12090     L%(T)=0
12100     I1=I1+1
12110     CA(I1)=T
12120  NEXT I
12125  XX=I1
12130  FOR I=1 TO 26
12140     IF L%(I)=0 GOTO 12160
12150     I1=I1+1: CA(I1)=I
12160  NEXT I
```

```
12500  B=1
12510  P=0
12520  FOR II=1 TO 5
12530     FOR JJ=1 TO 5
12540        T=CA(B+P)
12550        PA%(II,JJ)=T
12560        LI%(T)=II
12570        LJ%(T)=JJ
12580        P=P+XX
12590        IF (B+P) > 25 THEN B=B+1: P=0
12600        PRINT CHR$(T+64)
12610     NEXT JJ
12620     PRINT
12630  NEXT II
12640  LI%(10)=LI%(9)
12660  LJ%(10)=LJ%(9)
12670  RETURN
```

Program 11.3 (cont'd) Subroutine to Make a Scrambled and Transposed Alphabet Comments

12010 I1 is a pointer to the scrambled, but not transposed, alphabet CA.
12020 L% indicates whether or not a letter has been used (0 = used). Start off with all unused letters.
12025 Clear the keyboard input buffer.
12030 Make the letter J be *used.*
12040-12050
Enter the keyword.
12060-12120
Take letters from the keyword and put in CA.
12070 Next letter goes to T.
12080 If T has been used already, skip it.
12090 Mark T as used.
12100 Bump I1.
12110 Put T into CA at I1.
12125 Save the value of I1 in XX (the number of unique letters in the keyword).
12130-12160
Search the alphabet for any unused letters and put them into CA.

Now we are going to transpose the letters in CA and put them into PA. There were XX unique letters in the keyword. We are going to start with the first letter in CA, then the XX + 1, then the 2*XX + 1, and so forth. This is equivalent to reading down a column of the transposing block. When we reach the bottom, we will come back and take letters 2, XX+2, and so forth.

12500 B is set to 1. This, in effect, is the column pointer to the transposing block.
12510 P is set to 0, which corresponds to the row of the transposing block.
12520 For rows 1 to 5 of the key square.
12530 For columns 1 to 5.
12540 T is the $B+P^{th}$ letter of the scrambled alphabet of the transposing block.
12550 Put it in the key square.
12560–12570
Put its row and column in LI% and LJ%.
12580 Go to the next row of the transposing block.
12590 If it is off the end of the block, reset to row 0 and the next column.
12600 Print out the letter.
12640–12650
Make row and column of J be the same as those of I.

Hand Solution

For short messages of approximately one hundred letters, it is usual to give a "tip," or probable word or phrase. Moreover, the tip is usually so structured that it will "fit" into the crypt at only one or, at most, two places. The purpose of the tip is to give you a start at reconstructing the square that was used to encipher the message.

Suppose that we have the message

LZ XB FY BX LZ BX WY BX ZC GQ 20
XB KL HQ TK VO EN OX LZ FK YX 40
LC TM LM LZ WO GC TI EM NQ AQ 60
QB DN WK GM CN IN HU BH KB RP 80
FY UH SR LZ BX FE FY BX XU QO 100
LZ WY SE XB SO XO CZ SR EF HU 120
XY XB VK NY XK BG QB 134

with the tip, yo ud ea ra nd th re ew ea re fr om. The thing to look for is a repeated digram representing the re separated by two other digrams. The only place that this occurs is in the pair at 90 and 96. We can therefore line up the ciphertext and the tip as follows:

yo	ud	ea	ra	nd	th	re	ew	ea	re	fr	om
KB	RP	FY	UH	SR	LZ	BX	FE	FY	BX	XU	QO

and for each quadruple of letters we can construct pieces of the grid that could have given rise to these quadruples. For example, the quadruple

```
r a
U H
```

could have been in one row, in one column, or in a square, as follows:

```
             R
             U    R • U
R U • A H    •    •   •
             A    H • A
             H
```

where the dots indicate that there might or might not be other letters present in those locations. Remember that a row or column can "wrap around" (H•RU•A) and that a "square" can be flipped over several ways and may indeed be oblong rather than square:

```
R • U    U • R    A • H    H • A
•   •    •   •    •   •    •   •
H • A    A • H    U • R    R • U
```

The object now is to combine quadruples and, it is to be hoped, to limit the possible combinations and thus arrive at at least a partial reconstruction. To this end, look at the two quadruples, RE/BX and FR/XU. They give:

```
1) R B • E X    3) R • B    4) F X • R U    6) F • X
2) R               •   •    5) F               •   •
   B               X • E       X               U • R
   •                           •
   E                           R
   X                           U
```

We can't combine 1 with 4 because we would end up with six letters in one row. Nor can we combine 1 with 5 because 1 calls for R and X in one row whereas 5 calls for them in different rows. The same argument inhibits a combination of 1 with 6. Since 1 can't combine with any of the possible arrangements of FR/XU, it has to be discarded.

Exactly similar arguments lead us to discard 4 as a possible arrangement.

Although 2 can't combine with 5, it can combine with 6. Moreover, 5 can combine with 3, and 3 and 6 can combine. The result is

```
i)  R • U     ii)  F           iii)  R • B • U
    B              X • E             •   •   •
    •              •                 X • E • F
    E              R • B
    X • F          U
```

Now EW/FE is going to be constrained to either a row or a column since the E can't occupy two separate corners of a square.

```
          W
W E F     E
          F
```

Trying to combine either of these with i, ii, and iii, we are led to only one possible arrangement:

```
R •   B U
•
X • W E F
```

This is an ideal situation because we now know a good deal about the original grid and can proceed to fit other parts around it. The first piece to fit in is the quadruple EA/FY:

```
             E
             F     E • F
E F • A Y    •     •   •
             A     Y • A
             Y
```

This will fit in only as

```
R •   B U
•     • •
X • W E F
      • •
      Y A
```

Now that we have R, A, and U more or less pinned down, we can add RA/UH:

```
R •   B U
•     • •
X • W E F
•     • •
H •   Y A
```

Since U and R are in the diagram now, we can add the quadruple UD/RP:

```
             U
             R    U • R
U R • D P    •    •   •
             D    P • D
             P
```

Of these, the first and third are plausible. Thus we have either 1 or 2 below:

```
1) R D P B U    2) D       P
   •     • •       •       •
   X • W E F       R •   B U
   •               •     • •
   H • • Y A       X • W E F
                   •
                   H •   Y A
```

Now ND/SR can be added as 3, 4, or 5:

```
3) N S • D R    4) N    5) N • S
                   S       •   •
                   •       R • D
                   D
                   R
```

Neither 1 and 3 will mesh, nor will 1 and 4. Moreover, 2 and 3 are out as are 2 and 4 and 2 and 5. That leaves only 1 and 5, giving

```
R D P B U
• • • • •
X • W E F
• • • • •
H • • Y A
• • • • •
N S
```

We still have TH/LZ and OM/QO, neither of which fit in yet, but we can add the YO/KB group, giving

```
      O
R D P B U
• • • • •
X • W E F
• • • • •
H • • Y A
• • • K •
N S • • •
```

Since B and Y are on different rows and since the B row is full, we can eliminate the square configuration YO/KB. Note that the O may be in the NS row, or else the K may be, giving us one of the following:

```
N S     O
R D P B U        R D P B U
---------        ---------
X   W E F        X   W E F
---------        ---------
H       Y A      H     Y A
      K          N S   K
                       O
```

where the underscorings indicate that there is no tie between adjacent rows and that the diagram could be rearranged by shuffling the blocks. In each of these, the OM/QO quadruple will fit in only one way:

```
N S M O Q        R D P B U
R D P B U        ---------
---------        X   W E F
X   W E F        H     Y A
---------        N S   K
H     Y A            M O Q
      K
```

Armed with this information, let us go to the crypt and see how much we can decipher:

```
LZ  XB  FY  BX  LZ  BX  WY  BX  ZC  GQ
th  er  ea  re  th  re  e?  re

XB  KL  HQ   TK  VO  EN   OX   LZ  FK  YX
er      a n/?        x o/r n/?e th  e?  he

LC  TM  LM  LZ  WO  GC  TI  EM  NQ   AQ
            th  em              wo  q/? o/?

QB  DN  WK  GM  CN  IN  HU  BH  KB  RP
ou  rs  e?                  ar  ry  yo  ud
```

FY	UH	SR	LZ	BX	FE	FY	BX	XU	QO
ea	ra	nd	th	re	ew	ea	re	fr	om

LZ	WY	SE	XB	SO	XO	CZ	SR	EF	HU
th	e ?	o ? k ?	er	n m k ?	e n ?		nd	we	ar

XY	XB	VK	NY	XK	BG	QB
eh	er		o k h	? e n		ou

where the upper plaintext comes from the left-hand diagram and the lower plaintext comes from the right-hand. Reading out the plaintext we have so far, we get

> there are three -re----er -- an ----x one the -he-- ---- them ---- wo qo-- ourse -------arry you dear and three we are from the -o-ernmen- -nd we are her- -o he-- -ou

from the left-hand diagram. Let's put the other one aside until we are forced to abandon this one.

Near the end of the message, it looks as if the word *government* would fit in. Lacking anything better to do, we will try it, producing

```
eg  ov
WY  SE
```

or, diagramatically,

```
E W • G Y     O S • V E
W             S
•     E W     •
G     Y G     V     O S
Y             E     E V
```

The EG/WY fits in only one way, producing

```
N S M O Q
R D P B U
---------
X   W E F
---------
H   G Y A
      K
```

The OV/SE goes in as follows:

```
N S M O Q
R D P B U
---------
X V W E F
---------
H   G Y A
      K
```

Now at last we can put in the TH/LZ quadruple,

N	S	M	O	Q
R	D	P	B	U
X	V	W	E	F
H	Z	G	Y	A
L	T		K	

and the only two letters we are missing are C and I.

Filling in the crypt as we know it now, we obtain

LZ	XB	FY	BX	LZ	BX	WY	BX	ZC	GQ
th	er	ea	re	th	re	eg	re	?t	am
XB	KL	HQ	TK	VO	EN	OX	LZ	FK	YX
er		an	e	es	xo	ne	th	e	he
LC	TM	LM	LZ	WO	GC	TI	EM	NQ	AQ
	?s	?n	th	em			wo	qo	
QB	DN	WK	GM	CN	IN	HU	BH	KB	RP
ou	rs	e?		?l	l?	ar	ry	yo	ud
FY	UH	SR	LZ	BX	FE	FY	BX	XU	QO
ea	ra	nd	th	re	ew	ea	re	fr	om
LZ	WY	SE	XB	SO	XO	CZ	SR	EF	HU
th	eg	ov	er	nm	en	ta	nd	we	ar
XY	XB	VK	NY	XK	BG	QB			
eh	er	et	oh	el	py	ou.			

At this point we can read out the message as follows:

There are three great American lies. One: the check is in the mail, two: of course I will marry you, dear, and three: we are from the government and we are here to help you!

The final diagram is

N	S	M	O	Q
R	D	P	B	U
X	V	W	E	F
H	Z	G	Y	A
L	T	I	K	C

Other Aids to Solution

In a Playfair cipher, only certain letters may substitute for a given plaintext letter. These are the letters in the same row and the letter immediately beneath the plaintext letter in the key square. To see how this works, consider the key square

A	B	C	D	E
F	G	H	I	K
L	M	N	O	P
Q	R	S	T	U
V	W	X	Y	Z

Let the letter in question be A. The second letter of the pair can be any of the other letters in the square, but it can't be A itself. If the second letter is either B, C, D, or E, then A is enciphered as B. We can summarize the possible encipherment as follows:

Rule 1:	B	C	D	E	→	B
Rule 2:	F	L	Q	V	→	F
Rule 3:	G	M	R	W	→	B
Rule 3:	H	N	S	X	→	C
Rule 3:	I	O	T	Y	→	D
Rule 3:	K	P	U	Z	→	E

There are eight ways out of 24 that lead to B—the letter immediately to the right of A—and four ways of getting each of the other possible encipherments: C, D, E, and F. If we take a letter frequency count of the example we just solved, we get:

A: 1	H: 5	O: 6	V: 2
B: 14	I: 2	P: 1	W: 4
C: 5	J: 0	Q: 7	X: 15
D: 1	K: 7	R: 3	Y: 8
E: 5	L: 9	S: 4	Z: 8
F: 6	M: 4	T: 3	
G: 4	N: 6	U: 4	

The ten most popular letters are therefore X, B, L, Y, Z, K, Q, F, N, O.

Looking at the completed key square, the letters associated with E are F, X, V, W, and Y, and those associated with T are I, K, C, L, and S. Obviously, random fluctuations have managed to obscure the results. We would expect, given that the plaintext has not been distorted or otherwise manipulated, that E and T would be the most popular plaintext letters. As a result, F and I should be the most popular ciphertext letters by the argument given above. As it is, F is exceeded in popularity by seven other letters and I is one of the least frequent letters in the ciphertext. Of course, given large amounts of text to work with, statistical fluctuations will be smoothed away, and more reliable results can be obtained. Then, guessing that the most popular letters stand to the right of E and T or in the rows they occupy may help to reconstruct the key square.

In a similar vein, digram frequencies and digram reversals require substantial amounts of text before they can be of much use, although it never hurts to try the most popular digrams of the ciphertext as th or he.

One Last Point

The Playfair ciphers used in *The Cryptogram* are almost all constructed with a simpler scrambling scheme than the one we have been considering. The alphabet is mixed once with a keyword and then written into the key square from left to right, top to bottom. Thus, the keyword MAGNETIC would lead to the key square,

M	A	G	N	E
T	I	C	B	D
F	H	K	L	O
P	Q	R	S	U
V	W	X	Y	Z

As may be seen, this tends to leave the less popular letters of the alphabet more or less in order at the bottom of the square. To see how this can aid the analyst, consider the three possible reconstructions of Fig. 11.1 that were derived from the correctly placed tip of a recent example.

Assuming that a simple keyword alphabet was directly written into the key square, we can do a great deal of narrowing down right away. In the second row of 2, FC/XR/Y is not going to make an En-

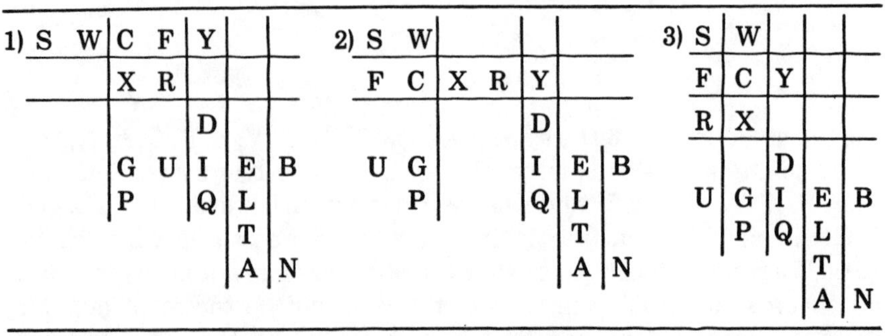

1)

S	W	C	F	Y		
		X	R			
				D		
		G	U	I	E	B
		P		Q	L	
					T	
					A	N

2)

S	W					
F	C	X	R	Y		
				D		
U	G			I	E	B
	P			Q	L	
					T	
					A	N

3)

S	W			
F	C	Y		
R	X			
		D		
U	G	I	E	B
	P	Q	L	
			T	
			A	N

Fig. 11.1 Three possible reconstructions.

glish word no matter how we switch it around, nor are the letters arrangeable in ascending alphabetical order: C F R X Y. We can thus "discard" arrangement 2, at least until all else fails. Similarly, in arrangement 1, the fifth line, P?/Q/L, can be reordered as L P ? Q, but if these are the "leftover" letters, there isn't any English letter to go in place of the question mark. Thus we can set 1 aside for the present, leaving us with arrangement 3. We obviously have to do some folding here to get this down to a 5×5 square. Since nothing we can fold in with T seems to make much of a word, we will assume that T is one of the leftover letters. Consequently, we should rotate the A/N to the top of the square, leaving T on the bottom row. Putting the letters P/Q/L in order and leaving some space between the L and the P for perhaps one or more of the letters M and O produces

F	A		C	Y	N
				D	
U	E		G	I	B
	L	-	P	Q	
	T				
R			X		
S			W		

If we read the top line as FANCY, that puts the B between the E and G, just right to start off the list of "leftovers." Either R/X or S/W goes on the last line and the other in row 2, giving us a 5×5 square. The unused letters are M, O, and H. If we put the row R/X into row 2, no English word is obviously suggested, but if we put row S/W into row 2, the word SHOW can be readily formed, giving the completed square:

F A N C Y
S H O W D
U E B G I
K L M P Q
R T V X Z

This makes a lot more sense after you do the square for yourself a few times rather than just reading about it.

Programmed Analysis

It would seem at first as if a computer would be ideal for reconstructing key squares from quadruples. After three days of work, however, I had written about six pages of code for merging and displaying partial reconstructions, and when I realized that I had not made allowance for the fact that rows and columns "wrap around," I threw up my hands in disgust, uttered several words that the *New York Times* would consider "unfit to print," and abandoned the project.

Nevertheless, there are still a couple of ways one can use a computer to help analyze a Playfair. First, it can be used to help search for the places a probable phrase will fit, and second, it can be used to display the partially deciphered message (see Program 11.4).

Program 11.4 Playfair Analysis

```
1   DIM T%(300)
2   DIM TP(100), KS(5,5),LR(26),LC(26)
10  GOSUB 10000 : REM READ IN CIPHERTEXT
20  GOSUB 10200 : REM REMOVE BLANKS
30  PRINT "ENTER TIP - USE NO BLANKS"
40  INPUT A$
45  L=LEN(A$)
50  FOR I=1 TO L
60     TP(I)=ASC(MID$(A$,I,1))-64
70  NEXT I

75  FOR IS=1 TO 2
77     XX=IS
80     FOR I1=IS TO L STEP 2
90        X=TP(I1)
100       Y=TP(I1+1)
110       FOR I2=I1+2 TO L STEP 2
120          IF X <> TP(I2) OR Y <> TP(I2+1) GOTO 130
125          R=0 : GOTO 135
130          IF X <> TP(I2+1) OR Y <> TP(I2) GOTO 140
132          R=1
135          S=I1 : K=I2-I1 : IS=2 : I1=L : I2=L
140       NEXT I2
150    NEXT I1
155 NEXT IS

157 P=1
160 IF R=1 GOTO 210
170 FOR I=1 TO J STEP 2
180    IF T%(I)=T%(I+K) AND T%(I+1)=T%(I+K+1) THEN
       F(P)=I : P=P+1
190 NEXT I
200 GOTO 235
210 FOR I=1 TO J STEP 2
220    IF T%(I)=T%(I+K+1) AND T%(I+1)=T%(I+K) THEN
       F(P)=I : P=P+1
230 NEXT I
```

```
235  PRINT "clear and home"
240  PRINT "MATCHES FOUND PT THEN CT
250  FOR K=XX TO L STEP 2
260     PRINT CHR$(TP(K)+64); CHR$(TP(K+1)+64);"  ";
270  NEXT K
280  PRINT
290  FOR I=1 TO P-1
300     FOR K=XX TO L STEP 2
310        Y=F(I)-S
320        PRINT CHR$(T%(Y+K)+64);
330        PRINT CHR$(T%(Y+K+1)+64);
340        PRINT"  ";
350     NEXT K
360     PRINT
370  NEXT I
380  FOR I=1 TO 26 : LR(I)=0 : LC(I)=0 : NEXT I
400  PRINT "ENTER KEY SQUARE — USE '- ' FOR
     UNKNOWNS"
410  FOR I1=1 TO 5
420     FOR J1=1 TO 5
430        GET A$ : IF A$="  " GOTO 430
440        PRINT A$
450        X=ASC(A$)-64
455        IF X < 1 OR X > 26 THEN X=ASC("-")-64 : GOTO 490
460        KS(I1,J1)=X
470        LR(X)=I1
480        LC(X)=J1
490     NEXT J1
500     PRINT
510  NEXT I1
515  LC(10)=LC(9) : LR(10)=LR(9)
520  FOR I=1 TO 5
530     KS(0,I)=KS(5,I)
540     KS(I,0)=KS(I,5)
550  NEXT I
600  FOR I=1 TO J STEP 26
610     FOR I1=1 TO 26 STEP 2
615        IF I+I1 > J THEN I1=26 : GOTO 630
620        PRINT CHR$(T%(I+I1-1)+64);CHR$(T%(I+I1)+64);"  ";
630     NEXT I1
640     PRINT
650     FOR I1=1 TO 26 STEP 2
655        IF I+I1 > J THEN I1=26 : GOTO 730
660        R1=LR(T%(I+I1-1))
670        R2=LR(T%(I+I1))
```

```
675         IF R1=0 OR R2=0 THEN PRINT"   ";GOTO 730
680         C1=LC(T%(I+I1-1))
690         C2=LC(T%(I+I1))
700         IF R1=R2 THEN PRINT
            CHR$(KS(R1,C1-1)+64);CHR$(KS(R1,C2-1)+64);" "; :
            GOTO 730
710         IF C1=C2 THEN PRINT
            CHR$(KS(R1-1,C1)+64);CHR$(KS(R2-1,C1)+64);" "; :
            GOTO 730
720         PRINT CHR$(KS(R1,C2)+64);CHR$(KS(R2,C1)+64);" "; :
            GOTO 730
730       NEXT I1
740       PRINT
750     NEXT I
760     GOTO 380
```

Program 11.4 (cont'd) Playfair Analysis Comments

Note: T% is the buffer to hold the ciphertext; TP is the buffer to hold the "tip" or probable word; KS is the 5×5 key square; LR is the row a letter occupies in the square; and LC is the column.

10–20
: Read in ciphertext and squeeze out blanks.

30–70
: Read in the tip, convert it to integers 1 through 26, and store in TP.

75 We are going to try the tip with and without the first letter.

77 XX saves the value of IS=1 if it includes the first letter and IS=2 if we skip the first letter. Note that we will try to find a pattern omitting the first letter only if we fail to find a pattern that includes it.

80–150
: Search for a repeat, XY . . . XY or a reversal, XY . . . YX, in the tip.

90–100
: X and Y are the letters of a pair pointed at by I1.

110–140
: Search down the tip to find a repeat (lines 120–125) or a reversal (lines 130–132); if a repeat, then R=0; if a reversal, then R=1.

135 S is the starting place of the pattern in the tip, and K is the space between the first and second occurrence.

157 Set P=1. P is a pointer to the table F(P) that holds all places in the ciphertext where the tip might fit.

160 Check the value of R (R=0 is a repeat; R=0 is a reversal).

170–200
: For a repeat, search the ciphertext for all matches. Store the location of each match in F(P).

210–230
Do the same for a reversal.

233 Clear the screen.

240–370
Print out the tip and the possible matches.

250–270
Print out the tip. IF XX=2, drop the first letter of the tip.

290–370
Using F(P) as a table of pointers into the ciphertext, print out all possible matches. Usually there will be only one. S represents how far into the tip we find the repeat or reversal. F(I) is the place in the ciphertext that the matching pattern was found so that Y=F(I)-S is the place to start printing the ciphertext. Again, XX worries about that first letter.

380 Clear LR(I) and LC(I)—the row and column of the 26 letters.

400–510
Get the user's best guess about the key square.

430–450
Get a character from the keyboard.

455 If it is not a letter, replace it with "-".

460–480
Put it in the key square and note its row and column in LR and LC.

495 Make J equivalent to I (in terms of row and column).

520–550
Make the 0 row equal the fifth row and the 0 column equal the fifth column. We will then not have to worry about a wrap around when decoding (left or up movements only).

600–750
Print a line of ciphertext followed by the translation of that line wherever it can be determined from the key square.

610 Print 13 pairs per line.

615 Test to see if you are out of text.

620 Print a pair of characters.

640 New line.

650–730
Print a translated line.

655 Check for end of text.

660 R1 is the row of the first character of the pair.

670 R2 is the row of the second character of the pair.

675 If either equals 0 because the character is not defined, print three blanks.

680–690
C1 and C2 are columns of the first and second letters in the pair.

700 If letters are in the same row.

710 If letters are in the same column.

720 If letters are on a diagonal.
740 New line.
760 Go back and ask for a new key square if the user has any new guesses based on what he has seen of the plaintext.

Problems for Chapter 11

1. ZY RT DV BW ME NZ VO YW DQ HZ
OU CR SX FK CQ VN RC WN OC BS
NS MP QM ZY CQ ID CM LE RU CZ
WX KM OZ FI BW ZE MD ZW PF YM
WC LB WV BW WG UY NO MP MZ TD
CB YV FN RV EO DB (*George Bernard Shaw*)

(Begins: YO UD EM AN DT OB ES HO TB)

2. QV BY VS SL AH GX KM QZ OX ZA
TW VS SL FH ZL XS ZL RT WN HZ
CS UQ AX SX RX BA CD PK AM TF
VS SX AH XS XM MQ CA WG VS FH
QB NT LQ ZK FQ GV XA FL SA KP
QB BT LO AH ZS EB ZC YB DF DU
MA SH CS LO XN

(TH ER EA RE PE OP LE IN TH IS WO RL DW)

3. TI RW QV MD IC WM VI PW SD EA
PM PH FP WA LT XI UF OD XI ES
FD GA HK UP SV MK VF DU EA WV
MY KH HG KI MA OU UY AP UP IE
SK AP CQ KO FH VF UP HP QI AP
HK ZX HX EB IS

(HE GO OD GU YS AL WA YS WI NA FT ER)

4. VR PE BM KC YD IO PV GP OK AB
SB AS HO NG KP XB EB TO XA UT
NO IO IU EX QT FP HD PO KW YD
UG HO NH ON KB QD CK LA QS KW
IZ AP LC EH

(Begins: IW OU LD RA TH ER ME NS HO UL)

5. ZU FQ MD GR ZU BR FD VS XD XV
SH UB PC DQ YG MP PD PC QD FN
DL GR ZU DI DQ TL XF GR ZU HF

OG YO NM KP KH RM ZG NX HS LD
ZG KG OF MI BR FD ZA UQ NK CF
EU WX OY GU WL XH WC PW KH OY
(*Johannes Brahms*)

(TH EV ER YB ES TX TH IN GS)

6. GU YO AP PK RM EB CY OM VI AD
UV EN WD WM CP KE UV UQ PV YU
MP AD PU XW FY AB GZ OB DP NY
CE DU XW UA VR RF ZT PC VR HF
UM PG VB GM MY ZY KU CE MU TO
ZO UW NF (*Oscar Wilde*)

(RE AL LY GO OD AL LT HE TI ME)

7. FX ZF LX VS IH ZI YD LM ZC YD
DY HZ QH AY HS NS FW GZ LH XM
VG WL MU IY HU BI SX XF GX RY
WN CL GY XY VE XK IH SX HZ SB
SV WG WL CP DL UM UH HU WI YK
MD (*H. L. Mencken*)

(IL LA LS OM AK EB ET TE RS)

8. UF EQ DE HD RC QU WH GW GU DX
LR GK RQ FU TU XV YU SG HD QE
BM ME MX ZK NU UF KS FO MN CR
NU RQ EG EI MX VL EG CD MR ON
UZ WB LP TU XV QF UX UT PN ZR
ET EX OU NX TU WC XD UA HM LQ
PG IX (*Alfred North Whitehead*)

(Ends: ST OW AR OS AV IC TO RY)

9. HU DB YH GC TX RQ CB EU RQ ZW
GX EA TX UH YF AN GL WH TX BC
VX GX VH TH LX LF QX ZP YV ZS
TF FP HU AB UZ LR CT MR PT PZ
WH YV KX XG GC OK EZ TX HY WM
LV OK YL WQ FE (*Mark Twain*)

(HE YS IM PL YS TA RE DW HE)

10. AU YV HV UV DW BO DK BX QH HW
PH LV EH DW IT TZ WA OA EH DR
RL UC ZO GV ZO MI RU UQ FZ DL

AO	ET	RE	YT	WZ	DR	HA	UI	QG	WI
YM	RD	TH	QW	UO	KH	DW	US	EM	WA
YT	QG	NQ	CD	KU	WC	WH	TD	HY	BQ
MB	ZM	KH	BQ	IT	IK	TI	RW	IC	GF

(*Jascha Heifetz*)

(OM PO SE RS FI RS TX TO)

12

Other Block Substitution Ciphers

The difference between a *stream cipher* and a *block cipher* is that in the former you can spit out each ciphertext letter as soon as the plaintext letter is read in, whereas in the latter you have to accumulate a number of letters before you can spit out anything. Transposition ciphers are all of the block kind, some requiring a group of letters (turning grill, for instance) and some requiring the whole message (columnar) before any output can be generated.

The substitution ciphers that we have examined have been stream ciphers—except for the Playfair, which deals with blocks of two letters at a time. While in practice that innovation does not represent a significant change or great delay in the generation of the ciphertext, it is a major change in principle for it opens the door to a number of interesting cipher systems that operate on blocks of several letters at a time.

Fractionated Morse

Many block-substitution ciphers involve the idea of *fractionations,* that is, the breaking up of a single letter into pieces and then combining the pieces of different plaintext letters in order to get a ciphertext letter. The simplest scheme of this sort is the one called *Fractionated Morse.* Plaintext letters are translated into Morse code dots (•) and dashes (–) with an x between letters and an xx between words to make up the intermediate text. The three symbols, • – x generate 27 possible patterns of symbols, taken three at a time, except that the pattern xxx cannot occur in the intermediate text. These 26 occurring patterns are mapped onto a keyword scrambled alphabet, and the ciphertext is read out. For example, Morse code equivalents of the letters of the alphabet are as follows:

A •-	G --•	M --	S •••	Y -•--
B -•••	H ••••	N -•	T -	Z --••
C -•-•	I ••	O ---	U ••-	
D -••	J •---	P •--•	V •••-	
E •	K -•-	Q --•-	W •--	
F ••-•	L •-••	R •-•	X -••-	

With the plaintext "now is the time for all," we invariably get the same intermediate text:

```
Plaintext:          n  o   w   i  s   t h   e
Intermediate text: -•x---x•--xx••x•••xx-x••••x•xx

                    t i  m e   f    o  r   a  l    l
                   -x••x--x•xx••-•x---x•-•xx•-x•-••x•-••xx
```

At this point, we choose the keyword alphabet based on SPILLED MILK:

S •••	M •x•	G --•	R x••	Y xx•
P ••-	K •x-	H ---	T x•-	Z xx-
I ••x	A •xx	J --x	U x•x	
L •-•	B -••	N -x•	V x-•	
E •--	C -•-	O -x-	W x--	
D •-x	F -•x	Q -xx	X x-x	

Looking up the symbols of the intermediate text three at a time, we get

```
Intermediate text: -•x---x•--xx••x•••xx-x••••x•xx-x••x--x•
Ciphertext:         F  H  T  Q  I  S  Z  R  I  A  N  K  N

                   xx••-•x---x•-•xx•-x•-••x•-••xx
                    Y  L  W  N  F  T  T  I  L  A
```

which is read out in groups of five letters as

FHTQI SZRIA NKNYL WNFTT ILA

Deciphering is the obvious inverse and restores the plaintext complete with word divisions.

To carry out enciphering and deciphering on a computer, it would probably be simplest to replace the dot, dash, and x by 1, 2, and 3, respectively. If one were truly interested in speed, one could output a ciphertext letter every time three symbols were collected in the intermediate text buffer, but in practice it would surely be simpler to generate all the intermediate text first and then produce the ciphertext in one burst.

Our previous message came out as an even multiple of three. Had it not, either or both of the terminal x's could have been dropped.

The analysis of Fractionated Morse is reasonably mechanical provided there is a "probable" word. If the tip is not located (for example, "ends with ----"), it is translated to Morse code, and from this an identifiable pattern is derived. Once the tip has been located, the ciphertext letters at this location are entered into a 26-letter list of the possible triples of symbols as they are disclosed from the tip. Doing so will give some clues about the structure of the alphabet, which is most likely a shifted-keyword scrambled one. Knowing that letters not in the keyword will be in alphabetical order is a great help in guessing the location of as yet unidentified letters. Partial deciphering, guessing at plaintext, and building up the cipher alphabet usually lead quite quickly to a solution. It is left as an exercise for the reader to construct an analysis program for cracking Fractionated Morse. A program for enciphering it is provided by Program 12.1.

Program 12.1 Enciphering Fractionated Morse

```
  1  DIM T%(200)
  2  DIM U%(200)
  3  DIM M%(1000),MC%(5,26)
  4  DIM CA(55)
 10  REM READ IN MORSE MATRIX DOT=1, DASH=2, LETTER
     SPACE=3
 20  FOR I=0 TO 26
 30     K=1
 40     READ X
 50     MC%(K,I)=X
 60     K=K+1
 70     IF X <> 3 GOTO 40
 80  NEXT I
 90  DATA 3,1,2,3,2,1,1,1,3,2,1,2,1,3,2,1,1,3,1,3,1,1,2,1,3
100  DATA 2,2,1,3,1,1,1,1,3,1,1,3,1,2,2,2,3,2,1,2,3,1,2,1,1,3
110  DATA 2,2,3,2,1,3,2,2,2,3,1,2,2,1,3,2,2,1,2,3,1,2,1,3
120  DATA 1,1,1,3,2,3,1,1,2,3,1,1,1,2,3,1,2,2,3,2,1,1,2,3
130  DATA 2,1,2,2,3,2,2,1,1,3

200  REM X-LATE TO INTERMEDIATE TEXT-MORSE CODE
230  P=0
240  FOR I=1 TO J
250     T=T%(I)
```

```
260      IF T< 1 OR T> 26 THEN T=0
270      K=0
280      K=K+1
290      P=P+1
300      M%(P)=MC%(K,T)
310      IF M%(P)<> 3 GOTO 280
320   NEXT I
330   P=P+1
340   M%(P)=3

400   REM X-LATE TO CT
410   IP=3*INT(P/3)
420   REM GET KEYWORD AND SHIFT
430   GOSUB 12000
440   K=0
450   FOR I=1 TO IP STEP 3
460      T=9*(M%(I)-1)+3*(M%(I+1)-1)+M%(I+2)
470      K=K+1
480      U%(K)=CA(T)
490   NEXT I
495   IP=K
500   REM PRINTOUT CT FROM BUFFER U%-IP CHARACTERS
510   GOSUB 10300
520   GOTO 200
```

Program 12.1 (cont'd) Fractionated Morse Comments

We are going to store a dot as 1, a dash as 2, and an end of letter and word space as 3.

10-130
: Read in the Morse code matrix. Each letter has up to five slots holding the pattern, ending with a 3. The 0 letter is for "space."

200-320
: Pick up the pattern for each letter in the plaintext (up to and including the 3) and put it into the intermediate text buffer, M%. P is the pointer to M% and K is the pointer into the letter pattern.

330-340
: Add one more 3 at the end of M% as a final word space.

410 Ip is the rounded down value of P. In Fractionated Morse, you keep or discard the two terminal 3's as required to make things come out even.

430 Get the keyword.

440 K is the pointer to the output buffer U%.

450-490
: Translate the intermediate text three symbols at a time to the ciphertext.

495 Save the number of output characters since the print routine destroys K.

510 Print out IP characters from U%.

Algebraic Systems

A second form of block cipher particularly well adapted to a computer is the algebraic system first proposed by Lester Hill in the June/July 1929 issue of the *American Mathematical Monthly*. He was the first to discuss an encrypting process based upon ordinary algebra.

The system involves a square matrix of size B equal to the block size. Letters in the plaintext are grouped in blocks of B letters, and one block is enciphered at a time. Plaintext letters are translated to numbers in any convenient fashion. A through Z may be mapped as 1 through 26 in order, or a "randomizing" procedure may be employed if desired.

Suppose that we have chosen a block size of 4. Then we require four equations, as follows:

$$\begin{aligned} C_1 &= 8P_1 + 6P_2 + 9P_3 + 5P_4 \\ C_2 &= 6P_1 + 9P_2 + 5P_3 + 10P_4 \\ C_3 &= 5P_1 + 8P_2 + 4P_3 + 9P_4 \\ C_4 &= 10P_1 + 6P_2 + 11P_3 + 4P_4 \end{aligned}$$

where P_1 through P_4 refer to the four letters of the plaintext block and C_1 through C_4, the four resulting ciphertext letters. All arithmetic is done modulo 26, and the resulting numbers (C_1 through C_4) are translated back to letters by the same mapping used to convert plaintext to numbers or by some other mapping.

The two number-to-alphabet mappings plus the coefficients of the equations form the key, which, as usual in real life, would be changed frequently for security purposes.

To decipher, we need the two number-to-letter maps plus a set of equations that is the "inverse" of the enciphering set. For the enciphering equations given above, the inverse equations are as follows:

$$\begin{aligned} P_1 &= 23C_1 + 20C_2 + 5C_3 + C_4 \\ P_2 &= 2C_1 + 11C_2 + 18C_3 + C_4 \\ P_3 &= 2C_1 + 20C_2 + 6C_3 + 25C_4 \\ P_4 &= 25C_1 + 2C_2 + 22C_3 + 25C_4 \end{aligned}$$

One of the problems with this scheme is that not every set of equations (every matrix) has a unique inverse, particularly if the arithmetic is done modulo 26, as it is here. Sinkov provides a very clear description of the problem of finding an inverse when one does exist. Similar discussions may be found in any text on algebra. If the inverse doesn't exist, then the ciphertext can't be decoded by anybody, and the system is relatively useless.

For a simplified system with a block size of 2 and mod 26 arithmetic, Sinkov shows that it is necessary and sufficient for the "determinant" to be an odd number not divisible by 13. If the equations for a block size of 2 are given by

$$C_1 = aP_1 + bP_2$$
$$C_2 = cP_1 + dP_2$$

then the "determinant" is

$$D = ad - bc$$

For example, the set of numbers, $a = 1$, $b = 2$, $c = 3$, and $d = 4$ have a determinant, $D = 4 - 6 = -2$, and are thus not satisfactory, but the set, $a = 1$, $b = 2$, $c = 3$, and $d = 5$, have a determinant, $D = 5 - 6 = -1$, which is fine.

To discover the inverse of a set of equations, there are formal methods, but for simple cases, such as a block size of 2, it is easier to reason the answer out. For example, given:

$$C_1 = P_1 + 2P_2$$
$$C_2 = 3P_1 + 5P_2$$

we can multiply the first equation by 3 and subtract the second from it, giving

$$3C_1 - C_2 = 3P_1 + 6P_2 - 3P_1 - 5P_2$$

or

$$P_2 = 3C_1 - C_2$$

Multiplying this result by 5, we can substitute it into the second original equation, giving

$$C_2 = 3P_1 + 15C_1 - 5C_2$$

Solving this for P_1, we get

$$3P_1 = 6C_2 - 15C_1$$

In this case, we can divide each coefficient conveniently by 3, which gives integers in each case, but we are usually not so lucky. When nonintegers would result from division, we multiply instead. The trick here is to get a coefficient for P_1 that is equal to 1 modulo 26. Since any number of the form $26 \cdot k+1$ is, of course, equal to 1 mod 26, we must search for a multiplier for the coefficient of P_1 that produces a number of this form. In this case, the search is brief. Since $3\times9=27$, which is 1 mod 26, multiplying each coefficient by 9 produces

$$27P_1 = 54C_2 - 135C_1$$

It will be no surprise to discover that 27=1, 54=2, and 135=5, all modulo 26. This produces the following pair of deciphering equations:

$$P_1 = -5C_1 + 2C_2$$
$$P_2 = 3C_1 - C_2$$

in which all arithmetic is again done modulo 26.

Algebraic systems such as this one have the advantage that each unique block of letters has a unique ciphertext equivalent (how else could we decode it?), which means that changing a single letter of a plaintext block may cause every letter of the ciphertext to change. Thus, the analyst is reduced to looking at statistics of N-grams where N is the block size. To begin with, not much is known of the statistics of anything larger than trigrams, and what is worse, the fluctuations of statistics for messages of reasonable length will be fierce. Thus, under normal circumstances, these systems are beyond amateur analysis. Note that Sinkov does present the solution of a digraphic system in his excellent text.

The disadvantage of algebraic systems, and of many other block systems as well, is that an error in a single bit will cause the loss of the entire block containing that bit. One therefore wants to choose a block size that will, on the one hand, maximize the difficulties of an enemy analyst and, on the other, minimize the amount of retransmission required by a noisy communication channel.

Seriated Playfair

The Playfair system can be made considerably more secure by breaking up the normal digrams of adjacent letters before encipherment. To do this, one chooses a *seriation index,* or what we have been calling a *block size.* Suppose that we choose a seriation index of 6. The message (our old favorite again) is written in blocks of 12 letters in two rows of six, as follows:

```
NOWIST  EFORAL  MENTOC
HETXIM  LGXOOD  OMEXYZ
```

Note that the final block is padded out with nulls. Encipherment is accomplished by the normal Playfair rules except that pairs are taken vertically: NH OE WT IX, and so forth. Note that when identical letters would have been positioned one above the other, a null has been inserted (an X replaces the I in the first block of the second row, for example). Since the letters of a pair, in this case, are formed six positions apart in the original text, normal digram frequencies will not be found but rather the frequencies of "random digrams" previously discussed.

This method introduces a transposition to the plaintext before encipherment. It would be equally possible to apply a transposition after normal Playfair encipherment instead of (or even in addition to) the encipherment before it. The combination of transposition and substitution is a powerful one. When the substitution is made by pairs, as in Playfair, the analyst is left with very little to work with unless he has strongly probable words or considerable text to work with, all enciphered using the same key.

ADFGVX

One of the best known uses of a combined substitution and transposition cipher was the ADFGVX system used by the Germans during the first World War. The letters were chosen because their Morse equivalents are quite distinct and unlikely to be confused one for another. The 26 letters of the alphabet, plus the ten digits, were written in scrambled order into a 6×6 square, as shown in Table 12.1.

Table 12.1 6×6 square of the ADFGVX system

	A	*D*	*F*	*G*	*V*	*X*
A	K	R	B	2	V	Q
D	6	F	9	P	5	I
F	G	1	J	E	Z	W
G	N	A	T	4	H	L
V	3	0	8	X	7	Y
X	U	S	M	C	D	O

The intermediate text was taken off as pairs of letters, first the row and then the column, as follows:

```
n  o  w  i  s  t  h  e  t  i  m  e
GA XX FX DX XD GF GV FG GF DX XF FG
```

The intermediate text was then written into a block and subjected to a columnar transposition:

2	5	3	1	4
G	A	X	X	F
X	D	X	X	D
G	F	G	V	F
G	G	F	D	X
X	F	F	G	

The columnar transposition then gave the ciphertext:

XXVDG GXGGX XXGFF FDFXA DFGF

This practice resulted in doubling the length of each message. This doubling could have been avoided by substituting back into the original square, but evidently it was felt that the distinctness of the six chosen letters and the consequent reduction in retransmission, not to mention the possibilities of errors on resubstitution, excused the expansion of the text.

Despite the apparent simplicity of this scheme, the best French cryptanalyst, Painvin, took over a month to solve the first batch of messages. Kahn (1) calls it the "toughest field cipher the world had yet seen."

The Germans used a smaller 5×5 grid based on the letters ADFGX when the system was first introduced. The interested reader could easily patch such a system together from parts of preceding programs. The scrambled and transposed square we used for the Playfair would serve well for this purpose, as would parts of the program for doing columnar transpositions. About all that would be new would be the necessity to read out the coordinates of a letter in the square rather than to make use of the Playfair rules.

Once again, an analysis of this cipher falls outside the scope of this book, which is a gentle way of saying that it exceeds the abilities of the author.

DES

In 1978, the National Bureau of Standards proposed a "Data Encryption Standard," otherwise known as the DES, to be used by all government data-processing centers for information of a private nature. The system involves a 64-bit key that controls 17 stages of substitution alternated with 16 stages of transposition. This system, first available as software, is now available as a single hardware chip to be placed between the CPU and a disk. Any data written to the disk will be automatically enciphered in 64-bit blocks and on the way back into main memory will be automatically deciphered. Thus, data stored on disk will be unreadable to anybody not possessing the correct key.

So far no one has suggested a method of analysis other than an exhaustive search of all 2^{64} keys. In a paper that has stirred a great deal of controversy, however, Diffie and Helman have suggested the design for a machine that will perform an exhaustive search of the keys. They estimate that at a cost of about $5000 their machine could take an enciphered record for which the plaintext equivalent is known and try one key after another until the enciphered plaintext matched the already enciphered record. At that point, any interested party would be in possession of the key for the entire disk and could read it at leisure.

Their machine relies on massive parallelism with the order of a million microcomputers, each searching part of the key space. The total cost of such a machine, by their estimate, would be around $20 million, and the $5000 figure merely represents the rent for half a day's use of the hardware. Clearly, such a machine is beyond the reach of the average hobbyist, but they insist it is not beyond the reach of a government or one of the major corporations. Since the DES was intended in large part to provide industrial security, their paper and their conclusions raise serious doubts about the utility of the DES.

13

The Bifid

Properly speaking, the Bifid and its close relative, the Trifid, are block ciphers and belong in the preceding chapter, but there is sufficient interest in the Bifid and enough of an analytic approach has been developed to warrant giving it a chapter of its own.

Both the Bifid ("two-footed") and Trifid ("three-footed") ciphers were developed by Felix Marie Delastelle, a French cryptologist, shortly before he died in 1902.

Enciphering

Enciphering in the Bifid system requires a scrambled or keyword alphabet plus a block length. The alphabet is written into a 5×5 grid whose coordinates (row and column number) are used to identify the plaintext letters (J is usually the omitted letter). So far, the system is very similar to the ADFGVX system. The coordinates in the square of each plaintext letter are written vertically—first the row, then the column—beneath the plaintext.

With the keyword BULLDOZER, we would get the square shown in Table 13.1.

Table 13.1 5×5 grid for the Bifid system

	1	*2*	*3*	*4*	*5*
1	B	U	L	D	O
2	Z	E	R	A	C
3	F	G	H	I	K
4	M	N	P	Q	S
5	T	V	W	X	Y

Our old message, "Now is the time for all good men," then becomes

```
n o w i s t h   e t i m e f o   r a l l g o o   d m e n

4 1 5 3 4 5 3   2 5 3 4 2 3 1   2 2 1 1 3 1 1   1 4 2 4

2 5 3 4 5 1 3   2 1 4 1 2 1 5   3 4 3 3 2 5 5   4 1 2 2
```

Any desired block length may be chosen, but odd numbers are popular. We will choose 7. The plaintext and its row of coordinates are divided into blocks of 7 with any leftover letters at the end forming a short block:

```
n o w i s t h | e t i m e f o | r a l l g o o | d m e n
              |               |               |
4 1 5 3 4 5 3 | 2 5 3 4 2 3 1 | 2 2 1 1 3 1 1 | 1 4 2 4
              |               |               |
2 5 3 4 5 1 3 | 2 1 4 1 2 1 5 | 3 4 3 3 2 5 5 | 4 1 2 2
```

Now the coordinates are read out in pairs, first all the row coordinates of a block, followed by the column coordinates. The odd (last) row coordinate of a block is paired with the first column number. Thus, for the first block we get

41 53 45 32 53 45 13

which are then back-substituted in the square to produce

```
41 53 45 32 53 45 13
 M  W  S  G  W  S  L
```

as the first seven letters of the ciphertext.

Completing the encipherment we obtain

MWSGWSL CIRUDUO EBFLPGY DAME

the last block being treated as 14 24 41 22.

Program 13.1 provides the enciphering process. Decipherment is the obvious reverse of this process.

Program 13.1 Enciphering a Bifid

```
1  DIM T%(200),M%(400),S%(200)
2  DIM CA(55),L%(26),LI%(26),LJ%(26),PA%(5,5)
10 REM GET KEYWORD SCRAMBLED AND TRANSPOSED
20 GOSUB 12000
```

```
  30  REM READ PT AND DEBLANK
  40  GOSUB 10000
  50  GOSUB 10200
  60  PRINT "ENTER BLOCK LENGTH"
  70  INPUT B
  80  REM GENERATE INTERMEDIATE TEXT
  90  GOSUB 1000
 100  REM GENERATE CT
 110  GOSUB 2000
 120  REM PRINT OUT CT
 130  GOSUB 10300
 140  PRINT: PRINT
 150  GOTO 10

1000  FOR I=0 TO J-B STEP B
1010     FOR K=1 TO B
1020        M%(2*I+K)=LI%(T%(I+K))
1030        M%(2*I+K+B)=LJ%(T%(I+K))
1040     NEXT K
1050  NEXT I
1060  R=J-I
1065  IF R=0 GOTO 1110
1070  FOR I1=1 TO R
1080     M%(2*I+I1)=LI%(T%(I+I1))
1090     M%(2*I+I1+R)=LJ%(T%(I+I1))
1100  NEXT I1
1110  RETURN

2000  REM GENERATE CT
2010  FOR I=0 TO J-1
2020     S%(I+1)=PA%(M%(2*I+1),M%(2*I+2))
2030  NEXT I
2040  RETURN
```

Program 13.1 (cont'd) Enciphering a Bifid Comments

The main program is a collection of subroutine calls. The keyword subroutine scrambles and transposes the keyword alphabet.

1000–1110

Translates from plaintext to intermediate text by looking up the coordinates of the letters one by one and writing them in the intermediate buffer M%. First we write a block of row coordinates, then a block of column coordinates and repeat.

2000–2040
Translate from intermediate text to ciphertext. Take coordinates in pairs and replace them by the letter in that location in the square.

Analysis

Two sources were used in developing this section. The first is an article in *The Cryptogram* by GIZMO (Jan.–Feb. 1979), and the second is a pamphlet available from the ACA called "Practical Cryptanalysis," Vol. II, by W. M. Bowers (1960).

There are two stages in analyzing a Bifid cipher. First one must obtain the block length and then reconstruct the key square. In *The Cryptogram*, Bifids are usually given with the letters grouped in blocks of the period length.

There are several methods of identifying the period if it is not known. The first is the one usually reserved for hand analysis because no computation is involved. We will call it the "method of repeats." This method relies on the fact that there may be repeats in the plaintext both of which happen to fall in odd or even positions of a block. The pattern one obtains depends on the length of the repeat, the length of the block, and the oddness or evenness of the position at which the repeat starts in the block.

If the repeat is four letters long, the block length is 7, and the repeat begins in position 1, we get the following pattern:

$$T_r\ H_r\ I_r\ S_r\ X_r\ Y_r\ Z_r$$

$$T_c\ H_c\ I_c\ S_c\ X_c\ Y_c\ Z_c$$

(T_rH_r)	(I_rS_r)	(X_rY_r)	(Z_rT_c)	(H_cI_c)	(S_cX_c)	(Y_cZ_c)
A	B	?	?	C	?	?

where A, B, C is the letter in the key square at the position given by (i,j).

Starting in position 3, we get

$$X_r\ Y_r\ T_r\ H_r\ I_r\ S_r\ Z_r$$

$$X_c\ Y_c\ T_c\ H_c\ I_c\ S_c\ Z_c$$

(X_rY_r)	(T_rH_r)	(I_rS_r)	(Z_rC_c)	(Y_cT_c)	(H_cI_c)	(S_cZ_c)
?	A	B	?	?	C	?

where this ABC will be the same as the previous ABC.

If the repeat starts in an even position, we get

$$X_r\ T_r\ H_r\ I_r\ S_r\ Y_r\ Z_r$$

$$X_c\ T_c\ H_c\ I_c\ S_c\ Y_c\ Z_c$$

(X_rT_r)	(H_rI_r)	(S_rY_r)	(Z_rX_c)	(T_cH_c)	(I_cS_c)	(Y_cZ_c)
?	P	?	?	Q	R	?

Notice that in general PQR will not be the same as ABC, nor will they be related in any simple fashion since the letter at (I_rS_r) is not the same as that at (I_cS_c) unless both I and S are on the diagonal of the key square.

For different length repeats, the pattern will be different as it will be for different block lengths, as follows:

Repeat four letters	*Starting point*	
Block length	*Odd*	*Even*
5	AB-C	P-QR
6	AB-CD	P--Q
7	AB--C	P--QR
8	AB--CD	P---Q

Repeat of five letters	*Starting point*	
Block length	*Odd*	*Even*
6	AB-CD	PQ-RS
7	AB--CD	PQ-RS
8	AB--CD	PQ--RS
9	AB---CD	PQ--RS

If only odd-period Bifids are considered, as is common in amateur circles, then any patterns that can be found in a message point to a unique period. Even admitting even periods, the patterns narrow down the possibilities to one or two periods.

A second method of determining the period was originally developed by Morgan (*The Cryptogram*, June–July 1946) and is presented by Bowers (*Practical Cryptanalysis*, vol. II). It is called the *Chi-square test* ("chi" is pronounced "ky" as in "sky").

The Chi-Square Test

This test for a period revolves around the fact that the enciphered letters in the first half of each block are substitutes for pairs of *row* coordinates, whereas in the last half of each block they stand for pairs of *column* coordinates. For an odd-period Bifid, the middle letter of each block, being of mixed ancestry, is ignored.

Unless the key square has been very carefully constructed for balance of frequencies about the diagonal, there is every reason to expect that the pairs of row coordinates (in their guise as ciphertext letters in the first half of each block) will have a different frequency distribution than the pairs of column coordinates (in their guise as ciphertext letters in the second half of each block). If we don't know the length of the period, we can try several periods, and it is likely that the one that shows the largest difference between the letters in the first half and the letters in the second half is the best guess for the real period.

To measure the differences between the letters in the first and second halves, we first count how many A, B, . . . , Z's occur in each half of the blocks. Suppose that there are A_1, B_1, . . . , Z_1's in the first half of all the blocks and A_2, B_2, . . . , Z_2's in the second half. For each letter we form the square of the difference divided by the sum and add up all the terms, as follows:

$$\chi^2 = \frac{(A_1-A_2)^2}{A_1+A_2} + \frac{(B_1-B_2)^2}{B_1+B_2} + \ldots + \frac{(Z_1-Z_2)^2}{Z_1+Z_2}$$

where χ is the Greek letter chi. Put more succinctly, if D_i is the difference for the ith letter and S_i is the sum of the number of occurrences, then

$$\chi^2 = \sum_{i=1}^{26} \frac{D_i^2}{S_i}$$

Index of Coincidence

Another approach to discovering the period of a Bifid is due to GIZMO and does not rely on a fortuitous arrangement of the key square. The argument goes this way. If you have guessed the proper period length and set up the ciphertext letters in a proper block,

$$\overset{1}{P}_r P_c \overset{1}{R}_r R_c \overset{1}{O}_r O_c \overset{1}{P}_r P_c \overset{1}{E}_r E_c \overset{1}{R}_r$$

$$R_c B_r B_c L_r L_c O_r O_c C_r C_c K_r K_c$$

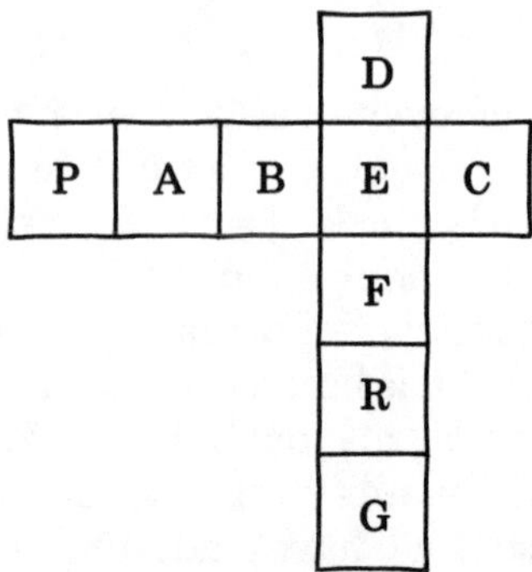

Fig. 13.1 Portion of the original key square.

then each vertical pair will represent a unique plaintext letter. If we look at the frequency distribution of these vertical pairs and compute the index of coincidence for the distribution, we might hope to find a large value when the proper block is reconstructed and a lower value for improper blocks.

Suppose that in the original key square the row that contained P and the column that contained R intersected at the letter E, as shown in Fig. 13.1. Then every time we find the row of P above the column of R we will get a plaintext E. Unfortunately, a number of other combinations will produce a plaintext E as well, for example: row of A/column of G or row of E/column of F. The existence of these alternative representations will significantly lower the index of coincidence when we compute it. If we have guessed wrong on the block length, however, the resulting vertical pairs will be completely random since they didn't come from real letters and thus will not have the uneven frequency distribution that real letters do. In counting up the number of times each vertical pair occurs, we must keep A_rB_c distinct from A_cB_c or A_cB_r. It will be sufficient to keep one set of counts for the odd positions in the reconstructed block and another for the even positions. Thus, in the block of ciphertext letters already established, (P_rR_c), (R_rB_c), (O_rL_c), (P_rO_c), (E_rC_c), and (R_rK_c) will go in one distribution count and (P_cB_r), (R_cL_r), (O_cO_r), (P_cC_r), and (E_cK_r) will go in the other. In fact, we can drop the subscripts since they will be uniquely determined by the trial block length and the oddness or evenness of the positions of the pairs.

GIZMO shows three examples of the use of the index of coincidence and the Chi-square. In his examples, the index of coincidence selected the correct period in each case, but the Chi-square was correct only two times out of three. When I applied Program 13.2 to eight recent examples of the Bifid from *The Cryptogram,* the index of coincidence selected the correct period four times and the Chi-square seven. Combining these eleven examples (our eight plus GIZMO's three), we find the index of coincidence to be correct about two-thirds of the time and the Chi-square correct about 80 percent of the time. When the two predictors agree, at least in this limited experiment, they select the correct period. When they do not agree, the odds are 2:1 that the Chi-square is correct and the index is wrong. Since the index of coincidence runs very slowly (because it has to search through the list of digrams every time), one might consider dropping it altogether and relying on the Chi-square alone.

Program 13.2 Bifid Helper I

```
10 REM DETERMINE PERIOD
20 REM READ AND SQUEEZE
30 GOSUB 10000
```

```
  40  GOSUB 10200
  45  PRINT "PERIOD IC"
  50  FOR P=3 TO 20
  55    FOR Q=1 TO 26: L1(Q)=0: L2(Q)=0: NEXT Q
  60    HP=INT(P/2)
  70    OD=P-2*HP
  75    S=0
  80    TA%(I)=0 : K=0
  90    FOR B=0 TO J-P STEP P
 100      FOR X=1 TO HP+OD
 110        F=T%(B+X)
 120        G=T%(B+X+HP)
 125        S=S+1
 130        GOSUB 1000
 140      NEXT X
 150      FOR X=1 TO HP
 160        L1(T%(X+B))=L1(T%(X+B))+1
 170        L2(T%(B+P+1-X))=L2(T%(B+P+1-X))+1
 180      NEXT X
 190    NEXT B
 200    IC=0
 210    GOSUB 2000
 220    GOSUB 3000
 230    PRINT P; IC*625; CS
 240  NEXT P
 250  STOP

1000  FOR Y=1 TO K
1010    IF F=TA%(Y) AND G=TB%(Y) THEN TC%(Y)=TC%(Y)+1 :
        RETURN
1020  NEXT Y
1030  K=K+1
1040  TA%(K)=F
1050  TB%(K)=G
1060  TC%(K)=I
1070  RETURN

2000  FOR Y=1 TO K
2010    IC=IC+TC%(Y)*(TC%(Y)-1)
2020  NEXT Y
2030  IC=IC/ (S*(S-1))
2040  RETURN

3000  CS=0
```

```
3010  FOR Z=1 TO 26
3015     IF L1(Z)+L2(Z)=0 GOTO 3030
3020     CS=CS+(L1(Z)-L2(Z))↑2/ (L1(Z)+L2(Z))
3030  NEXT Z
3040  RETURN
```

Program 13.2 (cont'd) Bifid Helper Comments

30–40
: Read in the ciphertext and squeeze out blanks.

50–240
: For each period from 3 to 20, compute the index of coincidence and Chi-square.

55 Clear the left- and right-half letter counts.

60 Compute the half period, HP. If P is even, HP=P/2, and if P is odd, HP=(P–1)/2.

70 Compute the oddness (OD=1) or evenness (OD=0) of the period.

75 Zero the count of digrams.

80 Set K to 0 so that when you bump it the first time, it will go to 1 and set TA%(I)=0, which won't match any letter.

90–190
: For all the blocks except the uneven remainder at the end.

100–140
: For each letter in the first half (through the middle letter if the period is odd), compute the index of coincidence.

110 F is the upper letter in the vertical pair.

120 G is the lower letter in the pair.

125 Add one to the count of digrams.

130 Go to the subroutine that counts digrams.

150–180
: Do the Chi-square part.

160 Count the letters in the left half of the block.

170 Count the letters in the right half of the block.

200 Clear the index of coincidence value.

210 Compute the IC.

220 Compute Chi-square.

230 Print the results.

1000–1070
: Count digrams.

1000–1020
: Search for the digram FG.

1010 If FG matches the digram, add one to the count.

1030 If we failed to find FG, add it to the list.

1040–1060
TA ← F, TB ← G, and TC is set to 1.

2000–2040
Compute IC, where

$$IC = \sum_{list} \frac{N_i(N_i-1)}{S(S-1)}$$

3000–3040
Compute Chi-square.
3015 If both are zero, skip it.
3020 Compute CS, where

$$CS = \sum_{i=1}^{26} \frac{D_i^2}{S_i}$$

Placing the Tip

Once the period has been determined, one can reconstruct the blocks into vertical pairs, as previously indicated. When the row coordinate of a letter happens to lie directly above the column coordinate of the same letter, as is the case with the A_r/A_c in this example,

$$X_r\ X_c\ A_r\ A_c\ B_r\ B_c\ F_r$$
$$F_c\ A_r\ A_c\ Q_r\ Q_c\ G_r\ G_c$$

this coincidence is called a *natural*, and it is obvious that the plaintext letter these coordinates came from can be none other than the letter A itself. Look back at the first two blocks of the message that we enciphered using the BULLDOZER square:

M_r	M_c	W_r	W_c	S_r	S_c	G_r		C_r	C_c	I_r	I_c	R_r	R_c	U_r
G_c	W_r	W_c	S_r	S_c	L_r	L_c		U_c	D_r	D_c	U_r	U_c	O_r	O_c
n	o	w	i	s	t	h		e	t	i	m	e	f	o

In the first block, both W and S are "naturals." In the second block, I_r/D_c produces i and U_r/O_c produces o. These are called *half-naturals,* in which one of the two coordinates of a plaintext letter gets enciphered as the letter itself. On average, this happens to about 8 letters in 24.

Using naturals, which are definite, as well as guesses about which letters in the block might produce half-naturals, it is usually easy to pin down the location of the tip, particularly since it will probably have been chosen with ease of placement in mind.

Program 13-3, which is an extension of Program 13.2, will try to place the tip in all possible positions, counting one for a half-natural match and two for a natural match. It will then print out the ten best fits (highest counts) and allow the user to choose among them.

Program 13.3 Bifid Helper II

This is the same program as Program 13.2 with the following additions:

```
  4  DIM TP%(50),R%(200),C%(200),B(11),LB(11)
 41  PRINT "DO YOU KNOW THE PERIOD?-TYPE Y OR N"
 42  GET A$: IF A$=" " GOTO 42
 43  IF A$="Y" GOTO 300

250  REM PLACE THE TIP
300  PRINT "WHAT IS THE PERIOD?"
310  INPUT P
320  HP=INT(P/2)
330  OD=P-2*HP
340  PRINT "ENTER THE TIP-NO BLANKS"
350  INPUT A$
355  TL=LEN(A$)
360  FOR I=1 TO TL
370     TP%=ASC(MID$(A$,I,1))-64
380  NEXT I
390  REM MAKE VECTORS OF ROW AND COLUMN ELEMENTS
     AR=1,AC=101
400  K=1
410  FOR B=0 TO J-P STEP P
415     C%(K)=T%(B+1)
420     FOR X=1 TO HP+OD
430        R%(K)=T%(B+X)
440        R%(K+1)=T%(B+X)+100
445        C%(K+1-OD)=T%(B+X+HP)+100
450        C%(K+2-OD)=T%(B+X+HP+1)
460        K=K+2
470     NEXT X
480     K=K-OD
490  NEXT B
495  B(11)=10000: FOR XX=1 TO 10: B(XX)=0: NEXT XX
500  IF OD=0 GOTO 610
510  REM FIND ODD PERIOD NATURALS
520  FOR I=0 TO B-TL
530     C=0
540     FOR K=1 TO TL
550        IF R%(I+K)=TP%(K) THEN C=C+1
```

```
560         IF C%(I+K)=TP%(K)+100 THEN C=C+1
570       NEXT K
580       GOSUB 4000
590    NEXT I
600    GOTO 700
610    REM DO IDENTICALS FOR EVEN PERIOD
620    FOR I=0 TO B-TL
630       C=0
640       FOR K=1 TO TL
650         IF TP%(K)=R%(I+K) AND TP%(K+1)=C%(I+K) THEN
            C=C+2
670       NEXT K
680       GOSUB 4000
690    NEXT I
700    PRINT: PRINT "PT='
710    FOR I=1 TO TL
720       PRINT CHR$(TP%(I)+64);
730    NEXT I
735    PRINT
740    FOR I=10 TO 1 STEP -1
745       IF B(I)=0 GOTO 830
750       PRINT LB(I),
760       FOR X=1 TO TL
765         T=R%(LB(I)+X): IF T> 100 THEN T=T-100: PRINT
            "reverse";
770         PRINT CHR$(T+64); "reverse off";
780       NEXT X
790       PRINT: PRINT,
800       FOR X=1 TO TL
805         T=C%(LB(I)+X): IF T> 100 THEN T=T-100: PRINT
            "reverse";
810         PRINT CHR$(T+64); "reverse off";
820       NEXT X
825       PRINT
830    NEXT I
840    STOP
4000   IF C< B(1) THEN RETURN
4010   FOR XX=2 TO 11
4020      IF C< B(XX) THEN B(XX-1)=C: LB(XX-1)=I: RETURN
4030      B(XX-1)=B(XX)
4040      LB(XX-1)=LB(XX)
4050   NEXT XX
4060   RETURN
```

Program 13.3 (cont'd) Bifid Helper II Comments

41–43
Ask if the user wants to skip the long process of identifying the period.

300 In either event (Y or N), you end up here asking what period to use.

320 HP is the half-period.

330 OD is the oddness (OD = 1 if odd; OD = 0 if even).

340–380
Enter the tip (probable word) and convert it to numbers.

390–490
We are going to set up the vectors of R%-row elements and C%-column elements in block formation. Letters left over after the end of the last full block will be ignored.

400 K is a pointer to the next element in R% and C%.

410 P is the period (block size), and B will point just to the left of the beginning of a block. We step along one block at a time.

415 Set up the first column elements of the block. If the period is even, this is left as it is. If the period is odd, it will be overwritten.

420–470
Steps through the letters that will make up this block.

430–450
Set up two letters in the R% and C/ vectors. Column designators get +100. Note when storing in C% that odd period letters go one to the left (−OD).

460 Bump K by 2.

480 If the period is odd (OD = 1), set K back one at the end of the block because, in writing the block, we wrote one into the next block in both R% and C%.

495 Set best (11) to a large number as a guard to keep from running off the list of ten best matches between the tip and the ciphertext, then clear the best array.

500 We have to match differently for odd periods and even periods.

510–600
Here we look for naturals and half-naturals (odd period).

520–590
For each starting position in the ciphertext that will allow a complete fit of the tip, count the number of naturals (worth 2 each) and half-naturals (worth 1 each).

530 Set the count to 0.

540–570
Step across the letters of the tip.

550 If the entry in R% is a row element and if it matches the tip letter, count 1.

560 If the entry in C% is a column element and if it matches the tip letter, count 1.

580 Go to 4000 to see if this count (C) is among the ten best so far.

600 Go to the "rejoin" point.

610–690
This is for even-period Bifids. Look for identicals as in 510–600 except that they should be adjacent pairs of letters in the tip (XX) that line up with the X-row/Y-row.

700–735
Print out the tip as given.

740–830
Print the ten best matches.

745 Skip if the count was 0.

760–780
Print the R% elements (if column designator, print reversed).

800–820
Print the C% elements. In each case, remove the "excess 100" (if column designator, print reversed.)

4000–4060
Same subroutine to sort ten best used previously.

When the period of a Bifid is even, the analysis is quite different. During enciphering, the intermediate text is identical, of course, regardless of what period is chosen. If the period is 4, then we take four vertical pairs at a time to convert from intermediate to ciphertext. Using the same square and message as before, we get

n	o	w	i	s	t	h	e
4	1	5	3	4	5	3	2
2	5	3	4	5	1	3	2

Reading off the coordinate pairs as 41, 53, 25, and 34, and then 45, 32, 51, and 32, we get

MWCI SGTG . . .

When we take the ciphertext and expand and block it, we get

M_r	M_c	W_r	W_c	S_r	S_c	G_r	G_c
C_r	C_c	I_r	I_c	T_r	T_c	G_r	G_c
n	o	w	i	s	t	h	e

When a pair of adjacent plaintext letters such as wi are such that the column of the first is equal to the row of the second ($w_c = 3$,

$i_r = 3$), the plaintext is reproduced "vertically" in the blocked ciphertext. The same thing happens with the st pair of the second block. These pairings are called *identicals*, and Program 13.3 is arranged to search for them when the period is even.

Reconstructing the Square

As in most ciphers of this general type, the analyst's approach is to try to reconstruct the key square. Once the tip has been placed, one has a number of equivalences of the form, $I_r = K_c$, that can be used for this purpose. Taking the Bifid by NEON from *The Cryptogram* (Jan.–Feb. 1980), we find the best fit of the tip to be

A_r	A_c	T_r	T_c	B_r	B_c	B_r	C_r	C_c	I_r	I_c	T_r	T_c	E_r
B_c	T_r	T_c	O_r	O_c	S_r	S_c	E_c	M_r	M_c	A_r	A_c	F_r	F_c
(b)	o	((t))	h	(b)	y	a	(c)	c	(i)	d	e	n	t

where the natural is circled twice and the half-naturals once. The second *c* of *accident* is not a natural because it lines up with a column designator in its row position. From this alignment, we know that the row of A is equal to the row of B, the column of A is the row of O, the row of T is the column of O, and so on. When we get a cross reference with the same value appearing in two different equations, we can combine the information.

Starting out, we write

A_r B_r
A_c O_r
T_r O_c
T_c H_r
O_r H_c

and the last item can go on the second row because O_r appears in both of them. Redundant information ($T_r = T_r$) is ignored. We end up with

1. A_r B_r D_c
2. A_c O_r H_c S_c E_c C_c M_r
3. T_r O_c B_c Y_r E_r
4. T_c H_r N_r F_c
5. S_r Y_c
6. M_c I_c D_r
7. F_r N_c

where the numbers are assigned arbitrarily. We now construct a trial square of seven rows and seven columns, knowing that eventually this

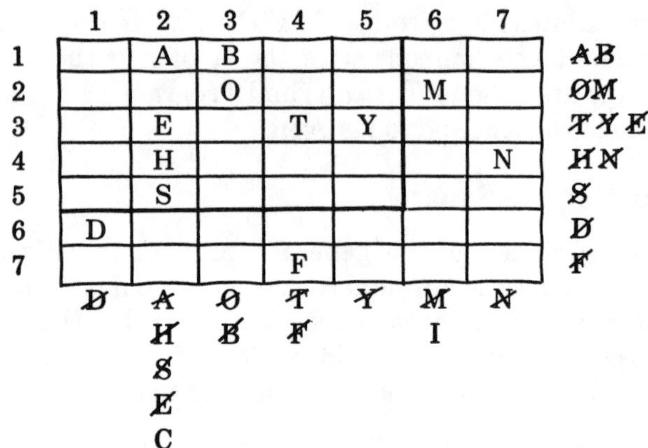

Fig. 13.2 Trial square.

square must collapse into a 5×5 grid. Outside the square we write whatever information we have. In row 1 we put A and B, and in column 1 we put D. In row 2 we put O and M, and in column 2 we put A, H, S, E, and C. Thus, we have the layout shown in Fig. 13.2.

When a letter appears in both a row and a column, we can enter it in the square and cross it off on the outside. We have done this in Fig. 13.2, and all the letters have been entered except I and C, about which we have no row information.

Now we can begin to apply the kind of logic that is very difficult to explain to a computer. Look at column 2. It has four letters entered in it and still has a C hanging on the outside. C, therefore, has to go into row 2, column 2. Row 7 with F in it is going to have to "fold into" one of the other rows. Row 3, column 4 is already occupied by T so 7 might go into row 1, 2, 4, or 5. But if row 7 maps into row i, then column 7 must map or fold into column i. Since the N of row 4, column 7 can't fold on top of the H of column 2, we can restrict the folding of 7 to either 1, 4, or 5. Similarly, row and column 6 can fold into 1, 3, 4, or 5.

Now it is time to go to the ciphertext and fill in what we know to see if we can make any clever guesses to extend our knowledge:

$X_rX_cC_rC_cL_rL_cE_r$ $P_rP_cW_rW_cG_rG_cX_r$ $S_rS_cF_rF_cK_rK_cA_r$ $T_rT_cI_rI_cA_rA_cT_r$

$E_cT_rT_cU_rU_cM_rM_c$ $X_cA_rA_cC_rC_cA_rA_c$ $A_cC_rC_cZ_rZ_cM_rM_c$ $T_cC_rC_cH_rH_cC_rC_c$

s c t h a c e

$M_rM_cT_rT_cX_rX_cB_r$ $K_rK_cN_rN_cL_rL_cR_r$ $T_rT_cH_rH_cV_rV_cO_r$ $T_rT_cI_rI_cB_rB_cW_r$

$B_cQ_rQ_cC_rC_cC_rC_c$ $R_cH_rH_cB_rB_cN_rN_c$ $O_cL_rL_cX_rX_cS_rS_c$ $W_cC_rC_cL_rL_cC_rC_c$

o h a h c h e

$A_rA_cT_rT_cB_rB_cB_r$	$C_rC_cI_rI_cT_rT_cE_r$	$F_rF_cD_rD_cI_rI_cE_r$	$U_rU_cF_rF_cG_rG_cE_r$
$B_cT_rT_cO_rO_cS_rS_c$	$E_cM_rM_cA_rA_cF_rF_c$	$E_cD_rD_cY_rY_cA_rA_c$	$E_cG_rG_cB_rB_cT_rT_c$
b o t h b y a	c c i d e n t	d b d	t
$H_rH_cK_rK_cY_rY_cM_r$	$P_rP_cI_rI_cD_rD_cB_r$	$O_rO_cN_rN_cT_rT_cG_r$	$K_rK_cK_rK_cA_rA_cD_r$
$M_cI_rI_cM_rM_cM_rM_c$	$B_cS_rS_cE_rE_cQ_rQ_c$	$G_cD_rD_cW_rW_cC_rC_c$	$D_cH_rH_cO_rO_cS_rS_c$
s m			b
$U_rU_cT_rT_cB_rB_cH_r$	$C_rC_cK_rK_cG_rG_cX_r$	$B_rB_cK_rK_cB_rB_cB_r$	$H_rH_cX_rX_cK_rK_cR_r$
$H_cQ_rQ_cC_rC_cR_rR_c$	$X_cO_rO_cM_rM_cM_rM_c$	$B_cL_rL_cA_rA_cC_rC_c$	$R_cZ_rZ_cD_rD_cH_rH_c$
h a	c	b a e a	
$Y_rY_cO_rO_cK_rK_cV_r$	$K_rK_cY_r$		
$V_cC_rC_cM_rM_cK_rK_c$	$Y_cU_rU_c$		
s c e			

Look at the fourth block of the first row, th--ace, which might well be "the race" or "the face." The combination I_r/C_c that would stand for e occurs also in block 8 following an h. Looking at the key square, we see that if I were in row 3, I_r/C_c would indeed be e. Let's put I in row 3 and see how things work out; we can always remove it if it doesn't. The square is now that shown in Fig. 13.3.

If we try to fold column 6, the only place it can go is into column 1. In order to maintain our equivalences, we must fold row 6 into row 1. Now row/column 7 can fold into 1 or 5 since 2 is blocked by the N-H conflict, 3 by the F-T conflict, and 4 by the F-N conflict.

In block 3, we have sc?, where the ? is given by F_r/C_c. If 7 folds into 1, F_r/C_c = A, and if it folds into 5, F_r/C_c = S, producing either

	1	2	3	4	5	6	7
1	-	A	B	-	-	-	-
2	-	C	O	-	-	M	-
3	-	E	-	T	Y	I	-
4	-	H	-	-	-	-	N
5	-	S	-	-	-	-	-
6	D	-	-	-	-	-	-
7	-	-	-	F	-	-	-

Fig. 13.3 7 × 7 grid.

	1	2	3	4	5
1	D	A	B	F	
2	M	C	O		
3	I	E		T	Y
4	N	H			
5		S			

Fig. 13.4 5 × 5 grid.

sca or scs. Since it's hard to make a word or combination of words out of scs, let's fold 7 into 1, giving the square shown in Fig. 13.4.

Going back to the ciphertext, we will now plug in all we know, adopting a shorthand to cut down on the amount of writing required. Each upper letter is to be combined with the letter below it and the letter below and to the right of it as long as they are in the same block:

```
XCLE    PWGX    SFKA    TIAT
ETUM    XACA    ACZM    TCHC
------i -------  sca---d theface

MTXB    KNLR    THVO    TIBW    ATBB
BQCC    RHBN    QLXS    WCLC    BTOS
o--h--a --hd--- ------c -he--e- bothbya

C ITE   FDIE    UFGE    HKYM    PIDB
EMAF    EDYA    EGBT    MIMM    BSEQ
ccident andbyde ---n--t no--ism --eba--

ONTG    KKAD    UTBH    CKGX    BKBB
GDWC    DHOS    HQCR    XOMM    BLAC
-in--h- ----b-a ---ha-- -c----- b---aea

HXKR    YOKV    KY
RZDH    VCMK    YU
-sce--- --ce--- ---
```

Following the tip, the plaintext is "both by accident and by de---n" and a reasonable guess is the word "design." In block 3, the word is probably "scanned" or "scarred"; in any event, it ends in "ed." Block 5 makes sense as "of the ?." Putting these into the block, we get the square shown in Fig. 13.5.

Plugging these back into the ciphertext, we can then guess that the beginning of the plaintext is "explosions have scarred the face of

	1	2	3	4	5
1	D	A	B	F	G
2	M	C	O		
3	I	E	X	T	Y
4	N	H	K	Q	
5		S	U		

Fig. 13.5 Revised 5 × 5 grid.

D	A	B	F	G
M	C	O	P	L
I	E	X	T	Y
N	H	K	Q	R
V	S	U	W	Z

Fig. 13.6 Completed key square.

the earth . . . " and completely fill in the key square as shown in Fig. 13.6. From this the reader can easily complete the plaintext.

Before presenting the program for Bifid Helper III, it will be necessary to make some changes to earlier sections. When trying to establish the period or to place the tip, it was possible to ignore the final partial block, but when the test message came out "now is the time for all goof @@@," I realized at once that my laziness would have to be corrected. The section of code that constructed the intermediate text (lines 410–490 of Program 13.3 works on a block-by-block basis. The terminal letters also form a block but of a shorter period. Putting the code for generating one block in a subroutine, we get the revised lines:

```
410  FOR B=0 TO J-P STEP P
420     GOSUB 6000
430  NEXT B
440  R=J-B
450  HP=INT(R/2)
460  OD=R-2*HP
470  GOSUB 6000

6000 C%(K)=T%(B+HP+1)
6010 FOR X=1 TO HP+OD
6020    R%(K)=T%(B+X)
6030    R%(K+1)=T%(B+X)+100
6040    C%(K+1-OD)=T%(B+X+HP)+100
6050    C%(K+2-OD)=T%(B+X+HP+1)
```

```
6060      K=K+2
6070   NEXT X
6080   K=K-OD
6090   RETURN
```

In order to get this entire program into an 8K PET, I was forced to reduce the maximum size of the ciphertext to 150 letters. (Cleverer programmers could undoubtedly reuse some of the vectors from earlier parts of the program to permit longer messages. Removal of spaces and the use of multiple statements per line saves considerable space at the expense of readability. Finally, careful planning was required to leave insufficient space for Program 13.4 before the subroutines used by Programs 13.2 and 13.3. Consequently, Program 13.4 begins with a jump over these subroutines.

Program 13.4 Bifid Helper III

```
   1   DIM T%(150)
   2   DIM TA%(150),TB%(150),TC%(150)
   3   DIM L1(26),L2(26)
   4   DIM TP%(50),R%(150),C%(150),B(11),LB(11)
   5   DIM KS%(9,9),RL%(26),CL%(26)

 840   GOTO 5000

5000   REM HELPER-3 TRANSLATE BACK TO PT
5010   FOR I=1 TO 26
5020      RL%(I)=0
5030      CL%(I)=0
5040   NEXT I

5060   PRINT "KEY SQUARE ROWS AND COLUMNS 1-9. O ROW/
       COLUMN MEANS UNASSIGNED. END EACH WITH /.
5070   FOR I=0 TO 9
5080      PRINT "ROW";I;"=";
5090      GET A$: IF A$="" GOTO 5090
5100      PRINT A$;
5110      T=ASC(A$)-64
5120      IF T=-17 GOTO 5145
5130      RL%(T)-I
5140      GOTO 5090
5145      PRINT
5150   NEXT I

5160   FOR I=0 TO 9
5170      PRINT "COLUMN";I;"=";
5180      GET A$: IF A$="" GOTO 5180
```

```
5185        PRINT A$
5190        T=ASC(A$)-64
5200        IF T=-17 GOTO 5225
5210        CL%(T)=I
5220        GOTO 5180
5225        PRINT
5230    NEXT I

5240    PRINT "ANY FOLDS? END WITH /"
5250    GET A$: IF A$="" GOTO 5250
5260    PRINT A$;
5270    X=ASC(A$)-ASC("0")
5280    IF X=-1 GOTO 5360
5290    PRINT "IS EQUAL TO";
5300    GET A$: IF A$="" GOTO 5300
5310    PRINT A$
5315    Y=ASC(A$)-ASC("0")
5320    FOR I=1 TO 26
5330        IF RL%(I)=X THEN RL%(I)=Y
5340        IF CL%(I)=X THEN CL%(I)=Y
5350    NEXT I
5355    GOTO 5250

5360    FOR I=0 TO 9
5370        FOR K=0 TO 9
5380            KS%(I,K)=0
5390        NEXT K
5400    NEXT I
5405    RL%(10)=RL%(9): CL%(10)=CL%(9)
5410    FOR I=26 TO 1 STEP -1
5420        IF RL%(I)=0 OR CL%(I)=0 GOTO 5440
5430        KS%(RL%(I),CL%(I))=I
5440    NEXT I

5600    FOR I=0 TO J-1 STEP 39
5610        FOR K=1 TO 39
5620            T=R%(I+K)
5630            IF T > 100 THEN T=T-100
5640            PRINT CHR$(T+64);
5650            IF I+K > J-1 THEN K=40
5660        NEXT K
5670        PRINT
5680        FOR K=1 TO 39
5690            T=C%(I+K)
5700            IF T > 100 THEN T=T-100
5710            PRINT CHR$(T+64);
5720            IF I+K > J-1 THEN K=40
```

```
5730        NEXT K
5740        PRINT
5750        FOR K=1 TO 39
5760           T=R%(I+K)
5770           S=C%(I+K)
5780           IF T< 100 THEN R=RL%(T)
5790           IF T> 100 THEN R=CL%(T-100)
5800           IF S< 100 THEN C=RL%(S)
5810           IF S> 100 THEN C=CL%(S-100)
5820           IF KS%(R,C)=0 THEN PRINT "-";: GOTO 5840
5830           PRINT CHR$(KS%(R,C)+64)
5840           IF I+K > J-1 THEN K=40
5850        NEXT K
5860        PRINT: PRINT
5870     NEXT I
5880     GOTO 5060
```

Program 13.4 (cont'd) Bifid Helper III Comments

5010–5040
Clear the row and column assignments for all letters. When the user inputs key square rows and columns, these vectors will hold them.

5070–5150
Enter the letters that belong on row i of the key square (the order on the row does not matter). If the user wants to leave any letters "unassigned," they may be entered as belonging to row 0 or column 0.

5090–5100
Get a letter and echo it to the screen.

5110–5120
Convert the letter to a number; if a slash, it marks the end of this row.

5130 Put the present row number (i) in RL% of this letter.

5140 Get another letter for this row.

5160–5230
Do the same thing for the columns of the key square.

5240–5350
Make a row/column number equivalent to another number by changing all occurrences of the first number to the second.

5250–5270
Get a digit (0–9), echo it, and convert it to a number (= X).

5280 If a slash, it will equal −1 after subtracting ASC("0"), which is 48. Other BASICS may require a different value.

5300 Get the other number (= Y).

5320–5350
Convert all occurrences of X to Y.

5355 Do it again until a slash is input.

5360–5400
Clear the key square.

5405 Make J the same as I.

5410–5440
Build the key square from the row/column designations of the letters. Do it from Z to A so that I wipes out J.

5600–5870
Print out the reconstructed blocks with the known plaintext. Use 39 letters per line.

5610–5660
Print a line of blocked ciphertext row elements.

5680–5730
Print a line of blocked ciphertext column elements.

5750–5850
Print the plaintext if it is known or else a "–".

5760–5770
T is the row element and S is the column element of this plaintext letter.

5780 If T < 100, use the RL%(T) as the row of the PT letter.

5790 If T > 100, use the CL%(T–100) as the row of the PT letter.

5800–5810
Do the same for the column of the PT letter.

5820 If the key square entry at this row/column is zero, no PT letter is known. Print a minus.

5830 Print the PT letter.

5880 Go back to ask for more row/columns of letters. Old information need not be repeated.

Problems for Chapter 13

1. Period 5 (ADVANCESCONFIDENTLY)

NMTIF QUPZX LRKPQ NIGIZ ISNTO
ITGHU NGTFQ PPLGE ELSHB DXZMY
IEGZC DPFMG LXPTT ITEIM FLQEU
ELHDY TBVYO KEVXG TTZAU NSTTV
TZEDT DFSYW LRUPK IMGNM LTUEQ
NYXQV MHISD RS (*Thoreau*)

2. Period 9 (MEANANDVINDICTIVE)

IIZTI TKASE TACUU LSQER MVZGH
XNOMT CQLGH EQWTG HSCCK OYMTL

EHGRP TQQFG HTLTE ERLIO GHEYT
VYOIM FTOIZ RCSCH UMNFM XVEHB
MKDTD LDCSE TM (*Somerset Maugham*)

3. Period 6 (ETHATICOULDBEJUSTA)
IXAAM XKTZY OWLRK WOIIP UNVNI
GCESF ZGSCS BLBVK AIYOD RAPLF
ZAKSC USOLX EKZIE COAKR XYKER
NNIPL RVAOI GHWSS NFYFK ZDMBZ
VCBAA AILW

4. Period 7 (KNOWBECAUSEIHAVE)
FXIYS YPROL ICUGI UEIRL YHOQS
PRBLG DSGHB NOLLU XTELZ HUSGQ
OEACZ KXBUN OCPIA EOAFU EWWHO
MBDHE USBTA OBSXR MKGLT TH

5. Period 8 (TIMESAYEARIHAVEM)
FWKBE PDEHE PVITC WRRAR ETNAV
THXNH RQLMI PTEOQ TFZKP TCFLH
YBNDB BHBLO FNTNT RCTYE HALOS
ZTNWX YHDBS QHIEC DVTYA DNKTE
CDHBP RXKDY S (*G. B. Shaw*)

6. (AFALSESTATEMENTBUTTHEOPPOSITE)
YEGOI MEZXZ UNAOK ISTSG OCXHV
PCABW NIADC DXHFL RABWE TIYEG
MUBEZ GAHNR ZSTOT QNWNX IXXNA
GLDQM BDWIU VULPH RRECL GQZRN
XIHAG L (*Niels Bohr*)

7. (ONERANAWAYTOSEAANDTHEOTHER)
ECQOE OREWN WNBVO BFSDS IUUME
OUUAK RNYHY WCSDQ PQUGT WWWOP
SKNCN TLUBE OOTEK YBWTN WEFSV
QTZUW MWIHS EOFSX HVNUY VCKIF
CYMUT UMEFM HTUAG I

8. (THEDISADVANTAGES)

CZUTW IGVOF OBHUC SMEQU YTONH
ENEGM EEZKW UZKAV ZEOUW WIHEG
UWHIH ZTQTL VNKWD IDVMD INWEN
LRIFW SWEIQ ZTHEP E

9. (ADIFFERENCEBETWEEN)

TQQHQ EMQAD UTQWB QWSBB EECEZ
DFSDP YSTAM XGMBG AEAHA UBBIC
VNAVL CQEVE ZHBMB SFOLV YYLUC
WLAVL CVEVE TZWYM HBNBS DE

(*John Erskine*)

10. (EVERYOTHERWORD)

FAEXI GZPYN KRSNA YWHCB QMVLU
OUSDW STONP VGDVN EHMPH KOUCD
OHTPA YVRNQ FIHCP FSOQV TOVRS
OXIHH DMRWR POIQQ QWZIB TDILH
UIYGD TIFKF XUQO (*Sydney Smith*)

14

Exercises for the Reader

At this point, we have covered only a small fraction of the ciphers that appear regularly in *The Cryptogram.* Many other systems that are equally interesting never appear there, and were we to attempt to include a chapter on every system known, this book would run to several times its present size. Worse yet, we would have deprived the reader of the fun of puzzling out systems for himself. Consequently, in this chapter we will mention briefly a number of appealing systems that appear more or less regularly in *The Cryptogram* since these are the ones on which the amateur cryptanalyst can easily test his burgeoning skills.

Key Phrase

The key phrase system is similar to simple substitution except that several plaintext letters may map onto a single ciphertext letter. The ciphertext alphabet is a *complete* 26-letter phrase that is written out against the plaintext alphabet with repeats left intact, as follows:

Plaintext:	A	B	C	D	E	F	G	H	I	J	K	L	M
Ciphertext:	G	I	V	E	M	E	L	I	B	E	R	T	Y

Plaintext:	N	O	P	Q	R	S	T	U	V	W	X	Y	Z
Ciphertext:	O	R	G	I	V	E	M	E	D	E	A	T	H

and the standard message generates the ciphertext as

```
n o w    i s    t h e    t i m e    f o r
O R E    B E    M I M    M B Y M    E R V
```

This is not nearly as hard to solve as it appears at first glance.

Ragbaby

Ragbaby is a polyalphabetic cipher based on a 24-letter keyword alphabet (J and X are eliminated) with shifts that may be called "ratcheted progressive." The shift is to the right (modulo 24) in the keyword alphabet, and successive letters in a word are each shifted one more place than the previous letter (progressive). When a new word is begun, the shift starts over again, one greater than for the previous word (ratcheted). If the keyword alphabet is:

M A G N E T I C B D F H K L O P Q R S U V W Y Z

the message becomes

Plaintext:	now	is	the	time	for
Shift:	123	23	345	4567	567
Ciphertext:	EQM	BW	BPD	DHIH	PVM

Tridigital

This is a form of controlled polyphonic (many pt letters to one ct letter). A keyword alphabet is written in three rows of nine, nine, and eight letters, and a second keyword, this time of ten letters, is used to generate a numerical key that is placed above the rows of the alphabet:

R	E	P	U	B	L	I	C	A	N
9	4	8	0	2	6	5	3	1	7
M	A	G	N	E	T	I	C	B	-
D	F	H	J	K	L	O	P	Q	-
R	S	U	V	W	X	Y	Z	-	-

M, D and R are enciphered by 9; A, F, and S by 4, and so forth; and 7 serves as a word separator:

now is the time
052754768276592

Checkerboard

The checkerboard cipher involves a key square constructed by any convenient means, say by writing a keyword alphabet in a clockwise spiral into the square. Then two or four five-letter words are chosen and written next to the square to serve as coordinates. Each plaintext letter becomes a pair of coordinate letters that intersect at the position of the plaintext letter in the key square. When four coordinate words are used, the coordinate letters may be taken from either of the words on the side and either of the words above, as shown in Fig. 14.1.

		B	R	O	W	N
		G	H	O	S	T
N	F	M	A	G	N	E
O	I	P	Q	R	S	T
I	G	O	Y	Z	U	I
S	H	L	X	W	V	C
E	T	K	H	F	D	B

Fig. 14.1 Checkerboard key square.

Thus, the letter M might be enciphered as NG, NB, FB, or FG, depending on the whim of the encipherer. In the less complex case when only two words are used, the encipherer is relieved of all these decisions.

Homophonic

The plaintext alphabet is straight, omitting the letter J, and there are four possible encipherings for each letter. The numbers 01, 02, 03, . . . , 99, 00 are divided into four groups of twenty-five that are assigned in order to the alphabet with the starting point of each group selected by a four-letter keyword. If the keyword is GREY, the assignment would be as follows:

A	B	C	D	E	F	G	H	I	K	L	M	N	O	P	Q	R	S	T	U	V	W	X	Y	Z
20	21	22	23	24	25	<u>01</u>	02	03	04	05	06	07	08	09	10	11	12	13	14	15	16	17	18	1
35	36	37	38	39	40	41	42	43	44	45	46	47	48	49	50	<u>26</u>	27	28	29	30	31	32	33	3
72	73	74	75	<u>51</u>	52	53	54	55	56	57	58	59	60	61	62	63	64	65	66	67	68	69	70	7
78	79	80	81	82	83	84	85	86	87	88	89	90	91	92	93	94	95	96	97	98	99	00	<u>76</u>	7

Thus, E might be enciphered by 24, 39, 51, or 82.

Grandpre

Grandpre is a combination checkerboard and homophonic. We pick eight words of eight letters, each of whose initial letters form a ninth word. Generally, all 26 letters occur, or their absence should be noted. The eight words are written horizontally and coordinates (1–8) are read out in pairs to form the ciphertext. Letters that occur more than once in the 8×8 square can be enciphered by any of the alternatives, as shown in Fig. 14.2.

	1	2	3	4	5	6	7	8
1	L	A	D	Y	B	U	G	S
2	A	Z	I	M	U	T	H	S
3	C	A	L	F	S	K	I	N
4	Q	U	A	C	K	I	S	H
5	U	N	J	O	V	I	A	L
6	E	V	U	L	S	I	O	N
7	R	O	W	D	Y	I	S	M
8	S	E	X	T	U	P	L	Y

Fig. 14.2 Grandpre key square.

```
M A G N E      N O R T H
T I C B D      E A S B C
F H K L O      D F G I K
P Q R S U      L M P Q U
V W X Y Z      V W X Y Z
```

Fig. 14.3 Key squares of the two-square cipher.

With this square, E could be enciphered by 61 or 82 and S by 18, 28, 35, 47, 65, 77, or 81.

Two-Square Cipher

The two-square cipher and the four-square cipher that follows are based on the Playfair. Two keyword alphabets are written into adjacent 5×5 squares, as shown in Fig. 14.3.

The plaintext is divided into pairs, the first letter being found in the left-hand square and the second in the right-hand. The opposite corners of the rectangle are read out as the ciphertext. If the letters happen to fall on the same row, then the reversed plaintext letters become the ciphertext:

```
no wi st he ti me
ON YH QN DI BF NT
```

Four-Square Cipher

Squares 1 and 3 of the four-square cipher are plain-ordered alphabets and squares 2 and 4 are keyed, as shown in Fig. 14.4.

Plaintext pairs are looked up in squares 1 and 3, and the ciphertext pair is read out from the opposite corners of the rectangle, as follows:

```
no wi st he ti me
LG YA SP BR SB OO
```

A	B	C	D	E	M	A	G	N	E
F	G	H	I	K	T	I	C	B	D
L	M	N	O	P	F	H	K	L	O
Q	R	S	T	U	P	Q	R	S	U
V	W	X	Y	Z	V	W	X	Y	Z
N	O	R	T	H	A	B	C	D	E
E	A	S	B	C	F	G	H	I	K
D	F	G	I	K	L	M	N	O	P
L	M	P	Q	U	Q	R	S	T	U
V	W	X	Y	Z	V	W	X	Y	Z

Fig. 14.4 Four-square cipher.

Conjugated Matrix Bifid

The Conjugated Matrix Bifid is exactly the same as an ordinary Bifid except that when the coordinates are translated back into letters, a second 5×5 key square is used rather than the original one.

6×6 Bifid

The 26 letters, plus the ten digits 1 through 0, are used in the 6×6 Bifid. The digits (in the cryptogram) must immediately follow the first ten letters of the alphabet (A–J), as shown in Fig. 14.5.

Otherwise, the 6×6 Bifid is the same as a 5×5 Bifid.

	1	*2*	*3*	*4*	*5*	*6*
1	M	A	1	G	7	N
2	E	5	T	I	9	C
3	3	B	2	D	4	F
4	6	H	8	J	0	K
5	L	O	P	Q	R	S
6	U	V	W	X	Y	Z

Fig. 14.5 The 6 × 6 bifid.

Trifid

The Trifid is a sort of cross between the Bifid and fractionated Morse. A keyword or scrambled alphabet, plus the symbol # makes a 27-letter sequence. To these are assigned the 27 different combinations of the digits 1, 2, and 3, taken three at a time, as follows:

M	A	G	N	E	T	I	C	B	D	F	H	J	K	L	O	P	Q	R	S	U	V	W	X	Y	Z	#
1	1	1	1	1	1	1	1	1	2	2	2	2	2	2	2	2	2	3	3	3	3	3	3	3	3	3
1	1	1	2	2	2	3	3	3	1	1	1	2	2	2	3	3	3	1	1	1	2	2	2	3	3	3
1	2	3	1	2	3	1	2	3	1	2	3	1	2	3	1	2	3	1	2	3	1	2	3	1	2	3

The plaintext is divided into groups of P letters where P is the period. The three-digit equivalences are written beneath the plaintext and then three digits are read off horizontally (within a group), looked up in the alphabet, and the alphabetic symbol that corresponds to the triplet is read out as ciphertext. With a period of 5, we get

n	o	w	i	s
1	2	3	1	3
2	3	2	3	1
1	1	2	1	2

and the intermediate text becomes 123, 132, 323, 111, 212, producing TCXMF.

Tri-Square

The tri-square cipher expands the plaintext by 50 percent, since each plaintext pair becomes a ciphertext triple. Three keyed squares are used in positions 2, 3, and 4 of the four-square cipher as shown in Fig. 14.6.

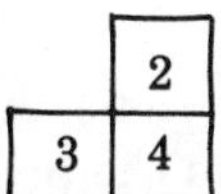

Fig. 14.6 Tri-square cipher.

The first letter of the plaintext pair is located in square 3 and the second in square 2. The first letter of the ciphertext triple may be any of the letters in the same column as the first plaintext letter in square 3. The middle of the ciphertext triple is the letter in square 4 at the intersection of the two plaintext letters, projected right from square 3 and down from square 2. The last of the triple is any letter from the row of the second plaintext letter in square 2. The tri-square is shown in Fig. 14.7.

Morbit

The Morbit cipher is very similar to Fractionated Morse. The plaintext is written in Morse code with x between letters and xx be-

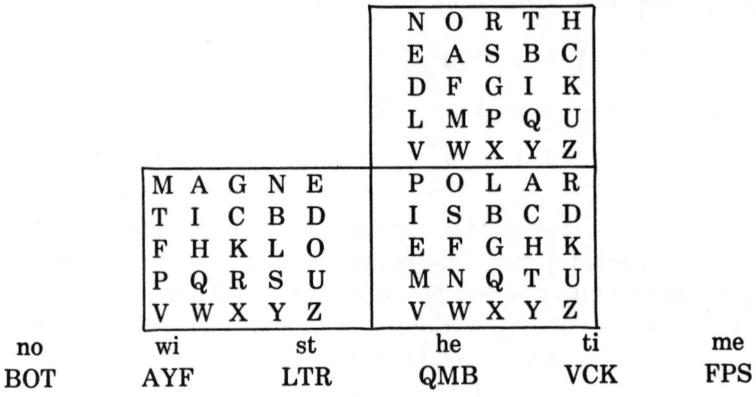

```
                      N O R T H
                      E A S B C
                      D F G I K
                      L M P Q U
                      V W X Y Z
          M A G N E   P O L A R
          T I C B D   I S B C D
          F H K L O   E F G H K
          P Q R S U   M N Q T U
          V W X Y Z   V W X Y Z
 no       wi     st    he     ti     me
 BOT      AYF    LTR   QMB    VCK    FPS
```

Fig. 14.7 The tri-square cipher.

tween words. Symbols are taken off in pairs and looked up against a key number-sequence derived from a nine-letter keyword, as follows:

```
Q U I L T I N G S
6 9 2 4 8 3 5 1 7
• • • – – – x x x
• – x • – x • – x
```

```
Plaintext:            n   o   w   i   s
Intermediate text:  –• x–––x•––xx•• x•••xx
Ciphertext:           4  1 8 5 8  7 6 5 6 7
```

Many other ciphers, both substitution and transposition, may be found, but if you have followed the text this far, you should probably join the ACA anyway, and one of the things they will send you is a pamphlet called "ACA and YOU" that details the ciphers normally found in *The Cryptogram.* Their current address (as of August 1980) for subscriptions is

American Cryptogram Association
1007 Montrose Avenue
Laurel, Maryland 20810

Failing that, try the publisher at

American Cryptogram Association
325 Carol Drive
Ventura, California 93003

May you have many happy hours wearing out pencils, erasers, and your computer, but never, oh never, your patience.

Appendix A
Letter Frequency per 10,000 Letters

Alphabetically		*By frequency*	
A:	805	E:	1250
B:	153	T:	925
C:	310	A:	805
D:	397	O:	760
E:	1250	I:	729
F:	231	N:	710
G:	195	S:	655
H:	542	R:	613
I:	729	H:	542
J:	16	L:	414
K:	66	D:	397
L:	414	C:	310
M:	254	U:	272
N:	710	M:	257
O:	760	F:	231
P:	202	P:	202
Q:	11	G:	195
R:	613	W:	188
S:	655	Y:	172
T:	925	B:	153
U:	272	V:	100
V:	100	K:	66
W:	188	X:	20
X:	20	J:	16
Y:	172	Q:	11
Z:	10	Z:	10
	10,000		

Appendix B
Terminal and Initial Letters

Terminal Letters

Percentage of all words ending in a given letter:

E: 20.2
S: 12.9
D: 10.5
T: 9.4
N: 8.8
R: 5.9
Y: 5.9 (increasingly in longer words)
O: 4.2 (mostly in two-letter words)

Initial Letters

Percentage of all words beginning with a given letter:

T: 15.9
A: 11.5 (mostly in three-letter words)
O: 7.2
S: 7.0
I: 6.8
W: 6.1
H: 5.4
C: 4.9 (increasingly in longer words)
B: 4.6

Appendix C (Opposite)
Frequency of English Digrams Without Regard to Word Boundaries

(Occurences per 10,000 Letters of Text)

Second letter of digram

First Letter of Digram	A	B	C	D	E	F	G	H	I	J	K	L	M	N	O	P	Q	R	S	T	U	V	W	X	Y	Z	
A	2	20	41	37	1	10	19	3	29	1	10	82	27	156	1	19	0	87	82	117	9	18	9	2	21	1	A
B	14	1	0	0	47	0	0	0	8	1	0	19	0	0	18	0	0	9	3	1	17	0	0	0	12	0	B
C	42	1	6	1	48	1	0	46	20	0	13	12	1	0	60	1	0	12	3	31	10	0	0	0	3	0	C
D	37	16	8	10	64	10	6	14	53	2	1	8	9	8	30	7	1	13	25	41	13	2	13	0	7	0	D
E	98	20	60	115	45	32	18	23	40	3	5	54	47	121	36	35	5	175	134	81	8	24	39	15	17	1	E
F	22	2	5	2	20	14	2	5	26	1	0	7	4	2	42	4	0	19	6	36	8	1	3	0	2	0	F
G	21	3	2	2	31	3	3	25	17	0	0	6	3	6	17	2	0	17	8	16	7	0	3	0	2	0	G
H	88	2	3	1	261	2	1	4	72	0	0	2	3	3	45	2	0	8	5	23	7	0	4	0	4	0	H
I	19	7	52	28	28	16	22	2	0	0	5	37	28	189	55	7	1	26	89	89	10	20	2	2	0	5	I
J	2	0	0	0	4	0	0	0	0	0	0	0	0	0	46	0	0	0	0	0	5	0	0	0	0	0	J
K	5	1	1	0	22	1	0	2	10	0	0	2	1	5	3	1	0	1	5	3	0	0	2	0	1	0	K
L	47	5	5	27	70	8	2	3	53	0	3	52	5	2	36	6	0	3	16	16	11	3	4	0	37	0	L
M	49	9	2	1	64	2	0	2	28	0	0	1	8	1	30	17	0	4	10	8	10	0	2	0	5	0	M
N	49	8	37	108	64	11	83	11	40	2	5	9	8	10	51	6	1	5	48	121	8	4	11	0	10	0	N
O	14	14	17	19	6	86	9	8	10	1	7	31	48	132	26	21	0	101	30	49	78	16	32	1	4	0	O
P	26	1	0	0	37	1	0	7	12	0	0	20	2	0	28	11	0	33	5	9	8	0	1	0	1	0	P
Q	0	0	0	0	0	0	0	0	0	0	0	0	0	0	0	0	0	0	0	0	11	0	0	0	0	0	Q
R	65	7	15	19	146	7	9	9	60	1	8	11	18	15	66	9	0	12	43	48	11	6	8	0	19	0	R
S	62	12	23	8	74	13	4	40	63	1	5	11	15	10	57	24	1	7	47	124	25	2	21	0	5	0	S
T	62	9	11	6	95	8	3	297	111	1	1	14	10	4	105	6	0	35	38	50	20	1	21	0	18	0	T
U	10	7	14	8	11	2	12	1	8	0	0	28	10	33	1	12	0	40	37	36	0	0	1	0	1	0	U
V	9	0	0	0	65	0	0	0	19	0	0	0	0	0	5	4	0	0	0	0	0	0	0	0	0	0	V
W	42	1	1	1	31	1	0	33	33	0	0	2	1	8	21	1	0	3	4	3	0	0	1	0	1	0	W
X	2	0	2	0	1	0	0	0	2	0	0	0	0	0	1	5	0	0	0	3	0	0	0	0	0	0	X
Y	17	7	7	5	12	6	2	7	12	1	1	4	7	3	23	6	0	4	17	19	1	1	9	0	1	0	Y
Z	2	0	0	0	4	0	0	0	1	0	0	1	0	0	0	0	0	0	0	0	0	0	0	0	0	1	Z
	A	B	C	D	E	F	G	H	I	J	K	L	M	N	O	P	Q	R	S	T	U	V	W	X	Y	Z	

Note: This table is based on the Brown tape which contains 4,743,925 letters. If the text contains "THE MAN," we will count a TH, an HE, an EM, etc. The frequency of QU per 10,000 letters is 11. The frequency of UQ is 0, rounding may have caused the totals in columns and rows to differ from each other and from the letter frequency given elsewhere.

Appendix D Frequency of Digrams Not Crossing Word Boundaries

(Occurrences per 10,000 Digrams)

Second letter of digram (columns); First Letter of Digram (rows)

	A	B	C	D	E	F	G	H	I	J	K	L	M	N	O	P	Q	R	S	T	U	V	W	X	Y	Z	
A	0	22	44	44	1	7	20	1	36	1	12	100	27	196	1	18	0	107	94	143	11	21	7	2	26	2	**A**
B	17	2	0	0	60	0	0	0	10	2	0	24	0	0	22	0	0	11	4	1	22	1	0	0	16	0	**B**
C	51	0	7	0	61	0	0	58	24	0	17	15	0	0	75	0	0	14	2	38	13	0	0	0	3	0	**C**
D	16	0	0	5	74	0	3	0	45	1	0	4	2	3	21	0	0	10	13	0	12	2	1	0	6	0	**D**
E	73	2	42	126	42	15	11	2	17	0	3	54	36	140	6	17	4	204	124	43	2	26	13	19	17	1	**E**
F	17	0	0	0	23	14	0	0	28	0	0	7	0	0	50	0	0	21	0	8	10	0	0	0	1	0	**F**
G	15	0	0	0	37	0	3	27	15	0	0	6	1	6	15	0	0	20	5	2	8	0	0	0	2	0	**G**
H	101	1	0	0	330	0	0	0	87	0	0	1	1	3	53	0	0	9	2	16	8	0	1	0	5	0	**H**
I	23	9	65	34	36	19	27	0	0	0	6	47	34	240	69	9	1	32	111	111	1	26	0	2	0	6	**I**
J	3	0	0	0	4	0	0	0	0	0	0	0	0	0	6	0	0	0	0	0	7	0	0	0	0	0	**J**
K	2	0	0	0	28	0	0	0	11	0	0	1	0	6	1	0	0	0	5	0	0	0	0	0	1	0	**K**
L	50	1	1	31	86	6	1	0	62	0	3	64	3	1	39	2	0	1	13	11	13	3	1	0	47	0	**L**
M	56	9	0	0	80	0	0	0	32	0	0	0	9	1	35	21	0	4	10	0	13	0	0	0	6	0	**M**
N	30	0	38	131	74	5	103	1	34	1	6	7	2	10	46	1	1	1	48	101	8	4	1	0	11	0	**N**
O	8	10	15	19	5	106	8	2	9	1	8	36	55	165	28	22	0	124	29	43	98	19	36	1	4	1	**O**
P	30	0	0	0	47	0	0	8	14	0	0	26	2	0	33	14	0	41	5	8	10	0	0	0	1	0	**P**
Q	0	0	0	0	0	0	0	0	0	0	0	0	0	0	0	0	0	0	0	0	13	0	0	0	0	0	**Q**
R	63	3	10	19	180	3	9	2	67	0	10	10	16	17	73	4	0	11	44	35	13	6	1	0	23	0	**R**
S	24	1	14	1	86	1	0	36	53	0	5	7	7	2	39	19	1	0	39	111	28	0	3	0	5	0	**S**
T	51	0	4	0	116	1	0	361	116	0	0	12	3	1	110	0	0	39	34	20	23	0	8	0	20	0	**T**
U	12	9	17	9	13	2	15	0	10	0	0	35	13	42	1	15	0	51	45	44	0	0	0	0	1	0	**U**
V	12	0	0	0	82	0	0	0	24	0	0	0	0	0	6	0	0	0	0	0	0	0	0	0	1	0	**V**
W	50	0	0	1	38	0	0	40	40	0	0	1	0	10	25	0	0	3	32	1	0	0	0	0	0	0	**W**
X	2	0	2	0	2	0	0	0	3	0	0	0	0	0	0	7	0	0	0	4	0	0	0	0	0	0	**X**
Y	2	1	1	1	12	0	0	0	3	0	0	1	2	1	17	2	0	1	11	2	0	0	1	0	0	0	**Y**
Z	2	0	0	0	5	0	0	0	1	0	0	0	0	0	1	0	0	0	0	0	0	0	0	0	0	1	**Z**
	A	B	C	D	E	F	G	H	I	J	K	L	M	N	O	P	Q	R	S	T	U	V	W	X	Y	Z	

Note: This table is taken from the Brown sample tape of 1,012,801 words containing 4,743,92 letters, giving 3,731,124 noncrossing digrams. If the text contain "THE MAN" we will count TH, an HE, an MA, an AN, and so on. We don't count EM because of the space between letter

Appendix E
Top 1000 Words from Brown Corpus

70008 THE
36475 OF
28937 AND
26245 TO
23530 A
21422 IN
10597 THAT
10100 IS
9816 WAS
9542 HE
9500 FOR
8769 IT
7291 WITH
7258 AS
7000 HIS
6767 ON
6391 BE
5383 AT
5347 BY
5253 I
5146 THIS
5133 HAD
4620 NOT
4394 ARE
4382 BUT
4371 FROM
4227 OR
3941 HAVE
3750 AN
3619 THEY
3562 WHICH
3439 ONE
3347 WERE
3292 YOU
3094 ALL
3037 HER
2859 SHE
2724 THERE
2719 WOULD
2670 THEIR
2653 WE
2619 HIM
2472 BEEN
2439 HAS
2331 WHEN
2252 WHO
2250 WILL
2219 NO
2218 MORE
2201 IF
2164 OUT
2160 ITS
2029 SO
1975 UP
1961 SAID
1910 WHAT
1817 ABOUT
1795 THAN
1791 INTO
1789 THEM
1773 CAN
1747 ONLY
1706 OTHER
1694 TIME
1646 NEW
1617 SOME
1599 COULD
1573 THESE
1516 TWO
1400 MAY
1388 FIRST
1377 THEN
1375 DO
1345 ANY
1339 LIKE
1321 MY
1317 NOW
1307 OVER
1303 SUCH
1253 OUR
1238 MAN
1185 ME
1174 EVEN
1162 MOST
1147 MADE
1077 AFTER
1069 ALSO
1069 WELL
1044 DID
1037 MANY
1016 BEFORE
1013 MUST
1002 YEARS
977 BACK
972 THROUGH
943 MUCH
939 WHERE
925 YOUR
924 WAY

923 DOWN
888 SHOULD
883 BECAUSE
880 LONG
876 EACH
872 JUST
862 STATE
851 PEOPLE
850 THOSE
840 TOO
839 HOW
839 MR
834 LITTLE
832 GOOD
816 WORLD
805 MAKE
797 VERY
793 YEAR
785 STILL
775 SEE
773 OWN
772 WORK
769 MEN
760 DAY
753 GET
750 HERE
747 OLD
730 BETWEEN
730 BOTH
730 LIFE
721 BEING
717 UNDER
704 THREE
700 NEVER
689 KNOW
686 SAME
684 LAST
683 ANOTHER
681 WHILE
678 US
674 OFF
672 MIGHT
670 GREAT
652 STATES
633 GO
632 COME
629 SINCE
627 AGAINST
626 RIGHT
622 CAME
620 TAKE
613 USED
603 HIMSELF
601 FEW
601 HOUSE
598 AMERICAN
594 USE
589 PLACE
585 DURING
583 HIGH
583 WITHOUT
580 AGAIN
566 HOME
564 AROUND
554 SMALL
552 HOWEVER
539 FOUND
537 MRS
532 PART
515 SCHOOL
515 THOUGHT
507 WENT
506 SAY
505 GENERAL
505 ONCE
497 UPON
492 EVERY
492 LEFT
492 WAR
490 DONT
485 DOES
482 GOT
482 UNITED
472 NUMBER
470 HAND
465 COURSE
465 S
462 WATER
461 UNTIL
459 ALWAYS
459 AWAY
456 PUBLIC
451 SOMETHING
447 FACT
446 LESS
442 THROUGH
440 FAR
438 PUT
436 HEAD
434 THINK
433 CALLED
433 SET
432 ALMOST
431 ENOUGH
428 END
426 TOOK
425 GOVERNMENT
424 NIGHT
420 YET
419 SYSTEM
417 BETTER
417 FOUR
414 NOTHING
413 TOLD
408 EYES
407 CITY
406 GOING
404 PRESIDENT
404 WHY
403 DAYS
403 PRESENT
402 POINT
401 DIDNT
401 LOOK
399 FIND
398 ASKED
398 SECOND
397 GROUP
397 LATER
397 NEXT
397 ROOM
397 SOCIAL
395 BUSINESS
395 KNEW
394 PROGRAM

393 GIVE
392 HALF
391 SIDE
386 FACE
386 TOWARD
386 WHITE
385 FIVE
385 LET
385 YOUNG
383 FORM
380 GIVEN
380 PER
379 ORDER
378 LARGE
377 SEVERAL
376 NATIONAL
375 IMPORTANT
373 POSSIBLE
373 RATHER
371 BIG
370 AMONG
370 CASE
369 OFTEN
368 EARLY
368 JOHN
368 THINGS
367 C
367 LOOKED
366 EVER
361 BECOME
361 BEST
360 NEED
359 WITHIN
357 FELT
355 ALONG
355 CHILDREN
353 SAW
351 CHURCH
351 LIGHT
350 POWER
343 LEAST
339 FAMILY
334 DEVELOPMENT
334 INTEREST
334 OTHERS
333 OPEN
333 THING
332 SEEMED
330 WANT
329 AREA
329 U
328 GOD
327 MEMBERS
327 MIND
326 HELP
325 COUNTRY
323 SERVICE
322 TURNED
321 DOOR
320 DONE
320 LAW
319 ALTHOUGH
318 WHOLE
316 LINE
315 PROBLEM
314 SENSE
313 CERTAIN
313 DIFFERENT
313 KIND
312 BEGAN
312 THUS
310 MEANS
309 MATTER
307 PERHAPS
306 NAME
306 TIMES
306 YORK
305 ITSELF
302 ACTION
302 HUMAN
301 ABOVE
298 WEEK
293 COMPANY
293 FREE
292 EXAMPLE
292 HANDS
291 LOCAL
291 SHOW
290 HISTORY
286 WHETHER
285 ACT
285 EITHER
285 GAVE
284 DEATH
284 FEET
284 TODAY
283 ACROSS
283 BODY
283 PAST
282 QUITE
281 TAKEN
280 ANYTHING
279 FIELD
279 HAVING
279 SEEN
279 WORD
278 CAR
276 EXPERIENCE
275 IM
275 MONEY
275 REALLY
274 CLASS
274 WORDS
273 ALREADY
271 COLLEGE
271 INFORMATION
271 TELL
270 B
270 MAKING
270 SURE
270 THEMSELVES
270 TOGETHER
269 FULL
268 AIR
268 SHALL
266 HELD
266 KNOWN
265 PERIOD
264 KEEP
264 POLITICAL
263 REAL
262 MISS
261 PROBABLY
259 CENTURY
259 QUESTION

259 SEEMS
258 BEHIND
258 CANNOT
256 MAJOR
256 OFFICE
253 BROUGHT
252 SPECIAL
252 WHOSE
251 BOY
251 COST
251 FEDERAL
249 ECONOMIC
249 SELF
249 SOUTH
248 PROBLEMS
247 HEARD
247 SIX
247 STUDY
246 AGO
246 BECAME
246 MOMENT
246 RUN
245 AVAILABLE
245 JOB
245 M
245 STREET
244 RESULT
244 SHORT
244 WEST
242 AGE
242 CHANGE
242 P
242 POSITION
241 BOARD
241 INDIVIDUAL
241 REASON
240 TURN
239 CLOSE
238 AREAS
237 AM
237 LOVE
237 SOCIETY
236 LEVEL
234 COURT
233 CONTROL
233 TRUE
232 COMMUNITY
232 FORCE
232 ILL
232 TYPE
231 FRONT
231 WIFE
229 CENTER
229 FUTURE
229 HARD
229 POLICY
229 SEEM
228 CLEAR
227 TOWN
226 VOICE
226 WANTED
226 WOMAN
225 COMMON
225 DEPARTMENT
225 GIRL
224 BLACK
224 PARTY
223 LAND
223 NECESSARY
223 SURFACE
223 TOP
222 FOLLOWING
222 RATE
222 SOMETIMES
222 TAX
221 E
221 MOTHER
221 MUSIC
220 STUDENTS
219 LOW
219 MILITARY
218 CHILD
218 FURTHER
218 THIRD
217 RED
217 UNIVERSITY
216 ABLE
216 EDUCATION
216 FEEL
216 PROVIDE
215 EFFECT
214 MORNING
214 NATIONS
213 TOTAL
212 NEAR
212 ROAD
212 STOOD
211 ART
210 D
210 FIGURE
210 OUTSIDE
209 NORTH
208 MILLION
208 WASHINGTON
207 LEAVE
207 VALUE
206 CUT
206 USUALLY
205 FIRE
205 PLAN
205 PLAY
205 SOUND
205 THEREFORE
204 ENGLISH
204 EVIDENCE
204 TABLE
203 BOOK
203 STRONG
202 RANGE
201 BELIEVE
201 LIVING
201 PEACE
201 VARIOUS
200 MEAN
200 MODERN
200 SAYS
200 SOON
198 LINES
198 LOOKING
198 SCHOOLS
198 SINGLE
197 ALONE
197 LONGER
197 MINUTES
197 PERSONAL

197 PROCESS
197 SECRETARY
196 GONE
196 IDEA
196 MONTHS
196 SITUATION
196 WOMEN
195 INCREASE
195 NOR
195 SECTION
194 AMERICA
194 PRESSURE
194 PRIVATE
194 STARTED
193 DARK
193 GROUND
192 DR
192 EAST
192 NATURE
192 STAGE
191 FINALLY
190 KEPT
189 CALL
189 FATHER
189 NEEDED
189 VALUES
188 GREATER
187 EXPECTED
187 VIEW
186 THATS
185 EVERYTHING
185 SPACE
185 TEN
185 UNION
184 BASIS
184 SPIRIT
183 BROWN
182 REQUIRED
182 TAKING
181 COMPLETE
181 CONDITIONS
181 EXCEPT
181 HUNDRED
181 LATE
181 MOVED
181 ONES
181 WROTE
180 HOURS
180 RETURN
180 SUPPORT
179 ATTENTION
179 HOUR
179 LIVE
179 PARTICULAR
179 RECENT
179 TH
178 DATA
178 HOPE
178 PERSON
177 BEYOND
177 COMING
177 DEAD
177 MIDDLE
177 N
177 ST
176 COLD
176 COSTS
176 ELSE
176 FORCES
176 HEART
176 MATERIAL
175 COULDNT
175 DEVELOPED
175 FEELING
175 FINE
175 STORY
174 INSIDE
174 LOST
174 READ
174 REPORT
174 RESEARCH
174 TWENTY
173 INDUSTRY
173 INSTEAD
173 MILES
173 SON
173 WALL
172 ADDED
172 AMOUNT
172 FOLLOWED
172 H
172 MAKES
172 MOVE
172 PAY
171 BASIC
171 CANT
171 INCLUDING
170 BUILDING
170 DEFENSE
170 HOLD
170 REACHED
170 SIMPLY
170 TRIED
169 CENTRAL
169 WIDE
168 COMMITTEE
168 EQUIPMENT
168 PICTURE
167 ISLAND
167 SIMPLE
166 ACTUALLY
166 CARE
166 RELIGIOUS
166 SHOWN
165 FRIENDS
165 RIVER
164 BEGINNING
164 GETTING
164 HIGHER
164 MEDICAL
164 RECEIVED
164 REST
164 SORT
163 BOYS
163 DOING
163 FLOOR
163 FOREIGN
163 TERMS
163 TRYING
162 INDEED
161 ADMINISTRATION
161 CENT
161 DIFFICULT
161 F
161 SUBJECT

160 ESPECIALLY
160 MEETING
159 EARTH
159 MARKET
159 PAPER
159 PASSED
159 WALKED
158 BLUE
158 BRING
158 COUNTY
158 LABOR
157 HALL
157 NATURAL
157 POLICE
157 SIMILAR
157 TRAINING
156 ENGLAND
156 FINAL
156 GROWTH
156 INTERNATIONAL
156 PROPERTY
156 TALK
156 WORKING
156 WRITTEN
155 CONGRESS
154 FOOD
154 GIRLS
154 NON
154 START
154 WASNT
153 ANSWER
153 HEAR
153 ISSUE
153 PURPOSE
153 SUDDENLY
153 WEEKS
153 WESTERN
152 NEEDS
152 STAND
152 YOURE
151 CONSIDERED
151 COUNTRIES
151 FALL
151 HAIR
151 LIKELY
151 NATION
150 LAY
150 SAT
149 CASES
149 COLOR
149 ENTIRE
149 FRENCH
149 HAPPENED
149 PAID
149 PRODUCTION
149 READY
149 RESULTS
149 SQUARE
148 DIFFERENCE
148 EARLIER
148 INVOLVED
148 MEET
148 STEP
148 STOCK
148 THINKING
148 WILLIAM
147 CHRISTIAN
147 CLUB
147 G
147 LETTER
146 AID
146 ANTI
146 INCREASED
146 LOT
146 MONTH
146 PARTICULARLY
146 R
146 WHOM
145 BELOW
145 EFFORT
145 KNOWLEDGE
145 LOWER
145 POINTS
145 SENT
145 TRADE
145 USING
144 INDUSTRIAL
144 SIZE
144 YES
143 BAD
143 BILL
143 CERTAINLY
143 EYE
143 IDEAS
143 T
143 TEMPERATURE
142 ADDITION
142 DEAL
142 DUE
142 METHOD
142 METHODS
142 MORAL
142 READING
141 DECIDED
141 DIRECTLY
141 KENNEDY
141 NEARLY
141 NEITHER
141 QUESTIONS
141 RECORD
141 SHOWED
141 STATEMENTS
141 THROUGHOUT
140 ANYONE
140 J
140 PROGRAMS
140 TRY
139 ACCORDING
139 MEMBER
139 PHYSICAL
139 SCIENCE
139 SERVICES
139 SOUTHERN
138 HOT
138 REMEMBER
138 SOVIET
138 STRENGTH
137 COMES
137 NORMAL
137 TROUBLE
137 UNDERSTAND
137 VOLUME
136 POPULATION
136 SUMMER
136 TRIAL

135 APPEARED
135 BED
135 CONCERNED
135 DISTRICT
135 LED
135 MERELY
135 SALES
135 STUDENT
134 DIRECTION
134 FRIEND
134 MAYBE
134 PIECE
134 RAN
133 ARMY
133 BLOOD
133 CONTINUED
133 DE
133 DEGREE
133 DIRECT
133 EVENING
133 GAME
133 GREEN
133 HUSBAND
133 LIST
133 LITERATURE
133 PLANE
132 ASSOCIATION
132 AVERAGE
132 CAUSE
132 GENERALLY
132 GEORGE
132 INFLUENCE
132 MET
132 PROVIDED
132 SEVEN
132 SYSTEMS
131 CHANCE
131 CHANGES
131 EASY
131 FORMER
131 FREEDOM
131 HELL
131 MEANING
131 OPENED
131 SHOT
131 SPRING
131 WAYS
131 WORKS
131 WRONG
130 FEAR
130 ORGANIZATION
130 PLANNING
130 SERIES
130 TERM
130 THEORY
129 ASK
129 EFFECTIVE
129 LEAD
129 MYSELF
129 RESPECT
129 STOPPED
129 WOULDNT
128 CLEARLY
128 EFFORTS
128 FORMS
128 GROUPS
128 MOVEMENT
128 PLANT
128 TRUTH
128 WORKED
127 BASED
127 BEAUTIFUL
127 CONSIDER
127 FARM
127 HORSE
127 HOTEL
127 MANS
127 NOTE
127 PRESS
127 SOMEWHAT
127 TREATMENT
126 ARMS
126 CHARGE
126 PLACED
125 APPARENTLY
125 CARRIED
125 FEED
125 HERSELF
125 HES
125 HIT
125 IVE
125 LENGTH
125 NUMBERS
125 OPERATION
125 PERSONS
125 RADIO
125 REACTION
124 BORN
124 MANNER
124 OH
124 RECENTLY
124 RUNNING
123 APPROACH
123 CHIEF
123 DEEP
123 EIGHT
123 IMMEDIATELY
123 LARGER
123 PERFORMANCE
123 PRICE
123 SUN
122 COUPLE
122 DAILY
122 GUN
122 LIVED
122 MAIN
122 STOP
122 STRAIGHT
121 HEAVY
121 IMAGE
121 L
121 MARCH
121 OPPORTUNITY
121 TECHNICAL
121 TEST
121 UNDERSTANDING
121 WRITING
120 ADDITIONAL
120 BRITISH
120 DECISION
120 DESCRIBED
120 DETERMINED
120 EUROPE
120 FISCAL
120 NEGRO

120 PROGRESS
120 SERVED
120 WINDOW
119 CARS
119 CHARACTER
119 QUALITY
119 RELIGION
119 REPORTED
119 RESPONSIBILITY
119 STEPS
118 APPEAR
118 SERIOUS
117 ACCOUNT
117 BALL
117 COMMUNIST
117 CORNER
117 DESIGN
117 LEARNED
117 MOVING
117 POST
116 ACTIVITY
116 FORWARD
116 PATTERN
116 POOL
116 POOR
116 SLOWLY
116 SPECIFIC
116 STAFF
116 TYPES
115 ACTIVITIES
115 AUDIENCE
115 CHOICE
115 FILLED
115 GROWING
115 JUSTICE
115 LATTER
115 LETTERS
115 NUCLEAR
115 OBTAINED
115 RETURNED
114 DEMOCRATIC
114 DOUBT
114 OBVIOUSLY
114 PARTS
114 PLANS
114 THIRTY
113 ESTABLISHED
113 FIGURES
113 FOOT
113 FUNCTION
113 INCLUDE
113 LEADERS
113 MASS
113 SAYING
113 STANDARD
113 STAY
112 ATTACK
112 CLOSED
112 CO
112 DRIVE
112 GIVES
112 SPEAK
112 WAITING
112 WHATEVER
111 COMPLETELY
111 COVERED
111 FAITH
111 HOSPITAL
111 LANGUAGE
111 RACE
111 SEASON
111 WISH
110 BUILT
110 DESIGNED
110 DISTANCE
110 EFFECTS
110 EXTENT
110 GLASS
110 INCOME
110 LACK
110 PRODUCTS
109 AHEAD
109 ANALYSIS
109 CORPS
109 ELEMENTS
109 EXISTENCE
109 EXPECT
109 FIRM
109 MARRIED
109 PRINCIPLE
109 THERES

Appendix F
Most Common Words by Length from Brown Corpus

This Appendix includes words appearing one hundred or more times in the Brown corpus in order of frequency for each length (for a total of 1060 words). Read across each row.

Number of words

One-letter words

2	A	I

Two-letter words

	OF	TO	IN	IS	HE	IT	AS	ON	BE	AT	BY	OR	AN
24	WE	NO	IF	SO	UP	DO	MY	ME	MR	US	GO		

Three-letter words

	THE	AND	WAS	FOR	HIS	HAD	NOT	ARE	BUT	ONE	YOU
	ALL	HER	SHE	HIM	HAS	WHO	OUT	ITS	CAN	NEW	TWO
	MAY	ANY	NOW	OUR	MAN	DID	WAY	TOO	HOW	SEE	OWN
	MEN	DAY	GET	OLD	OFF	FEW	USE	MRS	SAY	WAS	GOT
	FAR	PUT	SET	END	YET	WHY	LET	PER	BIG	SAW	GOD
	LAW	ACT	CAR	AIR	BOY	SIX	AGO	RUN	JOB	AGE	ILL
	TOP	TAX	LOW	RED	ART	CUT	NOR	TEN	SON	PAY	NOW
	LAY	SAT	AID	LOT	YES	BAD	EYE	DUE	TRY	HOT	BED
	LED	RAN	MET	ASK	HES	HIT	IVE	SUN	GUN	ARM	SEA
102	BIT	OIL	GAS								

Four-letter words

```
    THAT WITH THIS FROM HAVE THEY WERE BEEN WHEN WILL
    MORE SAID WHAT THAN INTO THEM ONLY TIME SOME THEN
    LIKE OVER SUCH EVEN MOST MADE ALSO WELL MANY MUST
    BACK MUCH YOUR DOWN LONG EACH JUST GOOD MAKE VERY
    YEAR WORK HERE BOTH LIFE KNOW SAME LAST COME CAME
    TAKE USED HIGH HOME PART WENT ONCE UPON LEFT DONT
    DOES HAND AWAY FACT LESS HEAD TOOK FOUR TOLD EYES
    CITY DAYS LOOK FIND NEXT ROOM KNEW GIVE HALF SIDE
    FACE FIVE FORM CASE JOHN EVER BEST NEED FELT OPEN
    WANT AREA MIND HELP DOOR DONE LINE KIND THUS NAME
    YORK WEEK FREE SHOW GAVE FEET BODY PAST SEEN WORD
    TELL SURE FULL HELD KEEP REAL MISS COST SELF WEST
    TURN LOVE TRUE TYPE WIFE HARD SEEN TOWN GIRL LAND
    RATE ABLE FEEL NEAR ROAD FIRE PLAN PLAY BOOK MEAN
    SAYS SOON GONE IDEA DARK EAST KEPT CALL VIEW LATE
    ONES HOUR LIVE DATA HOPE DEAD COLD ELSE FINE LOST
    READ WALL MOVE CANT HOLD WIDE CARE BEST SORT BOYS
    CENT BLUE HALL TALK FOOD HEAR FALL HAIR PAID MEET
    STEP CLUB ANTI WHOM SENT SIZE BILL DEAL ARMY GAME
    LIST EASY HELL SHOT WAYS FEAR TERM LEAD FARM MANS
    NOTE ARMS FEED BORN DEEP MAIN STOP TEST CARS BALL
    POST POOL POOR FOOT MASS STAY RACE WISH LACK FIRM
    NONE ROLE WONT DATE JAZZ NEWS UNIT CLAY JUNE NINE
234 RISE WALK HEAT POET
```

Five-letter words

	WHICH	THERE	WOULD	THEIR	ABOUT	OTHER	COULD	THESE	FIRST
	AFTER	YEARS	WHERE	STATE	THOSE	WORLD	STILL	BEING	UNDER
	THREE	NEVER	WHILE	MIGHT	GREAT	SINCE	RIGHT	HOUSE	PLACE
	AGAIN	SMALL	FOUND	EVERY	WATER	UNTIL	THINK	NIGHT	GOING
	POINT	DIDNT	ASKED	GROUP	LATER	WHITE	YOUNG	GIVEN	ORDER
	LARGE	AMONG	OFTEN	EARLY	ALONG	LIGHT	POWER	LEAST	THING
	WHOLE	SENSE	BEGAN	MEANS	TIMES	HUMAN	ABOVE	HANDS	LOCAL
	DEATH	TODAY	QUITE	TAKEN	FIELD	MONEY	CLASS	WORDS	SHALL
	KNOWN	SEEMS	MAJOR	WHOSE	SOUTH	HEARD	STUDY	SHORT	BOARD
	CLOSE	AREAS	LEVEL	COURT	FORCE	FRONT	CLEAR	VOICE	WOMAN
	BLACK	PARTY	MUSIC	CHILD	THIRD	TOTAL	STOOD	NORTH	LEAVE
	VALUE	SOUND	TABLE	RANGE	PEACE	LINES	ALONE	WOMEN	STAGE
	THATS	SPACE	UNION	BASIS	BROWN	MOVED	WROTE	HOURS	COSTS
	HEART	STORY	MILES	ADDED	MAKES	BASIC	TRIED	SHOWN	RIVER
	DOING	FLOOR	TERMS	EARTH	PAPER	BRING	LABOR	FINAL	GIRLS
	START	WASNT	ISSUE	WEEKS	NEEDS	STAND	YOURE	CASES	COLOR
	READY	STOCK	MONTH	BELOW	LOWER	TRACE	USING	IDEAS	MORAL
	COMES	TRIAL	SALES	MAYBE	PIECE	BLOOD	GREEN	PLANE	CAUSE
	SEVEN	WORKS	WRONG	FORMS	PLANT	TRUTH	BASED	HORSE	HOTEL
	PRESS	RADIO	CHIEF	EIGHT	PRICE	DAILY	LIVED	HEAVY	IMAGE
	MARCH	NEGRO	STEPS	STAFF	TYPES	DOUBT	PARTS	PLANS	DRIVE
	GIVES	SPEAK	FAITH	BUILT	GLASS	AHEAD	CORPS	VISIT	SCENE
	SERVE	REACH	MOUTH	WRITE	RHODE	SPENT	STYLE	HAPPY	RATES
216	TEETH	JAMES	ROUND	SIDES	TREES	BOOKS	KNOWS	MEANT	SHARE

Six-letter words

BEFORE SHOULD PEOPLE LITTLE STATES DURING AROUND SCHOOL
UNITED NUMBER COURSE ALWAYS PUBLIC THOUGH CALLED ALMOST
ENOUGH SYSTEM BETTER SECOND SOCIAL TOWARD RATHER THINGS
LOOKED BECOME WITHIN CHURCH FAMILY OTHERS SEEMED TURNED
MATTER ITSELF ACTION EITHER ACROSS HAVING REALLY MAKING
PERIOD BEHIND CANNOT OFFICE BECAME MOMENT STREET RESULT
CHANGE REASON CENTER FUTURE POLICY WANTED COMMON MOTHER
EFFECT FIGURE STRONG LIVING MODERN SINGLE LONGER MONTHS
GROUND NATURE FATHER NEEDED VALUES SPIRIT TAKING EXCEPT
RETURN RECENT PERSON BEYOND COMING MIDDLE FORCES INSIDE
REPORT TWENTY AMOUNT SIMPLY ISLAND SIMPLE HIGHER TRYING
INDEED MARKET PASSED WALKED COUNTY POLICE GROWTH ANSWER
LIKELY NATION ENTIRE FRENCH SQUARE LETTER EFFORT POINTS
METHOD NEARLY RECORD SHOWED ANYONE MEMBER SOVIET NORMAL
VOLUME SUMMER MERELY FRIEND DEGREE DIRECT GEORGE CHANCE
FORMER OPENED SPRING SERIES THEORY MYSELF GROUPS WORKED
CHARGE PLACED LENGTH MANNER LARGER COUPLE EUROPE FISCAL
SERVED WINDOW APPEAR CORNER DESIGN MOVING SLOWLY CHOICE
FILLED LATTER THIRTY SAYING ATTACK CLOSED SEASON EXTENT
INCOME EXPECT THERES PRETTY STRESS CITIES FOLLOW PLAYED
EASILY HARDLY THOMAS HEALTH ENERGY STATUS DEMAND SUNDAY
176 SUPPLY EVENTS RAISED UNLESS WEIGHT ACTUAL DOCTOR PLACES

Seven-letter words

THROUGH BECAUSE BETWEEN ANOTHER AGAINST HIMSELF WITHOUT
HOWEVER THOUGHT GENERAL NOTHING PRESENT PROGRAM SEVERAL
MEMBERS COUNTRY SERVICE PROBLEM CERTAIN PERHAPS COMPANY
EXAMPLE HISTORY WHETHER ALREADY COLLEGE CENTURY BROUGHT
SPECIAL FEDERAL SOCIETY CONTROL SURFACE FURTHER PROVIDE
MORNING NATIONS OUTSIDE MILLION USUALLY ENGLISH BELIEVE
VARIOUS LOOKING SCHOOLS MINUTES PROCESS SECTION AMERICA
PRIVATE STARTED FINALLY GREATER HUNDRED SUPPORT COULDNT
FEELING INSTEAD DEFENSE REACHED CENTRAL PICTURE FRIENDS
GETTING MEDICAL FOREIGN SUBJECT MEETING NATURAL SIMILAR
ENGLAND WORKING WRITTEN PURPOSE WESTERN RESULTS EARLIER
WILLIAM METHODS READING DECIDED KENNEDY NEITHER SCIENCE
TROUBLE STUDENT EVENING HUSBAND AVERAGE SYSTEM CHANGES
FREEDOM MEANING RESPECT STOPPED WOULDNT CLEARLY EFFORTS
CARRIED HERSELF NUMBERS PERSONS RUNNING WRITING BRITISH
QUALITY SERIOUS ACCOUNT LEARNED FORWARD PATTERN GROWING
JUSTICE LETTERS NUCLEAR FIGURES INCLUDE LEADERS WAITING
COVERED EFFECTS MARRIED LIMITED MACHINE APPLIED CURRENT
FACTORS STATION DESPITE CHARLES COUNCIL EXACTLY PLAYING
140 REASONS STUDIES BECOMES RELATED DROPPED OFFICER TALKING

Eight-letter words

AMERICAN BUSINESS NATIONAL POSSIBLE CHILDREN INTEREST ALTHOUGH
ANYTHING TOGETHER PROBABLY QUESTION ECONOMIC PROBLEMS POSITION
STUDENTS MILITARY EVIDENCE PERSONAL INCREASE PRESSURE EXPECTED
REQUIRED COMPLETE MATERIAL RESEARCH INDUSTRY FOLLOWED BUILDING
ACTUALLY RECEIVED TRAINING PROPERTY CONGRESS SUDDENLY HAPPENED
INVOLVED THINKING ADDITION DIRECTLY PROGRAMS PHYSICAL SERVICES
SOUTHERN REMEMBER STRENGTH APPEARED DISTRICT PROVIDED PLANNING
MOVEMENT CONSIDER SOMEWHAT REACTION RECENTLY APPROACH STRAIGHT
DECISION PROGRESS RELIGION REPORTED ACTIVITY SPECIFIC AUDIENCE
OBTAINED RETURNED FUNCTION STANDARD WHATEVER HOSPITAL LANGUAGE
DESIGNED DISTANCE PRODUCTS ANALYSIS ELEMENTS ATTITUDE CONTINUE
DIVISION REMAINED PREPARED DIRECTOR ORIGINAL OFFICERS STANDING
85 THOUSAND

Nine-letter words

	SOMETHING	PRESIDENT	IMPORTANT	DIFFERENT	POLITICAL	AVAILABLE
	COMMUNITY	NECESSARY	FOLLOWING	SOMETIMES	EDUCATION	THEREFORE
	SECRETARY	SITUATION	ATTENTION	DEVELOPED	INCLUDING	COMMITTEE
	EQUIPMENT	RELIGIOUS	BEGINNING	DIFFICULT	COUNTRIES	CHRISTIAN
	INCREASED	KNOWLEDGE	CERTAINLY	QUESTIONS	STATEMENT	ACCORDING
	CONCERNED	DIRECTION	CONTINUED	GENERALLY	INFLUENCE	EFFECTIVE
	BEAUTIFUL	TREATMENT	OPERATION	TECHNICAL	DESCRIBED	CHARACTER
	COMMUNIST	OBVIOUSLY	EXISTENCE	PRINCIPLE	INDICATED	DETERMINE
54	AFTERNOON	AGREEMENT	SUGGESTED	RELATIONS	RADIATION	MATERIALS

Ten-letter words

	GOVERNMENT	EXPERIENCE	THEMSELVES	INDIVIDUAL	DEPARTMENT
	UNIVERSITY	WASHINGTON	EVERYTHING	CONDITIONS	PARTICULAR
	ESPECIALLY	CONSIDERED	PRODUCTION	DIFFERENCE	INDUSTRIAL
	THROUGHOUT	UNDERSTAND	POPULATION	LITERATURE	APPARENTLY
	ADDITIONAL	DETERMINED	ACTIVITIES	DEMOCRATIC	COMPLETELY
29	IMPORTANCE	INTERESTED	COMMISSION	MANAGEMENT	

Appendix G
Pattern Words That Appear Two or More Times in the Brown Corpus

To find the words that have a particular pattern, replace the letters of the pattern with the successive letters of the alphabet, repeating letters as necessary. For example, the word *pattern* gives the key

ABCCDEF

The keys are sorted alphabetically, and below each key may be found the words that match the key. To keep the size of this Appendix down to manageable proportions, many of the less common English words were not included. Moreover, hyphens and apostrophes were deleted.

AA
CC
EE
MM
PP
SS
TT

AAA
AAA
BBB
MMM

AAB
EEG
EEL
MME

ABA
ADA
AIA
ALA
BEB
BIB
BOB
CDC
DAD
DID
EVE
EYE
GAG
HUH
LIL
MOM
NAN
NON
NUN
OSO
PAP
PIP
POP
PUP
SIS
SOS
TAT
TNT

ABB
ADD
ALL
ANN
APP
ASS
ATT
BEE
DOO
EGG
FEE
GEE
HEE
ILL
INN
LEE
MEE
ODD
OFF
PEE
SEE
TEE
TOO
WEE
WOO
YFF
ZOO

AABC
MMES
OOZE

ABAA
LULL
PAPP

ABAB
MAMA
OSOS
PAPA

ABAC
ADAM
ADAS
AFAR
AJAR
ALAN
ALAS
ARAB
AWAY
BABE
BABY
CDCS
COCK
CTCA
DADE
DIDN
DRDW
EDEN
EKED
ELEC
EVEN
EVER
EXEC
EYED
EYES
GAGE
GAGS
GOGH
LILA
LOLA
NINE
NONE
NUNS
ODOR
PIPE
PIPS
POPE
POPS
PUPS
RARE
SASH
SISK
TATE
TITO
TITS
VIVO

ABBA
ALLA
ANNA
ATTA
DEED
ESSE
MAAM
NOON
PEEP
SEES
TOOT
UHHU

ABBC
ABBE
ADDS
ALLY
AMMO
ANNE
ANNS
ASSN
ATTY
BEEF
BEEN
BEEP
BEER
BEES
BOOK
BOOM
BOON
BOOS
BOOT
COOK
COOL
COOP
DEEP
DEER
DOOM
DOOR
EDDY
EGGS
EMMA
FEED
FEEL
FEES
FEET
FOOD
FOOL
FOOT
GOOD
HEED
HEEL
HOOD
HOOF
HOOK
HOOP
HOOT
ILLS
INNA
JEEP
KEEL
KEEN
KEEP
LEES
LOOK
LOOM
LOON
LOOP
LOOT
MEEK
MEET
MOOD
MOON
MOOS
NEED
ODDS
OFFS
PEEL
PEER
POOL
POOR
REED
REEF
REEK
REEL
REES
ROOF
ROOM
ROOS
ROOT
SEED
SEEK
SEEM
SEEN
SEEP
SOON
TEEN
TOOK
TOOL
USSR
VEER
WEEK
WEEP
WOOD
WOOL

ABCA
ALMA
ALVA
ANTA
AREA
ASIA
BLOB
BOMB
BULB
CHIC
DEAD
DIED
DYED
EASE
EDGE
EIRE
ELSE
ERIE
GANG
GREG
HATH
HIGH
HUGH
HUSH
KICK
NEON
OHIO
ONTO
ORDO
OSLO
PIMP
PREP
PROP
PULP
PUMP
REAR
ROAR
SAMS
SANS
SAWS
SAYS
SBAS
SEAS
SETS
SHES
SIMS
SINS
SIRS
SITS
SKYS
SMUS
SOBS
SONS
SUBS
SUDS
SUMS
SUNS
TACT
TAFT
TART
TAUT
TENT
TEST
TEXT
THAT
THET
TILT
TROT

ABCB
ASKS
BEDE
COLO
DANA
DATA
DEAE
DENE
FETE
GALA
GENE
HERE
JAVA
LANA
LAVA
MANA
MERE
MONO
NARA
NOVO
PABA
PETE
POLO
RASA
RATA
SAGA
SARA
SHAH
SOLO
STAT
USES
VASA
WERE
WEVE
YERE

ABCC
BALL
BASS
BELL
BESS
BILL
BONN
BOSS
BUDD
BUFF
BULL
BURR
BUTT
BUZZ
CALL
CARR
CATT
CELL
COBB
CONN
CUFF
DELL
DILL
DOLL
DORR
DULL
DUNN
FALL
FELL
FILL
FOGG
FOSS
FREE
FULL
FUSS
FUZZ
GALL
GILL
GLEE
HALL
HAMM
HELL
HERR
HILL
HISS
HOSS
HUFF
HULL
ITLL
JAZZ
JEFF
JESS
KERR
KILL
KISS
KNEE
LASS
LESS
LOSS
LYNN
MALL
MANN
MARR
MASS
MATT
MESS
MILL
MINN
MISS
MOLL
MOSS
NOTT
NUFF
NULL
PALL
PASS
PENN
PILL
PITT
POLL
PULL
PUTT
RABB
RALL
ROLL
ROSS
RUSS
SELL
SILL
TALL
TASS
TELL
THEE
TILL
TODD
TOLL
TOSS
TREE
VENN
WALL
WATT
WELL
WILL
WITT
YALL
YELL

AABCA
EERIE

AABCD
AARON
LLOYD
OOZED

ABAAB
MAMMA

ABAAC
BOBBY
DADDY
LILLY
LOLLY
MOMMA
POPPY
PUPPY

ABABC
COCOA
MAMAS
PAPAL
PAPAS
VIVID

ABACA
ACALA

ABACC
AMASS

ABACD
ABACK
ADAGE
ADAIR
ADAMS
ADAPT
AGAIN
ALARM
AMAZE
APART
ARABS
AVAIL
AVANT
AWAIT
AWAKE
AWARD
AWARE
BABEL
BABES
BABIN
BABYS
BIBLE
BUBER
COCKY
CYCLE
DIDNT
DODGE
EDEMA
ELECS
ELECT
ELENA
ENEMY
ERECT
EVENT
EVERY
EXERT
FIFTH
FIFTY
GAGES
IDIOM
IDIOT
ILIAD
IRINA
IRISH
IVIES
LILAC
NANCY
NINTH
ODORS
OZONE
PAPER
PIPED
PIPES
POPES
PUPIL
RURAL
SUSAN
SUSHI
SUSIE
TITAN
TITER
TITLE
TITRE
TITUS
TOTAL
TUTOR
USUAL

ABBAB
BEEBE

ABBAC
ABBAS
ALLAN
ALLAY
ARRAY
ASSAM
ASSAY
BOOBY
COOCH
DEEDS
ELLEN
ERRED
ESSEX
ETTER
TEETH
TOOTH

ABBCA
EDDIE
SEEDS
SEEKS
SEEMS

ABBCB
ADDED
ASSES
ERROR
GEESE
KEENE
REESE

ABBCD
ABBEY
ABBOT
AGGIE
ALLEN
ALLEY
ALLOW
ALLOY
ANNES
ANNOY
ANNUM
APPLE
APPLY
ARROW
ASSET
ATTIC
BEECH
BEEPS
BEETS
BOOKS
BOONE
BOOST
BOOTH
BOOTS
BOOTY
BOOZE
COOKE
COOKS
COOKY
COOLS
COONS
COOSA
DOORS
ELLIS
EMMAS
ESSAY
FEEDS
FEELS
FOODS
FOOLS
GEELY
GOODS
GOODY
GOOSE
HEELS
HOODS
HOOFS
HOOKS
HOOPS
INNER
ISSUE
KEEPS
LEEDS
LOOKS
LOOMS
LOOSE
MCCAY
MEETS
MOODS
MOODY
MOONS
MOORE
MOORS
NEEDS
NEEDY
NOOSE
OCCUR
ODDLY
OFFER
OTTER
PEERS
POOLS
REEDY
ROOFS
ROOMS
ROOTS
SAAMI
TEENS
TOOKE
TOOLS
UPPED
UPPER
UPPON
UTTER
WEEDS
WEEKS
WOODS

ABCAA
GREGG
SWISS

ABCAB
EDGED
KAFKA
MIAMI
ONION
PAMPA
SENSE
VERVE

ABCAC
ELSES
ENDED
TESTS

ABCAD
ADLAI
AHEAD
ALGAE
ALTAR
AREAS
ASIAN
ATLAS
AXIAL
BARBS
BOMBS
BULBA
BULBS
CATCH
CHECK
CHICK
CHICO
CHUCK
CINCH
CLICK
CLOCK
CLUCK
COACH
COUCH
CRACK
DANDY
EAGER
EARED
EASED
EASEL
EATEN
EDGES
ELDER
ELMER
ENTER
ENVER
ETHEL
EXPEL
GANGS
GAUGE
GREGS
HIGHS
INDIA
IONIC
KHAKI
KICKS
LISLE
NOUNS
ORMOC
OTHON
PIMPS
PROPS
PUMPS
SCUSE
SLASH
SMASH
SPASM
TASTE
TASTY
TEATS
TENTH
TENTS
TEXTS
THATS
TILTS
TRITE
TRUTH
UNDUE
VALVE
ABCBA
CIVIC
LEVEL
MADAM
RADAR
REFER
ROTOR
SARAS
SEXES
SOLOS

ABCBB
MELEE
PFAFF

ABCBC
SLYLY

ABCBD
BANAL
BENET
BESET
BEVEL
BOSOM
CANAL
CIVIL
COLON
COLOR
DANAS
DEPEW
DEVEY
DEWEY
DIGIT
DONOR
DRURY
FATAL
FETED
FEVER
FEWER
GIVIN
GODOT
HEGEL
HELEN
HERES
HONOR
JAGAN
JAPAN
JEWEL
KASAI
KEYED
LABAN
LAMAR
LEGER
LEVER
LIMIT
MANAS
METED
METER
MEYER
MOTOR
MUCUS
NASAL
NATAL
NAVAL

ABCBD

NEVER NEWER NOGOL PAEAN PAGAN PARAY PETER REBEL RENEW REPEL REVEL RIGID SALAD SARAH SATAN SEVEN SEVER SEWER SOKOL STATE TARAS TIMID VEXED VISIT WEBER

ABCCA

SELLS SIMMS SKIIS

ABCCB

FREER GAMMA GREER JESSE KAPPA KITTI MOTTO ROCCO WANNA

ABCCC

BOSSS JESSS YEHHH

ABCCD

ALOOF BAGGY BALLS BARRE BARRY BASSO BELLA BELLS BELLY BENNY BERRA BERRY BETTY BILLS BILLY BLEED BLOOD BLOOM BONNS BREED BROOD BROOK BROOM BUDDY BUGGY BULLS BULLY BURRS BUTTS CALLS CANNY CAPPY CARRE CARRY CELLS CHEEK CHEER COMMA CREED CREEK CREEP CROOK CUFFS CURRY DANNY DECCA DELLA DENNY DEPPY DILLS DIZZY DOLLS DOLLY DONNA DUFFY DULLY DUMMY DUNNE FALLS FANNY FATTY FELLA FERRO FERRY FILLE FILLS FILLY FLEET FLOOD FLOOR FOGGS FOGGY FOLLY FREED FREES FULLY FUNNY FUSSY FUZZY GALLI GARRY GERRY GIBBS GIBBY GIDDY GLOOM GOLLY GONNA GOTTA GREED GREEK GREEN GREET GROOM GULLY GUMMY GUNNY HALLS HAPPY HARRY HELLO HELLS HERRY HETTY HILLS HOBBY HOFFA HUBBA HUBBY HURRY ISAAC IZAAK JELLY JENNY JERRY JIFFY JIMMY JOLLA JOLLY JOSSY KENNY KILLS KITTY KLEES KNEEL KNEES LARRY LASSO LEMMA LISSA LIZZY LOBBY MANNS MANNY MARRY MERRY MESSY MILLE MILLS MISSY MOLLY MUDDY MYRRH NILLY NOTTE OUTTA PENNY PERRY PETTY PEZZA PILLS PIZZA POLLS POSSE PROOF PUFFY PULLS PUSSY PUTTY QUEEN QUEER RABBI RALLY RICCO ROLLS ROSSI RUDDY SALLE SALLY SCOOP SECCO SHEEN SHEEP SHEER SHEET SHOOK SHOOT SIDDO SILLY SKEET SLEEK SLEEP SOGGY SOLLY SONNY SORRY SPEED SPOON STEEL STEEP STEER STOOD STOOL STOOP SUNNY SWEEP SWEET SWOOP TALLY TEDDY TELLS TERRA TERRY TOLLS TOMMY TREES TROOP TWEED VILLA WALLS WALLY WATTS WELLS WHEEL WILLY WITTY WORRY

ABCDA

ALPHA ANITA AORTA ARENA AROMA COMIC CONIC CUBIC DAMED DARED DATED DAVID DAZED DINED DIVED DOMED DOPED DOSED DOZED DREAD DRIED EAGLE ELITE ELSIE EMILE ENSUE ERNIE EVOKE EXILE GOING HANCH HARSH HATCH HITCH HOUGH HUNCH KNACK KNOCK LABEL LEGAL LIBEL LOCAL LOYAL MECUM NIXON OUTDO PLUMP RAZOR RECUR RIDER RIVER ROGER ROVER RUGER RULER RUMOR SAILS SALES SALTS SAMOS SANDS SATIS SAVES SCANS SCARS SCOTS SEALS SEAMS SEARS SEATS SECTS SENDS SHAWS SHEDS SHIPS SHOES SHOPS SHOTS SHOWS SHUNS SIDES SIGNS SILOS SINGS SITES SITUS SIZES SKIES SKINS SLIPS SLITS SLOTS SLUGS SLUMS SNOWS SOAPS SOCKS SOFAS SOILS SOLES SONGS SORES SORTS SOULS SPANS SPIES SPOTS SPURS STANS STARS STAYS STEMS STEPS STIRS STOPS STUBS STUDS SUITS TACIT TAINT TAUNT TEMPT THANT THEFT TIBET TIGHT TOAST TRACT TRAIT TREAT TROUT TRUST TWIST WIDOW WOHAW

ABCDB

AGING ALGOL ANTON ARBOR ARDOR ARGER ARMOR ASHES BEALE BEAME BELGE BERLE CARLA CEASE COMBO CONGO CORSO DEFOE DENSE DRIER DRYER FENCE GENRE GYPSY HAFTA HEARE HEAVE HEDGE HENCE INJUN ISLES JELKE KATYA KEANE KEMPE KNOWN LANZA LAURA LEASE LEAVE LEDGE LEYTE MALTA MANIA MARIA MERGE NERVE ORDER PANZA PASHA PAULA PEACE PEALE PERSE PESCE POLIO PORTO PRIOR REINE ROMEO SANTA SEIZE SERGE SERVE SIEPI SOCIO START STINT STOUT STRUT TEASE TENSE TERSE THIGH TOKYO TORSO TRUER TSARS UNION USERS VERGE VERSE WEAVE WEDGE WHICH YALTA

ABCDC

ADELE AIDED ALIBI AMICI BASES BASIS BOSIS BUSES BUSTS CANON CASES CASTS CHILI CLARA CONAN COSTS CYSTS DESKS DETAT DIANA DISCS DISKS DOSES DRAMA DRYLY DURER FADED FISTS FUROR FUSES GASES GASPS GHANA GUSTS HOEVE HONAN HOSES HOSTS IRENE JADED JESUS JUROR KYOTO LENIN LINEN LISTS LOSES LTURU MANIN MASKS MASTS MISTS MOLAL MOSES NESTS NIECE NOSES OASES OMAHA OSAKA PESTS PHOTO PIECE PLAZA POSTS PROTO REAMA RESTS RISES RISKS ROSES RUSKS SCENE SHYLY SIDED SIEGE SPADA STEVE TASKS THEME THERE THESE TUSKS VASES WADED WESTS WHERE WRYLY

ABCDD

ABYSS AGREE AMISS BEALL BLESS BLISS BLUFF BRAGG BRASS BRETT CHESS CHILL CLASS CLIFF CRASS CRISS CROSS DRESS DRILL DROSS DWELL FLYNN FROMM GAUSS GLASS GLENN GRASS GRATT GRILL GRIMM GROSS GRUBB GRUFF GUESS IDYLL KEYSS KNOLL MCKEE PAREE PRATT PRESS QUELL QUILL RADII RUPEE SCOTT SHALL SHANN SHELL SKIFF SKILL SKULL SMALL SMELL SNIFF SPELL SPREE STAFF STALL STIFF STILL STUFF SWELL TABOO THREE TRILL UDALL VIALL WEISS WOLFF WYATT YOULL ZEISS

AABCDE

EERILY LLOYDS

ABAABC

PEPPER

ABAACD

BOBBED BOBBIE BUBBLE DADDYS GOGGLE LILLYS POPPED PUPPET SUSSEX TUTTLE

ABABBC

COCOON

ABABCA

ACACIA

ABABCD

LILIAN PIPING REREAD TITIAN VIVIAN

ABACAD

ELEVEN

ABACBD

HUHMUN MEMBER

ABACDA

AGATHA ALASKA AZALEA DODGED EMERGE SUSANS

ABACDB	ABBACC	ABBCDC	KEENLY	ABCACD	GANGES	REFERS	CITIES	REJECT	HOLLOW
DEDUCE	EMMETT	ARROYO	LEEWAY	CAUCUS	GARGLE	REVERT	CITING	REMEDY	KENNEL
SESAME		POORER	LOOKED	INSIST	GAUGED	TENETS	COLONY	REPEAL	KITTIS
	ABBACD	WOODED	LOOKIT	IODIDE	GINGER		COLORS	REPEAT	KIZZIE
ABACDC	AFFAIR		LOOKUP		GOUGED	ABCBBD	DAMAGE	REPENT	LEGGED
KIKUYU	ANNALS	ABBCDD	LOOMED	ABCADA	HIGHER	BAZAAR	DECEIT	RESENT	LESSEN
	ASSAIL	ABBOTT	LOOMIS	ARMATA	HIGHLY	REDEEM	DECENT	REVEAL	LESSER
ABACDD	ATTACH	ACCESS	LOOSEN	EUGENE	HITHER		DEFEAT	RIDING	LETTER
AMADEE	ATTACK		LOOTED	STASIS	HOTHAM	ABCBCB	DEFECT	RISING	LIZZIE
	ATTAIN	ABBCDE	MCCLOY		HUGHES	BANANA	DESERT	ROBOTS	MILLIE
ABACDE	EFFECT	ACCENT	MEEKLY	ABCADB	HUSHED	ROCOCO	DEVERY	SAFARI	MINNIE
ADAGIO	EMMERT	ACCEPT	MOORED	INDIAN	IDLING		DIVINE	SALAMI	MORROW
AMAZED	OPPOSE	ACCORD	MOORES	LESLIE	IGNITE	ABCBCD	DIVING	SALARY	NASSAU
AMAZON		ACCUSE	OCCUPY	PEOPLE	INCITE	LINING	DONORS	SAVAGE	PEGGED
APATHY	ABBCAD	ADDING	OCCURS	PROPER	INDIAS	LINING	FACADE	SELECT	PENNED
ARABIC	ANNUAL	AFFECT	OFFEND		INDIES	MINING	FILING	SELENA	PETTED
ARABLE	APPEAL	AFFIRM	OFFERS	ABCADC	INSIDE		FINISH	SICILY	SELLER
AWAITS	APPEAR	AFFORD	OFFICE	BARBER	INTIMA	ABCBDA	FINITE	SIDING	SETTER
AWAKEN	EDDIES	AGGIES	OFFSET	EXTENT	INVITE	DEFEND	FIRING	SILICA	SORROW
AWARDS		ALLIED	POODLE	TACTIC	IODINE	DEPEND	FIXING	STATED	TAPPAN
BABIES	ABBCBA	ALLIES	POORLY	TASTES	IRVING	GIVING	FUTURE	STATEN	TELLER
CICERO	DEEMED	ALLOWS	ROOFED		KICKED	MIRIAM	GALAXY	STATIC	TILLIE
COCKED		ALLOYS	ROOKIE	ABCADD	KUNKEL	SALADS	GENEVA	STATUE	VESSEL
CYCLES	ABBCBB	APPLES	ROONEY	EXCESS	LODLEY	SARAHS	HAZARD	STITCH	WILLIE
DEDUCT	ASSESS	ARREST	ROOTED	THATLL	LUBLIN	SEWERS	HEREBY	TIMING	WILLIS
ENEMYS	VOODOO	ARRIVE	SEEING		MADMEN	STATES	HEREIN	TIRING	YELLED
ENERGY		ARROWS	SOONER	ABCADE	MARMON	STATUS	HERESY	VACANT	YELLER
EVELYN	ABBCBC	ASSENT	SOOTHE	ABLARD	NERNST		HIDING	VARANI	
EVENLY	NEEDED	ASSERT	TOOBIN	ABLAZE	ODIOUS	ABCBDB	HIKING	VIRILE	ABCCDA
EVENTS		ASSIGN	TOODLE	ABOARD	ORIOLE	CABANA	HIRING	VISION	DAMMED
EXEMPT	ABBCBD	ASSUME	WEEKLY	AFLAME	OXFORD	CANADA	HONORS	WABASH	DIPPED
EXERTS	ASSIST	ASSURE	WOODEN	AFRAID	POMPEY	HAVANA	HONOUR	WERENT	DOGGED
EYEING	BEEFED	ATTEND	WOOLEN	AHMADS	PROPEL	PANAMA	JEWELS	WIPING	DONNED
FIFTHS	DEEPER	ATTIRE		ALBANY	PULPIT	RECEDE	JOYOUS	WIRING	DOTTED
IDIOMS	ERRORS	BOOGIE	ABCAAD	ALWAYS	PUMPED	SAHARA	LEGEND		DUBBED
LELAND	FEEDER	BOOKED	EILEEN	AMEAUX	PURPLE	SECEDE	LEVERS	ABCCAD	DULLED
LILACS	FEELEY	BOOKER	ESTEEM	ARCADE	ROARED	SERENE	LIBIDO	LITTLE	HURRAH
MEMOIR	KEELER	BOOTHS	EXCEED	BARBED	ROURKE	SEVERE	LIKING		RITTER
MEMORY	KEEPER	BOOTLE	GRIGGS	BOMBED	SANSOM		LIMITS	ABCCBA	ROBBER
MOMENT	LEERED	COOKED	PHIPPS	BOMBER	SEASON	ABCBDC	LIVING	HANNAH	RODDER
NINETY	MEEKER	COOLED		BOMBUS	SENSOR	DETECT	LUXURY	REDDER	ROLLER
PAPERS	PEEKED	COOLER	ABCABA	BRIBED	SIESTA	SUBURB	MANAGE		RUBBER
PAPIER	PEELED	COOMBS	SENSES	BUSBOY	SUNSET	VISITS	MERELY	ABCCBC	RUNNER
POPISH	PEERED	COOPED		CANCEL	TASTED		MEREST	HORROR	SALLYS
POPLAR	REELED	COOPER	ABCABC	CANCER	TILTED	ABCBDD	METEOR	WEDDED	SHEETS
PUPILS	SEEMED	DEEGAN	MURMUR	CHECKS	TINTED	HAWAII	METERS		SNEERS
RARELY	SEEPED	DEEPLY	TULTUL	CIRCLE	TRUTHS	RECESS	MILIEU	ABCCBD	SPEEDS
RARITY	VEERED	DOOLIN		CIRCUS	TURTLE		MIXING	BALLAD	STEELS
SISTER		EBBING	ABCABD	CLICHE	TWITCH	ABCBDE	MOLOCH	BEGGED	SWEETS
SYSTEM	ABBCCD	EFFORT	ALKALI	CLICKS	UNDULY	AIDING	MOROSE	BETTER	SWOOPS
TITERS	COOLLY	ERRAND	MADMAN	CLOCKS	UNJUST	AILING	MOTORS	BILLIE	TAPPET
TITLED	WOOLLY	ERRANT	MIAMIS	CLUCKS	UNRULY	AIMING	MUTUAL	BONNOR	TURRET
TITLES		FEEBLY	MORMON	CONCUR	UPTURN	AIRILY	NEWEST	BORROW	WILLOW
TOTALS	ABBCDA	FOOLED	OCLOCK	CRACKS	VALVES	AUBURN	NIKITA	BOTTOM	
UNUSED	DOOMED	FOOTED	ONIONS	DEADLY		AUGUST	NOBODY	CALLAS	ABCCDB
URUNDI	SAAMIS	GOODIS	REARED	ELDERS	ABCBAB	AUTUMN	PALACE	COMMON	HETTIE
		HOOKED	REGRET	ELDEST	REVERE	BEHELD	PALATE	COTTON	ISAACS
ABBABB	ABBCDB	HOOKUP	SENSED	ENTERS		BENETS	PARADE	DALLAS	JENNIE
CEECEE	ASSETS	HOOPER	TESTED	ERNEST	ABCBAD	BEREFT	PETERS	DELLER	JESSIE
	ATTEST	HOOVER	UNSUNG	EXCEPT	AEGEAN	BITING	PILING	FELLED	KETTLE
ABBABC	ESSAYS	HOOVES	VELVET	EXPECT	DIVIDE	CELERY	PITIED	FENNEL	METTLE
INNING	FEEBLE	INNATE		EXPERT	GARAGE	CEMENT	POROUS	FOLLOW	NELLIE
	ISSUES	ISSUED		EXTEND	LEVELS	CEREAL	REBELS	GOSSON	PEBBLE
	NEEDLE	KEEGAN		GADGET	MADAME	CETERA	RECENT	HEMMED	SETTLE

ABCCDB

TESSIE TORRIO

ABCCDC

BOSSES BREEZE BUSSES CANNON CHEESE FREEZE GANNON GREECE GREENE HOSSES KENNAN KISSES LOSSES MASSES MESSRS MIRROR MISSES NODDED PADDED PASSES PETTIT POSSES RUNNIN SLEEVE STEELE TERROR TOSSES WADDED

ABCCDD

COFFEE MILLSS WELLSS

ABCCDE

BALLED BALLET BALLOT BANNED BANNER BARRED BARREL BARREN BATTED BATTEN BATTER BATTLE BEGGAR BELLOW BELLUM BIDDER BIGGER BILLED BITTEN BITTER BLOODY BLOOMS BONNER BONNET BOTTLE BREEDS BROODS BROODY BROOKE BROOKS BUDDHA BUFFER BUFFET BUGGED BULLET BURROW BUTTED BUTTER BUTTON BUZZED BUZZES CALLED CALLER CANNED CANNOT CAPPED CATTLE CELLAR CHEEKS CHEERS CHEERY CHOOSE COFFIN COLLAR COLLIE COMMIT COPPER CORRAL COTTEN CROOKS CUPPED CUPPLY CUTTER DAMMIT DAPPER DENNIS DIFFER DIGGER DILLON DINNER DIPPER DOLLAR DOLLEY DONNAY DUFFEL DULLER DULLES DUTTON FALLEN FANNED FATTER FELLOW FERRIS FIDDLE FIGGER FILLED FILLES FINNEY FITTED FLEETS FLOODS FLOORS FREELY FREEST FULLER FURROW GALLEY GALLON GALLOP GASSED GIBBON GIFFEN GLOOMY GODDAM GOSSIP GOTTEN GREEDY GREEKS GREENS GROOMS GROOVE GUNNAR HADDIX HAMMER HAPPEN HARRIS HARROW HIDDEN HISSED HITTER HOBBES HOPPED HOPPER HOTTER HUDDLE HUGGED HUMMED HUTTON IZAAKS JABBED JAGGED JAMMED JARRED KILLED KILLER KISSED KITTEN KITTYS LADDER LAGGED LAPPED LATTER LESSON LIPPED LITTER LOGGED LUGGED MADDEN MAGGIE MANNED MANNER MARRED MARROW MASSED MATTEI MATTER MIDDAY MIDDLE MILLER MISSED MOLLIE MOLLYS MOPPED MORRIS MULLEN MULLER MURRAY MUTTON MUZZLE NARROW NASSER NIGGER NORRIS NOZZLE PALLID PALLOR PARRIS PASSED PATTED PATTER PENNYS PERRIN PILLAR PILLOW PINNED POLLEN POSSUM POTTED POTTER PUFFED PULLED PULLEN PULLEY PUZZLE QUEENS RABBIT RABBLE RAGGED RAMMED RAPPED RATTLE RIBBON RIDDEN RIGGED RIMMED RIPPED RIPPLE ROBBED ROBBIE ROLLED RONNIE ROTTEN RUBBED RUGGED RUSSET RUSSIA SADDLE SAGGED SAPPED SIMMER SINNED SINNER SIPPED SITTER SKIING SLEEPY SMOOTH SOBBED SOCCER SODDEN SONNET SORREL SPEECH SPEEDY SPOOKY SUDDEN SUFFER SULLAM SULLEN SUMMED SUMMER SUMMIT SUMMON SUPPER SUPPLY TAGGED TALLER TANNED TANNER TAPPED TENNIS TIPPED TISSUE TOLLEY TOPPED TORRID TOSSED TROOPS TUGGED TUNNEL TUSSLE VALLEY VOLLEY WAGGED WALLED WALLET WALLYS WARREN WHEELS WILLED WINNER WOBBLE WOBBLY YARROW YELLOW

ABCDAA

LOWELL LUBELL STRESS

ABCDAB

ANDEAN CHURCH DECADE DECIDE DELUDE DORADO EDITED ERASER GEORGE NAVONA ORATOR RETIRE TENITE TOMATO

ABCDAC

ANYWAY COERCE ENSUES RETORT

ABCDAD

ELUDED ERODED EVADED EXUDED TAHITI TRUSTS TWISTS

ABCDAE

ABROAD ACTUAL ADRIAN AERIAL AFGHAN AFLOAT AMORAL ANIMAL ARENAS AROMAS ASTRAY BRUMBY CALICO CHANCE CHOICE CLINCH CLUTCH COURCY CROUCH CRUNCH CYNICS DAVIDS EAGLES EARNED EASIER EASTER ECHOED ECHOES EITHER ELATED EMILES ENSUED ENVIED ERASED ESTHER ETCHED EVOKED EVOKES EXILED GRUDGE HEIGHT HOUGHS IMPAIR IRONIC KNOCKS KODYKE LABELS LAPELS LASTLY LATELY LIABLE LIKELY LIVELY LOCALE LONELY LORDLY LOUDLY LOVELY NADINE NAIRNE NAMING NOTING NUGENT OPTION OREGON PETIPA PROMPT REBORN RECORD REFORM REGARD REMARK REPORT RESORT RETARD RETURN REWARD RIDERS RIGORS RIVERS ROBERT ROGERS ROTARY RULERS RUMORS SADISM SAFEST SPARSE SPLASH SPOUSE SQUASH TAUNTS THIRTY TRACTS TRAITS TREATS TREATY TWENTY UNIQUE UNTRUE USEFUL VOTIVE

ABCDBA

DEFIED DENIED ENGINE EVOLVE MUSEUM NATHAN NERIEN NORTON NOTION PUSHUP READER RENDER SELVES SERIES SERVES SEYNES STARTS STILTS STUNTS WARSAW

ABCDBB

DECREE DEGREE

ABCDBC

BERGER COSMOS HERTER INTENT JENSEN LONDON MERCER MERGER OUTPUT PAYDAY PERIER PICNIC RUMDUM TORPOR WEDGED WERNER

ABCDBD

BEARER CEASES HEADED HEARER HERDED KANSAS LEASES LENSES NEARER SEXTET STRATA TENDED TORSOS VERSES WELDED

ABCDBE

ANTONY ANYONE ARTERY ARTURO BALKAN BALZAC BASHAW BATEAU BEAKER BEATEN BEAVER BECKET BEGLEY BELIED BELIEF BELTED BETSEY BIRDIE BOLIOU BOSTON BOUTON CAESAR CANVAS CARNAL CASBAH CASUAL CAUSAL CEASED CENTER CONVOY CORDON COWBOY CUPFUL DEALER DENIES DENVER DEXTER DIARIO DOCTOR DREARY DRIERS DUGOUT ENDING ERHART FABIAN FACIAL FEARED FENCED FENCES FENDER FIBRIN FLATLY FORGOT FUNGUS GALWAY GEARED GENDER GLADLY GLIBLY GORDON GORTON HAIJAC HARLAN HEADER HEALED HEALER HEAPED HEATED HEATER HEAVED HEAVEN HEBREW HEDGES HEISER HELPED HELPER HEMPEL HEROES HESTER INFANT INJUNS INLAND INSANE INTEND INVENT JAGUAR JERKED JERSEY JULIUS KELSEY KERNEL LANDAU LARVAE LAWMAN LAYMAN LEADEN LEADER LEAKED LEANED LEAPED LEASED LEAVES LEDGER LESTER LEVIES LIQUID LOTION LUCIUS MANIAC MANUAL MEAGER MEANES MELIES MELTED MERGED MERGES MEYNER MICKIE MIDAIR MIJBIL MONROE MORTON MOSCOW

ABCDBE
MOTION
NEARED
NECKED
NEPHEW
NERVES
NESTED
NESTER
ORDERS
ORNERY
OUTRUN
PANTAS
PAULAS
PEAKED
PECKED
PEYSER
PIDGIN
POIROT
POISON
PURSUE
RACIAL
RADIAL
RAMEAU
REFLEX
REFUEL
REINED
RELIED
RELIEF
RELIES
RENTED
RESTED
REUBEN
REVIEW
RHYTHM
SCARCE
SCOTCH
SEALED
SEAMEN
SEATED
SECRET
SEIDEL
SEIZED
SELDEN
SERGEI
SERVED
SLOWLY
SUBDUE
TAIWAN
TARZAN
TEAMED
TEASED
TEMPER
TENDER
TERMED
THIGHS
UNDONE
UNIONS
UNKIND
VARIAN
VEILED
VERSED
VERTEX
VESTED
VICTIM
VIOLIN
VIRGIL
VIRGIN
WEAKEN
WEAKER
WEASEL
WEAVER
WEAVES
WEIDER
WELTER
WESKER
WESLEY
WEXLER
WITHIN

ABCDCA
ALICIA
AURORA
CLINIC
CRITIC
ENGAGE
ESTATE
PHILIP
SCENES
SWEDES
TENANT

ABCDCB
POTATO
PREFER
REVIVE
UNEVEN

ABCDCD
CRISIS

ABCDCE
BOLDLY
CALMLY
CANONS
CHEWED
CLEVER
COLDLY
CONANT
CONING
CREWEL
DRAMAS
DREXEL
ELICIT
ENTITY
FLEXED
FRIGID
FUELED
GILELS
GRAHAM
JURORS
LIEDER
MILDLY
MISUSE
NIECES
OBEYED
OMELET
OPENED
OPENER
ORIGIN
OWNING
PETITS
PHOTOS
PIECES
PLANAR
PROTON
QUEBEC
RESIST
ROTATE
SARTRE
SCALAR
SEAMAN
SEIZIN
SMILIN
SOLELY
SPIRIT
STALAG
STEREO
SWEDEN
TAILIN
THEMES
THERED
THERES
TRIVIA
TUNING
UNIFIL
VIEWED
VIEWER
WANING
WHERED
WHERES
WILDLY
ZONING

ABCDDA
SHELLS
SKIFFS
SKILLS
SKULLS
SMELLS
SPELLS
SPILLS
STAFFS
STALLS
STILLS
SWELLS

ABCDDB
NEISSE
STREET
UNSEEN
UPKEEP

ABCDDC
APOLLO
CAREER
INDEED
PIAZZA
PIERRE
YVETTE

ABCDDE
AGREED
AGREES
ASLEEP
BAILLY
BLUFFS
BRASSY
CHERRY
CHILLS
CHILLY
CHOPPY
CHUBBY
CLAMMY
CLIFFS
CRUMMY
DRESSY
DRILLS
FLURRY
FREDDY
FRILLS
FROMMS
GAULLE
GHETTO
GLADDY
GLASSY
GRANNY
GRASSY
GRILLE
GRITTY
GROSSE
GRUBBY
INDOOR
JOHNNY
KNOTTY
LAGOON
MAROON
ORALLY
PRETTY
QUARRY
REALLY
RUPEES
SALOON
SCHOOL
SCOTTY
SCREEN
SHABBY
SHAGGY
SHERRY
SHIMMY
SIENNA
SIERRA
SKINNY
SLOPPY
SPLEEN
STAFFE
STUBBY
STUCCO
STUFFY
THREES
THYNNE
VACUUM
VIENNA
WHOLLY
WOLFFS

ABCDEA
ADELIA
AFRICA
AGENDA
ANDREA
ANEMIA
ANGOLA
ANTHEA
CEDRIC
CELTIC
COGNAC
COSMIC
DAMNED
DANCED
DARNED
DARTED
DASHED
DEMAND
DEVOID
DIALED
DONALD
DOWNED
DRAPED
DUCKED
DUMPED
EDIBLE
EDYTHE
ELAINE
EMPIRE
ENABLE
ENDURE
ENSURE
ENTIRE
ENZYME
EQUATE
ESCAPE
EUROPE
EXCISE
EXCITE
EXCUSE
EXPOSE
GAMING
GAPING
GAZING
GEHRIG
HEALTH
HEARTH
HIRSCH
KODIAK
LAUREL
LAWFUL
LETHAL
LIONEL
MAGNUM
MEDIUM
MOSLEM
MUSLIM
NAGRIN
NAPKIN
NATION
NEIMAN
NELSON
NEWMAN
NEWTON
NIEMAN
NORMAN
NOTHIN
PICKUP
RAISER
RANCOR
RANGER
RATHER
RECTOR
RENOIR
REPAIR
RICHER
RINKER
ROCKER
ROSTER
SAINTS
SALONS
SAUCES
SAXONS
SCALES
SCORES
SCOURS
SCOUTS
SCRAPS
SCREWS
SEDANS
SHADES
SHAFTS
SHAKES
SHAPES
SHARES
SHARKS
SHAWLS
SHIFTS
SHINES
SHIRES
SHIRTS
SHOALS
SHOCKS
SHORES
SHORTS
SHOUTS
SHREDS
SHRUBS
SHRUGS
SHUCKS
SHUNTS
SIGHTS
SIRENS
SKIRTS
SKOPAS
SKYROS
SLACKS
SLAVES
SLICES
SLIDES
SLOANS
SLOPES
SMILES
SMITHS
SNACKS
SNAILS
SNAKES
SNOPES
SOLIDS
SOLVES
SOMERS
SOUNDS
SOUTHS
SPACES
SPADES
SPARKS
SPEAKS
SPECKS
SPENDS
SPICES
SPIKES
SPIRES
SPLITS
SPOKES
SPORES
SPORTS
SQUADS
STAGES
STAINS
STAIRS
STAKES
STAMPS
STANDS
STEAKS
STEINS
STICKS
STINGS
STOCKS
STONES
STORES
STORMS
STOVES
STRAPS
STRAWS
STRAYS
STRIPS
STUMPS
STYLES
SUITES
SWAMPS
SWEARS
SWIFTS
SWINGS
SWORDS
SZOLDS
TABLET
TALENT
TAOIST
TARGET
TAUGHT
THIRST
THREAT
THRIFT
THROAT
THRUST
THWART
TICKET
TOILET
TRUEST
TYRANT
WINDOW
YEARLY

ABCDEB
ABSORB
ADORED
ARMOUR
ARTHUR
BEADLE
BEATIE
BECAME
BECOME
BEFORE
BEHAVE
BEINGE
BESIDE
BETIDE
BEWARE
BRAVER
BUREAU
CAMERA
CAPITA
CENTRE
CESTRE
CRATER
DAKOTA
DEBATE
DEFINE
DELUGE
DELUXE
DEMISE
DEMURE
DENOTE
DERIVE
DESIRE
DEVICE
DEVISE
DEVOTE
DRAPER
DRAWER
DRIVER
EDMUND
EDWARD
ENSIGN
FELICE
FELINE
FEMALE
FLORAL
FOREGO
GALENA
GARCIA
GENTLE
GLOBAL
GLYCOL
GRADER
GRAVER
GROVER
INTERN
JEROME
KEMBLE
KROGER
KRUGER
LAGUNA
LEAGUE
LEGUME
MANILA
MARINA
MARTHA
MENACE
MIYAGI
NAUSEA
NEGATE
PAMELA
PETRIE
PONCHO
PRAYER
PRIEUR
REBUKE
RECIPE
RECITE
REDUCE
REFINE
REFUGE
REFUSE
REGIME
RELATE
RELIVE
REMAKE
REMOTE
REMOVE
REPOSE
REPUTE
RESALE
RESCUE
RESIDE
RESUME
REVISE
SABINA
SALIVA
SCENIC
SECURE
SEDATE
SEMITE
SENATE
SENILE
SEWAGE
SHEATH
SHILOH
STRAIT
STRICT
STUART
SYDNEY
SYRUPY
TABULA
TEMPLE
TENURE
THOUGH
THRUSH
TORINO
TRADER
TRAGER
TREMOR
UNBORN
UNISON
USAGES
UTMOST
VAGINA
VENICE
VESOLE
WRITER

ABCDEC
ARCTIC
ARTIST
AVENGE
AVENUE
BARKER
BASILS
BENSON
BODIED
BORDER
BUNYAN
BURNER
BUSHES
CANYON
CARMER
CARTER
CASEYS
CORDER
CORNER
CREATE
DARKER
DASHES
DENTON
DISHES
DUNCAN
EDGING
EUSTIS
EVADNA
EXTANT
FARMER
FERVOR
FIERCE
FIRMER
FISHES
FORMER
GARTER
GASHES
GOETHE
GREASE
GUNMAN
GUNMEN
HANGIN
HANSEN
HARBOR
HARDER
HARPER
HECTIC
HEYDAY
HINTON
INTACT
JUDGED
KENYON
LARGER
LASHES
LATENT
LATEST
LINDEN
LUNION
LYNDON
MARKER
MARTYR
MASONS
MORTAR
MURDER

ABCDEC
NUDGED
OATNUT ONSETS OUTFIT OUTLET OUTSET PARKER PARLOR PATENT PATHET PHEDRE PIERCE PLASMA PLEASE PLEDGE POMHAM PORTER POTENT PUSHES RAGING RANKIN REHASH RESINS RUANDA RUNYON RUSHES SIDLED SPECIE STEVIE SUNKEN SWERVE THENCE THEYRE THEYVE TREBLE TURNER TWELVE UPROAR UPSETS URGING VISTAS WANTON WARMER WASHES WASTES WHENCE WISHES WORKER YORKER

ABCDED
ABUSES
ADHERE AGNESE APIECE ARISES ARLENE BANDED BEASTS BLASTS BOASTS BONDED BURSTS

CANDID CAUSES CENSUS CHASES CHESTS CIUDAD CLOSES COASTS CRESTS CRISES CURSES EIGHTH EXISTS FAUSTS FEASTS FOLDED FRIEZE FROSTS GHOSTS GILDED GOADED GRADED GUESTS GUIANA GUIDED HANDED HORSES HOSAKA HOUSES JACOPO KODAMA LANDED LAPSES LOADED MEANIN MINDED MOBUTU MOLDED MORSES MUSTNT NEVADA NOISES NURSES PAUSES PAVESE PHASES POISES RAISES REPNIN SANDED SCHEME SHADED SONATA SORDID SPHERE THESIS TRADED VERNON VERSUS WINDED WORDED WRISTS

ABCDEE
ACROSS
APOGEE BEFALL BOXELL BYPASS ENROLL JAMESS LEVITT LEWISS LOUISS MARISS MIZELL NORELL ONEILL ORCUTT ORWELL POWELL REBUFF RECALL REFILL RUNOFF SHRILL SQUALL SQUIBB STROLL TARIFF THEYLL THRILL UNLESS YANKEE

ABAABCD
LILLIAN
MAMMALS PEPPERY

ABAACDD
BABBITT

ABAACDE
BABBLED
BOBBIES BOBBING BOBBSEY BUBBLED BUBBLES GIGGLED GIGGLES LULLABY MAMMOTH NENNIUS POPPING PUPPETS SESSION

ABABCCD
LOLOTTE

ABABCDE
COCONUT
GAGARIN VIVIDLY

ABACADA
ALABAMA

ABACADD
EVERETT

ABACADE
ADAMANT
ELEMENT EVEREST INITIAL UNUSUAL

ABACBDE
FIFTIES
LILTING MEMBERS

ABACCAD
OCONNOR

ABACDAE
ARABIAN
AZALEAS EJECTED ELECTED EMERGED EMERGES ENEMIES ERECTED EXERTED IDIOTIC

ABACDBA
DEDUCED

ABACDBD
MIMESIS

ABACDBE
MIMETIC
TITANIC

ABACDCE
CECILIA
ELEAZAR EVENING IMITATE JEJUNUM

ABACDDE
FIFTEEN
TOTALLY USUALLY

ABACDEA
EXECUTE
SISTERS SYSTEMS

ABACDEB
ADAPTED
PAPRIKA

ABACDEC
ABANDON
DODGING

ABACDED
AWARDED

ABACDEE
EYEBALL

ABACDEF
ACADEMY
AGAINST ALARMED ALASTOR AMATEUR AMAZING ANALOGY ANALYST ANALYZE ANARCHY ANATOMY APACHES AVAILED AVARICE AWAITED BABYLON CACKLED COCKPIT COCTEAU CYCLIST DODGERS ELEANOR ELECTOR ELEGANT ELEGIAC EMERALD EMERSON ETERNAL EYEBROW EYELIDS MEMOIRS MEMPHIS MOMENTS MUMBLED POPULAR SUSPECT SUSPEND SUSTAIN TOTALED

ABBABCA
ACCACIA

ABBABCD
INNINGS

ABBACAD
ILLICIT

ABBACCD
ADDABBO

ABBACDA
ESSENCE

ABBACDC
OPPOSES

ABBACDE
AFFAIRS
APPAREL ARRANGE ARRAYED ASSAULT ATTACKS EFFECTS OPPOSED OTTOMAN PEEPING

ABBCABD
ARREARS

ABBCADB
ATTRACT
OSSEOUS

ABBCADC
APPEASE

ABBCADE
ACCLAIM
APPEALS APPEARS APPLAUD ISSUING

ABBCBDA
SEEKERS

ABBCBDE
DEEPEST
FEELERS HEELERS KEENEST LOOKOUT MEEKERS WEEKEND

ABBCDAE
ARRIVAL
ESSAYED LOOSELY NEEDING

ABBCDBA
WOODROW

ABBCDBC
SEEDBED

ABBCDBE
BEECHER
NEEDLES ROOFTOP

ABBCDCE
ALLEGED
KEENING KOONING OFFERED UTTERED

ABBCDEA
ROOSTER

ABBCDEB
ASSERTS
ASSIGNS ASSUMES ASSURES ATTEMPT ILLEGAL SEEPAGE TEENAGE

ABBCDEC
IMMENSE
OFFENSE SEEKONK

ABBCDED
ACCUSES
ARRESTS

ABBCDEE
ADDRESS
ELLIOTT ILLNESS

ABBCDEF
ACCENTS
ACCEPTS ACCOUNT ACCRUED ACCUSED ADDICTS AFFECTS AFFIXED AFFORDS AFFRONT ALLEGRO ALLOWED ANNOYED APPLIED APPLIES APPOINT APPROVE ARRIVED ARRIVES ASSUMED ASSURED ATTENDS ATTUNED BOOKIES BOOKING BOOSTED COOKIES COOKING COOLANT

COOLERS COOLEST COOLING COOPERS DEEGANS DOORMAN DOORMEN DOORWAY EFFORTS ERRATIC FEEDING FEELING FOOLING FOOLISH FOOTING GOODBYE GOODMAN GOODWIN HOODLUM IMMORAL KEELSON KEEPING LEERING LEESONA LOOKING LOOMING LOOTING MCCRADY MEETING MOONLIT MOORISH NEEDHAM OFFICER OFFICES PEELING PEERING POOLING POOREST REENACT ROOKIES ROOMING ROOTING SEEBOHM SEEKING SEEMING SEEPING SOOTHED TOOLING UNNAMED UTTERLY VEERING WEEKDAY WEEPING

ABCAADE
EILEENS
EXCEEDS PROPPED TROTTED

ABCABCB
BARBARA
MARMARA

ABCABCD
TARTARY

ABCABDC
RETREAT

ABCABDD
CARCASS
REDRESS

ABCABDE
ALKALIS
CONCORD KICKING MANMADE POMPOUS REGRETS SAUSAGE VELVETY WAYWARD

ABCACDC
INSISTS

ABCACDE
IMBIBED
PROPOSE TUITION

ABCADAE
ABRAHAM
ENTERED EUGENES INHIBIT

ABCADBA
ATLANTA

ABCADBC
GRIGORI
PREPARE

ABCADBD
INDIANA

ABCADBE
AERATED
CIRCUIT DISDAIN ELDERLY GREGORY INDIANS KOLKHOZ PEOPLES TACTUAL

ABCADCC
FULFILL

ABCADCE
CHECKED
GARGERY PURPORT SENSING

ABCADCE
TACTICS
TORTURE

ABCADDE
ADMASSY
AURALLY
ESTELLA

ABCADEA
ALBANIA
EXPENSE
GOUGING
SEASONS
SENSORS

ABCADEB
REWRITE
SEASIDE
TEXTILE
TEXTURE

ABCADEC
AERATOR
CONCERN
INSIDES
SPOSATO

ABCADED
CONCEDE
EMPEROR
EPHESUS

ABCADEE
BARBELL
KICKOFF
LAWLESS
POMPEII

ABCADEF
ADVANCE
ALVAREZ
AMIABLE
ARCADES
ARIADNE
ASHAMED
ATHALIE
AVIATOR
BOMBERS
BOMBING
BURBANK
CALCIUM
CATCHER
CATCHES
CHECKUP
CHICAGO
CHICKEN
CHUCKLE
CIRCLED
CIRCLES
CLICHES
CLICKED
COACHES
CONCAVE
CONCEAL
CONCEPT
CONCERT
CONCURS
COUCHED
CRACKED
CRACKLE
CRICKET
CROCKED
CRUCIAL
EAGERLY
ECHELON
EUGENIA
EXCERPT
EXPECTS
EXPERTS
EXTENDS
FORFEIT
GADGETS
GINGHAM
HIGHEST
HIGHWAY
IMPINGE
IMPIOUS
INCITED
INDICES
INFIELD
INSIGHT
INVITED
INVITES
IONIZED
KUNKELS
LUBLINS
MAHMOUD
NUANCES
OCTOBER
ORIOLES
OSBORNE
OSMOTIC
PIEPSAM
PROPHET
PUMPING
PUMPKIN
PURPOSE
REARING
RECRUIT
REFRAIN
REXROTH
ROARING
ROURKES
SENSORY
SENSUAL
SLASHED
SMASHED
SUBSIDE
SUBSIDY
SUDSING
SWISHED
TACTFUL
TACTILE
TANTRUM
TASTING
TESTIFY
TESTING
TEXTUAL
UNLUCKY
UPSURGE
WARWICK

ABCBAAD
LASALLE

ABCBABD
LEVELED
REVERED

ABCBADA
DIVIDED
MINIMUM

ABCBADB
RESERVE
REVERSE

ABCBADE
AWKWARD
DIVIDES
GARAGES
MINIMAL
MONOMER
STETSON

ABCBBDE
STETTIN

ABCBCCB
CASASSA

ABCBCDD
ONENESS

ABCBCDE
LUMUMBA

ABCBDAB
TORONTO

ABCBDAE
DEFENDS
DEPENDS
MIRIAMS
RIVIERA
SOLOIST

ABCBDBD
RECEDED
SECEDED

ABCBDBE
BEVELED
BEYELER
CABANAS
CARAVAN
CARAWAY
JEWELED
JEWELER
METERED
MILITIA
MOLOTOV
PAJAMAS
RENEWED
SEVERED
SOKOLOV
SOLOMON
STATUTE

ABCBDCA
SUBURBS

ABCBDCB
DETENTE

ABCBDCE
DECENCY
VACANCY

ABCBDDB
MOROCCO

ABCBDDE
COLONNA
FATALLY
FILIPPO
PALAZZO

ABCBDEA
AUGUSTA
DAMAGED
HOWORTH
SAVAGES
SELECTS
STATUES
TINIEST

ABCBDEB
BATAVIA
BAVARIA
DEFENSE
DESERVE
DIMITRI
JAMAICA
KATANGA
MALARIA
RECEIVE
RELEASE
REVENGE
REVENUE
UNKNOWN

ABCBDEC
COLONEL
CORONER
DESERTS
DONOVAN
VISIONS

ABCBDED
GENESIS
NEMESIS
PARADED

ABCBDEF
AUDUBON
BALANCE
BENEATH
BENEFIT
BENELUX
BEVERLY
BOLOGNA
BOROUGH
CAMARET
CAPABLE
CATALOG
CAVALRY
CEREALS
CITIZEN
COLOGNE
COLORED
DAMAGES
DANAHER
DEFEATS
DEFECTS
DEVELOP
DIGITAL
DOLORES
DOROTHY
FEDERAL
GENERAL
GENETIC
HAZARDS
HERETIC
HONORED
JEWELRY
LARAMIE
LEGENDS
LIAISON
LIMITED
MACABRE
MALAISE
MANAGED
MANAGER
MANAGES
MASARYK
METEORS
NOBODYS
PALACES
PARABLE
PARADES
PARADOX
PARAGON
PARASOL
PAYABLE
PITIFUL
POTOMAC
RAVAGES
RECEIPT
REGENTS
REJECTS
RENEWAL
REPEATS
REVEALS
RIGIDLY
SEVENTH
SEVENTY
SEVERAL
SILICON
SIMILAR
SOJOURN
STATELY
STATING
STATION
STATURE
TAXABLE
TEHERAN
TIDINGS
TUBULAR
VACATED
VETERAN
VICIOUS
VIKINGS
VISIBLE
VISIBLY
VISITED
VISITOR

ABCCADE
BELLBOY

ABCCBCA
GINNING

ABCCBCD
BAGGAGE
HORRORS
WINNING

ABCCBDA
SELLERS
SORROWS

ABCCBDC
DIGGING
RIGGING
VESSELS

ABCCBDD
FERRELL
ROSSOFF

ABCCBDE
BALLADS
BALLAST
BARRAGE
BIDDING
BILLING
BILLION
BOTTOMS
CABBAGE
COMMONS
DESSERT
DITTIES
FILLING
FISSION
FITTING
FOLLOWS
GALLANT
HAGGARD
HISSING
HITTING
KENNEDY
KENNETH
KIDDING
KILLING
KISSING
LETTERS
MASSAGE
MILLING
MILLION
MISSILE
MISSING
MISSION
PASSAGE
POLLOCK
RIDDING
RIPPING
SABBATH
SIPPING
SITTING
TAMMANY
TELLERS
VERREAU
WALLACE
WARRANT
WILLIAM
WILLIES
WILLING
YIDDISH

ABCCDAA
SUCCESS

ABCCDAB
TAFFETA

ABCCDAC
NAGGING

ABCCDAE
COLLECT
CONNECT
CORRECT
COSSACK
NODDING
RAPPORT
ROBBERS
ROBBERY
RUNNERS
SUGGEST
SUPPOSE
TAPPETS

ABCCDBA
SETTLES

ABCCDBC
TERRIER

ABCCDBE
BELLIED
BELLIES
BERRIES
HALLWAY
MISSAIL
NETTLED
PEBBLES
PEDDLER
PENNIES
SETTLED
SETTLER
VILLAIN

ABCCDCA
SLEEVES
STEELES

ABCCDCC
POSSESS

ABCCDCD
SPEEDED

ABCCDCE
BREEZES
CANNING
CHEERED
CUNNING
FANNING
FERRARO
GREETED
KENNANS
KNEELED
LUGGAGE
MANNING
MIRRORS
PENNANT
RUNNING
SLEEVED
SNEEZED
STEEPED
STEEPER
STEERED
SWEENEY
SWEETER
WHEELED
WHEELER

ABCCDDE
BALLOON
SUCCEED

ABCCDEA
DAZZLED
GETTING
ROTTGER
SADDLES
SIMMONS
SINNERS
SITTERS
SOMMERS
SONNETS
SUFFERS
SUMMERS
TORRENT

ABCCDEB
MESSAGE TERRACE TROOPER

ABCCDEC
BARRIER BEGGING BUGGING CARRIER CODDLED FITTEST HOTTEST HUDDLED HUGGING LESSONS LOGGING MUDDIED MUSSELS RAGGING RIDDLED RUSSIAS SADDLED SAGGING STEEPLE TISSUES WAGGING WARRIOR

ABCCDED
BELLINI BLOODED CHOOSES COLLEGE FELLINI FLOODED

ABCCDEE
CARROLL FARRELL GANNETT GODDESS HAMMETT HARRISS KIMMELL MERRILL MERRITT MINNETT RUSSELL WADDELL

ABCCDEF
BAFFLED BALLETS BALLOTS BANNERS BARRELS BARRING BATTENS BATTERS BATTERY BATTING BATTLES BEDDING BEGGARS BELLMAN BELLOWS BETTING BIDDERS BIGGEST BLOOMED BOTTLED BOTTLES BUDDIES BUFFALO BULLETS BULLIES BULLOCH BURROWS BUTTONS BUZZING CALLERS CALLING CALLOUS CANNERY CARRIED CARRIES CARROTS CELLIST COLLAGE COLLINS COMMAND COMMEND COMMENT COMMIES COMMITS COMMUNE COMMUTE COPPERY CORRUPT COTTAGE CROOKED CROONED CURRENT CUTTERS CUTTING DABBING DERRICK DIFFERS DIFFUSE DINNERS DISSENT DOLLARS DOTTING DUFFERS DULLEST FALLING FALLOUT FELLING FELLOWS FINNEYS FLEEING FOLLIES FORREST FREEDOM FREEING FREEMAN FREEWAY FULLEST FUSSING GALLERY GALLEYS GALLIUM GALLONS GALLOWS GARRICK GIFFENS GOBBLED GODDAMN GROOMED GROOVED GROOVES GUNNERS GUTTERS HALLECK HAMMOCK HAMMOND HAPPENS HAPPIER HAPPILY HARRIET HERRICK HERRING HESSIAN HILLMAN HILLYER HITTERS HOBBIES HOBBLED HOFFMAN HOLLAND HOPPING HOPPLES HUMMING HURRAYS HURRIED JABBING JAGGERS JESSICA JITTERS JUTTING KENNARD KITTENS LAPPING LATTERS LATTICE LESSING LETTING LIPPMAN LITTERS LUBBOCK MADDENS MAGGIES MAGGOTS MANNERS MAPPING MARRIED MARRIES MASSEUR MASSIVE MATTERS MATTHEW MATTING MERRILY MESSIAH MESSING MILLAYS MILLERS MISSTEP MITTENS MOLLIFY MOPPING MOTTLED MUFFLED MUFFLER MULLERS MULLINS NARROWS NIGGERS NOZZLES PADDING PASSING PASSION PASSIVE PATTERN PATTIES PATTING PENNOCK PETTING PILLAGE PILLARS PILLOWS POLLING POTTERS POTTERY PUDDLES PUFFING PULLEYS PULLING PURRING PUTTING PUZZLED PUZZLES RABBITS RALLIES RAPPING RATTLED REDDISH RIBBONS RIDDLES RIPPLES ROBBING ROBBINS RODDING ROLLING ROTTING RUBBING RUBBISH RUFFIAN RUFFLED RUSSIAN SCOOPED SCOOTED SELLING SETTING SHEERAN SHOOTER SHOOTIN SIZZLED STOOPED SUFFICE SUMMARY SUMMATE SUPPORT SWEETLY SWOOPED TALLIES TALLYHO TAPPING TELLING TENNIAL TERRAIN TOLLEYS TOPPING TOPPLED TOSSING TUNNELS VALLEYS VECCHIO VILLAGE WATTLES WEDDING WEMMICK WETTING WIGGLED WILLARD WILLCOX WINNERS WOBBLED WOLLMAN WORRIED WORRIES YELLING ZIFFREN

ABCDAAD
ELYSEES

ABCDAAE
LEGALLY LOCALLY LOWELLS LUCILLE OAKWOOD OUTDOOR OUTLOOK

ABCDABA
DECIDED DELUDED

ABCDABC
GIORGIO

ABCDABE
AIRMAIL BOURBON CHURCHS DECADES DECIDES FAIRFAX GEORGES HEATHEN HEATHER INCLINE MAXIMAL ORATORS ORATORY RETIRED RETIRES SILESIA TEMPTED

ABCDACA
DREADED

ABCDACE
ABIGAIL EASIEST ITALIAN SPONSOR THEATER TREATED UNTRUTH

ABCDADA
MINUMUM

ABCDADC
ACETATE

ABCDADE
EMINENT IRONING LABELED

ABCDAEA
EXTREME MAXIMUM OKAMOTO SARPSIS SPOUSES

ABCDAEB
PROSPER TRACTOR TRAITOR

ABCDAEC
ARCHAIC AVERAGE AVOCADO HATCHET LOYALTY OUTPOST THEATRE WIDOWED

ABCDAED
ACREAGE IMAGING TRENTON

ABCDAEE
ENDLESS EXPRESS NOMINEE TRUSTEE

ABCDAEF
ABREAST AIRWAYS ALREADY ANIMALS ASPHALT CHANCED CHANCES CHOICES COUNCIL CYNICAL DWINDLE EARNEST EASTERN ESCHEAT EVIDENT FATEFUL FEARFUL GEORGIA GLASGOW GRUDGES HARSHLY HATCHED HAUGHTY HEIGHTS HITCHED HUNCHED IMAGINE IMPLIED IMPLIES INFLICT INQUIRE INQUIRY INSPIRE IOCSIXF IOCSIXG ITALICS ITCHING KNOCKED KNUCKLE LOBULES LOCALES NADINES NOMINAL OBVIOUS OMINOUS OUTCOME PLUMPED PROMPTS RAMIREZ RECORDS REFORMS REGARDS REMARKS REPORTS RETURNS REWARDS ROBARDS ROBERTA ROBERTS ROSTRUM RUMORED SAMPSON SATISFY SIMPSON STEPSON TACITLY TAUNTED THAXTER TIBETAN TIGHTEN TIGHTLY TIMOTHY TOASTED TRAFTON TRUSTED TWISTED TWISTER

ABCDBAC
MUSEUMS

ABCDBAD
WARSAWS

ABCDBAE
CARMACK DIOXIDE ENGINES EVOLVED GARBAGE NOTIONS RAMPART READERS RENDERS RUPTURE TIDBITS

ABCDBBA
ANTENNA

ABCDBBC
MONSOON

ABCDBBE
BETWEEN BOYHOOD DECREES DEGREES GENTEEL SEAWEED UNCANNY VARLAAM

ABCDBCA
SERVERS

ABCDBCB
BENZENE

ABCDBCC
DISMISS

ABCDBCD
JENSENS
RINGING
SINGING

ABCDBCE
ANIONIC
BARNARD
BERGERS
BINDING
CHATHAM
FINDING
FORLORN
HARVARD
HERBERT
LENIENT
LINKING
LONDONS
MERCERS
MERGERS
MINCING
NURTURE
OUTPUTS
PERIERS
PICNICS
RINSING
SECRECY
SINKING
TERPERS
WARFARE
WHETHER
WINDING
WINKING

ABCDBDC
ORDERED
SIGNING

ABCDBDE
HEARERS
LACTATE
PRAIRIE

ABCDBEA
DESCEND
ENHANCE
SANDALS
SECRETS
SIXTIES
TEMPEST
TOPCOAT

ABCDBEB
BELIEVE
RELIEVE

ABCDBEC
BOSTONS
MOSCOWS
PINCIAN
PURSUER
REDHEAD
SIGHING
SUNBURN
WESKERS

ABCDBED
ANTONIO
BIRDIED
GEYSERS
INCENSE
INTENSE
JERSEYS
POISONS
PURSUES
SOMEONE
STANTON
STARTER
SUBDUED

ABCDBEE
BECKETT
BOYCOTT
CANVASS
GINMILL
JACKASS
MEYNELL
WENDELL

ABCDBEF
AIRLINE
ANYONES
ARMORED
BALKANS
BANDAGE
BARGAIN
BASTARD
BELIEFS
BEQUEST
BERKELY
BIRDIES
CAETANI
CALVARY
CAPTAIN
CENTERS
CHEKHOV
COMFORT
COMPOSE
COMPOST
CONFORM
CONTOUR
COWBOYS
CULTURE
DEALERS
DEAREST
DESCENT
DIARIES
DICTION
DIGNITY
DISLIKE
DOCTORS
DOGTOWN
ENDINGS
FANTASY
FERMENT
FERVENT
FICTION
FISHING
FORMOSA
GARLAND
GIRLISH
GORDONS
GORTONS
HEAVENS
HEAVERS
HELMETS
HELPERS
HENLEYS
HERSELF
HOLYOKE
HORMONE
INFANCY
INFANTS
INTENDS
INTONED
JANUARY
KERNELS
LEADERS
LIFTING
LIGNITE
LIMPING
LIQUIDS
LISTING
LITHIUM
MALRAUX
MANDATE
MANUALS
MAYFAIR
MAYNARD
MIJBILS
MOTIONS
NEAREST
NEGLECT
NEPHEWS
NISHIMA
NORFOLK
NOXIOUS
ORDERLY
PACKAGE
PACKARD
PAGEANT
PERCENT
PERFECT
PIANIST
PICKING
POGROMS
PROGRAM
PURSUED
PURSUIT
RADIANT
RAMEAUS
RAMPANT
RANSACK
RAPHAEL
REAVEYS
REFLECT
RELIEFS
REQUEST
RESPECT
REUVENI
REVIEWS
RHYTHMS
SALVAGE
SEGMENT
SERPENT
SIGNIFY
STARTED
STILTED
STRATUM
STRETCH
TEMPERS
TENSELY
TERSELY
UNLINED
VANTAGE
VARIANT
VERMEJO
VICTIMS
VIEWING
VULTURE
WEAKEST
WEIGELS
WESTERN
WISHING
WORKOUT
YARDAGE

ABCDCAB
ESTATES

ABCDCAD
OPINION

ABCDCAE
CLINICO
CLINICS
CRITICS
ENGAGED
ENGAGES
GEOLOGY
PHILIPS
TENANTS
THERETO
TRINITY

ABCDCBB
USELESS

ABCDCBE
BREWERS
BREWERY
DEITIES
GRANARY
PREFERS
REVIVED
SYNONYM
UNITING
UTILITY

ABCDCDA
GAINING

ABCDCDE
ASININE
JOINING
LETITIA
RAINING
SHINING
VEINING
WHINING

ABCDCEA
BATHTUB
EDIFICE
ENTITLE
GUIDING
SPIRITS
STEVENS
SWEDENS
TEACART

ABCDCEB
PENANCE

ABCDCEC
NIAGARA
PRECEDE

ABCDCED
BLATANT
BONANZA
DAISIES
PRETEXT
PRONOUN

ABCDCEE
AGELESS
AVERELL
BAILIFF
GALILEE
THERELL

ABCDCEF
ABIDING
ABILITY
AGILITY
AMOROUS
APOLOGY
ARIDITY
ARISING
AWNINGS
BAILING
BICYCLE
BIOLOGY
BOILING
BOUQUET
BRAVADO
BRITISH
CEILING
CLEMENS
CONANTS
DRIVING
ECONOMY
EDITING
EDITION
FAILING
FAIRIES
FAIRING
FINANCE
LUEGERS
MAILING
NOISILY
ONESELF
ORIGINS
OXALATE
PEASANT
PHALANX
PORTRAY
PRABANG
PRESENT
PRETEND
PREVENT
PRICING
PRIMING
PROMOTE
PROTONS
PROVOKE
PROVOST
RAIDING
RAILING
RAISING
REVIVAL
RIOTOUS
ROILING
ROTATED
ROTATES
SAILING
SCENERY
SIEBERN
SLIDING
SMILING
SPIRITO
SUICIDE
TENANCY
THEREBY
THEREIN
THEREOF
THERESA
TRIVIAL
TWOFOLD
UNAWARE
UNIFIED
UNIFIES
UTILIZE
VIEWERS
WAILING
WAITING
WHEREAS
WHEREBY
WHEREIN
WHEREOF
WHITING
WIENERS
WRITING
ZEALAND

ABCDDAE
EMITTED
IDYLLIC

ABCDDBA
STREETS

ABCDDBE
SCHAACK

ABCDDCA
DRESSED
PHILLIP
RIEGGER
STEPPES

ABCDDCB
BRENNER
GRAMMAR
PRESSER

ABCDDCD
DRESSES
GUESSES
PRESSES

ABCDDCE
ABETTED
BLESSED
BLOSSOM
CAREERS
CROSSON
DWELLER
GRATTAN
GRIFFIN
GUESSED
KIEFFER
LOESSER
PRESSED
SHELLEY
SMELLED
SPELLED
STEMMED
STEPPED
SWELLED

ABCDDEA
CLASSIC
DRAGGED
DRILLED
DRIPPED
DROPPED
DRUGGED
DRUMMED
SALOONS
SCHOOLS
SCOTTYS
SCREENS
SIERRAS

ABCDDEB
CRUPPER
DRUMMER
FLANNEL
REISSUE
SEATTLE
SWALLOW
TRAPPER
TRIGGER
TRIMMER
WRAPPER

ABCDDEC
FREDDIE
JANSSEN
ODYSSEY
WHADDYA

ABCDDED
BRANNON
BRENNAN
CLASSES
CROSSES
GLASSES
PLODDED
PRODDED
SKIDDED
SQUEEZE
STUDDED
TRUSSES

ABCDDEF
BDIKKAT
BLOTTED
BLURRED
BRAGGED
BRIMMED
BRITTEN
BRITTLE
CHANNEL
CHATTED
CHATTER
CHILLED
CHIPPED
CHOPPED
CLAPPED
CLASSED
CLATTER
CLIPPED
CLOGGED
CLUBBED
CRAMMED
CROPPED
CROSSED
DRIZZLE
FLAPPED
FLIPPED
FLOGGED
FLOPPED
FLUTTER
FREDDYS
GHETTOS
GLADDEN
GLADDYS
GLIMMER
GLITTER
GRABBED
GRILLED
GRINNED
GRIPPED
GROKKED
GROSSLY

ABCDDEF
HYANNIS
INDOORS
JOHNNIE
KNITTED
KNOTTED
LAGOONS
LAISSEZ
OMITTED
OVERRUN
PHYLLIS
PLANNED
PLANNER
PLATTER
PLOTTED
PLUGGED
PLUMMER
POUSSIN
PRUSSIA
QUARREL
SCANNED
SCARRED
SCATTER
SCOFFED
SHALLOW
SHATTER
SHIPPED
SHIPPER
SHUDDER
SHUFFLE
SHUTTER
SKILLED
SKILLET
SKIMMED
SKIPPED
SLAMMED
SLAPPED
SLIPPED
SLIPPER
SLUGGED
SLUGGER
SMALLER
SNAPPED
SNIFFED
SNUBBED
SOUFFLE
SPANNED
SPILLED
SPITTLE
SPOTTED
SPURRED
STABBED
STAFFED
STAGGER
STALLED
STARRED
STELLAR
STIFFLY
STIRRED
STIRRUP
STOPPED
STOPPER
STUBBLE
STUFFED
STUNNED
SWOLLEN
TAUSSIG
THINNER
TRAFFIC
TRAPPED
TRIMMED
TRIPPED
TROLLEY
WHIPPED
WHIPPLE
WHIZZED
WRAPPED
WRITTEN

ABCDEAA
SADNESS
SINLESS
STRAUSS

ABCDEAB
CORTICO
ESCAPES
HIBACHI
INSULIN
NEPTUNE
REQUIRE
RESTORE
STYLIST

ABCDEAC
CREVICE
EARLIER
ENDOWED
ENDURED
LINCOLN
MUSLIMS

ABCDEAD
CADENCE
CONTACT
EPITHET
OBANION

ABCDEAE
EXCUSES
EXPOSES
SIAMESE
TAOISTS
THRUSTS
VERNAVA

ABCDEAF
ABYSMAL
ADRENAL
AFRICAN
AMELIAS
ANGULAR
AQUINAS
AROUSAL
ARSENAL
ARTISAN
AZTECAN
COMPACT
CONDUCT
CONVICT
DEMANDS
EDYTHES
ELAPSED
EMPIRES
EMPTIED
EMPTIER
EMPTIES
ENABLED
ENABLES
ENACTED
ENDURES
ENJOYED
ENTRIES
ENZYMES
EQUATED
ERUPTED
ESCAPED
EUROPES
EVICTED
EXALTED
EXCITED
EXCUSED
EXHALED
EXISTED
EXPIRED
EXPOSED
FALSIFY
FORTIFY
GIZENGA
HEALTHY
IBRAHIM
INERTIA
INHERIT
INTERIM
INVALID
ISLAMIC
LARGELY
LAUCHLI
LAURELS
LIGHTLY
LOVABLE
LUCKILY
MAGNUMS
MEDIUMS
NAKTONG
NAPKINS
NATIONS
NEARING
NESTING
NEWTONS
NOTHING
NUMBING
NURSING
OCZAKOV
ORATION
OUTFLOW
OUTGROW
OVATION
PERHAPS
RAIDERS
RANGERS
RAPTURE
RAYBURN
RECTORS
REPAIRS
RICHARD
RICHERT
RIOTERS
RIVALRY
RODGERS
ROSBURG
RUMFORD
SAWDUST
SELFISH
SLOWEST
SPANISH
SUNRISE
SWADESH
SWEDISH
TALENTS
TARGETS
THIRSTY
THREATS
THRIFTY
THROATS
TICKETS
TOILETS
TRIBUTE
TWELFTH
URANIUM
WINDOWS

ABCDEBA
ANDRENA
DEBATED
DECAYED
DECRIED
DEFINED
DELAYED
DENOTED
DEPOSED
DERIVED
DESIRED
DEVISED
DEVOTED
EVASIVE
GNAWING
NEWSMEN
RECOVER
SEMITES
SENATES
STRAITS
SURPLUS
THOUGHT
TURNOUT

ABCDEBB
REFUGEE

ABCDEBC
BESIDES
DESIRES
ENTRANT
MENCKEN
REDUCED
RESIDES
SANDMAN
VERNIER
WERTHER

ABCDEBD
INSTANT
INTERNE
JOHNSON
MEASLES
SCIENCE
SOUNION

ABCDEBE
ATHLETE
BEARDED
HABITAT
REFUSES
RESIDED

ABCDEBF
ALVEOLI
ANCIENT
ANTHONY
BASEMAN
BEACHES
BEADLES
BEARDEN
BECOMES
BEHAVED
BEHAVES
BELATED
BELCHED
BELOVED
BENCHED
BENCHES
BENTLEY
BERATED
BISCUIT
BLANDLY
BLEAKLY
BLINDLY
BLUNTLY
BOREDOM
BRAVERY
BREVARD
BROKERS
BUILDUP
BUREAUS
CAMERAS
CAPITAL
CARLOAD
CLEANLY
CLEARLY
CLOSELY
COMPSON
CONTROL
CRATERS
CURIOUS
DEBATES
DEFINES
DELANEY
DELIVER
DENOTES
DERIVES
DEVICES
DRAPERS
DRAPERY
DRAWERS
DRIVERS
DUBIOUS
EDWARDS
ENGLAND
ENSUING
EPITAPH
FACTUAL
FAIRWAY
FEATHER
FEMALES
FURIOUS
GATEWAY
GENTLER
GROCERS
GROCERY
GROWERS
HALFWAY
HANDBAG
HARTMAN
HEARTED
HEAVIER
HEINKEL
HORIZON
HOUSTON
INFERNO
KEMBLES
KINETIC
KINSHIP
KIWANIS
KNOWING
KROGERS
KRUGERS
LADGHAM
LAOTIAN
LEAGUER
LEAGUES
LEARNED
LEATHER
LOVEJOY
MAGICAL
MARINAS
MARITAL
MARSHAL
MARTIAN
MATHIAS
MAYORAL
MELTZER
MENACED
MERITED
MONITOR
MUSIQUE
NATURAL
NEGROES
NEITHER
NESTLED
NUCLEUS
OERSTED
ORCHARD
PARKWAY
PARTIAL
PASCHAL
PEONIES
PERCHED
PILGRIM
PLAINLY
PORTION
PRAYERS
PRIMARY
PROCURE
PROVERB
QUANTUM
QUINTUS
RACEWAY
RADICAL
RAILWAY
REACHED
REACHES
REACTED
RECITED
REDUCES
REFINED
REFUSED
REFUTED
REGIMES
RELATED
RELATES
RELAXED
RELAXES
RELAYED
REMOVED
REMOVES
RENAMED
REPLIED
REPLIES
REPUTED
RESCUED
RESUMED
REVISED
RITCHIE
SAMOVAR
SCRATCH
SECURED
SEIGNER
SIBERIA
SNORING
SNOWING
SOMEHOW
STEALTH
SULPHUR
TEACHER
TEACHES
TEMPLES
TRACERS
TRADERS
UNDOING
URINARY
VAGINAL
VATICAN
VAUGHAN
VITAMIN
WARHEAD
WEATHER
WEBSTER
WEIGHED
WRITERS
YEARNED

ABCDECA
DREAMED
MALCOLM
SHELVES
SPECIES
TANGENT

ABCDECB
BATISTA
BEDSIDE
CREAMER
DESPISE
DREAMER
GENUINE
GREATER
GRENIER
PREMIER
PROCTOR

ABCDECC
DISCUSS
HOSTESS

ABCDECD
BANGING
CONTENT
DISEASE
FASTEST
FAUSTUS
FLEDGED
HANGING
HANSENS
LONGING
ORESTES
PLEDGED
RANGING
REDONDO
SWINGIN
THINKIN

ABCDECE
AMENDED
ARTISTS
BLENDED
CLEARER
GREASES
MONTANA
PLEADED
PLEASES
WIELDED
YIELDED

ABCDECF
AIRPORT
ALERTED
AQUEOUS
AVENUES
AVERTED
BANKING
BENDING
BERNARD

ABCDECF
BOATMAN
BORDERS
BRITAIN
BURNERS
BUSIEST
CANYONS
CARMERS
CARPORT
CHAPMAN
CHATEAU
CHEAPER
CHEATED
CHESTER
CLEANED
CLEANER
CLEARED
COASTAL
CONFINE
CONSENT
CONTEND
CONVENT
CORNERS
CREAKED
CREASED
CREATED
CREATES
CURSORY
DANCING
DENTING
DENYING
DIAGRAM
DISPOSE
DRIFTIN
ECSTASY
EMOTION
EROSION
FARMERS
FASCISM
FASCIST
FENCING
FIEDLER
FIELDER
FINLAND
FLECKED
FOREARM
FORWARD
FRESNEL
FRITZIE
GLEAMED
GRACIAS
GRADUAL
GREASED
HANDING
HARBERT
HARBORS
HARBURG
HARPERS
HEARSAY
HERFORD
HUNTING
HYDRIDE
HYDRIDO
INVOLVE
JENKINS
KOEHLER
LANDING
LENDING
MANKIND
MENDING
MERCURY
MORTARS
MUNDANE
MURDERS
NITRATE
NORBERG
NURSERY
OUTLETS
PANTING
PARKERS
PATENTS
PENDING
PERFORM
PERJURY
PIERCED
PLATEAU
PLEASED
PLEDGES
PORTERS
PUNGENT
QUERIED
QUERIES
QUICKIE
RANGONI
RANKING
RAUCOUS
RENTING
ROADWAY
ROUNDUP
SANDING
SATIETY
SCANDAL
SCENTED
SENDING
SHELTER
SLENDER
SMEARED
SNEAKED
SNEAKER
SOLIDLY
SOLUBLE
SPARTAN
SPATIAL
SPEAKER
SPECTER
SPENCER
STEALER
STEAMED
STENGEL
STEPHEN
STEUBEN
SURGERY
SWEATER
TENDING
TENDONS
THEOREM
THOMSON
URGINGS
VENDING
VINCENT
VOLUBLE
WANTING
WASPISH
WILHELM
WORKERS
WRECKED
YORKERS

ABCDEDA
SCHEMES
SINUOUS
SONATAS
SPHERES

ABCDEDB
ADHERED
ALCOHOL
BRIEFER

ABCDEDC
FOREVER
MODELED
MONAGAN
PACIFIC
SUVOROV
WIDENED

ABCDEDD
FORESEE

ABCDEDE
IMPEDED
SCHERER

ABCDEDF
AEROSOL
ALTERED
ANGELES
ARDUOUS
ASPIRIN
BOGEYED
BRIEFED
BURNING
CLOSEST
CONSIST
COVERED
COVETED
DAWNING
DEFICIT
DICTATE
DYNAFAC
EARNING
EXHIBIT
FATUOUS
FIREMEN
FRIEZES
HOWEVER
INDEXES
INTEGER
ISFAHAN
KILOTON
LEANING
LIBRARY
LIKENED
LOWERED
MEANING
MORNING
OPENING
PANELED
PEACOCK
PERDIDO
PERSIST
POLITIC
POWERED
QUIETED
QUIETER
REGULUS
REMNANT
RIPENED
RUNAWAY
SATIRIC
SCREWED
SEMITIC
SHAEFER
SOBERED
SURVIVE
TAMIRIS
TAPERED
TENUOUS
THIEVES
TUNISIA
TURNING
USHERED
VERNONS
WARNING
WATERED
WEANING
WHOEVER
WORLDLY
YAWNING

ABCDEEA
IERULLI
SARKEES
SCRIPPS

ABCDEEB
CAMILLA
CEZANNE
MADONNA
MARELLA
SABELLA
TOBACCO
TYRANNY

ABCDEEC
CANTEEN
REDWOOD

ABCDEED
CAYENNE
FAYETTE
GAZETTE
GISELLE
MICELLE
PALETTE

ABCDEEF
AWFULLY
BEDROOM
BIZARRE
CARTOON
CARWOOD
CORELLI
CRUELLY
DILEMMA
DRYFOOS
EMBASSY
EQUALLY
FINALLY
HAPGOOD
HEYWOOD
IDEALLY
IMPASSE
JAYCEES
MAHZEER
MANHOOD
MAUREEN
MELISSA
MIDWEEK
MORALLY
MYNHEER
ORVILLE
ORWELLS
PICASSO
PIONEER
PLATOON
PLYWOOD
POWELLS
PROCEED
RECALLS
SEAFOOD
SHRILLY
SIBYLLA
SIXTEEN
THRILLS
UNHAPPY
VERLOOP
VITALLY
YANKEES

ABCDEFA
ALGEBRA
ALGERIA
AMERICA
ARIZONA
ASTERIA
ASTORIA
AUSTRIA
CALORIC
CERAMIC
CHAOTIC
CHRONIC
CRYPTIC
DANGLED
DEFRAUD
DIAMOND
DILATED
DILUTED
DONATED
DOUBLED
DOUBTED
DRAFTED
DRAINED
DRAWLED
DRIFTED
DROWNED
ECLIPSE
EDUCATE
ELUSIVE
EMBRACE
EMULATE
ENDORSE
ENFORCE
ENLARGE
ENSLAVE
EPICURE
EPISODE
EPITOME
ERUDITE
ESQUIRE
EXAMINE
EXAMPLE
EXCLUDE
EXPANSE
EXPLODE
EXPLORE
GASPING
GELDING
GLARING
GLAZING
GLOWING
GRAYING
GRAZING
GROPING
GROWING
ISRAELI
LEXICAL
LIBERAL
LITERAL
LOGICAL
LYRICAL
MODICUM
NEWBORN
ORLANDO
RANCHER
REACTOR
REALTOR
REGULAR
RUSTLER
SACHEMS
SAILORS
SALYERS
SAMPLES
SATIRES
SAUCERS
SAVINGS
SCREAMS
SEATONS
SECANTS
SECONDS
SECTORS
SERIOUS
SERMONS
SEWARDS
SHADOWS
SHAKERS
SHARPES
SHAYNES
SHIELDS
SHOVELS
SHOWERS
SHRINES
SHRINKS
SIDNEYS
SIGNALS
SIGNERS
SINGERS
SLOCUMS
SLOGANS
SLUICES
SOPHIAS
SOURCES
SOVIETS
SPACERS
SPREADS
SPRINGS
SQUARES
SQUIRES
STABLES
STALINS
STEARNS
STORIES
STRAINS
STRANDS
STREAKS
STREAMS
STRIDES
STRIKES
STRINGS
STRIPES
STRIVES
STROKES
STUDIES
STUDIOS
SUBMITS
SUITORS
SULTANS
SUNDAYS
SURVEYS
SYMBOLS
TONIGHT
TORMENT
TOURIST
TRANSIT
TRUMPET
WHITROW
WINSLOW

ABCDEFB
ACRYLIC
ADMIRED
ADOPTED
ADVISED
ANTIGEN
ARBITER
ASPECTS
BECAUSE
BEDTIME
BROADER
BROILER
BROTHER
CADENZA
CALENDA
CALINDA
CENSURE
CHERISH
CREATOR
CROWDER
CRUISER
DEBACLE
DECLARE
DECLINE
DEPRIVE
DESPITE
DRINKER
DRUNKER
DYNASTY
ESKIMOS
FEATURE
FERTILE
FESTIVE
GENTILE
GERMANE
GESTURE
HEROINE
INHUMAN
ISLANDS
KEYHOLE
KEYNOTE
LECTURE
LEISURE
MAGENTA
MATILDA
MAZURKA
MEASURE
MONTERO
MYSTERY
NECKTIE
NIKOLAI
PERFUME
PLAYFUL
PLEURAL
PORTAGO
PORTICO
PRINTER
REALIZE
RECLUSE
REDOUTE
REPLACE
RESIDUE
RESOLVE
RESPITE
SEIZURE
SERVICE
SERVILE
SOPRANO
STARLET
STEWART
STUDENT
TENABLE
TENSILE
THROUGH

ABCDEFB

TRAILER TROUSER UNCLEAN VEHICLE VENTURE VESTIGE VOLCANO WELCOME WELFARE

ABCDEFC

ACETONE ANSWERS ANYBODY ARGUING AUDITED AUSTINS AWESOME BASKETS BEDFORD BISHOPS BREATHE BROGLIO BUSHELS CASTLES CASTROS CONDEMN CONSIGN CONTAIN CURATOR CUSTOMS CZARINA DESIGNS DETROIT DOSAGES DUNGEON ENTRUST EXTRACT FARTHER FOSTERS FUNSTON FURTHER GARDNER GARVIER GASEOUS GASKETS GODSEND GONTRAN GOSPELS GRANDMA GRENADE HANDGUN HELPFUL INDUCED INSECTS INSULTS JOSEPHS JUANITA KARSNER LANTERN LISTENS MANSION MASTERS MENTION MENUHIN MOSQUES MUSCLES MUSKETS MYSTICS OPERATE OVERDUE OYSTERS PARTNER PASTORS PATIENT PATRIOT PENSION PISTOLS PISTONS POSTERS PRECISE PREFACE PRELUDE PREMISE PRESIDE PRESUME PROVISO PUSHERS RADIOED RESULTS ROYALTY RUNDOWN SHRIVER STAMINA STERILE STIMULI SUNDOWN SYMPTOM TENSION THROWER TORQUER TRACHEA TPEMBLE UPDATED WINGMAN WINSTON WISMANS WITHOUT WRESTLE ZURCHER

ABCDEFD

ABSENCE ADVERSE ALUSIKS BAPTIST BIZERTE BRANDON BRIDGED BRUSHES BULGING BUNDLED CADMIUM CENSORS CHARTER CHRISTI CLASHES CLINTON CLOSETS COMEDIE CONTEST CONTEXT COUNTIN COURIER COUSINS CRADLED CROSBYS CULTIST DENTIST DISTANT DISTORT DIVERSE DRUNKEN DUNKIRK EGOTIST FLASHES FRESCOS FUELOIL GANTLET HANDLED HUDSONS HUNDRED INVERSE JUDGING KAISERS KINDRED KONISHI LICENSE LINEAGE LODGING MARSHES MATSUOS MERGING MILEAGE MIRANDA MYCENAE OBSERVE PANSIES PARSONS PERALTA PERSONS PHYSICS PLAYBOY PORNSEN PREMIUM PRISONS PROTECT PROTEST PSYCHIC PURGING QUARTER REASONS REUNION ROMANZA SELKIRK SHARPER SHORTER SILENCE SINATRA SMARTER STAGING STUDIED SURGING THURBER TRUDGED TWIRLER VERANDA WATSONS WILSONS

ABCDEFE

ABILENE ACHIEVE ADJUSTS ADMIRER ADVISES AROUSES AUSTERE AVOIDED BLINDED BOARDED BOUNDED BRANDED BREASTS BRUISES BRUMIDI BURMESE CABRINI CHINESE CHRISTS CLAUSES CLOUDED COMPETE CORPSES COURSES CROWDED DYNASTS FARNESE FOCUSES FORESTS FOUNDED GEROSAS GUARDED HEARSTS HYGIENE IMPOSES INVADED JURISTS KETOSIS LABORER LUMIERE MALTESE MARLENE MARTINI MOLIERE MOUNDED NAIVETE NOWHERE OBSCENE OPTIMUM PHRASES POLTAVA POUNDED PRAISES PRIESTS QUARTET QUINTET RAPISTS ROUNDED SCHIELE SINCERE SOUNDED STYRENE SUPREME TERMINI TIEPOLO UNAIDED WOUNDED

ABCDEFF

ACTRESS AIMLESS AIRLESS ARTLESS BADNESS BARNETT BURGESS BUSHELL COMPASS CONFESS CORNELL COYNESS CURTISS CYPRESS DRYNESS DRYWALL FITNESS GODLESS HAPLESS HARNESS HASKELL HAZLITT IMPRESS INSTALL JOBLESS LAXNESS LEAVITT LIONESS MACNEFF MADNESS MAXWELL OVERALL PAYROLL PERLUSS PICKOFF PITFALL PLAYOFF PROCESS PROFESS PROWESS SCHMITT SCHRAMM SHAMPOO SHAWNEE SHERIFF SITWELL TAKEOFF THOMASS TOYNBEE WINLESS WITNESS

ABAABCBD

PEPPERED

ABAACDCE

TATTERED

ABAACDEA

SESSIONS

ABAACDEF

BUBBLING

ABABCDAD

MOMOYAMA

ABABCDEF

COCONUTS LALAURIE

ABACADAE

ALABAMAS

ABACADCE

INITIATE

ABACADEF

ARAPACIS ELEMENTS ELEVENTH INITIALS

ABACBDBE

TETHERED

ABACBDEC

BIBLICAL

ABACCDEE

ODONNELL

ABACDACD

NONSENSE

ABACDAEF

EMERGENT

ABACDBCE

NINETIES POPULOUS

ABACDBEA

ANACONDA

ABACDBEC

PIPELINE

ABACDBEF

TITANIUM VIVACITY

ABACDCCA

NINETEEN

ABACDCEF

AWAITING EVENINGS IMITATED IMITATES

ABACDDEF

TOTALLED

ABACDEAD

SUSPENSE

ABACDEAF

ELEVATED ENERGIES EXECUTED TOTALITY

ABACDEBA

DEDUCTED

ABACDEBF

ETERNITY GIGANTIC MEMORIES PEPTIDES

ABACDEDF

AWAKENED

ABACDEFA

ELEGANCE EVERYONE EXERCISE MOMENTUM SUSPECTS

ABACDEFB

ACADEMIC MEMBRANE MEMORIZE

ABACDEFC

ELECTRIC

ABACDEFD

EMERGING EMERSONS EVERYDAY

ABACDEFE

ANALYSES ANALYSIS ANALYSTS

ABACDEFG

ADAPTERS ADAPTING ALACRITY AMATEURS ANALYSED ANALYTIC ANALYZED ANALYZER ANALYZES AWARDING COCKTAIL EJECTION ELECTION ELECTORS ELECTRON ELEPHANT ELEVATOR EMERALDS EMERITUS ERECTING ERECTION EVENTUAL EXECUTOR EXEMPLAR EXERTING EYEBROWS HOHLBEIN IRISHMAN MEMORIAL NONWHITE POPULACE SYSTEMIC TOTALING TUTORING

ABBABBCD

ASSASSIN

ABBACBDE

BEEBREAD

ABBACCDE

APPALLED

ABBACDAB

ESSENCES

ABBACDAE

EFFECTED ILLINOIS

ABBACDCE

IMMINENT OPPONENT

ABBACDEB

ASSAULTS

ABBACDEF

APPARENT ARRANGED ASSAILED ASSAYING ATTACHED ATTACHES ATTACKED ATTACKER ATTAINED EMMERICH

ABBACDEF
OPPOSING
OPPOSITE

ABBCABDE
WOODWORK

ABBCADBE
ATTRACTS

ABBCADCE
APPEALED
APPEARED
APPEASED

ABBCADDE
ANNUALLY

ABBCADEC
WOODWARD
WOODWIND

ABBCADEF
ALLIANCE
APPLAUSE
APPRAISE
ASSUAGED

ABBCBBCD
ASSESSED

ABBCBBDE
ASSESSOR

ABBCBDBA
DEEPENED

ABBCBDEF
ASSISTED
ATTITUDE
WEEKENDS

ABBCDABE
ACCURACY

ABBCDAEF
ACCOLADE
ACCURATE
ALLOCATE
APPROACH
ARRIVALS
ARROGANT
EFFLUENT
ILLUSION
ILLUSIVE
IMMUNITY
OFFSHORE

ABBCDBAE
LOOPHOLE

ABBCDBCE
ATTESTED
FOOTNOTE
GOODBODY

ABBCDBEE
HEEDLESS
NEEDLESS
PEERLESS

ABBCDBEF
ANNOUNCE

ABBCDCEF
ADDITION
ADDITIVE
AFFINITY
ARRIVING
FOOTSTEP
OFFICIAL

ABBCDDEF
ALLOTTED
OCCURRED

ABBCDEAC
ROOSTERS

ABBCDEAE
APPESTAT
ELLIPSES

ABBCDEAF
APPROVAL
ASSYRIAN
OCCASION

ABBCDEBF
ANNOYING
ATTEMPTS
DOORKNOB
INNOCENT
TEENAGER
WEEKLIES

ABBCDECE
APPENDED
ATTENDED
OFFENDED
OFFENSES

ABBCDECF
ACCENTED
ACCEPTED
AFFECTED
ARRESTED
ASSENTED
ASSERTED
IMMERSED
OFFENDER
WOODSIDE

ABBCDEDC
APPETITE

ABBCDEDF
EFFICACY
IMMANENT
LOOSENED

ABBCDEFB
ADDICTED
ANNISTON

ABBCDEFC
ASSEMBLE
LEESONAS
WOODLAND

ABBCDEFD
ALLEGING

ABBCDEFE
ACCORDED
AFFORDED
OCCLUDED

ABBCDEFF
ASSIGNEE
COOLNESS
DOORBELL
FOOTBALL
GOODNESS
ROOTLESS
WOODRUFF

ABBCDEFG
ACCIDENT
ACCOSTED
ACCOUNTS
ACCRUING
ACCUSING
AFFIRMED
AFFLUENT
ALLEGORY
ALLERGIC
ALLOWING
ALLUSION
APPENDIX
APPLYING
APPROVED
ASSEMBLY
ASSIGNED
ASSORTED
ASSUMING
ASSURING
ATTORNEY
BEETLING
BOOKCASE
BOOKLETS
BOOSTING
COOLIDGE
DOORSTEP
DOORWAYS
FEEDBACK
FEELINGS
HOODLUMS
ILLUSORY
IMMATURE
IMMORTAL
ISSUANCE
MCCARTHY
MCCAULEY
MEETINGS
OCCIDENT
OCCUPANT
OCCUPIED
OCCUPIES
OFFERING
OFFICERS
SOOTHING
UTTERING
WOODBURY

ABCAADAD
EXCEEDED

ABCAADAE
ESTEEMED

ABCAADEF
GROGGINS
ONLOOKER

ABCABADE
ETCETERA
INFINITE
INFINITY

ABCABCDE
CORCORAN
MURMURED

ABCABDAE
ENGENDER

ABCABDBE
HATHAWAY

ABCABDCE
PALPABLE

ABCABDEA
ENTENDRE
SAUSAGES

ABCABDEB
ECLECTIC

ABCABDEF
ALKALINE
COLCORDS
MONMOUTH
TORTOISE

ABCACDAE
AGRARIAN

ABCACDED
PROPOSES

ABCACDEF
INSISTED
PROPOSAL
PROPOSED

ABCADAAE
OCTOROON

ABCADABE
INVITING
TEKTITES

ABCADACE
IONIZING

ABCADAEC
IGNITION

ABCADAEF
ACHAEANS
EASEMENT
ETHEREAL
INCISIVE
INHIBITS

ABCADBAE
ATLANTAS

ABCADBCE
GRIGORIS
PINPOINT
PREPARED
PREPARES

ABCADBDE
TORTUOUS

ABCADBEB
REPRIEVE
RETRIEVE

ABCADBED
GREGORIO

ABCADBEE
GRIGORSS

ABCADBEF
ATLANTIC
ATLANTIS
CIRCLING
CIRCUITS
GORGEOUS
PROPERLY
PROPERTY
THATCHED

ABCADCBE
TACTICAL

ABCADCCE
FULFILLS

ABCADCEF
AVIATION
PURPORTS
TORTURED
TORTURES

ABCADDAD
EMBEDDED
EXCESSES

ABCADDAE
EXPELLED

ABCADDED
ADMASSYS

ABCADEAC
ENDEARED

ABCADEAD
ALBANIAN

ABCADEAE
ARKANSAS
EXPENDED
EXPENSES
EXTENDED

ABCADEAF
ALSATIAN
ENMESHED
EXPECTED

ABCADEBF
CRACKERS
ENTERING
INCIDENT
ONCOMING
SEASONED
TEXTILES
TEXTURED
TEXTURES

ABCADECF
COACHMAN
CONCERNS
HITHERTO
INTIMATE
SEASONAL
SUNSHINE

ABCADEDA
SENSUOUS

ABCADEDE
CONCEDED

ABCADEDF
CANCELED
CRUCIFIX
EMPERORS

ABCADEEB
CALCUTTA

ABCADEEF
KIRKWOOD
MUSMANNO
TARTUFFE
TEXTBOOK

ABCADEFA
ENSEMBLE
ENVELOPE

ABCADEFB
ADVANCED
CONCERTO
DEADLINE
SEASHORE
SENSIBLE
TESTICLE

ABCADEFC
CIRCULAR
INDICTED
INSIDERS
INSIGHTS

ABCADEFD
BARBECUE
CONCEIVE
EXTERIOR

ABCADEFE
CONCRETE
ISTIQLAL
OBSOLETE
PURPOSES
SUBSIDED

ABCADEFF
HIGHBALL

ABCADEFG
ABLATION
ADJACENT
ADVANCES
AERATION
ALMAGEST
AUDACITY
BOMBINGS
CATCHERS
CATCHING
CHECKING
CHICAGOS
CHICKENS
CHOCTAWS
CHUCKLED
COACHING
COACHMEN
CONCEALS
CONCEITS
CONCEPTS
CONCERTS
CONCHITA

ABCADEFG
CONCLAVE
CONCLUDE
CRACKING
CRICKETS
DEADLOCK
ENDEAVOR
EXCERPTS
EXPERTLY
EXTERNAL
GANGSTER
GINGERLY
HIGHLAND
HIGHROAD
HIGHWAYS
INDICATE
INDIRECT
INTIMACY
IODINATE
PAMPHLET
PROPHECY
PROPHETS
RECRUITS
REPRINTS
REPRISAL
REPROACH
SENSIBLY
SLASHING
SUBSPACE
TANTRUMS
TASTEFUL
TINTABLE
TWITCHED

ABCBAABD
LEVELLED
REFERRED

ABCBAADE
REFERRAL

ABCBABDE
DECEDENT
DIVIDING
MINIMIZE
REVEREND
REVERENT

ABCBADBC
RESERVES

ABCBADBD
REVERSES

ABCBADBE
RESERVED
REVERSED
REVERTED
SEMESTER

ABCBADEA
DIVIDEND

ABCBADEB
TELETYPE

ABCBADEF
CAPACITY
LEVELING
REVERSAL
SINISTER
TAXATION

ABCBCDBA
REMEMBER

ABCBCDEF
LUMUMBAS

ABCBDABA
DEFENDED
DEPENDED

ABCBDABE
DEFENDER

ABCBDACE
SOKOLSKY

ABCBDAEA
SOLOISTS
STATUSES

ABCBDAEF
RESEARCH

ABCBDBCA
TENEMENT

ABCBDBCE
DIVISIVE
MONOTONE
MONOTONY

ABCBDBEA
STATUTES

ABCBDBEB
MAHAYANA

ABCBDBEF
CARAVANS
CAVANAGH
CEMETERY
CIVILIAN
DEFERENT
DIMINISH
DIVINITY
DIVISION
DOMOKOUS
FILIPINO
LIMITING
MONOPOLY
NAGASAKI
NIHILIST
RIGIDITY
SEVERELY
SICILIAN
VEHEMENT
VENEREAL
VICINITY
VIRILITY
VISITING

ABCBDCBA
DETECTED
DETESTED

ABCBDCEF
CEREBRAL
DETECTOR
STATUARY
SUBURBAN

ABCBDDBD
MANASSAS

ABCBDDBE
HAWAIIAN
REBELLED
RECESSED
REPELLED
SAVANNAH
TOMORROW

ABCBDDEC
COLOSSAL

ABCBDDED
COLOSSUS
PARALLEL

ABCBDDEF
HARASSED
MOROCCAN

ABCBDEBA
DECEASED
DECEIVED
DEFEATED
DESERTED
DESERVED
RECEIVER

ABCBDEBC
CANADIAN
DESERVES

ABCBDEBD
AUGUSTUS

ABCBDEBE
DEFENSES
RELEASES

ABCBDEBF
CEMENTED
DECEMBER
PARAXIAL
PEDERSEN
RECEIVED
RECEIVES
REJECTED
RELEASED
RELENTED
REMEDIES
REPEALED
REPEATED
RESENTED
REVEALED
REVENUES
SELECTED
UNENDING

ABCBDECD
MANAGING

ABCBDECF
COLONELS
CORONARY
CORONERS
HONORING
YOKOSUKA

ABCBDEDE
HONOLULU

ABCBDEDF
HONORARY

ABCBDEEF
MUTUALLY

ABCBDEFA
HEREWITH
SALARIES
SARACENS
STATIONS
STITCHES

ABCBDEFB
BEVERAGE
CALABRIA
CASANOVA
COLORADO
CORONADO
DELEGATE
GENERALE
GENERATE
NAKAMURA
PASADENA
RESEMBLE
SARATOGA

ABCBDEFC
CATALYST
COLONIAL
COLORFUL
LITIGANT
MOTORIST
VENETIAN
VISITORS

ABCBDEFD
DAMAGING
DAMASCUS
FINISHES
MILITANT
PARASOLS
SOLOVIEV

ABCBDEFE
JAPANESE
KASAVUBU

ABCBDEFF
PITILESS

ABCBDEFG
BALAFREJ
BALAGUER
BALANCED
BENEDICK
BENEFITS
BOROUGHS
CALAMITY
CATALOGS
CEREMONY
CILIATED
CITIZENS
COLONIES
COLORING
DEMEANOR
DEVELOPS
DILIGENT
DIVINELY
EPIPHANY
FANATICS
FEVERISH
FINISHED
GALAXIES
GENERALS
GENEROUS
HEGELIAN
HEREDITY
HEREUNTO
HOROWITZ
JEREBOHM
JEREMIAH
LAVATORY
LUXURIES
MAGAZINE
MALADIES
MANAGERS
MEREDITH
METERING
MILITARY
MINISTER
MINISTRY
MOROSELY
PAGANISM
PARADIGM
PARADING
PARADISE
PARANOID
PEDESTAL
PETERSON
PITIABLE
POROSITY
RECEDING
RECEIPTS
RECENTLY
RELEVANT
RIDICULE
SALARIED
SAVAGELY
SECEDING
SERENITY
SEVERITY
STITCHED
TELEGRAM
VACATION
VAGABOND
VETERANS
VIGILANT

ABCCADEF
BELLBOYS
PASSPORT

ABCCBADE
SUFFUSED

ABCCBCDE
WINNINGS

ABCCBDBE
CARRAWAY
LESSENED

ABCCBDEA
SITTINGS

ABCCBDEC
BORROWER
DESSERTS
MISSILES
MISSIONS
NARRATOR
PASSAGES

ABCCBDEF
BARRACKS
BELLETCH
BILLIKEN
BILLIONS
BORROWED
BOTTOMED
COMMONLY
FILLINGS
FOLLOWED
FOLLOWER
GUTTURAL
HELLENIC
KENNEDYS
MILLIONS
PALLADIO
WARRANTS
WILLIAMS
WILLINGS

ABCCDAEA
SUGGESTS

ABCCDAEC
COSSACKS

ABCCDAEF
COLLECTS
CONNECTS
DOGGEDLY
SUPPOSED

ABCCDBEA
SETTLERS

ABCCDBEC
WIGGLING

ABCCDBEF
CARRIAGE
HALLMARK
HILLSIDE
MARRIAGE
PEDDLERS
RIDDLING
RIPPLING
SIZZLING
SURROUND
VILLAINS

ABCCDCAD
SWEETEST

ABCCDCBE
CREEPERS

ABCCDCEA
SLEEPERS
STEELERS
SWEENEYS

ABCCDCEF
CELLULAR
FERRAROS
GREENEST
JENNINGS
KENNINGS
MANNINGS

ABCCDDEA
SUCCEEDS

ABCCDDEF
BALLOONS

ABCCDEAA
SUPPRESS

ABCCDEAD
COMMENCE
COMMERCE

ABCCDEAF
CURRENCY
DISSUADE
TORRENTS

ABCCDEBC
CORRIDOR
MESSAGES

ABCCDEBD
VITTORIO

ABCCDEBF
BELLOWED
DALLOWAY
GLOOMILY
HARRIMAN
KNEELING
MELLOWED
MORRISON
SLEEPILY
TERRACED
TERRACES
TROOPERS

ABCCDECA
SPEECHES
STEEPLES

ABCCDECF
BARRIERS
CARRIERS
FREEDMEN
GULLIBLE
SULLENLY
SYLLABLE
WARRIORS

ABCCDEDA
DIFFERED
GREENING

ABCCDEDE
SUFFERER

ABCCDEDF
BATTERED
BUFFERED
BUFFETED
COLLEGES
HAMMERED
HAPPENED
HOLLERED
LITTERED
MANNERED
MATTERED
MUTTERED
PUCCINIS
SUFFERED
TERRIFIC

ABCCDEEC
RUSSELLS

ABCCDEEF
BALLROOM
CONNALLY
HAMMETTS
JOLLIFFE
PARRILLO
POZZATTI

ABCCDEFA
DIFFUSED
GREETING
SERRATUS
SETTINGS
SUPPLIES
SUPPORTS

ABCCDEFB
COMMANDO
HELLFIRE
MISSOURI
SYMMETRY
TERRIBLE

ABCCDEFC
DISSENTS
FINNEGAN
HAGGLING
HESSIANS
JUGGLING
NARROWER
PASSIONS
RUSSIANS
TENNYSON

ABCCDEFD
BECCARIA
TORRENCE

ABCCDEFF
FULLNESS
LIPPMANN

ABCCDEFG
BAFFLING
BATTLING
BITTERLY
BLEEDING
BLOOMING
BREEDING
BROODING
BROOKLYN
BUDDHISM
BUDDHIST
BULLETIN
BULLSHIT
CARRYING
CHEERFUL
CHOOSING
COLLAGEN
COLLAGES
COLLAPSE
COLLARED
COMMANDS
COMMENTS
COMMUNAL
COMMUNES
COMMUTED
COMMUTER
COMMUTES
COTTAGES
CREEPING
CURRENTS
DABBLING
DAZZLING
DISSOLVE
EARRINGS
FLEETING
FLOODING
FLOORING
FREEDOMS
FREEHAND
FREEWAYS
FREEZING
FULLBACK
FUNNIEST
FURROWED
GALLERYS
GARRISON
GREENISH
HALLOWED
HAPPIEST
HARRISON
HORRIBLE
HORRIBLY
HUDDLING
HUMMOCKS
HURRYING
KILLPATH
LATTIMER
MARRYING
MEDDLING
MULLENAX
NARROWED
NARROWLY
PATTERNS
PILLARED
POSSIBLE
POSSIBLY
PULLINGS
PULLMANS
PULLOVER
PUZZLING
RALLYING
RATTLING
SETTLING
SHOOTING
SLEEPING
SMOOTHED
SMOOTHER
SMOOTHLY
SPEEDILY
SPEEDING
STEERING
STOOPING
SUDDENLY
SUFFRAGE
SULLIVAN
SUMMONED
SUPPLANT
SUPPLIED
SUPPLIER
SWEEPING
SWOOPING
TERRIBLY
TOPPLING
VILLAGES
WEDDINGS
WHEELING
WHEELOCK
WHOOPING
WORRYING

ABCDAABE
RECURRED

ABCDAADA
STRESSES

ABCDAADE
LABELLED
STRESSED

ABCDAAEF
OUTDOORS
THROTTLE

ABCDABAE
ARICARAS

ABCDABCD
BERIBERI

ABCDABCE
PHOSPHOR

ABCDABDE
LIVELIER

ABCDABED
INSTINCT
LIFELIKE

ABCDABEE
BASEBALL
NEARNESS

ABCDABEF
BOURBONS
CHURCHES
DECADENT
HITCHING
INCLINED
LEAFLETS
POSTPONE
TOMATOES

ABCDACBE
RETORTED

ABCDACEA
SPONSORS

ABCDACEF
ACTUATED
COINCIDE
CRESCENT
ESTHETIC
ITALIANS
THEATERS
THIRTIES
TWISTING

ABCDADEA
EMINENCE

ABCDADED
MCNAMARA

ABCDADEE
LIFELESS
LOVELESS

ABCDADEF
CYNICISM
DECIDING
MAXIMIZE
MOVEMENT
RETIRING
RIGOROUS

ABCDAEAF
EXTREMES
IMPLICIT
MAXIMUMS
ORTHODOX
TRUSTETH

ABCDAEBA
RECORDER
REFORMER
REPORTER

ABCDAEBC
HENCHMEN

ABCDAEBE
RECORDED
REGARDED
RETARDED
REWARDED

ABCDAEBF
COERCION
HATCHWAY
HOUGHTON
KNOCKING
NUMINOUS
RAILROAD
REFORMED
REMARKED
REPORTED
RESORTED
RETURNED
SALESMAN
TRACTORS
TRAITORS

ABCDAECF
ADENAUER
AVERAGED
AVERAGES
AVOCADOS
CHARCOAL
CLENCHED
EPIDEMIC
ITEMIZED
MONUMENT
TREATIES
TWENTIES

ABCDAEDF
ADRIATIC
SADISTIC
SALESMEN
TOGETHER

ABCDAEED
TRUSTEES
WELDWOOD

ABCDAEEF
ACTUALLY
THIRTEEN

ABCDAEFA
DWINDLED
EVIDENCE
SIMPSONS
SPLASHES
TIGHTEST

ABCDAEFB
MELAMINE
REMARQUE

ABCDAEFC
ABEYANCE
AMENABLE
AMONASRO
COERCIVE
ROSARIES

ABCDAEFD
LANDLORD
OUTGOING
RESTRICT

ABCDAEFE
INQUIRER
OUTMODED

ABCDAEFF
HEMPHILL
NUMBNESS

ABCDAEFG
ACQUAINT
ADORABLE
ALPHABET
ANIMATED
AROMATIC
BACKBONE
BLUMBERG
BRISBANE
CHANCERY
CHOICEST
CLUTCHED
CLUTCHES
COUNCILS
CROUCHED
CRUTCHES
DAVIDSON
DREADFUL
ESOTERIC
GEORGIAN
GEORGIAS
GERAGHTY
HATCHING
HUMPHREY
HUTCHINS
IMAGINED
IMAGINES
IMPAIRED
INQUIRED
INSPIRED
INTRIGUE
IRONICAL
KNUCKLED
KNUCKLES
LABELING
LOCALITY
LOYALIST
NICKNAME
NOMINATE
OPTIONAL
OUTBOARD
OUTCOMES
PROMPTED
PROMPTLY
PROSPECT
RESTRAIN
SPARSELY
SPLASHED
SQUASHED
TEMPTING
TOASTING
TREATING
TRIPTYCH
TRISTANO
TRUSTING
UNIQUELY
WESTWARD

ABCDBAAE
ENGINEER

ABCDBABD
RENDERED

ABCDBAEF
INSANITY
RUPTURED

ABCDBBAD
ANTENNAE

ABCDBBEF
STRATTON
STRUTTED
VARLAAMS

ABCDBCBE
HERBERET

ABCDBCEB
PERVERSE
SENTENCE

ABCDBCEF
CORPORAL
FINDINGS
FRAGRANT
INTENTLY
MARGARET
PRIORITY
SHEPHERD
TENDENCY
TOULOUSE

ABCDBDCE
KOINONIA

ABCDBDEF
FLAILING

ABCDBEAC
DESCENDS

ABCDBEAF
ARTERIAL
ENHANCED

ABCDBEBA
REVIEWER

ABCDBEBB
KEDGEREE

ABCDBEBF
BELIEVED
BELIEVER
BELIEVES
BESIEGED
CENTERED
LEAVENED
MENDERES
REFLEXES
RELIEVED
RELIEVES
REVIEWED
TEMPERED
VIRGINIA
WEAKENED

ABCDBECD
PURSUERS

ABCDBECF
LAUDANUM
VALUABLE

ABCDBEDA
SOMEONES

ABCDBEDC
MOREOVER

ABCDBEDE
INTENDED

ABCDBEDF
ARTERIES
INCENSED
INVENTED
REFLEXLY
UNFENCED

ABCDBEEF
BECKETTS
CASUALLY
MANUALLY
RUEFULLY

ABCDBEFA
DISLIKED
DOCTORED
RADIATOR
SEGMENTS
SERPENTS

ABCDBEFB
ASBESTOS
DECREASE
FANTASIA
PERCEIVE
SEQUENCE
TASMANIA

ABCDBEFC
BASTARDS
CULTURAL
DISLIKES
HESPERUS
OUTBURST
RADIATED
RESPECTS

ABCDBEFD
BANDAGED
CONSOLES
DISTINCT
INTONACO
PURSUITS

ABCDBEFE
BEQUESTS
CANVASES
COMPOSES
PIANISTS
REQUESTS

ABCDBEFF
FLAWLESS
PROGRESS

ABCDBEFG
AIRFIELD
AIRLINES
BANDAGES
BARGAINS
BURGUNDY
CAMPAIGN
CAPTAINS
CARVALHO
CASUALTY
CHISHOLM
COMFORTS
COMPOSED
COMPOSER
COMPOUND
CONFORMS
CONSOLED
CONTOURS
CULTURED
CULTURES
DISCIPLE
EVOLVING
FOXHOLES
GALVANIC
GEOMETRY
GORBODUC
HEAVENLY
HORMONES
INFANTRY
INVENTOR
KIPLINGS
LEUKEMIA
LIONIZED
MAJDANEK
MALRAUXS
MEDIEVAL
METRECAL
MICHIGAN
MIDNIGHT
MOTIONAL
MUSCULAR
ORDERING
PACKAGED
PACKAGES
PAGEANTS
PARLANCE
PARTAKES
PEACEFUL
POISONED
PROGRAMS
PURSUANT
PURSUING
RADIANCE
RAPHAELS
REAGENTS
REFLECTS
RHYTHMIC
SALVADOR
SCARCELY
SCARCITY
SCORCHED
SECRETLY
SERGEANT
STARTING
STARTLED
STRATEGY
TAXPAYER
TENDERLY
UNWANTED
VARIABLE
VERBENAS
WESLEYAN
WESTERLY
WORKOUTS

ABCDCAAC
PHILIPPI

ABCDCADE
OPINIONS

ABCDCAEB
CLINICAL

ABCDCAEF
AIRCRAFT
CRITICAL
OILCLOTH
PRECEPTS

ABCDCBAA
SELFLESS

ABCDCBEA
SYNONYMS

ABCDCBEC
PRESERVE

ABCDCBEE
HELPLESS

ABCDCBEF
CITATION
FOLKLORE
POTATOES
WILDLIFE

ABCDCCDC
OBSESSES

ABCDCCDE
OBSESSED

ABCDCDAE
ENTITIES

ABCDCDBE
PLUGUGLY

ABCDCDEF
PETITION
REVIVING

ABCDCEAB
HEADACHE

ABCDCEAC
HIAWATHA
SRELEASE

ABCDCEAF
CLEMENCY
ELICITED
ENTITLED
ENTITLES
ISOTONIC
ISOTOPIC
OPTATION
SURPRISE

ABCDCEBA
ELIGIBLE
NOTATION

ABCDCEBC
ENGAGING

ABCDCEBF
CLEVERLY
RESISTED
ROTATION

ABCDCECD
WHEREVER

ABCDCECE
PRECEDED

ABCDCECF
DROMOZOA
PROTOCOL
PROTOZOA
WHENEVER

ABCDCEDA
DOWNWIND

ABCDCEDF
PRETEXTS
PRONOUNS

ABCDCEEC
CHEYENNE

ABCDCEEF
OPERETTA

ABCDCEFA
DOWNWARD
RESISTOR
SUICIDES
TWILIGHT

ABCDCEFB
ECONOMIC
GERTRUDE
READABLE
THOROUGH

ABCDCEFC
CLEMENTE
PRESENCE
PRETENCE
PRETENSE
XRELEASE

ABCDCEFD
HOMEMADE
OXIDISED
PEASANTS
PORTRAIT
PRESENTS
SKELETAL

ABCDCEFF
FONDNESS
FORTRESS
KINDNESS

ABCDCEFG
ALTITUDE
APTITUDE
BICYCLES
CANONIST
CLEMENTS
CRIMINAL
DISASTER
DRAMATIC
DROPOUTS
EDITIONS
EROMONGA
FINANCED
FINANCES
LATITUDE
MAILINGS
ORIFICES
ORIGINAL
PORTRAYS
PRETENDS
PREVENTS
PROFOUND
PROMOTED
PROMOTES
PROSODIC
PROVOKED
PROVOKES
REVIVALS
ROTATING
SCIMITAR
SKELETON
SPIRITED
UNABATED
UNITIZED
UTILIZED
UTILIZES
VOEGELIN
WARDROBE
WRITINGS

ABCDDAEF
ABERRANT

ABCDDBCA
REAPPEAR

ABCDDBEE
MEANNESS

ABCDDBEF
BAULLARI

ABCDDCAB
TEAMMATE

ABCDDCAE
OMISSION
PHILLIPS

ABCDDCBD
DRESSERS

ABCDDCBE
BRENNERS
SNIFFING
STACCATO

ABCDDCDA
GRINNING

ABCDDCDE
CHINNING
SPINNING
THINNING

ABCDDCEA
GRIPPING
SHELLEYS

ABCDDCED
BLOSSOMS
CROSSONS

ABCDDCEF
CHILLING
CHIPPING
DRILLING
DRIPPING
DWELLERS
EMISSION

ABCDDCEF
FLIPPING
GRIFFITH
OMITTING
PHILLIES
QUITTING
SCABBARD
SHIPPING
SKIDDING
SKIMMING
SKIPPING
SLIPPING
SPILLING
SPITTING
STIRRING
SWIMMING
TRIMMING
TRIPPING
WHINNIED
WHIPPING
WHIRRING

ABCDDEAD
CLASSICS

ABCDDEAF
REAFFIRM
SCOTTISH
SLUGGISH
SMALLEST
SNOBBISH

ABCDDEBA
SWALLOWS

ABCDDEBC
PRESSURE

ABCDDEBF
CRITTERS
DRUMMERS
GAUSSIAN
SNAPPING
SNELLING
UNERRING

ABCDDECB
PRETTIER

ABCDDECF
CHERRIES

ABCDDEDE
UNHEEDED

ABCDDEDF
CHANNING
MCFEELEY
PLANNING
SCANNING
SCREENED
SQUEEZED
STUNNING

ABCDDEFA
GRABBING
GROKKING
GUESSING
SHUTTERS
SKIPPERS
SLIPPERS
SLUGGERS
STIFFENS
SWIMMERS

ABCDDEFB
AGREEING
BLISSFUL
WINOOSKI

ABCDDEFC
DIARRHEA
ROUSSEAU

ABCDDEFD
BRUSSELS
CHUGGING
CLOGGING
DRAGGING
POUSSINS
SKILLFUL
SLUGGING

ABCDDEFF
DUMBBELL
SHERRILL

ABCDDEFG
BLESSING
BLIZZARD
BLOTTING
BOUFFANT
BRITTANY
CHANNELS
CHATTING
CHOPPING
CLANNISH
CLAPPING
CLASSIFY
CLIFFORD
CRANNIES
CRIPPLED
CROSSING
CROSSMAN
DRESSING
DROPPING
DRUMMING
DWELLING
EMISSARY
FLAPPING
FLATTERY
FRETTING
GLADDENS
GLOSSARY
GLUTTONS
PLANNERS
PLODDING
PLOTTING
PRESSING
PRETTILY
PSYLLIUM
PUISSANT
QUARRELS
SCAFFOLD
SCHOONER
SCUDDING
SCURRIED
SCUTTLED
SHABBILY
SHEDDING
SHOPPING
SHUFFLED
SHUTTING
SKULLCAP
SLAMMING
SLAPPING
SLEDDING
SLIPPERY
SLOPPING
SMALLPOX
SMELLING
SMUGGLED
SNOBBERY
SNUGGLED
SPARRING
SPELLING
SPOTTING
STALLING
STALLION
STARRING
STEPPING
STOPPING
STUBBORN
STUFFING
SWELLING
TRAPPING
WITHHELD
WITHHOLD
WRAPPING

ABCDEAAF
EIGHTEEN
OVERLOOK

ABCDEABA
DEMANDED

ABCDEABC
EINSTEIN

ABCDEABF
HAVISHAM
INCOMING
INDEXING
INDUCING
INSURING
INVADING
INVOKING
MARKSMAN
NATIONAL
REPAIRED
REQUIRED
REQUIRES
RESTORED
UNSTRUNG
WATERWAY

ABCDEACB
IGNORING

ABCDEACF
ACTIVATE
ENTIRETY
FRUITFUL
LINCOLNS
REDBIRDS

ABCDEADF
ABUNDANT
CONTACTS
EPITHETS
OBANIONS
SOMERSET
TALENTED
THREATEN

ABCDEAEF
ADVOCACY
IDENTITY

ABCDEAFA
EMANUELE
SURMISES
SWADESHS

ABCDEAFB
ARMCHAIR
CLERICAL
INACTION
INVASION
RECOURSE
RESOURCE

ABCDEAFC
ADEQUATE
OVERCOME
OVERDONE
TUNGSTEN

ABCDEAFD
ABSTRACT
ALIENATE
OKLAHOMA

ABCDEAFE
ARTISANS
DISORDER
EXISTENT
INFERIOR
INTERIOR

ABCDEAFG
ADEQUACY
ADVOCATE
AFRICANS
AIRPLANE
ARBOGAST
ASPIRANT
CHAUNCEY
CHEMICAL
CONDUCTS
CONVICTS
CORTICAL
DISLODGE
EARLIEST
ELOQUENT
ENTIRELY
EUROPEAN
FAITHFUL
FANCIFUL
FORCEFUL
HARDSHIP
HAUNCHES
IDEALISM
IDEALIST
IDENTIFY
IMPERIAL
IMPLYING
IMPOSING
IMPUNITY
IMPURITY
INACTIVE
INERTIAL
INJURIES
LAUGHLIN
NOTHINGS
NUISANCE
ORATIONS
OVERCOAT
OVERLOAD
OVERSOFT
RAYBURNS
RHETORIC
RICHARDS
RICKARDS
SURMISED
TAPESTRY
THWARTED
VANDIVER

ABCDEBAA
SETHNESS

ABCDEBAD
ROCKFORK
SIDEWISE

ABCDEBAF
ALVEOLAR
ANDRENAS
EIGHTIES
ENJOINED
ENTWINED
ESPOUSED
INSOMNIA
RECOVERY
ROCHFORD
ROCKPORT
TAILGATE
THOUGHTS
TURNOUTS

ABCDEBBF
DEVOTEES
NOTEBOOK
REFUGEES

ABCDEBCC
RESTLESS

ABCDEBCD
DOWNTOWN
MAINTAIN
SENTIENT
TINGLING

ABCDEBCF
BRETHREN
CONFRONT
CRITERIA
DISGUISE
HARDWARE
PINCHING
RUNDFUNK
TINKLING
UNEARNED
VITALITY

ABCDEBDA
SCIENCES

ABCDEBDC
MISERIES

ABCDEBDE
JOHNSONS

ABCDEBDF
HANDMADE
LANGUAGE
MAINLAND

ABCDEBEF
ATHLETES
RIPENING

ABCDEBFA
ENTRANCE
SIMPKINS

ABCDEBFB
KEROSENE
LEBANESE
PANORAMA
PROCURER

ABCDEBFC
BISCUITS
FIGHTING
FIGURING
LIGHTING
LONGHORN
MEDFIELD
SIGHTING

ABCDEBFD
DISTRICT
LIFETIME
LIKEWISE
LONESOME
MARSHALS
NAMESAKE
OERSTEDS

ABCDEBFE
LAUREATE
TRAVERSE

ABCDEBFF
FEARLESS
HEADLESS
MARSHALL
RAINFALL
RECKLESS
WEAKNESS

ABCDEBFG
ABSORBED
ANTOINES
ATHLETIC
BACKWARD
BACKYARD
BEARDENS
BINOMIAL
CAPITALS
CONTROLS
DELIVERS
DELIVERY
DIETRICH
DILATION
DILUTING
DILUTION
DISUNITY
DOWNPOUR
EASTWARD
FAIRWAYS
FEATHERS
FIDELITY
FIELDING
FINALITY
FOREMOST
FURLOUGH
GLOBULIN
HALFBACK
HARDTACK
HEAVIEST
HINDUISM
HORIZONS
INSTANCE
INTERNAL
JUNCTURE
LAMINATE
LANDMARK
LEAGUERS
LEATHERS
LINGUIST
LIPCHITZ
LIPSTICK
LIVSHITZ

ABCDEBFG
LOVEJOYS
MACREADY
MAHOGANY
MARTIANS
MARYLAND
MELTZERS
MINORITY
MISCHIEF
MISTRIAL
MONITORS
MURTAUGH
ORCHARDS
PATHWAYS
PIERCING
PILGRIMS
PILOTING
PITCHING
PORTIONS
PROCURED
RADICALS
REGIMENT
REMOTELY
RESIDENT
RIEFLING
SABOTAGE
SALUTARY
SANITARY
SECURELY
SEDATELY
SEDIMENT
SIMPLIFY
SOMEBODY
STRICTLY
TEACHERS
THRASHED
UNGAINLY
UNICONER
UNSIGNED
VALIDATE
VANGUARD
VITAMINS
WILSHIRE
YIELDING
YORKTOWN

ABCDECAF
ANTIETAM
CONVINCE
SEACOAST
SKIRMISH
TANGENTS

ABCDECBA
DESPISED
REVOLVER

ABCDECBC
PREMIERE

ABCDECBD
SCIATICA

ABCDECBE
BATISTAS
DREISERS

ABCDECBF
AIRSTRIP
ARTISTRY
RENOWNED
REVOLVED
SENTINEL
UNIFYING

ABCDECCB
MELVILLE

ABCDECCF
WILFULLY

ABCDECDA
GLINTING
GRINDING

ABCDECDC
DISEASES

ABCDECDD
CAREFREE

ABCDECDE
BRINGING
CLINGING
CRINGING
SLINGING
STINGING
SWINGING

ABCDECDF
ARTISTIC
AUTISTIC
BLINDING
BLINKING
CONTENTS
DISTASTE
DRINKING
GAIETIES
LONGINGS
PAINTING
PATENTED
POINTING
PRINTING
SHOWDOWN
STINKING
THINKING

ABCDECEB
STAGNANT

ABCDECEC
MURDERER

ABCDECED
BORDERED
MURDERED
REIGNING

ABCDECEF
CATHETER
CONVENED

ABCDECFA
DISPOSED
EVALUATE
GRIEVING
SARTORIS
SCANDALS
SHELTERS
SNEAKERS
SPEAKERS
SPENCERS
STENGELS
STEPHENS
SWEATERS
TRANSACT

ABCDECFB
CHILDISH
DENOUNCE
PERFORCE
STALWART

ABCDECFC
FASCISTS

ABCDECFD
IMPROPER
OUTDATED
WEIGHING

ABCDECFE
GREATEST
OVERSEAS
QUIETIST
STANDARD

ABCDECFF
VIEWLESS

ABCDECFG
AIRBORNE
AIRPORTS
ARISTIDE
BLENHEIM
BRIEFING
BRITAINS
BUILDING
CHAPLAIN
CLAIMANT
CLEANERS
CLIMBING
CONFINED
CONFINES
CONTENDS
CONTINUE
DIAGRAMS
DISPOSAL
DRAINAGE
DRAWBACK
DRIFTING
EMOTIONS
ENORMOUS
EXISTING
FAIRVIEW
FIELDERS
FIERCELY
FIREARMS
FLAGRANT
FORMERLY
FREQUENT
FRICTION
GLORIOUS
GRADUATE
HARBORED
HYDRIDES
INVOLVED
INVOLVES
IRENAEUS
LANDINGS
MANKINDS
MORIARTY
MORTARED
OBEDIENT
OVERHEAD
PATHETIC
PERFORMS
PHANTASY
PHARMACY
PLAYMATE
POITRINE
PRISTINE
QUATRAIN
QUIETISM
RANGONIS
SEABOARD
SHIFTING
SHIRKING
SITUATED
STICKING
STIFLING
STIRLING
SWIRLING
TANGENCY
THAILAND
THIEVING
TRIFLING
TWIRLING
UNAFRAID
UNDERDOG
WHIRLING
WRITHING
ZIEGFELD

ABCDEDAA
SAMENESS

ABCDEDAC
SEMITISM

ABCDEDAF
MARITIME
NOTICING
OBLIVION
STOICISM

ABCDEDBD
CENSUSES

ABCDEDBE
DOMINION
FAMILIAL

ABCDEDBF
ALCOHOLS
FAMILIAR
HUMOROUS
INDECENT
INHERENT
MAGICIAN
PARISIAN
POSITION
VERIFIED
VOLITION

ABCDEDCA
SUVOROVS

ABCDEDCF
ACTIVITY
FUTILITY

ABCDEDDF
FORESEEN

ABCDEDEB
FEMININE

ABCDEDEF
BERNINIS
DEFINING
DRAINING
JUSTITIA
REFINING
STAINING
TRAINING

ABCDEDFA
DICTATED

ABCDEDFB
DECISIVE
DEFINITE
DELAWARE
ECSTATIC
ENVISION
ETHICIST
MEDICINE
POLITICO
SEPARATE

ABCDEDFC
CLEAVAGE
INTEREST
MODIFIED
THEODORE
TUNISIAN

ABCDEDFD
CONSISTS
PERSISTS

ABCDEDFE
AEROSOLS
OPTIMISM

ABCDEDFF
CARELESS
FAREWELL
HOPELESS
IDLENESS
LIKENESS
MALENESS
MEGAWATT
NAMELESS
TIMELESS
TIRELESS

ABCDEDFG
ACTIVISM
ADHERENT
ADMIRING
ADVISING
AMBITION
AUDITION
AUTONOMY
AVOIDING
BASEMENT
BRUISING
BUCKSKIN
BURNINGS
CANDIDLY
CHARTRES
CLAIMING
COHERENT
CRUISING
DEBILITY
DECISION
DELIRIUM
DERISION
DERIVING
DESIRING
DEVILISH
DICTATES
DICTATOR
EARNINGS
EXCITING
EXHIBITS
FACILITY
FAMILIES
FELICITY
FLUIDITY
FOREHEAD
FRUITION
FUGITIVE
HANDEDLY
HOMICIDE
HUMIDITY
HUMILITY
IDEOLOGY
INFRARED
JUDICIAL
LYRICISM
LYRICIST
MATUNUCK
MEANINGS
MINDEDLY
MOBILITY
MOBILIZE
MODIFIER
MODIFIES
MORNINGS
MUSICIAN
NOBILITY
NOTIFIED
NOWADAYS
OPENINGS
ORBITING
PACIFISM
PACIFIST
PAVEMENT
PAVILION
PEACOCKS
PLEASANT
POLICIES
POLICING
POLITICS
POSITIVE
PRAISING
PROBABLE
PROBABLY
PURIFIED
RAPIDITY
RATIFIED
RECITING
RELIGION
RELIVING
REMNANTS
RESIDING
REVISION
SOLIDITY
STRIDING
STRIKING
STRIVING
SURVIVAL
SURVIVED
THEOLOGY
THRIVING
TRAILING
TYPIFIED
VALIDITY
VENOMOUS
VIGOROUS
VOMITING
WARNINGS

ABCDEEAF
ENROLLED
EQUIPPED

ABCDEEBA
CADILLAC

ABCDEEBE
DEMURRER

ABCDEEBF
BEGOTTEN
CEZANNES
DIMAGGIO
REBUFFED
REBUTTED
RECALLED

ABCDEECF
REDWOODS

ABCDEEDB
UNCOMMON

ABCDEEDC
MISDEEDS

ABCDEEDE
CARESSES
IMBEDDED

ABCDEEDF
CARESSED
DISARRAY
IMPELLED
INFERRED
MICELLES

ABCDEEFB
ADMITTED
DEBONNIE

ABCDEEFD
OILSEEDS
SHOETTLE

ABCDEEFE
BAILEEFE
PICASSOS

ABCDEEFG
BACILLUS
BEDROOMS
CARTOONS
DILEMMAS
FOCUSSED
INCURRED
MAHZEERS
METALLIC
PIONEERS
PLATOONS
POCASSET
PROCEEDS
REBUTTAL
SCRAGGLY
SCRUBBED
SHRILLED
SHRUGGED
SQUATTED
STRAGGLE
STRIPPED
STROLLED
STRUGGLE
THRILLED
THROBBED

ABCDEFAA
EMPLOYEE
NORDMANN
SICKNESS
SKINLESS
SLOWNESS
SOFTNESS
SPOTLESS
SUBGROSS

ABCDEFAB
ANGLICAN
DESLONDE
EDUCATED
MEALTIME
MEANTIME
NECKLINE
SHREWISH
TEMPLATE

ABCDEFAC
ENDORSED
NUTRIENT
STEPWISE

ABCDEFAD
CONTRACT
EPISODES
OPERATOR
TOLERATE
WINSLOWS

ABCDEFAE
ATHENIAN
CLARENCE
EMBODIED
SHORTEST

ABCDEFAF
ECLIPSES
EMPHASES
EXCLUDED
EXPANDED
EXPLODED
EXPLORER
EXTRUDED
TOURISTS

ABCDEFAG
ABNORMAL
ADONIRAM
ALGERIAN
AMERICAN
AMERICAS
AUSTRIAN
BARTLEBY
BATHROBE
CERAMICS
CHADWICK
COMEBACK
CONFLICT
DELTOIDS
DIAMONDS
DOCKSIDE
EARTHMEN
EMBARKED
EMBODIES
EMBRACED
EMBRACES
EMPLOYED
EMPLOYER
EMPLOYES
ENCLOSED
ENFORCED
ENFORCES
ENGRAVED
ENGULFED
ENLARGED
ENLISTED
ENRICHED
ESCORTED
EXAMINED
EXAMINER
EXAMINES
EXAMPLES
EXCLUDES
EXPLORED
EXPORTED
KENTUCKY
KOWALSKI
LAVISHLY
LIBERALS
LINEARLY
LONSDALE
NESTLING
NOCTURNE
OBJECTOR
ORTHICON
OVERFLOW
RANCHERS
REACTORS
REALTORS
REGISTRY
REGULARS
REINHARD
SHOWCASE
SIGNPOST
SIMPLEST
SUITCASE
TENACITY
THICKETS
TONIGHTS
TRIPLETS
UNDERCUT

ABCDEFBA
ANGELINA
DEATHBED
DECANTED
DECLARED
DECLINED
DEPARTED
DEPICTED
DEPLORED
DEPLOYED
DEPRAVED
DEPRIVED
DERANGED
DESIGNED
DESTINED
DETACHED
DETAILED
DETOURED
DRUNKARD
GNASHING
REGISTER
REMINDER
SEARCHES
SERVICES
STUDENTS

ABCDEFBB
PEDIGREE

ABCDEFBC
CREATURE
DONATION
FLEXIBLE
GESTURES
HANDYMAN
LENGTHEN
LUSCIOUS
MACKINAC
RESIDUES
RESOLVES
TREASURE

ABCDEFBD
BRADFORD
CENSURES
JOHNSTON
MEASURES

ABCDEFBE
CRUISERS
GOVERNOR
LINGERIE
RELISHES
ROBINSON
TROUSERS

ABCDEFBF
ATHEISTS
DIALYSIS
FIBROSIS
HERALDED
LECTURER
NEUROSES
RELOADED
REMANDED
REMINDED

ABCDEFBG
ANYTHING
AURELIUS
BEAUTIES
BECKONED
BEGUILED
BELONGED
BESTOWED
BETRAYED
BLITHELY
BROCHURE
BROTHERS
CALENDAR
CARDINAL
CARNIVAL
CENSORED
COHESION
CONVEYOR
CRAWFORD
CREATORS
DECLARES
DECLINES
DEPLORES
DEPUTIES
DESIGNER
DIABETIC
DIATOMIC
DRINKERS
ENABLING
ENACTING
ENDURING
ENJOYING
ENSURING
ENVIRONS
EPIGRAPH
FEATURED
FEATURES
GESTURED
GRINDERS
HABITUAL
HANDICAP
HERCULES
HISTORIC
HYDROXYL
INDOLENT
INFLUENT
INHUMANE
INSOLENT
KEYNOTES
LECTURED
LECTURES
LOCATION
LUMINOUS
MADRIGAL
MARGENAU
MARGINAL
MATERIAL
MATERNAL
MEASURED
MELODIES
MILSTEIN
MONTEROS
NAUTICAL
NEWCOMER
NIKOLAIS
NUMEROUS
ORDINARY
PAKISTAN
PANDORAS
PARENTAL
PARSIFAL
PARTISAN
PASTORAL
PERFUMED
PERVADES
PSALMIST
PUBLIQUE
RAILHEAD
RATIONAL
REALIZED
REALIZES
REASONED
RECKONED
REGAINED
REMAINED
REPLACED
REPLACES
RESIGNED
RESOLVED
RESULTED
RETAINED
REUNITED
REVAMPED
SATURDAY
SAUCEPAN
SEARCHED
SLIGHTLY
SLOVENLY
SNARLING
SNEAKING
SOLUTION
SORPTION
STRENGTH
TACLOBAN
TRAILERS
TREASURY
VASCULAR
VEHICLES
VENTURED
VENTURES
VICTORIA
VOCATION
WEIGHTED
WELCOMED
WORKSHOP

ABCDEFCA
DRENCHED
ESTIMATE
NORTHERN
SKETCHES
SPURIOUS
SYMPTOMS

ABCDEFCB
BEGRUDGE
GRANULAR
KNOWLTON
NECKLACE
PREACHER
RELIABLE
RESPONSE

ABCDEFCC
BUSINESS
CALDWELL
CHEROKEE
DISTRESS
MISTRESS

ABCDEFCD
ALUMINUM
BROWNLOW
CREDITED
DANGLING
DISTRUST
FRESCOES
JANGLING
LITERATE
MANSIONS
MCGEORGE
MISTRUST
MOLECULE
OINTMENT
PENSIONS
PRESUMES
SOMETIME
TENSIONS

ABCDEFCE
CONSTANT
DISPENSE
DISPERSE
STEADIED

ABCDEFCF
PREMISES

ABCDEFCG
ABORTION
ADOPTION
AGENCIES
ANTIDOTE
ANYBODYS
BLACKMAN
BLEACHED
BREASTED
BREATHED
BREATHES
BURGLARS
BURGLARY
BUTYRATE
CAUTIOUS
CHAIRMAN
CONDEMNS
CONTAINS
CZARINAS
DENOTING
DIAGONAL
DISABUSE
DISCLOSE
DOUBTFUL
EXTRACTS
FLETCHER
FORBEARS
FRECKLES
FRESHMEN

ABCDEFCG
GARDNERS
GRANDMAS
GRENADES
GUARDIAN
HANDGUNS
HANDLING
HARCOURT
HARTFORD
IGNORANT
JEHOVAHS
LANTERNS
LONGHAND
MATURITY
MENACING
MENTIONS
MOUTHFUL
MULTIPLE
MULTIPLY
NAUTILUS
OPERATED
OPERATES
ORNAMENT
PANELING
PARTNERS
PATIENTS
POLITELY
PREACHED
PREFACED
PRESUMED
PUNCHING
QUIXOTIC
SILENTLY
SKETCHED
SOLEMNLY
SPECIMEN
STAIRWAY
STEADIER
STEICHEN
THEORIES
THOMPSON
TORQUERS
TREMBLED
ULTIMATE
UNLIKELY
VOLATILE
WRENCHED
WRENCHES
WRETCHED
YOUTHFUL

ABCDEFDA
DIGESTED
DIRECTED
DIVERTED
GLANCING
GRANTING
GRUNTING
NAPOLEON
SELKIRKS
SILENCES

ABCDEFDB
ECLIPTIC

ABCDEFDC
ABSENCES
APERTURE
INDEBTED
JONATHAN
OBSERVES
OVERTURE

ABCDEFDD
BARTLETT
HONEYBEE

ABCDEFDE
AVENGING
CHANGING
CHANSONS
LOUNGING
OBSERVER
PLUNGING

ABCDEFDF
ASCENDED
BAPTISTS
CONTESTS
DENTISTS
LICENSES
PROTESTS
SHIELDED
THREADED

ABCDEFDG
ALDERMEN
BOUNCING
BOUNDING
BRANDONS
BROADWAY
CHANTING
CHARTERS
CHRISTIE
COLUMBUS
COMEDIES
CONTEXTS
COUNTING
COVERLET
DEARBORN
DEVOTION
FABULOUS
FEBRUARY
FOUNDING
FRONTING
GOVERNED
HAUNTING
HUNDREDS
INFECTED
INFESTED
INGESTED
INJECTED
INSERTED
INVERTED
INVESTED
LAVENDER

LICENSED
LODGINGS
LOGISTIC
MANEUVER
MATERIEL
MOUNTING
MOURNERS
NEBULOUS
NOVEMBER
NUCLEOLI
OBJECTED
OBSERVED
ORIENTED
PAYCHECK
PERIODIC
PLANKING
PLANTING
PLUNKING
POUNDING
POYNTING
PRACTICE
PRANCING
PRECINCT
PREMIUMS
PROTECTS
PUBLICLY
QUARTERS
ROADSIDE
ROCKLIKE
ROUNDING
SCREAMED
SHANTUNG
SILENCED
SLANTING
SOUNDING
SPENDING
SQUEAKED
SQUEALED
STANDING
STARBIRD
STOLIDLY
STREAKED
STREAMED
TAKEOVER
TALIESIN
THANKING
THURBERS
UNDERSEA
UNHEATED
UNVEILED

ABCDEFEA
DAMPENED
DARKENED
SCHIELES
STIMULUS
STYRENES
SUBTILIS

ABCDEFEB
HESITATE
PATRICIA
TRAVELER

ABCDEFEC
BUDGETED
GARDENER

ABCDEFED
BURDENED
HARDENED
HINDERED
PONDERED
POWDERED
SPECIFIC
WANDERED
WONDERED

ABCDEFEF
BUCHANAN

ABCDEFEG
ACHIEVED
ACHIEVES
ADMIRERS
ANSWERED
BETRAYAL
BOTHERED
BROWNING
BRUMIDIS
CARBOLOY
CARNEGEY
CARPETED
CHASTITY
CHISELED
CHURNING
CLEANING
COMPETED
CONTRARY
CONVEYED
COVENANT
CROWNING
DELICACY
DIABETES
DIAMETER
DISHONOR
DOMINANT
DROWNING
EXPLICIT
FALTERED
FASTENED
FATHERED
FILTERED
FINGERED
FLOWERED
FOSTERED
FROWNING
GATHERED
GHOREYEB
GIVEAWAY
GLOWERED
HAMPERED
HASTENED
HORSEMEN
HUNKERED
JACKETED
LABORERS
LATHERED

LEARNING
LINGERED
LISTENED
LISTENER
LITERARY
MACKEREL
MARKETED
MARTINIS
MARVELED
MASTERED
MOISEYEV
MOLIERES
MORTGAGE
MOURNING
NUMBERED
PENDULUM
PHONEMES
PICKETED
POIGNANT
PREGNANT
PROHIBIT
PROLIFIC
PROSTATE
PUCKERED
QUANTITY
RESONANT
RIFLEMEN
SANCTITY
SCHAEFER
SHIVERED
SHOVELED
SHOWERED
SHRIEKED
SICKENED
SOFTENED
SOFTENER
SURVEYED
TIMBERED
TRAVELED
UPHEAVAL
VIRTUOUS
WHATEVER
WHITENED
WINTERED
WITHERED
YEARNING
ZODIACAL

ABCDEFFA
MUSHROOM
SHERIFFS

ABCDEFFB
GIOVANNI
MARIETTA

ABCDEFFC
FIORELLO
GREVILLE
OLIVETTI

ABCDEFFD
BANSHEES

ABCDEFFE
COQUETTE
GIUSEPPE
LAGUERRE
NOUVELLE
ROULETTE
SOUVANNA
WILMETTE

ABCDEFFG
ARTFULLY
BAREFOOT
BATHROOM
BRUTALLY
DISCREET
DISMALLY
FLAXSEED
FORMALLY
FOURTEEN
HANDBOOK
KATHLEEN
LIBRETTO
LOCKHEED
MANVILLE
MAXWELLS
MENTALLY
NORMALLY
OVERALLS
PAROLEES
PATRONNE
PENGALLY
SEXUALLY
SHERWOOD
SOCIALLY
SOWBELLY
TAKEOFFS
TEASPOON
TRUJILLO
UMBRELLA
VERBALLY
VISUALLY
WOEFULLY
YEARBOOK

ABCDEFGA
ANTISERA
CATHOLIC
DIALYZED
DISABLED
DISARMED
DISOWNED
DISPUTED
DIVORCED
ELSINORE
ENVIABLE
EURYDICE
EXCHANGE
EXPOSURE
GAMBLING
GLEAMING
GOLDBERG

GOULDING
GRASPING
GROUPING
GUARDING
HEYDRICH
NEGATION
NITROGEN
NOBLEMAN
PAWNSHOP
REDACTOR
SANFORDS
SARDINES
SCHOLARS
SEAPORTS
SECTIONS
SENATORS
SERVANTS
SETBACKS
SHACKLES
SHERMANS
SHINGLES
SHOWINGS
SIDEWAYS
SKEPTICS
SKOLMANS
SNATCHES
SOCIETYS
SOLDIERS
SOLVENTS
SOYBEANS
SPACIOUS
SPECIOUS
STANLEYS
STEROIDS
STEWARDS
STOMACHS
SUBJECTS
SUBPENAS
SURFACES
SWATCHES
SWITCHES
TOLERANT
TOUGHEST
TRANSMIT
WITHDRAW
WITHDREW

ABCDEFGB
ADJOINED
ADJUSTED
ADSORBED
ANDERSON
BACTERIA
BEATRICE
BLOMDAHL
BONTEMPO
BRIGHTER
BRUCKNER
CAROLINA
DECORATE
DEFIANCE
DELICATE
DELPHINE
DESCRIBE

ABCDEFGB

DESOLATE DEVIANCE FEASIBLE FLEXURAL FRONTIER GLYCEROL GRANDEUR HEADLINE HERITAGE LEMONADE MEDIOCRE MENARCHE MOSQUITO NEGATIVE PEMBROKE PEROXIDE PERSUADE PRISONER PRODUCER REGULATE RELATIVE RELIANCE RESOLUTE ROSTAGNO SKIPJACK STRAIGHT SYMPATHY SYMPHONY TEAHOUSE TRANSFER UNBROKEN UNFROZEN UNSPOKEN WESTMORE WRANGLER LARKSPUR LUNATION LUNCHEON MECHANIC MISTAKES MONDRIAN MUSICALS NOSTRILS ORDAINED OUTRIGHT OVERCAME OVERSIZE OVERTAKE OVERTIME PANTHEON PASTURES PENTAGON PLEASURE POSTURES PREAMBLE PRECLUDE PRESTIGE RESPONDS ROSEBUDS SANCTION STRANGER STRONGER SURVEYOR THEORIZE TURNOVER UPSTAIRS URETHANE WASHINGS WRECKAGE HOUSMANS INSECURE INSTRUCT JUVENILE LAUGHING LIBERACE LIBERATE MAESTROS MCKENZIE MODERATE MOLINARI MONSTERS MOUNTAIN NARCOTIC OBSTRUCT OLDSTERS PARDONED PAWTUXET PERSIANS PLASTICS PRODUCED SCHEDULE SCREVANE SHADOWED SUBTRACT TIRESOME TOWNSMEN TUXAPOKA UNDERLIE VERSIONS VOLCANIC WARSHIPS WESTPORT WHISKERS WHISPERS YOSEMITE LIGHTEST MCLENDON NEBRASKA PARODIED PATIENCE PRUDENCE SUPERIOR SYLVANIA TRANSOMS UNIVERSE UTENSILS VIOLENCE

ABCDEFGC

ANECDOTE AUSPICES BENJAMIN BRETAGNE CHRYSLER COSTUMES CREATIVE CREDIBLE CUSHIONS DIRECTOR DISPLAYS DISPUTES FASHIONS FESTIVUS FOSDICKS FUNCTION HOSTAGES HUMANISM HUSBANDS INDUCTED INDULGED INTERACT JUNCTION JUSTICES KIDNAPED KINGSTON

ABCDEFGD

ADHESIVE ALTHOUGH ANTELOPE APOSTLES BLISTERS BOURCIER BRISTLES CAPSULES CLOSEUPS CLUSTERS COHESIVE CONTEMPT CONTRAST COUGHING COURTIER COVERAGE CRANSTON CRYSTALS DISLOYAL DISTRACT DOWNTURN EVANSTON FARTHEST FOUNTAIN FRANKLIN GONZALEZ GRANDSON GRUESOME

ABCDEFGE

ADVISERS ADVISORS ANTERIOR ATKINSON AUDIENCE CARNEGIE CHABRIER CHARGING CHARTIST CHESTNUT CHROMIUM CONSERVE CONVERGE CONVERSE DEPOSITS ERIKSONS FAINTEST FLORENCE FORAGING GAUNTLET HESITANT IMPOTENT INCREASE JACKSONS LAURENCE LAWRENCE

ABCDEFGF

ABOUNDED ANYWHERE CASHMERE CHEMISTS CHORUSES COMPLETE CONFIDED CONQUETE DISCRETE EMPHASIS FLORISTS FUJIMOTO GLIMPSES GLORIANA GROUNDED GYMNASTS HARVESTS IMPULSES INCLUDED INTERAMA MECHOLYL NECROSIS NEUROSIS ORCHESIS PROMISES PROVIDED SHROUDED SPLENDID STAMPEDE STRANDED UNFOLDED UNLOADED VIRTUOSO

ABCDEFGG

BALDNESS BOLDNESS BULTMANN CALMNESS CAMPBELL CATSKILL CHAIKOFF CHINLESS COLDNESS COLQUITT COMPRESS CONGRESS COVERALL CROMWELL DAMPNESS DARKNESS DASHIELL DISAGREE DIVORCEE DOUGLASS DOWNFALL DOWNHILL DUTCHESS EICHMANN FAIRNESS FIRMNESS FLATNESS HARDNESS HARMLESS HOLINESS KILOWATT MINDLESS MITCHELL OVERFALL PAINLESS PRINCESS RATCLIFF RICHNESS RUTHLESS SHIFLETT SNOWBALL SNOWFALL UGLINESS WAITRESS WALITZEE WINDFALL

ABAABCDBA

SASSAFRAS

ABAABCDBE

MAMMALIAN

ABAACDEFG

LULLWATER

ABABCDEFG

LALAURIES

ABACADCEF

INITIATED INITIATES INITIATOR

ABACADEEF

INITIALLY UNUSUALLY

ABACADEFB

ELEMENTAL

ABACADEFG

ALABASTER

ABACCDEDF

UNUTTERED

ABACDAEDF

AVAILABLE

ABACDAEFA

EMERGENCE

ABACDAEFG

ADAPTABLE EMERGENCY ENERGETIC

ABACDBDEF

AMAZEMENT

ABACDBEAF

ANACONDAS

ABACDBEFG

VIVACIOUS

ABACDCAEF

IMITATING IMITATION

ABACDCEFE

AGAMEMNON

ABACDCEFG

IMITATORS

ABACDDECF

FIFTEENTH

ABACDEAFG

SUSPENSOR

ABACDEBFG

MOMENTOUS PAPERBACK

ABACDECFD

ABANDONED

ABACDEDFF

AWARENESS

ABACDEDFG

ABASEMENT ANALOGOUS SUSPICION

ABACDEEFG

COCHANNEL

ABACDEFAF

EXERCISES

ABACDEFAG

EVERYONES EXERCISED NONDRYING

ABACDEFBA

DEDICATED

ABACDEFBG

ACADEMICS ANALYZING DEDICATES MEMORIZED

ABACDEFDF

SUSPENDED

ABACDEFDG

ACADEMIES POPULARLY SUSPECTED

ABACDEFEG

AWAKENING ITINERARY

ABACDEFGA

ELECTRODE EXECUTIVE

ABACDEFGB

DEDUCTIVE ELECTORAL MEMORABLE

ABACDEFGC

NANTUCKET

ABACDEFGD

APARTMENT EVERYBODY

ABACDEFGH

AMAZINGLY ANALEPTIC ANALOGIES ANARCHIST APARTHEID COCKTAILS DEDUCTION ELECTIONS ELECTRONS ELEPHANTS ELEVATION EXECUTION EXECUTORS EXEMPLIFY EXEMPTION MEMORIALS MOMENTARY NONVERBAL POPULATED SUSTAINED

ABBABCDEF

TEETERING

ABBACADAE
ATTAKAPAS

ABBACADEF
APPARATUS

ABBACCDEF
APPALLING

ABBACDAEF
ASSAILANT

ABBACDCDE
ATTAINING

ABBACDCEF
IRRITATED
OPPONENTS

ABBACDECD
ARRANGING

ABBACDEFA
EFFECTIVE

ABBACDEFB
ECCENTRIC

ABBACDEFG
ANNAPOLIS
ARRAIGNED
ASSAULTED
ATTACHING
ATTACKERS
ATTACKING
EFFECTING
ESSENTIAL
IMMIGRANT
IRRITABLE
IRRITABLY

ABBCADBEF
ATTRACTED

ABBCADEAF
APPRAISAL

ABBCADECF
WOODWARDS

ABBCADEFE
APPLAUDED

ABBCADEFG
ACCLAIMED
ALLIANCES
APPEALING
APPEARING

ABBCBBDEB
ASSESSORS

ABBCBBDEF
ASSESSING

ABBCBDAED
ASSISTANT

ABBCBDCEF
ASSISTING

ABBCBDEFG
ATTITUDES
ZOOLOGIST

ABBCCDEFG
ROOMMATES

ABBCDABEF
ANNOYANCE

ABBCDACEF
ERRONEOUS

ABBCDADEC
ALLSTATES

ABBCDAEBF
ALLOCABLE
ALLOWABLE
MCCORMICK

ABBCDAECF
UNNATURAL

ABBCDAEFC
IMMEDIATE

ABBCDAEFD
ILLUSIONS

ABBCDAEFG
ALLIGATOR
ALLOCATED
ALLOWANCE
APPLIANCE
ARROGANCE
ASSURANCE
ILLUMINED
IMMEDIACY

ABBCDBAED
AGGREGATE

ABBCDBAEF
LOOPHOLES

ABBCDBCEF
FOOTNOTES

ABBCDBDEF
ATTRITION

ABBCDBEFC
ATTENTIVE

ABBCDBEFD
ATTENTION

ABBCDBEFG
ANNOUNCED
ANNOUNCER
ANNOUNCES

ABBCDCAEF
EFFICIENT

ABBCDCCEF
MCCLELLAN

ABBCDCEBF
ALLEGEDLY

ABBCDCEFD
FOOTSTEPS

ABBCDCEFG
ADDITIONS
ADDITIVES
OCCIPITAL
OFFICIALS

ABBCDDEFF
MCCONNELL

ABBCDDEFG
MCCULLERS
OCCURRING

ABBCDEADB
ATTENDANT

ABBCDEAFC
ALLEVIATE

ABBCDEAFD
OCCASIONS

ABBCDEAFG
ACCOMPANY
APPLICANT
ASSOCIATE
GOODNIGHT
IMMENSITY
IMMERSION

ABBCDEBBA
FOOLPROOF

ABBCDEBBF
DOOKIYOON
ILLEGALLY

ABBCDEBCF
ATTEMPTED

ABBCDEBDE
INNOCENCE

ABBCDEBFG
TEENAGERS
WOODSMOKE

ABBCDECED
ASSIGNING

ABBCDECFG
ADDICTION
AFFIRMING
IMMENSELY
OFFENDERS

ABBCDEDCC
LOOSENESS

ABBCDEDCF
APPETITES

ABBCDEDFG
ROOSEVELT

ABBCDEECF
DOOLITTLE

ABBCDEEDB
ADDRESSED

ABBCDEEDE
ADDRESSES
ILLNESSES

ABBCDEEDF
OPPRESSED

ABBCDEEFC
AGGRESSOR

ABBCDEFAG
OCCLUSION

ABBCDEFBG
ATTRIBUTE
BEETHOVEN
OCCUPANCY

ABBCDEFCC
INNESFREE

ABBCDEFCG
ASSEMBLED
FOOLISHLY

ABBCDEFDG
ATTENDING

ABBCDEFEG
AGGRIEVED

ABBCDEFFG
FOOTBALLS
WOODRUFFS

ABBCDEFGB
IRREGULAR

ABBCDEFGC
ASSERTIVE
OFFENSIVE
UTTERANCE

ABBCDEFGD
ALLOTMENT
ALLUSIONS
COOPERATE
DEERSKINS

ABBCDEFGE
AFFLUENCE

ABBCDEFGG
APPOINTEE

ABBCDEFGH
ACCEPTING
ACCIDENTS
ACCORDING
ACCOUNTED
ACCRETION
AFFECTING
AFFECTION
AFFLICTED
AFFORDING
ALLEGORIC
APPOINTED
ARRESTING
ASSERTING
ASSERTION
ASSUREDLY
ATTORNEYS
COOLIDGES
COOPERMAN
FOOLHARDY
MOONLIGHT
OCCUPANTS
OCCUPYING
OFFERINGS
OFFSPRING
SEEMINGLY
UNNOTICED
UPPERMOST

ABCAACDEB
REARRANGE

ABCAADEFG
EXCEEDING
ONLOOKERS

ABCABADEF
INFINITUM

ABCABCDEF
MURMURING

ABCABDBAA
SENSELESS

ABCABDBEF
HAPHAZARD
REPRESENT

ABCABDCBE
RETREATED

ABCABDDBE
REGRETTED
REPRESSED

ABCABDEBF
REFRESHED

ABCABDEFG
CASCADING
MONMOUTHS
PERPETUAL
PROPRIETY

ABCACDABE
INSISTING

ABCACDEBD
INSISTENT

ABCACDEDF
PROPONENT

ABCACDEFD
PROPOSALS

ABCACDEFG
ARMAMENTS
CHOCOLATE
DEODORANT
PROPOSING

ABCADAEBF
INCIPIENT

ABCADAEFB
TENTATIVE

ABCADAEFC
EASEMENTS
INSIDIOUS

ABCADAEFG
EPHEMERAL
INHIBITED
INHIBITOR
INVISIBLE
INVISIBLY
SUBSYSTEM

ABCADBCAE
HIGHLIGHT

ABCADBEBF
INDIGNANT
PERPLEXED
RETRIEVED

ABCADBEFG
GREGORIUS
PREPARING

ABCADCBEF
CALCULATE

ABCADCCEF
FULFILLED

ABCADCEFB
ENTERTAIN

ABCADCEFG
PURPORTED

ABCADDAEF
EXCELLENT

ABCADDEFA
EXCESSIVE

ABCADDEFG
UNHURRIED

ABCADEADE
IMPINGING

ABCADEADF
ALBANIANS

ABCADEAEE
BUMBLEBEE

ABCADEAFA
ELSEWHERE

ABCADEAFF
EAGERNESS

ABCADEAFG
ADVANTAGE
EXPEDIENT
OBNOXIOUS

ABCADEBAB
ESTERASES

ABCADEBBF
BOMBPROOF

ABCADEBCE
INCIDENCE

ABCADEBEF
INDIGENES

ABCADEBFA
TESTAMENT

ABCADEBFG
DEADLIEST
HIGHPOINT
INCIDENTS
TIPTOEING

ABCADECBF
RETRACTED

ABCADECDF
CONCERNED

ABCADECFG
INTIMATED
TWITCHING

ABCADEDBC
TESTIFIES

ABCADEDBF
TESTIFIED

ABCADEDFA
SUBSIDIES

ABCADEDFB
SENSITIVE

ABCADEDFG
CRUCIFIED
REWRITING
SUBSIDIZE

ABCADEEDB
PROPELLER

ABCADEEFG
CONCETTAS
CONCURRED

ABCADEFAC
ENSEMBLES

ABCADEFAG
EDGEWATER
ENVELOPES

ABCADEFBG
CONCERTOS
ENDEARING
RECRUITED
REPRINTED
TENTACLES

ABCADEFCG
CONCEDING

ABCADEFDG
ADVANCING
BARBECUED
BARBECUES
CONCEALED
CONCEIVED
CONCEIVES
CONCERTED
EXTENDING
SUBSTRATE

ABCADEFEB
ISTIQLALS

ABCADEFEG
SEASONING

ABCADEFFD
CHECKBOOK

ABCADEFFG
ARMADILLO

ABCADEFGA
EXPENSIVE
EXPERTISE
EXTENSIVE
SUNSHADES

ABCADEFGB
REPRODUCE

ABCADEFGC
INDICATED
IODINATED
SENSATION

ABCADEFGD
EPHESIANS
EXTENSION
GANGSTERS

ABCADEFGE
CONCIERGE
EXPECTANT
REPRISALS

ABCADEFGF
CONCLUDED

ABCADEFGH
CHECKLIST
CIRCULATE
CLOCKWISE
CONCLUDES
CRACKPOTS
ENDEAVORS
EXCELSIOR
EXCEPTION
EXPECTING
GEOGRAPHY
HIGHLANDS
INDICATES
INDICATOR
INVIOLATE
PAMPHLETS
PROPHETIC
PURPOSELY
PURPOSIVE
SUBSTANCE
TESTIMONY

ABCBAABDE
LAVALLADE

ABCBAADEF
REFERRALS
REFERRING
SECESSION

ABCBABDEB
REFERENCE
REVERENCE

ABCBABDEF
MINIMIZED

ABCBADBEA
SEMESTERS

ABCBADCEF
INANIMATE

ABCBADEAF
DIVIDENDS
REPERTORY

ABCBADEFA
RESERVOIR

ABCBADEFG
AWKWARDLY
CAPACITOR
RESERVING
REVERSING

ABCBCDBAE
REMEMBERS

ABCBCDEFB
CATATONIA

ABCBDABDE
DEPENDENT

ABCBDABEF
DEFENDERS

ABCBDAEBF
REHEARSED

ABCBDAECF
STATESMAN

ABCBDAEDF
DEFENDANT
DEFENDING
DEPENDING
REHEARSAL
STATESMEN

ABCBDAEFG
UNINJURED

ABCBDBCAE
TENEMENTS

ABCBDBEFA
SICILIANS

ABCBDBEFB
DEFERENCE
VEHEMENCE

ABCBDBEFC
POTOWOMUT

ABCBDBEFD
DIVISIONS

ABCBDBEFG
CIVILIANS
CIVILIZED
DIVISIBLE
KARAMAZOV
KAYABASHI
MONOLOGUE
STATUTORY

ABCBDCBAE
PARAGRAPH

ABCBDCEFB
DETECTIVE
RETENTIVE

ABCBDCEFD
DETENTION
RETENTION

ABCBDCEFF
COLORLESS

ABCBDCEFG
DETECTING
DETECTION
DETECTORS
VACANCIES

ABCBDDBEC
DETERRENT

ABCBDDBEF
TOMORROWS

ABCBDDECF
COROLLARY

ABCBDDEDF
PARALLELS

ABCBDDEFD
PERENNIAN

ABCBDDEFG
COLONNADE
COLOSSEUM
HARASSING
NECESSARY
NECESSITY
PERENNIAL
REBELLING
REBELLION
RECESSION
RETELLING

ABCBDEAFG
TELEPATHY

ABCBDEBAF
RECEIVERS

ABCBDEBBD
SEVENTEEN

ABCBDEBCF
CANADIANS
FINISHING

ABCBDEBDF
KATANGANS

ABCBDEBFC
DETERGENT

ABCBDEBFG
GALATIANS
MACAULAYS
NOTORIOUS
VENEZUELA

ABCBDECFA
CATALYTIC

ABCBDECFG
ANONYMOUS
MITIGATES

ABCBDEDFB
STATEMENT

ABCBDEDFG
DECEIVING
RECEIVING
UNANIMITY

ABCBDEFAG
NEVERSINK
UNANIMOUS

ABCBDEFBA
DELEGATED
DEVELOPED
SEVENTIES

ABCBDEFBC
HEREAFTER
RESEMBLES

ABCBDEFBF
SERENADED

ABCBDEFBG
BENEFITED
BEVERAGES
DELEGATES
DEVELOPER
FANATICAL
GENERATED
GENERATES
LUXURIOUS
RELEGATED
RESEMBLED
TELEVISED
VENERATED

ABCBDEFCB
METEORITE

ABCBDEFCF
CATALYSTS
EPIPHYSIS
MOTORISTS

ABCBDEFCG
LITIGANTS

ABCBDEFDB
PENETRATE

ABCBDEFDG
BALANCING
COWORKERS
SIMILARLY

ABCBDEFEC
PARAMETER

ABCBDEFEG
PARASITIC

ABCBDEFFE
HONOTASSA
LAFAYETTE

ABCBDEFFG
GENERALLY
PITIFULLY
STATEROOM

ABCBDEFGA
DIXIELAND
SALACIOUS

ABCBDEFGB
CELEBRATE
DECEPTIVE
DEFECTIVE
DEFENSIVE
DETERMINE
RECEPTIVE
RELEVANCE
SELECTIVE
TELEPHONE
TELESCOPE
VEGETABLE
VENERABLE

ABCBDEFGC
CELESTIAL
RIDICULED

ABCBDEFGD
ANONYMITY
GENERATOR
MACARTHUR
MINISTERS
PARASITES
STATEWIDE

ABCBDEFGE
DILIGENCE
SOJOURNER

ABCBDEFGF
COLONISTS
PARALYSIS

ABCBDEFGH
AUGUSTINE
CATALOGUE
CELEBRITY
CITIZENRY
COLOMBIAN
DECEPTION
DEFEATING
DEFECTION
DESERTION
DESERVING
HAZARDOUS
HOLOCAUST
HONORABLE
HONORABLY
JEREBOHMS
LEGENDARY
LEVERKUHN
MAGAZINES
MEREDITHS
MINIATURE
PARALYZED
PARALYZES
PARAMOUNT
RECEPTION
REJECTING
REJECTION
RELEASING
RELEVANCY
REPEATING
RESENTFUL
REVEALING
SELECTING
SELECTION
STATIONED

ABCBDEFGH
TELEGRAMS
TELEGRAPH
VACATIONS
VIGILANCE

ABCCADCEF
LYTTLETON

ABCCBDBEF
COMMODORE

ABCCBDCBE
WELLESLEY

ABCCBDDBB
TENNESSEE

ABCCBDEBF
COMMOTION
CORROSION
MESSENGER

ABCCBDECF
WILLINGLY

ABCCBDEDF
LESSENING

ABCCBDEFA
MILLIGRAM
NARRATION

ABCCBDEFC
COLLOIDAL

ABCCBDEFF
WILLIAMSS

ABCCBDEFG
BATTALION
BILLIKENS
BORROWING
COMMODITY
CORROSIVE
DIFFICULT
FOLLOWERS
FOLLOWING
GALLANTRY
JEFFERSON
LETTERING
NARRATIVE
SUCCUMBED
WARRANTED

ABCCDAADA
SUCCESSES

ABCCDAAEF
SUCCESSOR

ABCCDABEF
CURRICULA
MERRIMENT

ABCCDAEBF
COLLECTOR

ABCCDAECF
TERRITORY

ABCCDAEDF
COLLECTED
CONNECTED
CORRECTED
ROBBERIES
SUGGESTED
TILLOTSON

ABCCDAEFG
CORRECTLY
MERRIMACK
SHEEPSKIN
SUPPOSING

ABCCDBCCE
HILLBILLY

ABCCDBDEF
WALLPAPER

ABCCDBEFF
BLOODLESS

ABCCDBEFG
CARRIAGES
HALLMARKS
MARRIAGES

ABCCDCCDC
POSSESSES

ABCCDCCDE
POSSESSED

ABCCDCEFB
CELLULOSE
MENNONITE

ABCCDCEFG
CUNNINGLY

ABCCDDEBF
COFFEEPOT

ABCCDDEDE
SUCCEEDED

ABCCDEADF
COMMENCED

ABCCDEBBF
HOLLYWOOD

ABCCDEBCF
CORRIDORS

ABCCDEBFF
PENNILESS

ABCCDEBFG
BARRICADE
CANNIBALS
DIFFUSING
DIFFUSION
PILLORIED
WORRISOME

ABCCDECAA
SWEETNESS

ABCCDECBA
GREENBERG

ABCCDECFA
SYLLABLES

ABCCDECFG
GREENLEAF
ZIMMERMAN

ABCCDEDBF
COLLISION
TERRIFIED
TERRIFIES

ABCCDEDCE
PESSIMISM

ABCCDEDFA
GOSSIPING

ABCCDEDFC
BITTEREST

ABCCDEDFG
DIFFERENT
HORRIFIED
NULLIFIED

ABCCDEEBF
MILLENNIA

ABCCDEEFF
COMMITTEE

ABCCDEEFG
COMMITTED
GODDAMMIT

ABCCDEFAG
GREETINGS
NARROWING

ABCCDEFBC
CONNEXION
MISSOURIS

ABCCDEFBD
GILLESPIE

ABCCDEFBE
COMMUNION

ABCCDEFBG
COLLUSION
POLLUTION

ABCCDEFDC
SURRENDER

ABCCDEFDF
COMMENDED

ABCCDEFDG
BALLISTIC
BATTERIES
COMMENTED
GREENLAND
PASSENGER
PATTERNED

ABCCDEFEG
CATTLEMEN
FATTENING
HAPPENING
MADDENING

ABCCDEFFG
HALLOWEEN

ABCCDEFGA
DISSOLVED
MANNERISM
SUPPLIERS

ABCCDEFGC
CARRYOVER
COMMUNISM
GODDAMNED
JANNEQUIN

ABCCDEFGD
BALLESTRE
BLOODSHED
COLLEAGUE
CORRELATE

ABCCDEFGE
MOCCASINS
RUMMAGING
SUPPORTER

ABCCDEFGF
BUDDHISTS
COMMANDED
COMMUNESE
HILLSBORO

ABCCDEFGG
HAPPINESS

ABCCDEFGH
BATTERING
BELLOWING
BULLETINS
BUTTERFLY
CALLOUSED
COLLAPSED
COMMANDER
COMMUNIST
COMMUNITY
COMMUTING
CORRUPTED
CURRENTLY
GARRYOWEN
GREENWICH
HARROWING
HOLLERING
HURRICANE
HURRIEDLY
KILLPATHS
MINNESOTA
MISSHAPEN
MULLIGANS
MUTTERING
PATTERSON
PUNNISHED
PUTTERING
SMOOTHING
SUFFERING
SUMMARIZE
SUMMATION
SUNNYVALE
SUPPLYING
SUPPORTED
SYMMETRIC
VONNEGUTS
YELLOWING

ABCDAABEF
RECURRENT

ABCDAAEBF
REMARRIED

ABCDAAEFG
RECURRING
STRESSFUL
STRESSING

ABCDABAEF
DECIDEDLY

ABCDABEAF
INTRINSIC

ABCDABECB
DECADENCE

ABCDABECF
EPILEPTIC

ABCDABEDC
INSTINCTS

ABCDABEEC
BASEBALLS

ABCDABEFE
UNFOUNDED

ABCDABEFF
CHURCHILL

ABCDABEFG
CHURCHMEN
PHOSPHATE
POSTPONED
UNCOUNTED

ABCDACAEB
INTUITION

ABCDACAEF
INTUITIVE

ABCDACBEF
SALESLADY

ABCDACEFB
ESTHETICS

ABCDACEFE
COINCIDED

ABCDACEFG
COINCIDES
CRESCENDO
SPONSORED

ABCDADCEF
AGITATION

ABCDADEDF
HITCHCOCK
INSTITUTE

ABCDADEFG
EMINENTLY
MAXIMIZES
MOVEMENTS

ABCDAEABF
INQUIRING
INSPIRING

ABCDAEAFG
EXTREMELY
INABILITY
INQUIRIES
ITEMIZING
ORTHODOXY

ABCDAEBAF
REFORMERS
REPORTERS

ABCDAEBCF
PERIPHERY

ABCDAEBEF
PROSPERED

ABCDAEBFA
SINUSOIDS

ABCDAEBFD
CONSCIOUS
RIVERSIDE

ABCDAEBFG
BRADBURYS
RAILROADS

ABCDAECAF
ENTREATED
TWENTIETH

ABCDAECDF
DWINDLING

ABCDAECFA
TREATMENT

ABCDAECFB
ANIMATION

ABCDAECFG
EPIDEMICS
IMAGINARY
MONUMENTS
SCARSDALE
SNOWSTORM

ABCDAEDFA
SATISFIES

ABCDAEDFG
LOVELIEST
SATISFIED

ABCDAEEAE
EXPRESSES

ABCDAEEAF
EXPRESSED

ABCDAEEDF
ENDLESSLY

ABCDAEEFG
EXPRESSLY

ABCDAEFAD
EVIDENCED

ABCDAEFAG
EPICENTER
EVIDENCES
EXCHEQUER

ABCDAEFBG
ENAMELING
LEGALIZED
REMARQUES
ROBERTSON

ABCDAEFCG
ACTUALITY
ALEXANDER
EPIDERMIS
EXTREMITY
INTRICATE

ABCDAEFDC
RESTRICTS

ABCDAEFDG
LANDLORDS
WENTWORTH

ABCDAEFEG
MANOMETER
RETURNING
TIGHTENED

ABCDAEFFG
COMICALLY
FEARFULLY
NOMINALLY
UNEQUALLY

ABCDAEFGA
ARIMATHEA
EXONERATE

ABCDAEFGC
ALEXANDRE
REGARDING

ABCDAEFGD
PROSPECTS
RESTRAINT
TIMETABLE

ABCDAEFGE
AVERAGING
DAVIDSONS

ABCDAEFGF
LOYALISTS

ABCDAEFGG
PLUMPNESS

ABCDAEFGH
ARCHANGEL
BACKBENDS
BUCKBOARD
CATECHISM
CLUTCHING
CROUCHING
EARNESTLY
EVIDENTLY
EXUBERANT
GERAGHTYS
HAWTHORNE
INFLICTED
INTRIGUED
INTRIGUES
LAMPLIGHT
LOYALTIES
NOMINATED
OBVIOUSLY
OMINOUSLY
OUTBOARDS
RECORDING
REMARKING
REPORTING
RESORTING
REWARDING
RIVERBANK
SALISBURY
SLAPSTICK
SPLASHING
UNTOUCHED

ABCDBAAEF
ENGINEERS

ABCDBABEF
LIABILITY

ABCDBAECF
RENDERING

ABCDBAEFG
INGENIOUS
NATHANIEL
TALKATIVE

ABCDBCAEB
INTENTION

ABCDBCCEA
DISMISSED

ABCDBCCEF
DISMISSAL

ABCDBCEBA
SENTENCES

ABCDBCEBF
SENTENCED

ABCDBCECF
CONSONANT

ABCDBCEFA
SHEPHERDS

ABCDBCEFB
PEACEABLE

ABCDBCEFG
CORPORATE
FRAGRANCE
PITUITARY

ABCDBDEFG
LACTATING

ABCDBEABA
DESCENDED

ABCDBEACD
INVENTIVE

ABCDBEACF
INTENSITY

ABCDBEAFB
INVENTION

ABCDBEAFD
INCENTIVE
INTENSIVE

ABCDBEAFG
INFANTILE
INGENUITY
INTENSIFY

ABCDBEBAF
REVIEWERS

ABCDBEBCB
SANTAYANA

ABCDBEBDD
CEASELESS

ABCDBEBFA
DIGNIFIED

ABCDBEBFB
BELVEDERE

ABCDBEBFC
BESIEGERS

ABCDBEBFD
POISONOUS

ABCDBEBFE
VIRGINIAN

ABCDBEBFG
BELIEVERS
BELIEVETH
COSMOLOGY
DECREMENT
SIGNIFIED
SOCIOLOGY
SOPHOMORE
VIABILITY
VIOLINIST
VIRGINIAS
VIRGINITY

ABCDBECEF
ARTHRITIS
POISONING

ABCDBECFB
VENGEANCE

ABCDBECFG
CONJOINED
VERTEBRAL
WEDNESDAY

ABCDBEDEF
MOTIONING

ABCDBEDFG
BELIEVING
CONTORTED
FANTASTIC
INTENSELY
RADIATION
REVIEWING
VARIATION

ABCDBEEBA
DEPRESSED

ABCDBEEBC
MANHATTAN

ABCDBEEFA
DISTILLED

ABCDBEEFG
FORGOTTEN

ABCDBEFAB
TEMPERATE

ABCDBEFAG
INDONESIA
RADIATORS
SUBMUCOSA

ABCDBEFBA
DECREASED
SEQUENCES

ABCDBEFBE
WESTERNER

ABCDBEFBF
DECREASES

ABCDBEFBG
ENHANCING
FERMENTED
NEGLECTED
PERCEIVED
PERCEIVES
PERFECTED
PERMEATED
PERMEATES
REFLECTED
REQUESTED
RESPECTED
SEPTEMBER
VITRIOLIC

ABCDBEFCF
OUTBURSTS

ABCDBEFCG
CENTERING
STRATFORD

ABCDBEFDA
STRETCHES

ABCDBEFDG
GIRLISHLY
PAWCATUCK
SECRETARY
SOMNOLENT
STRETCHED

ABCDBEFEG
COMPONENT
WEAKENING
WHICHEVER

ABCDBEFGA
REFLECTOR
SOPHOCLES
TURBULENT
YESTERDAY

ABCDBEFGB
CASTANEDA
DESPERATE
LAGUARDIA
PEACETIME

ABCDBEFGC
DISCIPLES
HENDERSON

ABCDBEFGD
DAMNATION
INDENTURE
UNTENABLE

ABCDBEFGE
COMPOSERS
FANTASIES
PACKAGING
SALVAGING

ABCDBEFGF
CATHARSIS
CONGOLESE
GIANICOLO
MAGDALENE
PROTRUDED

ABCDBEFGH
AIRFIELDS
BEAVERTON
CAMPAIGNS
COMPOSING
COMPOSITE
COMPOSURE
COMPOUNDS
CONFORMED
DEPLETION
FERVENTLY
FICTIONAL
GEOMETRIC
INVENTORS
INVENTORY
KATHARINE
LANCASTER
LAWMAKERS
LAWMAKING
MANDATORY
ORDERINGS
OUTNUMBER
PERFECTLY
POTBOILER
PROGRAMED
RANSACKED
REFUELING
REPLENISH
SALVATION
SECRETION
SEGMENTAL
STARTLING
STRATEGIC
TAXPAYERS
TURQUOISE
VALUATION
VARIABLES

ABCDCACEF
CRITICISM
CRITICIZE

ABCDCAEFD
CHARACTER

ABCDCAEFG
GEOLOGIST
UNPOPULAR

ABCDCBBCE
PREFERRED

ABCDCBBDE
USELESSLY

ABCDCBCEF
UTILITIES

ABCDCBECD
PRESERVES

ABCDCBECF
PRESERVED

ABCDCBEFG
CLEVELAND
FREDERICK

ABCDCCEAF
OBSESSION

ABCDCCEFD
OBSESSIVE

ABCDCDEAF
PROTOTYPE

ABCDCDEFG
PETITIONS

ABCDCEABF
HEADACHES
SKOLOVSKY

ABCDCEAFA
SURPRISES

ABCDCEAFE
STEVENSON

ABCDCEAFG
SURPRISED

ABCDCEBCF
FINANCING

ABCDCEBDF
FINANCIAL

ABCDCEBEA
SEAFARERS

ABCDCEBFG
BIOLOGIST
FINANCIER

ABCDCECFG
ABILITIES
PHONOLOGY
PIECEMEAL
PRECEDENT
PRIMITIVE
UTILIZING

ABCDCEDFG
PRONOUNCE
RESISTING
THEREFROM

ABCDCEECF
CHEYENNES

ABCDCEFAB
THEREWITH

ABCDCEFAC
RESISTORS

ABCDCEFAG
ECONOMIES

ABCDCEFBG
CEILINGED
ECONOMICS
NEOCORTEX
PROMOTERS

ABCDCEFCB
PRETENDER

ABCDCEFCD
PRESENCES

ABCDCEFCF
PRETENDED

ABCDCEFCG
PRESENTED
PREVENTED
PROMOTION

ABCDCEFDC
THEREFORE
WHEREFORE

ABCDCEFDG
EMANATING
HOMEMAKER
PORTRAITS
SMILINGLY

ABCDCEFEG
PORTRAYAL
WHOSOEVER

ABCDCEFGA
ECONOMIZE
ELIMINATE

ABCDCEFGC
BENINGTON
DISASTERS

ABCDCEFGD
EMANATION

ABCDCEFGE
DRAMATIST
RESISTANT

ABCDCEFGF
PRIVILEGE

ABCDCEFGG
GUARANTEE

ABCDCEFGH
APOLOGIES
BROXODENT
CANONIZED
CARTRIDGE
CRIMINALS
DRAMATIZE
ECONOMIST
GLOBOCNIK
LENINGRAD
ORIGINALS
ORIGINATE
PENINSULA
PORTRAYED
PRECEDING
PRESENTLY
PROLONGED
PROMOTING
SPIRITUAL
THEREUPON
TREVELYAN
UNABASHED
WHEREUPON

ABCDDAEFD
AGREEABLE

ABCDDBCAE
REAPPEARS

ABCDDBEDF
SCREECHED

ABCDDBEFC
STREETCAR

ABCDDCABE
TEAMMATES

ABCDDCAED
OMISSIONS

ABCDDCECD
FLANNAGAN

ABCDDCEFG
BRILLIANT
CLIPPINGS
GRAMMATIC
OVERREACH
QUIZZICAL
TRIMMINGS

ABCDDEABF
REASSURED

ABCDDEACB
CLASSICAL

ABCDDEAFG
EBULLIENT

ABCDDEBCD
PRESSURES

ABCDDEBEF
PROFFERED
TRIGGERED

ABCDDEBFG
SWALLOWED

ABCDDECFD
PRETTIEST

ABCDDECFG
CLASSMATE
CRIPPLING
DRIZZLING

ABCDDEDFG
AGREEMENT

ABCDDEFAA
SMALLNESS
STILLNESS

ABCDDEFBF
BRASSIERE

ABCDDEFBG
GRILLWORK

ABCDDEFCD
ROUSSEAUS

ABCDDEFDG
BRASSNOSE
SCHOOLBOY

ABCDDEFED
SHUDDERED

ABCDDEFEG
CHANNELED
CHATTERED
CLATTERED
CLUTTERED
FLATTENED
FLATTERED
FLUTTERED
QUARRELED
SCATTERED
SCREENING
SHATTERED
SHUTTERED
SPATTERED
STAGGERED
STAMMERED
STIFFENED
SWAGGERED

ABCDDEFFG
CLASSROOM
GUERRILLA
SMALLWOOD

ABCDDEFGA
GRAPPLING
SMUGGLERS
STALLIONS
SWELLINGS

ABCDDEFGC
DIARRHOEA

ABCDDEFGD
BLESSINGS
THREESOME

ABCDDEFGE
CHALLENGE

ABCDDEFGH
DWELLINGS
OSULLIVAN
PRETTYMAN
SCALLOPED
SCHOOLING
SHUFFLING
SQUEEZING
THREEFOLD
TRAPPINGS
VACUUMING

ABCDEAAFD
PINEAPPLE

ABCDEAAFG
MIDSUMMER
OVERLOOKS
SURPASSED

ABCDEABAF
ENLIVENED

ABCDEABBA
ETIQUETTE

ABCDEABCD
EINSTEINS

ABCDEABCF
RACETRACK

ABCDEABFE
KOLPAKOVA
TEAMSTERS

ABCDEABFG
HIROSHIMA
HOUSEHOLD
NATIONALS
RIVALRIES
TOMBSTONE
WATERWAYS

ABCDEACFG
ACTIVATED
ANTIPATHY
AUTOMATED
AUTOMATIC
CORKSCREW
WHIRLWIND

ABCDEADBF
INVARIANT

ABCDEADFF
NAKEDNESS

ABCDEADFG
ABUNDANCE
CONTACTED
OVERLORDS
THREATENS

ABCDEAECF
SHORTSTOP

ABCDEAEDC
PRECIPICE

ABCDEAEFG
EXPONENTS
FORTIFIED
RANCOROUS
REPAIRING
REQUIRING
TRADITION

ABCDEAFAG
EMPOWERED
IMPOLITIC

ABCDEAFBC
DONALDSON
RESOURCES

ABCDEAFBE
INVASIONS

ABCDEAFBG
ARMCHAIRS
CONDUCTOR
FRANKFURT
HEALTHIER
REPAIRMEN

ABCDEAFCA
CLIMACTIC
STANISLAS

ABCDEAFCB
IDEALIZED

ABCDEAFCG
AXIOMATIC
OVERCOMES
OVERTONES

ABCDEAFDC
ABSTRACTS

ABCDEAFDG
ALIENATED
HEALTHILY
INHERITED
INJURIOUS
LANDSLIDE
OCTAGONAL
OVERBOARD

ABCDEAFEC
DISORDERS

ABCDEAFED
INDELIBLE

ABCDEAFEG
CONFUCIUS
DEMANDING
INTERIORS
SPOKESMEN

ABCDEAFGA
AUSTRALIA
ELOQUENCE
EXISTENCE
NEWTONIAN

ABCDEAFGB
ACROBATIC
ADVOCATED
ASPIRANTS
SPACESHIP

ABCDEAFGC
CONFUCIAN
SYMPOSIUM

ABCDEAFGD
CONDUCTED
HEALTHFUL

ABCDEAFGE
HARDSHIPS
IMPATIENT

ABCDEAFGF
UNCLOUDED

ABCDEAFGG
HAVERHILL

ABCDEAFGH
ABERNATHY
ADMIRABLE
ADMIRABLY
AIRPLANES
AMBULANCE
AVOIDANCE
CHEMICALS
CONDUCIVE
CONVICTED
EUROPEANS
EXCITEDLY
HAMPSHIRE
IDENTICAL
INAUDIBLE
INHABITED
INSCRIBED
MATRIMONY
OUTSPOKEN
RESTORING
SECLUSION
SPOKESMAN
SPORTSMAN
SPORTSMEN
STEAMSHIP
THRUSTING

ABCDEBABF
ARBITRARY
RECOVERED

ABCDEBAEF
ARBITRATE

ABCDEBAFA
SURPLUSES

ABCDEBAFG
GOITROGEN
INDEMNITY
TABULATED

ABCDEBBFG
NOTEBOOKS

ABCDEBCDF
AMENDMENT
MAINTAINS

ABCDEBCFA
DISGUISED

ABCDEBCFF
INEPTNESS

ABCDEBCFG
CONFRONTS
CRITERION
HABITABLE
IMPROMPTU
PRIMARIES
PRIMARILY
SATURATED
SOURDOUGH
TEMPLEMAN

ABCDEBDAF
ENSCONCED

ABCDEBDCF
STRUCTURE

ABCDEBDFG
AESTHETIC
INCARNATE
INSTANTLY
LANGUAGES
PATRIARCH

ABCDEBEFG
AMUSEMENT
IMPLEMENT
WHITEHEAD

ABCDEBFAB
STRICTEST

ABCDEBFAG
ENCHANTED
ENCOUNTER
ENGLANDER
ENTRANCED

ABCDEBFBA
DELIVERED
SUMPTUOUS

ABCDEBFBC
GENTLEMEN

ABCDEBFBG
FEATHERED
HEXAMETER
LITORIGIN

ABCDEBFCG
LONGHORNS

ABCDEBFDC
DISTRICTS
VIENTIANE

ABCDEBFEG
DRAPERIES
FRUSTRATE
GROCERIES
HABITANTS
NAUSEATED
PROSTRATE
TRAVERSED

ABCDEBFFC
BIENVILLE

ABCDEBFFE
CHILDHOOD

ABCDEBFFG
BASICALLY
DUTIFULLY
HENRIETTA
MAGICALLY
NATURALLY
PARTIALLY
RADICALLY

ABCDEBFGA
SAVOYARDS
SCRATCHES
SEDIMENTS
SOMEBODYS

ABCDEBFGB
PORTFOLIO
RESIDENCE

ABCDEBFGC
BOSPHORUS
FURIOUSER
GENTLEMAN
INSTANCES
PENDLETON
PRESCRIBE
RESIDENTS

ABCDEBFGD
GARIBALDI

ABCDEBFGE
BROKERAGE
FLEDGLING
FOREGOING
PALISADES

ABCDEBFGF
LINGUISTS
MISGUIDED

ABCDEBFGG
CLOUDLESS

ABCDEBFGH
ABSORBING
ARMSTRONG
ATHLETICS
BACKWARDS
BACKYARDS
CURIOUSLY
FAVORABLE
FAVORABLY
FIRELIGHT
FURIOUSLY
HEARTEDLY
HILARIOUS
JUNCTURES
KNOWINGLY
LAMINATED
LANDMARKS
MARYLANDS
NAVIGATOR
PUNCTURED
REGIMENTS
REPUTEDLY
SCRATCHED
SHEATHING
SHORTHAND
THRESHOLD
UNCHANGED
VICARIOUS

ABCDECABF
INVOLVING

ABCDECAFG
CONVINCED
PRINCIPAL
PRINCIPLE

ABCDECBAF
NEGLIGENT

ABCDECBCF
PREMIERES

ABCDECBFA
SENTINELS

ABCDECBFG
GENUINELY
NEWLYWEDS
SITUATION
VISCOSITY

ABCDECCBF
BEDRIDDEN

ABCDECCEC
ABSCESSES
HOSTESSES

ABCDECCFA
DISCUSSED

ABCDECCFC
DISCUSSES

ABCDECDEF
CONTENTED

ABCDECDFD
CONSENSUS

ABCDECDFG
PAINTINGS

ABCDECECF
CONFINING
MURDERERS

ABCDECEFA
MICROCOSM
NUTRITION

ABCDECEFG
NUTRITIVE

ABCDECFAA
STEPHENSS

ABCDECFAG
EMACIATED
ENCIRCLED
EVACUATED
EVALUATED

ISOTROPIC

ABCDECFBA
DENOUNCED

ABCDECFBC
PERFORMER

ABCDECFBG
MURDEROUS
PERFORMED

ABCDECFCD
CONTINENT

ABCDECFCG
CONVENING
SHELTERED

ABCDECFDG
OVERHEARD

ABCDECFEA
STANDARDS

ABCDECFED
CONDENSED

ABCDECFEF
CONTENDED

ABCDECFEG
CONSENTED
CONTENDER
REACTANTS
REDUNDANT

ABCDECFFG
CONTINUUM
GRADUALLY
HEADWALLS
SPATIALLY
WITHSTOOD

ABCDECFGA
DISGUSTED

ABCDECFGB
RECONCILE

ABCDECFGC
OBEDIENCE

ABCDECFGD
GRADUATED

ABCDECFGE
TRACEABLE

ABCDECFGF
FORWARDED
PROGNOSIS

ABCDECFGH
APOSTOLIC
BOATYARDS
BORDERING
BUILDINGS
CHAMPAGNE
CHARLAYNE
CLAIMANTS
CONGENIAL
CONTINUAL
CONTINUED
CONTINUES
EMOTIONAL
FRANCAISE
FREQUENCY
GRADUATES
MURDERING
PLAYMATES
POITRINES
POTENTIAL
PRAGMATIC
QUADRATIC
REVOLVING
WITHSTAND

ABCDEDAFG
AUXILIARY
OBLIVIOUS
OVERGROWN

ABCDEDBAF
CANDIDACY

ABCDEDBBF
COURTROOM

ABCDEDBEF
LIBRARIAN

ABCDEDBFC
ALCOHOLIC
POSITIONS

ABCDEDBFD
INFERENCE

ABCDEDBFG
CANDIDATE
DEFICIENT
DICTATING
LIBRARIES
MAGICIANS
MULTITUDE
RECIPIENT

ABCDEDCFG
CHILDLIKE

ABCDEDEFF
ALONENESS

ABCDEDEFG
PARTITION
PHILOLOGY
SURVIVING

ABCDEDFAB
ESCAPADES

ABCDEDFAC
CLEARANCE

ABCDEDFAG
EPICYCLES
EURIPIDES
EXHIBITED
HIERARCHY

ABCDEDFBA
SEPARATES

ABCDEDFBE
ENVISIONS

ABCDEDFBG
HERNANDEZ
MEDICINES
PERSISTED
SATIRICAL
SEPARATED
SOLICITOR

ABCDEDFCA
SURVIVORS

ABCDEDFCF
INTERESTS

ABCDEDFCG
INAUGURAL
MUNITIONS
QUOTATION
WHITETAIL

ABCDEDFDB
DESTITUTE

ABCDEDFDG
HIMALAYAS

ABCDEDFFG
CHARTROOM

ABCDEDFGA
STRIVINGS

ABCDEDFGB
CAFETERIA
REPAYABLE
SEPARABLE

ABCDEDFGC
BASEMENTS
FASCICLES
MUSICIANS

POLITICAL

ABCDEDFGD
ADHERENCE
MADELEINE
NICARAGUA

ABCDEDFGE
BUCKSKINS
DECISIONS
DOMINICAN
PHEASANTS
REVISIONS
UPRISINGS

ABCDEDFGF
LOUISIANA
LYRICISTS

ABCDEDFGG
BLINDNESS
BLUNTNESS
FRANKNESS

ABCDEDFGH
ACROPOLIS
ADHERENTS
AMBITIONS
AMBITIOUS
AUDITIONS
AUTOCODER
AUTONOMIC
CONSISTED
DELICIOUS
DICTATORS
EMPIRICAL
FOREHEADS
FORTITUDE
GRATITUDE
HYPEREMIA
HYPEREMIC
INCAPABLE
JUDICIARY
MALICIOUS
MOBILIZED
MODIFIERS
MUNICIPAL
PAVEMENTS
PAVILIONS
RELIGIONS
RELIGIOUS
SLOANAKER
SOLICITED
SOVEREIGN
SUBTITLED
UNLIMITED

ABCDEEAFG
ANCILLARY

ABCDEEBAF
CADILLACS

ABCDEEBCF
BEACHHEAD

ABCDEEBFG
BEGINNERS
CAPILLARY
NIGHTTIME
RECOMMEND

ABCDEEDAF
OCTILLION

ABCDEEDBF
COTILLION
UNFITTING
UNWILLING

ABCDEEDEC
BEGINNING

ABCDEEDFC
INTELLECT

ABCDEEDFF
COWESSETT

ABCDEEDFG
ADMISSION
ADMITTING
RAMILLIES
SPLITTING
THRILLING

ABCDEEFAE
EMBASSIES

ABCDEEFBE
BEFUDDLED

ABCDEEFBG
ARTILLERY
CARIBBEAN
INCESSANT

ABCDEEFCA
STRIPPERS

ABCDEEFCD
SATELLITE

ABCDEEFCG
INCORRECT
SHRUBBERY

ABCDEEFDG
CHAUFFEUR
DISAPPEAR
SIXTEENTH
UNSETTLED

ABCDEEFEF
PROCEEDED

ABCDEEFEG
PIONEERED

ABCDEEFGA
SQUABBLES
STRUGGLES

ABCDEEFGC
INTERRUPT

ABCDEEFGE
STRADDLED

ABCDEEFGG
HUMANNESS

ABCDEEFGH
CARESSING
POTASSIUM
RECALLING
SCHAFFNER
SCHELLING
SCRUBBING
SQUATTING
STRAPPING
STROLLING
STRUGGLED
STRUMMING
THROBBING
UNHAPPILY
UNMARRIED

ABCDEFAAG
EMPLOYEES
LIBERALLY
LITERALLY
LOGICALLY

ABCDEFABC
CHEMISCHE

ABCDEFABE
ENACTMENT

ABCDEFABG
ANGLICANS
DISCREDIT
EMPHYSEMA
ENDOWMENT
ENJOYMENT
INCEPTING
INCLUDING
INDOCHINA
INFORMING
INJECTING
INSULTING

ABCDEFACD
ALTERNATE

ABCDEFACE
OVERSHOES

ABCDEFACG
AFTERMATH
INTEGRITY
ISOLATION
NUTRIENTS

ABCDEFADG
CONTRACTS
IMPARTIAL
INTERVIEW
OPERATORS
TIDEWATER
TOLERATED

ABCDEFAEG
ADVERSARY
AFTERWARD
ATHENIANS
IMPENDING
REGULARLY
TORMENTED

ABCDEFAFC
MINUTEMEN

ABCDEFAFG
EXPLORERS

ABCDEFAGA
AMERICANA
DISBANDED
DISCARDED
SCLEROSIS
SUITCASES
SYNTHESIS

ABCDEFAGB
AEROSPACE
DEQUINDRE
INCEPTION
INCLUSION
INDUCTION
INFECTION
INFLATION
INJECTION
INTRUSION
INVERSION
REINFORCE
TRICKSTER

ABCDEFAGC
ASTRONAUT
MINUTEMAN
SANDERSON

ABCDEFAGD
INFECTIVE

ABCDEFAGG
EMPTINESS

ABCDEFAGH
AFORESAID
AMERICANS
ASCERTAIN
AUTOGRAPH
CHRONICLE
CONFLICTS
ELISABETH
ELIZABETH
EMPLOYERS
EQUIPMENT
FORGETFUL
FRIGHTFUL
IMPROVING
IMPROVISE
INCLUSIVE
INJUSTICE
INTRUSIVE
ISOLATING
MALFORMED
MULTNOMAH
NOCTURNAL
REINHARDT
SERIOUSLY
TRUNCATED

ABCDEFBAE
REGISTERS
ROQUEMORE

ABCDEFBAG
DRUNKARDS
INORGANIC
LEISURELY
REMINDERS
RETAILERS

ABCDEFBBC
HONEYMOON

ABCDEFBBF
STARLETTE

ABCDEFBBG
DEPORTEES

ABCDEFBCB
TREASURER

ABCDEFBCD
BANDSTAND
CARDBOARD
LINGERING
SENTIMENT
WEINSTEIN

ABCDEFBCE
HEARTBEAT
TREASURES

ABCDEFBCG
CHERISHED
COURTEOUS
CREATURES
CURVATURE
DONATIONS
DORMITORY
FURNITURE
TINKERING
TREASURED
VIOLATION

ABCDEFBDC
SIGNALING
UNDEFINED

ABCDEFBDG
LIBERTIES

ABCDEFBEG
DISBELIEF
GOVERNORS
LICENSING

ABCDEFBFC
LIGHTNING

ABCDEFBFD
PERTINENT

ABCDEFBFG
LISTENING
PERMANENT
SICKENING

ABCDEFBGA
DASHBOARD
ENDURANCE
MICROFILM
SAILBOATS
SATURDAYS
SOLUTIONS
STRENGTHS
SUBGROUPS

ABCDEFBGB
ASTERISKS
BELVIDERE
MARIJUANA

ABCDEFBGC
BEDSPREAD
DESIGNERS
DETRIMENT
DIGESTING
HISTORIES

ABCDEFBGD
DIGESTIVE
DIONYSIAN
DIRECTIVE
MACDONALD
MONSTROUS
PARENTAGE

ABCDEFBGE
DIMENSION
WORKSHOPS

ABCDEFBGF
INFLUENCE
INSOLENCE

ABCDEFBGG
HEAVINESS
MERCILESS
READINESS
WATERFALL
WEARINESS

ABCDEFBGH
BACKSTAGE
BATHYRANS
BEAUCLERK
BICKERING
BOURGEOIS
BROCHURES
BROTHERLY
CALENDARS
CARDINALS
CARTILAGE
CONESTOGA
DIRECTING
DIRECTION
DISABLING
DISARMING
DISMAYING
DISPARITY
DIVERSION
DIVERSITY
DIVERTING
EPISCOPAL
FASCINATE
FILTERING
FRACTURES
HANDCLASP
HEMPSTEAD
HERCULEAN
HIJACKING
HISTORIAN
HOUSEWORK
INFLUENZA
INSURANCE
LANDSCAPE
LIMOUSINE
LOATHSOME
LOCATIONS
LUXEMBURG
MADRIGALS
MARSICANO
MATERIALS
MIGRATION
MISTAKING
NEWCOMERS
NISCHWITZ
PATRONAGE
PICKETING
PICTORIAL
PICTURING
PNEUMONIA
PONDEROUS
RAINCOATS
RATIONALE
REPAYMENT
ROADBLOCK
SAFEGUARD
SANCTUARY
SCEPTICAL
SINCERITY
TOUCHDOWN
UNSTAINED
VIBRATION
VICTORIAN
VICTORIES
VIEWPOINT
VIOLATING
VISUALIZE
WASTELAND
WESTFIELD

ABCDEFCAB
ESTIMATES

ABCDEFCAE
ULTIMATUM

ABCDEFCAF
SCIENTIST

ABCDEFCAG
CONSTANCY
ENTRUSTED
ESTIMATED
EXTRACTED
OXIDATION
STAIRCASE
TRANSLATE

ABCDEFCBA
DETONATED

ABCDEFCBC
RESPONSES

ABCDEFCBE
STALEMATE

ABCDEFCBF
WISCONSIN

ABCDEFCBG
GRAVEYARD
MENTIONED
NECKLACES
PENSIONER
PREACHERS
STAMINATE
TRADEMARK

ABCDEFCCG
CALDWELLS
HELPFULLY
STOCKROOM

ABCDEFCDA
SOMETIMES

ABCDEFCDD
FRESHNESS

ABCDEFCDE
BLACKJACK

ABCDEFCDG
CHALIDALE
MOLECULES
PHENOMENA
QUINZAINE
TWINKLING

ABCDEFCEA
DISPENSED
DISPERSED

ABCDEFCEB
UNITARIAN

ABCDEFCED
CONDEMNED
CONSTANTS

ABCDEFCEG
ORIENTING
PATRIOTIC
PATRISTIC

ABCDEFCFG
FURTHERED

ABCDEFCGA
DISCLOSED
ELABORATE
ERADICATE
SPECIMENS
STAIRWAYS

ABCDEFCGB
BLACKMAIL
BRIGADIER
CHENOWETH

ABCDEFCGC
GUATEMALA

ABCDEFCGD
EXTRACTOR
GUITARIST

ABCDEFCGE
WHOLESOME

ABCDEFCGF
THOMPSONS

ABCDEFCGG
ALERTNESS
CLEARNESS
GREATNESS

ABCDEFCGH
AMORPHOUS
ANIMOSITY
AUTHENTIC
BERNHARDT
BLANCHARD
BLEACHERS
BOATSWAIN
BRISTLING
CHAMPLAIN
CLUBHOUSE
CONTAINED
CONTAINER
DIAPHRAGM
EDITORIAL
FAIRCHILD
FIREWORKS
FRIVOLITY
GUARDIANS
IGNORANCE
MOLECULAR
MOTIVATED
MOTIVATES
MUTILATED
OLEANDERS
ORNAMENTS
PATIENTLY
PLANETARY
PRECISELY
PRESIDENT
PREVALENT
QUIVERING
SCULPTURE
SHIELDING
SHIVERING
STEINBERG
SWITCHING
TECHNICAL
TRICKLING
UNHITCHED
WHISTLING

ABCDEFDAG
NAPOLEONS
OVERTHROW
ROSENBERG
SOCIALISM
SOCIALIST

ABCDEFDBC
INTERMENT

ABCDEFDBD
CLIENTELE
INTERVENE

ABCDEFDBG
UNDERWENT

ABCDEFDCG
ANTIQUITY
JONATHANS
OVERTURES
PRACTICAL
VANISHING

ABCDEFDDG
HONEYBEES
NOSEBLEED

ABCDEFDEA
SOCIETIES

ABCDEFDEC
OBSERVERS

ABCDEFDED
INTERFERE

ABCDEFDEF
SPRINGING

ABCDEFDEG
CONTESTED
KAMIENIEC
PROTECTED
PROTESTED
REMINDING
SHRINKING
SQUINTING
VARIETIES

ABCDEFDFE
DESIGNING

ABCDEFDFG
CHARTERED
RATIONING

ABCDEFDGA
DISTORTED
HUNDREDTH

ABCDEFDGC
INTERCEPT
INTERSECT
SPECTACLE

ABCDEFDGD
SOMEWHERE

ABCDEFDGE
LOGISTICS
UNDERWEAR

ABCDEFDGG
GOVERNESS
PLAINTIFF
POWERLESS
QUIETNESS
TOMBIGBEE

ABCDEFDGH
ACHIEVING
ADVERSELY
AMBIGUITY
ARMISTICE
BREAKFAST
BROADCAST
CHRISTIAN
CHRISTINE
CURIOSITY
DEPICTING
DEVIATION
DEVOTIONS
DIVERGENT
DRUNKENLY
EXPIATION
FEBRUARYS
FELONIOUS
FEROCIOUS
GALOPHONE
HOMESTEAD
IMPERFECT
INVERSELY
MANEUVERS
MELODIOUS
MODIFYING
PLAINTIVE
POLISHING
PRACTICED
PRACTICES
PRECINCTS
PSYCHICAL
PUBESCENT
QUARTERLY
QUIESCENT
SAXOPHONE
SENIORITY
SYNTHETIC

ABCDEFEAA
SCORELESS
SHAPELESS
SPINELESS

ABCDEFEAB
METRONOME
STALINIST

ABCDEFEBA
RECTIFIER

ABCDEFEBC
CONDITION
DESTINIES

ABCDEFEBD
DENSITIES

ABCDEFEBG
CERTIFIED
COALITION
HESITATED
INCLEMENT
NEWSPAPER
PETRIFIED
REALITIES
STABILITY
STERILITY
STUPIDITY
TRAVELERS
UNFAILING
UNSMILING

ABCDEFECA
MYSTICISM
SPECIFIES

ABCDEFECG
ABOLITION
BRAZILIAN
CONFIDING
PROVISION
SACRIFICE
SPECIFIED

ABCDEFEDB
AGONIZING
ATONEMENT

ABCDEFEDC
INTERPRET

ABCDEFEDF
UKRAINIAN

ABCDEFEDG
CAPTIVITY
FERTILITY
GENTILITY
HOSTILITY
PHYSICIST

ABCDEFEEA
RACKETEER

ABCDEFEEG
CONFEREES

ABCDEFEFC
REGAINING

ABCDEFEFG
ADJOINING
COMBINING
DECLINING
EXAMINING
HEPATITIS
OBTAINING
OUTLINING
RECLINING
REMAINING
RETAINING
STRAINING

ABCDEFEGA
ESPLANADE
EXQUISITE

ABCDEFEGB
MYTHOLOGY
RESONANCE

ABCDEFEGC
BEGUILING
LISTENERS

ABCDEFEGD
FORGIVING

ABCDEFEGF
COMBATANT
COMPETENT
JUSTINIAN

ABCDEFEGG
PRICELESS
VAGUENESS
WHITENESS
WHOLENESS

ABCDEFEGH
ABORIGINE
ACHIEVERS
ACQUIRING
AMPLIFIED
AMPLIFIER
ANTHOLOGY
ARISTOTLE
ASTRONOMY
BROWNINGS
CHARITIES
CLARIFIED
COGNITIVE
COMPILING
DARWINISM
DECLIVITY
DEPRIVING
DIAMETERS
DISPARATE
DOMINANCE
FRIVOLOUS
GIVEAWAYS
GLAMOROUS
GLORIFIED
GRATIFIED
JUSTIFIED
MACHINIST
MAGNIFIED
MOISEYEVA
MORTGAGES
ORDINANCE
PATHOLOGY
PHYSICIAN
PLACEMENT
POETIZING
POIGNANCY
PRECISION
PREGNANCY
PRESIDING
PREVISION
PROLIXITY
PROMISING
PROVIDING
PROXIMITY
PUBLICITY
QUALIFIED
QUALIFIES
QUALITIES
REALIZING
REJOICING
RETAILING
SERVICING
SINCERELY
SPECTATOR
STABILIZE
SUPREMELY
SYNAGOGUE
VERMILION
YEARNINGS

ABCDEFFAC
MUSHROOMS

ABCDEFFAG
ACQUITTAL
ENGROSSED

ABCDEFFBG
CONFESSOR
PERMITTED
PERSONNEL

ABCDEFFCB
PROCESSOR
PROFESSOR

ABCDEFFCG
GREVILLES

ABCDEFFEA
DISPELLED

ABCDEFFEB
TRAVELLER

ABCDEFFEC
UNDRESSED

ABCDEFFEF
ACTRESSES
CONFESSES
PROCESSES
WITNESSES

ABCDEFFEG
COMPELLED
CONFERRED
CONFESSED
HARNESSED
IMPRESSED
PROCESSED
PROFESSED
SCHAEFFER
TRAVELLED
WITNESSED

ABCDEFFGD
OUTRIGGER
TEASPOONS

ABCDEFFGH
ACQUITTED
BACKWOODS
FORBIDDEN
INSTALLED
KIDNAPPER
MARCELLUS
PATROLLED
SUBMITTED
TRUJILLOS
UMBRELLAS
UNSKILLED

ABCDEFGAA
SNODGRASS
STAINLESS

ABCDEFGAB
AMSTERDAM
ICELANDIC
RECAPTURE
STRONGEST
TERMINATE

ABCDEFGAC
COSMETICS
SYMBOLISM

ABCDEFGAD
SOUTHEAST
SOUTHWEST
SUPERVISE

ABCDEFGAE
CONSTRUCT
EXPOSURES

ABCDEFGAF
NILPOTENT
SLIGHTEST

ABCDEFGAG
EXPOUNDED
MELODRAMA
THEORISTS

ABCDEFGAH
ABDOMINAL
ADVERBIAL
ANCESTRAL
CATHOLICS
COWARDICE
ELONGATED
ENCRUSTED
ESTRANGED
EXCHANGED
EXCHANGES
EXCLAIMED
EXHAUSTED
EXPLAINED
EXPLOITED
GOULDINGS
GROUPINGS
HILPRECHT
NEGOCIANT
NORTHLAND
NUMBERING
OBJECTION
OPERATION
RAINSTORM
WITHDRAWN

ABCDEFGBA
CINEMATIC
DECLAIMED
DECORATED
DELIGHTED
DEPOSITED
DESCRIBED
DESTROYED
EVOCATIVE
REMAINDER
TRANSPORT

ABCDEFGBB
BLACKWELL

ABCDEFGBC
CONFUSION
CONTAGION
DESCARTES
DESCRIBES
ENGRAVING
PREMATURE
REDOUBLED

ABCDEFGBD
CRUSADERS
DISREPAIR
PRISONERS
UNDERGONE
UNDERLINE
UNDERMINE

ABCDEFGBE
BURLESQUE
COVINGTON
DESTROYER
MODERATOR
PROCEDURE
TRANSFERS

ABCDEFGBF
ACQUIESCE
ANDERSONS
COMPANION
DERVISHES
DIALECTIC
ENLARGING
POSTERIOR

ABCDEFGBG
DIAGNOSIS
PERSUADED
RESPONDED

ABCDEFGBH
ANSWERING
BACTERIAL
BENIGHTED
BEWITCHED
BRUCKNERS
BRUSHFIRE
CAROLINAS
CATHEDRAL
CENTURIES
CERVANTES
COMPEYSON
COUNSELOR
CREDITORS
DELPHINES
DRUGSTORE
ENFORCING
ESTABLISH
FORMATION
FRAMEWORK
FRONTIERS
HEADLINES
INCUMBENT
INDULGENT
INFORMANT
JERUSALEM
LAODICEAN
LUCRETIUS
LUDICROUS
ORCHESTRA
PAROCHIAL
PATROLMAN
PENALIZED
PENALTIES
PLAUSIBLE
PRODUCERS
RECLAIMED
RECOUNTED
REGULATED
RELATIVES
RENOVATED
STIMULATE
STIPULATE
TRANSFORM
TRENCHARD
UNFOLDING
UNLOADING

ABCDEFGCA
EXTRICATE
MAUSOLEUM
SANCTIONS
STRANGERS

ABCDEFGCB
FREIGHTER
GROSVENOR
KRETCHMER
SYNCHRONY

ABCDEFGCC
LINDEMANN

ABCDEFGCD
FRENCHMEN
INTEGRATE
OUTSKIRTS
PREDICTED
TOLERABLE
UNDERSIDE

ABCDEFGCE
PLEASURES

ABCDEFGCF
ARCHITECT
PREJUDGED

ABCDEFGCG
BOTANISTS
CONTADINI

ABCDEFGCH
ANECDOTES
AUTHORITY
BRAHMSIAN
CARPENTRY
CASTROISM
CHEVROLET
CHIEFTAIN
CLERGYMEN
CONDAMINE
CONFIDENT
CONFUSING
CONGRUENT
CONSUMING
CRAFTSMAN
DESPOTISM
DIRECTORS
DIRECTORY
DISCOURSE
DISHONEST
ENIGMATIC
EVOLUTION
FLOWERPOT
FUNCTIONS
HALTINGLY
LUNCHEONS
MECHANICS
MONTAIGNE
NORTHWARD
OVERSIZED
PANTHEONS
PONDERING
PREAMBLES
PREVAILED
PROBATION
PROFUSION
PROLUSION
PURGATORY
SCRIPTURE
THACKERAY
UNEARTHED
UNHEALTHY
URETHANES
WANDERING
WONDERING

ABCDEFGDA
DATELINED
DISREGARD
SCHEDULES
TRANSIENT
TRENCHANT

ABCDEFGDB
PERVASIVE
STEAMBOAT

ABCDEFGDC
BILATERAL
FOREIGNER
INSTRUCTS

ABCDEFGDD
CRISPNESS

ABCDEFGDE
ADHESIVES
DECORATOR
GREATCOAT
SCHEDULED
WHOLESALE

ABCDEFGDG
CONTRASTS

ABCDEFGDH
BEAUTIFUL
BLANCHING
BRUTALITY
CERTAINTY
COGNIZANT
COURTIERS
COURTYARD
CULTIVATE
DARTMOUTH
FORTUNATE
FOUNTAINS
HEXAGONAL
LAUNCHING
LIBERATED
MANKOWSKI
MENTALITY
MIGRATORY
MODERATES
MORTALITY
MOUNTAINS
NARCOTICS
NOVELTIES
ORGIASTIC
PANKOWSKI
POSTERITY
POSTULATE
SWINBURNE
THORNBURG
UNDERGOES
UNLEASHED
UNRELATED
VIOLENTLY
WATERSHED
ZEALOUSLY

ABCDEFGEA
DISCERNED
GROUNDING
ROCHESTER
SHORTCUTS
SUPERIORS

ABCDEFGEB
DEBUTANTE
DEPARTURE
NEGOTIATE
ORCHESTER

ABCDEFGEC
BARTENDER
CARPENTER
FRANCESCA
HARVESTER
HUNGARIAN
MYSTERIES
WORCESTER

ABCDEFGED
CHESTNUTS
OURSELVES
VALENTINE

ABCDEFGEF
BELONGING

ABCDEFGEG
INCREASES
PROTEASES

ABCDEFGEH
ALIGNMENT
ASCENDING
AUDIENCES
AUGMENTED
BROADSIDE
BYZANTINE
CHABRIERS
CLEANSING
CONGEALED
CONGESTED
CONVERTED
DEBUNKING
DECANTING
DEMOCRACY
EXPANDING
EXPLOSION
FISHERMEN
FRANCESCO
FRANCISCO
FROSTBITE
INCREASED
INFLECTED
INSOLUBLE
INSPECTED
LAWRENCES
POLYESTER
POLYETHER
PROJECTED
REALISTIC
SCHOLARLY
SUBJECTED
SUBMERGED
TRAGEDIES
TRIBESMEN

ABCDEFGFA
DISOBEYED
GARDENING
GOVERNING
STRENUOUS

ABCDEFGFC
HARTWEGER
PYROMETER
SCRIVENER

ABCDEFGFD
FERDINAND

ABCDEFGFE
BLUNDERED
BROADENED
SMOLDERED
THUNDERED

ABCDEFGFG
SLANDERER
TOSCANINI

ABCDEFGFH
AMBIGUOUS
BECKONING
BLACKENED
BLISTERED
CHAMBERED
CLAMBERED
CLUSTERED
COMPLETED
COMPLETES
COMPLEXES
CONQUERED
COUNSELED
COUNTERED
DARKENING
FLICKERED
GLISTENED
HACKNEYED
HASTENING
HOLSTERED
IMPETUOUS
JOURNEYED
KILOMETER
LIGHTENED
MOISTENED
PANTOMIME
PLASTERED
POLICEMEN
PROMINENT
REASONING
RECKONING
ROUGHENED
SHARPENED
SHORTENED

ABCDEFGFH
SHRIVELED
SLACKENED
SMOTHERED
SNICKERED
SOFTENING
TEMPORARY
THICKENED
UNCOVERED
UNSCREWED
WHISPERED

ABCDEFGGA
DISAGREED
LIVERPOOL
SNOWBALLS

ABCDEFGGB
ADULTHOOD
DEAUVILLE
RIMANELLI
TYPICALLY

ABCDEFGGC
DISAGREES
UNDERWOOD

ABCDEFGGD
ASHEVILLE
CATSKILLS

ABCDEFGGF
AFTERNOON
CIGARETTE
GABRIELLE
OLGIVANNA
PIROUETTE
PRINCESSE

ABCDEFGGH
BERNOULLI
BLACKFEET
BULTMANNS
CAREFULLY
CENTRALLY
CHARLOTTE
EICHMANNS
ETHICALLY
FALSEHOOD
GRANVILLE
GUIDEBOOK
HANDCUFFS
HOPEFULLY
MCAULIFFE
MEDICALLY
MUSICALLY
NASHVILLE
PAINFULLY
SPECIALLY
TEARFULLY
UNDERFOOT
UNDERTOOK
VIRTUALLY
VOLUNTEER
WESTBROOK
WISTFULLY

ABCDEFGHA
CHROMATIC
DIAGNOSED
DISPLACED
DISPLAYED
DISRUPTED
DISTURBED
DOMINATED
EMPHASIZE
ENCLOSURE
ENCOURAGE
ENDURABLE
ENJOYABLE
ENTOURAGE
EQUITABLE
ESPIONAGE
EXCLUSIVE
EXPLOSIVE
GATHERING
GLOWERING
MAGNETISM
MECHANISM
MODERNISM
NORWEGIAN
SANDBURGS
SCHNABELS
SCHUBERTS
SCULPTORS
SHIPMENTS
SHORTAGES
SHOULDERS
SHUTDOWNS
SIDEWALKS
SKYLIGHTS
SQUADRONS
STOCKINGS
THERAPIST

ABCDEFGHB
ADJOURNED
AYLESBURY
DESIGNATE
DESIRABLE
DYSTROPHY
GERALDINE
GERMINATE
HYPOCRISY
ISLANDERS
ISOPLETHS
MEANWHILE
PLENTIFUL
PSITHYRUS
RECOGNIZE
RECTANGLE
REPULSIVE
REPUTABLE
SCHEMATIC
SEDUCTIVE
SEMBLANCE
TECHNIQUE
UNCERTAIN
VENTRICLE
VERITABLE
VERSATILE
VESTIBULE
WEARISOME

ABCDEFGHC
ABSOLUTES
AESCHYLUS
CUSTOMERS
DISCOUNTS
DISCOVERS
DISTANCES
DREAMLIKE
DYSTOPIAS
FESTIVALS
HOSPITALS
INTROJECT
KINGSTOWN
METHODIST
MODULATED
NIETZSCHE
OBSTACLES
OPERATIVE
PREJUDICE
SPECULATE
STEPHANIE
UPGRADING

ABCDEFGHD
ADJECTIVE
ADVENTURE
ADVERTISE
BUDGETING
CONSIDERS
CONSUMERS
CORTLANDT
DOGMATISM
DRESBACHS
FIREPLACE
FORMALISM
FRENCHMAN
GERMANIUM
GERSHWINS
GRIEVANCE
HIBERNATE
HYPERBOLE
INTERFACE
INTERLUDE
MILESTONE
MISERABLE
NORTHEAST
NORTHWEST
OBJECTIVE
OTHERWISE
OUTSIDERS
PALESTINE
PAWTUCKET
PLATONIST
PRINCETON
QUESTIONS
SOMEPLACE
SPOTLIGHT
TOLERANCE
TULAREMIA
UNDERTAKE
UNWELCOME
WAREHOUSE
WORTHIEST

ABCDEFGHE
ANCESTORS
ARLINGTON
ASKINGTON
BANISTERS
BURNSIDES
CALDERONE
CAMPSITES
CATHERINE
CHRISTMAS
DISREPUTE
EXPANSION
FORTESCUE
GLYCERINE
GRAPEVINE
GROTESQUE
HOUSEWIFE
INDUSTRYS
INVESTORS
KATHERINE
LEXINGTON
NOSTALGIA
PENSACOLA
PROMENADE
PROSECUTE
REMINGTON
ROUNDHEAD
SHORELINE
STONEWARE
SYMINGTON
THOUSANDS
WHITEFACE

ABCDEFGHF
BRIGHTEST
FERGUSONS
FURNISHES
HAMBURGER
IMPORTANT
IMPOTENCE
KNOWLEDGE
MISJUDGED
PUBLISHES
RELUCTANT
RESULTANT
UNBRIDLED
VARNISHES
VIRULENCE

ABCDEFGHG
ASTOUNDED
COMPRISES
CONQUESTS
FORECASTS
HUMORISTS
NOVELISTS
ORGANISMS
PARTHENON
PURCHASES
QUASIMODO
SACRILEGE
VOCALISTS

ABCDEFGHH
AWFULNESS
BLACKNESS
BOUNDLESS
COUNTLESS
DAUNTLESS
DOUBTLESS
ENCOMPASS
FORESTALL
FRUITLESS
KOHNSTAMM
MATCHLESS
MILWAUKEE
NIGHTFALL
RIGHTNESS
ROUGHNESS
THICKNESS
TOUGHNESS
WORTHLESS

ABACADCABE
INITIATING

ABACADCAEB
INITIATION

ABACADCAEF
INITIATIVE

ABACADEFGH
ELEMENTARY

ABACBDEFGH
MEMBERSHIP

ABACDADEFG
ADAPTATION

ABACDCAEFG
IMITATIONS

ABACDCCADE
NINETEENTH

ABACDEAFGE
SUSPENSION

ABACDECFCG
ABANDONING

ABACDEDFBA
SUSPICIOUS

ABACDEDFGA
SUSPICIONS

ABACDEFACA
EVERYWHERE

ABACDEFAGG
EYEWITNESS

ABACDEFCGB
ELECTRICAL

ABACDEFCGH
DEDICATION
SYSTEMATIC

ABACDEFDAG
ANARCHICAL

ABACDEFDBA
NONFICTION

ABACDEFEFG
SUSTAINING

ABACDEFEGD
SUSTENANCE

ABACDEFEGH
EXERCISING
MEMORIZING

ABACDEFFAF
EYEGLASSES

ABACDEFGAC
ANALYTICAL

ABACDEFGAH
ANATOMICAL
EXECUTIVES

ABACDEFGBF
BABYLONIAN

ABACDEFGBG
PEPTIDASES

ABACDEFGBH
ALARMINGLY
ENERVATING
POPULATION

ABACDEFGDH
APARTMENTS
EVERYBODYS

ABACDEFGGH
EVENTUALLY

ABACDEFGHA
MEMORANDUM

ABACDEFGHB
DEDUCTIBLE

ABACDEFGHC
ELECTRONIC

ABACDEFGHI
AMATEURISH
DEDUCTIONS
EVERYTHING
EXECUTIONS
EXEMPTIONS
POPULARISM
POPULARITY
SUSPECTING

ABBACADEBF
TEETOTALER

ABBACDCAEF
IRRITATING
IRRITATION

ABBACDEAFG
IRRIGATION

ABBACDEDAF
OPPOSITION

ABBACDEDFG
APPARITION

ABBACDEFBG
ECCENTRICS

ABBACDEFCD
ILLITERATE

ABBACDEFDA
EFFECTUATE

ABBACDEFDB
ATTAINMENT

ABBACDEFGB
ATTACHMENT
ESSENTIALS

ABBACDEFGC
TOOTHBRUSH

ABBACDEFGH
APPARENTLY
IMMIGRANTS

ABBCADAEFC
APPEARANCE

ABBCADAEFG
AGGRAVATED

ABBCADBEFG
ATTRACTING
ATTRACTION
ATTRACTIVE

ABBCADEAFE
APPRAISALS

ABBCADEFGH
APPLAUDING

ABBCBBDCEF
ASSESSMENT

ABBCBDAEDB
ASSISTANTS

ABBCBDAEFG
ASSISTANCE

ABBCBDEAFG
IMMEMORIAL

ABBCBDEFGH
REELECTION

ABBCDACEFD
IRRADIATED

ABBCDAEAFG
IMMOBILITY

ABBCDAECFG
AFFIDAVITS

ABBCDAEFCG
ALLOCATION
IRRATIONAL

ABBCDAEFGB
ASSURANCES

ABBCDAEFGH
ACCURATELY
ACCUSATION
ALLOWANCES
APPLIANCES
APPROACHED
APPROACHES

ABBCDBEFBG
ANNOUNCING

ABBCDBEFGH
ANNOUNCERS
WOONSOCKET

ABBCDCAEDF
EFFICIENCY

ABBCDCAEFG
AFFILIATED

ABBCDCBCEF
IRREVERENT

ABBCDCCEFG
MCCLELLANS

ABBCDCEAFC
ACCELERATE

ABBCDCEAFG
ACCUMULATE
ASSIMILATE

ABBCDCEFAG
ADDITIONAL

ABBCDCEFCA
ASSINIBOIA

ABBCDCEFFG
OFFICIALLY

ABBCDCEFGH
IRRELEVANT
OFFICIATED

ABBCDDECFG
MCCULLOUGH

ABBCDDEFBE
OCCURRENCE

ABBCDDEFGC
ACCESSIBLE

ABBCDEADBF
ATTENDANTS

ABBCDEADFC
ATTENDANCE

ABBCDEAFBC
ACCEPTANCE

ABBCDEAFBG
ACCORDANCE

ABBCDEAFCG
APPLICABLE
OCCASIONAL

ABBCDEAFGB
ASSOCIATES

ABBCDEAFGC
ACCEPTABLE
ALLEGIANCE

ABBCDEAFGH
APPLICANTS
ASSOCIATED
OCCASIONED

ABBCDEBFGH
ATTEMPTING
INNOCENTLY

ABBCDEDFGC
ROOSEVELTS

ABBCDEEACE
OPPRESSORS

ABBCDEEFAG
OPPRESSION

ABBCDEEFGD
AGGRESSIVE
OPPRESSIVE

ABBCDEEFGH
ADDRESSING
AGGRESSION

ABBCDEFAAD
FOODSTUFFS

ABBCDEFACB
INNOVATION

ABBCDEFACG
IMMATERIAL

ABBCDEFAEF
ACCOUNTANT

ABBCDEFAGC
ASSEMBLAGE

ABBCDEFAGD
APPRECIATE

ABBCDEFAGH
IMMORALITY

ABBCDEFBGH
ATTRIBUTED
ATTRIBUTES

ABBCDEFCGE
ELLIPSOIDS

ABBCDEFCGH
IMMACULATE

ABBCDEFEGD
AMMUNITION

ABBCDEFEGH
APPETIZING

ABBCDEFGAH
ACCIDENTAL
OCCUPATION

ABBCDEFGBH
ACCOMPLICE

ABBCDEFGCB
ASSEMBLIES

ABBCDEFGDE
ACCREDITED

ABBCDEFGDH
ALLOTMENTS
COOPERATED

ABBCDEFGEH
ACCOUNTING
ASSIGNMENT
ILLUSTRATE

ABBCDEFGFG
AGGLUTININ

ABBCDEFGGH
APPOINTEES

ABBCDEFGHB
ASSERTIONS

ABBCDEFGHC
IRRESOLUTE

ABBCDEFGHD
APPRENTICE

ABBCDEFGHI
ACCOMPLISH
ACCRETIONS
ACCUSINGLY
ACCUSTOMED
AFFECTIONS
ASSEMBLING
ASSUMPTION
COORDINATE
OCCIDENTAL

ABCABADEFG
INFINITELY

ABCABCCDEB
CINCINNATI

ABCABCDBEF
BARBARIANS

ABCABDAEAD
ENGENDERED

ABCABDAEFG
INVINCIBLE

ABCABDBEFD
REPRESENTS

ABCABDCEFG
RETREATING

ABCABDDEFB
REPRESSIVE

ABCABDDEFG
REGRESSION
REPRESSION

ABCABDEFCA
TANTAMOUNT

ABCABDEFCB
PROPRIETOR

ABCABDEFCG
CONCORDANT

ABCABDEFDB
PERPETUATE

ABCABDEFEB
PROPRIETER

ABCABDEFGH
RECREATION
REFRESHING

ABCACBDECF
PROPORTION

ABCACDEBFE
INSISTENCE

ABCACDEDFG
PROPONENTS

ABCADACEFG
INDIVIDUAL

ABCADAEABF
INHIBITING

ABCADAEAFB
INHIBITION

ABCADAEBCF
INCIPIENCY

ABCADAEFAG
ATHABASCAN

ABCADAEFCG
INTIMIDATE

ABCADAEFGA
SUBSYSTEMS

ABCADAEFGH
INHIBITORS
INHIBITORY
.

ABCADBCAEF
HIGHLIGHTS

ABCADBEBEF
DISDAINING

ABCADBEFDG
PROPERTIES

ABCADBEFGH
DISDAINFUL
GREGARIOUS
PERPLEXING

ABCADCBEFG
CALCULATED

ABCADCCBEC
ZIGZAGGING

ABCADCCDEF
FULFILLING

ABCADCEFGA
CONCENTRIC

ABCADCEFGH
PROPIONATE
PURPORTING

ABCADDAECA
EXCELLENCE

ABCADDAECF
EXCELLENCY

ABCADDAEFG
AMBASSADOR

ABCADEAEEF
BUMBLEBEES

ABCADEAFGA
EXPERIENCE

ABCADEAFGB
RETROGRADE

ABCADEAFGH
ADVANTAGES
EXPEDIENCY

ABCADEBDFG
SUBSEQUENT

ABCADEBFAC
TESTAMENTS

ABCADEBFGC
ANTAGONIST

ABCADEBFGH
ANTAGONISM
INCIDENTAL
INDIGENOUS

ABCADECFCG
CONCERNING

ABCADECFFG
TRUTHFULLY

ABCADECFGH
INTIMATELY

ABCADEDAFB
INVITATION

ABCADEDBDF
SUBSTITUTE

ABCADEDCFG
PROPITIOUS

ABCADEDFBA
SENSITIVES

ABCADEDFBG
SENSITIZED

ABCADEDFGA
ENTERPRISE

ABCADEDFGD
PROPAGANDA

ABCADEDFGE
SUBSIDIZED

ABCADEDFGH
SUBSIDIARY

ABCADEEFBC
CONCESSION

ABCADEEFCG
CONCURRENT

ABCADEFABD
IODINATION

ABCADEFABG
INDICATING

ABCADEFADG
IODINATING

ABCADEFAGB
INDICATION

ABCADEFAGH
EXPERIMENT
INDICATIVE
INFIDELITY

ABCADEFBFG
OLEOPHILIC

ABCADEFBGC
RETROSPECT

ABCADEFBGG
DEADLINESS

ABCADEFCGH
SUBSCRIBED

ABCADEFDGA
SUBSTRATES

ABCADEFDGC
INDISPOSED

ABCADEFDGH
CRUCIFYING

ABCADEFEBD
INCITEMENT

ABCADEFECG
CONCEIVING

ABCADEFEGF
CHICKASAWS

ABCADEFEGH
CONCRETELY
EXPEDITING
EXPEDITION
RECRUITING
TURTLENECK

ABCADEFGAC
ENDEAVORED

ABCADEFGAH
EISENHOWER
EMPEDOCLES

ABCADEFGBC
CONCEPTION
CONCLUSION

ABCADEFGBE
INDICTMENT
REPRODUCED

ABCADEFGBH
ENVELOPING
PURPOSEFUL
REPRODUCES

ABCADEFGCA
SENSATIONS

ABCADEFGCB
PREPOLYMER

ABCADEFGCH
CONCLUDING
PROPULSION

ABCADEFGDE
EXTENSIONS

ABCADEFGDH
EXPECTANCY
FARFETCHED
HYPHENATED

ABCADEFGEA
SUBSPECIES

ABCADEFGEH
PROPHESIED

ABCADEFGGH
ESPECIALLY
EXPECIALLY
EXTERNALLY
INDISCREET

ABCADEFGHA
SUBSTANCES

ABCADEFGHE
SKYSCRAPER

ABCADEFGHI
CIRCULATED
CONCEPTUAL
CONCLUSIVE
EXCEPTIONS
GEOGRAPHIC
INDICATORS
INDIRECTLY
SENSUALITY
SUBSECTION
UNSUITABLE

ABCBABDBCE
MINIMIZING

ABCBABDEBF
REFERENCES

ABCBADCBEF
PARAPHRASE

ABCBADEDFG
CAPACITIES

ABCBADEFAB
REPERTOIRE

ABCBADEFAC
RESERVOIRS

ABCBADEFGB
REVERSIBLE

ABCBCDBABE
REMEMBERED

ABCBCDEFGH
UNANALYZED

ABCBDABDEA
STATISTICS

ABCBDABDEB
DEPENDENCE

ABCBDABDEF
DEPENDENCY
DEPENDENTS

ABCBDAEDFE
REHEARSALS

ABCBDAEDFG
DEFENDANTS

ABCBDAEFBA
RESEARCHER

ABCBDAEFGB
DEPENDABLE

ABCBDBCBEF
MONOTONOUS

ABCBDBEBFG
DIVINITIES
VISIBILITY

ABCBDBEEFG
CARAVAGGIO

ABCBDBEFGA
DIMINISHED

ABCBDBEFGE
DIMINISHES
KAYABASHIS

ABCBDBEFGH
DIVISIONAL
LOCOMOTIVE
MONOPOLIES
MONOPOLIZE
SALAMANDER
SIMILITUDE

ABCBDCBAEF
PARAGRAPHS

ABCBDCEFBG
DETECTIVES

ABCBDCEFGB
DETECTABLE
DETESTABLE

ABCBDDEDEF
PARALLELED

ABCBDDEFGH
REBELLIOUS

ABCBDEAECF
MANAGEMENT

ABCBDEBFCG
DETERGENTS

ABCBDEBFEF
UNINTENDED

ABCBDEBFGC
VENEZUELAN

ABCBDEBFGH
DETERGENCY
REPEATEDLY

ABCBDECBFD
MITIGATING

ABCBDECBFF
RELENTLESS

ABCBDECBFG
LITIGATION

ABCBDECEFG
FATALITIES

ABCBDEDBFG
LIMITATION
VISITATION

ABCBDEDEFG
REPETITION

ABCBDEDFBA
STATEMENTS

ABCBDEDFGH
VEGETATION

ABCBDEFAGH
EPIPHYSEAL

ABCBDEFBCG
BENEVOLENT
MILITARILY

ABCBDEFBDE
RESENTMENT

ABCBDEFBGA
MILITARISM

ABCBDEFBGD
DIVINATION
MILITARIST
MINISTRIES

ABCBDEFBGH
DEVELOPERS
DIMINUTIVE
HOMOZYGOUS
RIDICULING
SIMILARITY

ABCBDEFCBG
METEORITES

ABCBDEFCFG
METEORITIC

ABCBDEFCGH
CATAPULTED
PARAMETRIC
STATIONARY
TOPOGRAPHY

ABCBDEFDBG
PENETRATED

ABCBDEFDGB
REPENTANCE

ABCBDEFECB
HERETOFORE

ABCBDEFECG
PARAMETERS

ABCBDEFEGD
GENETICIST

ABCBDEFEGH
BENEFICIAL
CAPABILITY
FANATICISM
TELEVISION

ABCBDEFGBA
DETERMINED

ABCBDEFGBH
CELEBRATED
CELEBRATES
CEREMONIES
COLORATION
DEBENTURES
DETERMINES
MANAGERIAL
TELEPHONED
TELEPHONES
TELESCOPED
VEGETABLES

ABCBDEFGCA
GENERATING

ABCBDEFGCH
HEREDITARY

ABCBDEFGDE
COLORATURA
HARANGUING

ABCBDEFGDH
GENERATORS
PETERSBURG
VETERINARY

ABCBDEFGEH
RIDICULOUS

ABCBDEFGFH
MINISTERED

ABCBDEFGHA
SELECTIONS

ABCBDEFGHB
DEFENSIBLE
GENERALIZE
PETERHOUSE

ABCBDEFGHC
GENERATION
VENERATION

ABCBDEFGHD
DELEGATING

ABCBDEFGHE
HOMOGENATE

ABCBDEFGHG
IONOSPHERE

ABCBDEFGHI
BENEFACTOR
CALAMITOUS
CATALOGUED
CATALOGUES
CELEBRANTS
CEREMONIAL
COPOLYMERS
CUMULATIVE
DELEGATION
DEVELOPING
FEDERALISM
FEDERATION
FEVERISHLY
FILIBUSTER
GENERALITY
GENEROSITY
GENEROUSLY
HEREABOUTS
HOMOSEXUAL
PEDESTRIAN
REDEMPTION
RESEMBLING
REVELATION
SANATORIUM
STATIONERY

ABCCADEFGD
LITTLEPAGE

ABCCADEFGH
BILLBOARDS

ABCCBADEDF
MILLIMETER

ABCCBADEFD
DIFFIDENCE

ABCCBCBDEF
MILLILITER

ABCCBDBEFG
DISSIMILAR

ABCCBDEBFC
BETTERMENT
MESSENGERS

ABCCBDEFAG
MILLIGRAMS

ABCCBDEFBG
PASSAGEWAY

ABCCBDEFEG
BORROMINIS
COLLOQUIUM

ABCCBDEFGA
DISSIPATED

ABCCBDEFGC
COLLOQUIAL

ABCCBDEFGD
PIDDINGTON

ABCCBDEFGE
JEFFERSONS

ABCCBDEFGH
COMMONWEAL
DIFFICULTY
MISSIONARY
NARRATIVES

ABCCDAAEBF
SUCCESSFUL

ABCCDAAEFA
SUCCESSORS

ABCCDAAEFD
SUCCESSIVE

ABCCDAAEFG
SUCCESSION

ABCCDABEBF
CURRICULUM

ABCCDABEFC
CURRICULAR

ABCCDAEBFG
COLLECTORS

ABCCDAEFBC
CONNECTION

ABCCDAEFBG
COLLECTION
CORRECTION

ABCCDAEFCG
CONNECTING

ABCCDAEFGC
SUGGESTING

ABCCDAEFGD
COLLECTIVE
CONNECTIVE
SUGGESTIVE

ABCCDAEFGH
COLLECTING
SUGGESTION
SUPPOSEDLY

ABCCDBEBFC
SETTLEMENT

ABCCDBEFGF
SURROUNDED

ABCCDCBEFG
BALLPLAYER

ABCCDCCEBF
POSSESSION

ABCCDCCEFD
POSSESSIVE

ABCCDCCEFG
POSSESSING

ABCCDCEFBA
MANNINGHAM

ABCCDCEFBG
TERRORIZED

ABCCDCEFGC
BENNINGTON

ABCCDCEFGH
CUNNINGHAM

ABCCDDEFGH
SUCCEEDING

ABCCDEAAEF
SUPPRESSED

ABCCDEAFDG
CURRENCIES

ABCCDEAFEG
COMMENCING

ABCCDEAFGH
COMMERCIAL
DUSSELDORF

ABCCDEBBFG
HOLLYWOODS

ABCCDEBFFG
PICCADILLY

ABCCDEBFGH
BARRICADES

ABCCDECBFE
DISSENSION

ABCCDECFFE
LAMMERMOOR

ABCCDECFGD
SWEETHEART

ABCCDECFGE
COMMITMENT

ABCCDECFGH
SUCCINCTLY

ABCCDEDAFD
BESSARABIA

ABCCDEDBFE
COLLISIONS

ABCCDEDFGD
DIFFERENCE

ABCCDEDFGH
FOSSILIZED
SUFFICIENT

ABCCDEEBFA
MILLENNIUM

ABCCDEEDAA
SUDDENNESS

ABCCDEEDBF
COMMISSION

ABCCDEEDFG
COMMITTING

ABCCDEEFFG
COMMITTEES

ABCCDEEFGH
COMMISSARY

ABCCDEFBBG
DONNYBROOK

ABCCDEFBEG
DISSENTING

ABCCDEFBGA
SADDLEBAGS

ABCCDEFBGD
DINNERTIME

ABCCDEFBGH
CORRESPOND
DISSECTION
DISSOLVING
PASSIONATE

ABCCDEFCAA
SPEECHLESS

ABCCDEFCGH
GREENFIELD
MUSSORGSKY

ABCCDEFDGC
PASSENGERS

ABCCDEFDGG
BITTERNESS

ABCCDEFDGH
HIPPODROME
HORRIFYING
LAPPENBERG
TERRIFYING

ABCCDEFEGH
BOTTLENECK
HAPPENINGS
SUPPLEMENT

ABCCDEFGAA
SMOOTHNESS

ABCCDEFGBE
CODDINGTON

ABCCDEFGBH
CORRUPTION

ABCCDEFGCD
SUMMERTIME

ABCCDEFGCG
COMMUNISMS

ABCCDEFGCH
CARRUTHERS
CHEEKBONES

ABCCDEFGDH
COLLEAGUES
CORRELATED

ABCCDEFGEA
SUPPORTERS

ABCCDEFGEB
SORRENTINO

ABCCDEFGEH
COMMANDING
COMMENDING
COMMENTING

ABCCDEFGFC
MUSSOLINIS

ABCCDEFGGC
GREENVILLE

ABCCDEFGGF
WILLAMETTE

ABCCDEFGGH
CHEERFULLY

ABCCDEFGHA
GETTYSBURG
SUFFERINGS

ABCCDEFGHC
GREENHOUSE

ABCCDEFGHD
COLLEGIATE
HASSELTINE
SUMMERDALE

ABCCDEFGHE
BARRINGTON
HARRINGTON
MINNESOTAS

ABCCDEFGHG
COMMUNISTS

ABCCDEFGHH
BATTENKILL

ABCCDEFGHI
BROOKFIELD
COLLAPSING
COMMANDERS
COMMENTARY
COMMUNITYS
CORRUGATED
CORRUPTING
FELLOWSHIP
MIDDLETOWN
PITTSBURGH
SUMMARIZED
SUPPORTING
SUPPORTIVE

ABCDABCEFD
PHOSPHORUS

ABCDABEBFC
RETIREMENT

ABCDABECFG
GEORGETOWN

ABCDABEDFF
LIVELINESS

ABCDABEFAG
ENTRENCHED

ABCDABEFCG
CARICATURE
ORATORICAL

ABCDABEFDG
CHURCHYARD

ABCDABEFEG
POSTPONING

ABCDABEFFG
CHURCHILLS
LIKELIHOOD
LIVELIHOOD

ABCDABEFGD
IMPRIMATUR

ABCDABEFGH
EMBLEMATIC

ABCDACEFAG
UBIQUITOUS

ABCDACEFDG
SPONSORING

ABCDADEDFC
INSTITUTES

ABCDADEDFG
INSTITUTED
MAXIMIZING

ABCDADEFGH
RIGOROUSLY

ABCDAEAFDC
INELIGIBLE

ABCDAEAFDG
IMPLICITLY

ABCDAEAFGH
INQUISITOR
TEMPTATION

ABCDAEBCFD
PROSPEROUS

ABCDAEBCFG
PERIPHERAL

ABCDAEBEFF
UNIQUENESS

ABCDAEBFBG
HEIGHTENED

ABCDAEBFGB
RESURGENCE

ABCDAEBFGH
PROSPERITY
REPORTEDLY
SINUSOIDAL

ABCDAECDFF
LONELINESS

ABCDAECFAG
TREATMENTS

ABCDAECFGH
MONUMENTAL

ABCDAEDFGB
REMARKABLE

ABCDAEDFGH
REMARKABLY

ABCDAEEFAB
THIRTEENTH

ABCDAEEFGA
EXPRESSIVE

ABCDAEEFGH
EXPRESSING
EXPRESSION
EXPRESSWAY

ABCDAEFABE
INTRIGUING

ABCDAEFABG
INFLICTING

ABCDAEFAGB
INFLICTION

ABCDAEFAGH
GRUDGINGLY

ABCDAEFBFC
TIGHTENING

ABCDAEFBGG
REGARDLESS

ABCDAEFBGH
APOCALYPSE
ECUMENICAL

ABCDAEFCAF
CONSCIENCE

ABCDAEFCAG
EXIGENCIES

ABCDAEFCBB
USEFULNESS

ABCDAEFCGH
ALEXANDERS

ABCDAEFDBA
NOMINATION

ABCDAEFDBG
RESTRICTED

ABCDAEFDFG
MONTMARTRE

ABCDAEFDGG
LOVELINESS

ABCDAEFDGH
SATISFYING

ABCDAEFEBE
TRASTEVERE

ABCDAEFEGH
LOCALITIES

ABCDAEFFGH
CHANCELLOR

ABCDAEFGAH
ENUMERATED

ABCDAEFGBH
RESTRAINED

ABCDAEFGCG
EXTREMISTS

ABCDAEFGCH
BLAUBERMAN
STRASBOURG

ABCDAEFGDC
FOREFINGER
RESTRAINTS

ABCDAEFGDH
RESORCINOL
THEATRICAL

ABCDAEFGGH
IRONICALLY

ABCDAEFGHA
ALEXANDRIA
EXUBERANCE

ABCDAEFGHC
INEVITABLE

ABCDAEFGHD
COUNCILMAN

ABCDAEFGHF
HUTCHINSON

ABCDAEFGHI
ABREACTION
ACQUAINTED
BELABORING
IMPLICATED
IMPRISONED
INEVITABLY
ORTHOPEDIC
RECORDINGS
REMBRANDTS
RIVERBANKS

ABCDBAEDBF
REITERATED

ABCDBAEFGB
PERCEPTIVE

ABCDBAEFGH
PERCEPTION
PERCEPTUAL

ABCDBCAEBF
INTENTIONS

ABCDBCCBEF
DISMISSING

ABCDBCCEFG
CENTENNIAL

ABCDBCEBFG
PERVERSELY

ABCDBCECFD
CONSONANTS

ABCDBCECFG
PRIORITIES

ABCDBCEFBG
SEGREGATED
TENDENCIES

ABCDBDBEFG
FICTITIOUS

ABCDBDEFGH
UNFINISHED

ABCDBEABFE
YESTERYEAR

ABCDBEAFBG
INVENTIONS

ABCDBEAFDG
INCENTIVES

ABCDBEAFEG
DESCENDANT
DESCENDING

ABCDBEAFGH
INTANGIBLE

ABCDBEBFDC
MISGIVINGS

ABCDBEBFGH
VICTIMIZED

ABCDBECADB
INTONATION

ABCDBECBFF
TENDERNESS

ABCDBECFGE
WEDNESDAYS

ABCDBECFGF
CONFOUNDED

ABCDBEDFGH
RADIATIONS
VARIATIONS

ABCDBEEBFG
HEIDEGGERS

ABCDBEEFGE
CANVASSERS

ABCDBEEFGH
DEPRESSING
DEPRESSION

ABCDBEFAGB
INJUNCTION

ABCDBEFBAG
VINDICTIVE

ABCDBEFBGH
DISCIPLINE
KULTURBUND

ABCDBEFCCG
CULTURALLY

ABCDBEFCGH
DOSTOEVSKY

ABCDBEFDGA
SECRETARYS

ABCDBEFDGH
DISTINCTLY
HOMEOWNERS

ABCDBEFEFD
BARGAINING

ABCDBEFEGH
COMPONENTS
STRATIFIED

ABCDBEFFEF
PROGRESSES

ABCDBEFFEG
PROGRESSED

ABCDBEFFGB
PROGRAMMER

ABCDBEFFGH
PROGRAMMED

ABCDBEFGAB
ARTERIOLAR

ABCDBEFGAC
NEGLECTING
YESTERDAYS

ABCDBEFGAH
REFLECTORS

ABCDBEFGBH
BEQUEATHED
PERSECUTED

ABCDBEFGCH
CONSORTING

ABCDBEFGDG
GORTONISTS

ABCDBEFGDH
ARTERIOLES

ABCDBEFGGA
TENDERFOOT

ABCDBEFGGD
SANDALWOOD

ABCDBEFGGH
PEACEFULLY

ABCDBEFGHA
DISFIGURED
HENCEFORTH
HENGESBACH
SACRAMENTS

ABCDBEFGHB
PERCENTAGE
REFLECTIVE
RESPECTIVE

ABCDBEFGHC
CASUALTIES
SANDALPHON

ABCDBEFGHD
BIRMINGHAM
GEOCENTRIC
PROGRAMING
UNDENIABLE
VINDICATED

ABCDBEFGHE
LIQUIDATED
WILMINGTON

ABCDBEFGHF
TURBULENCE

ABCDBEFGHG
COMPOUNDED

ABCDBEFGHH
MOTIONLESS

ABCDBEFGHI
CAMPAIGNED
COMFORTING
CONFORMIST
CONFORMITY
DECREASING
DICTIONARY
HEIDENSTAM
HEUVELMANS
LEADERSHIP
PERFECTING
PERFECTION
PROTRUDING
REFLECTING
REFLECTION
RENDEZVOUS
REQUESTING
RESPECTFUL
RESPECTING
SACRAMENTO
STRETCHING
UNSINKABLE
VALUATIONS

ABCDCAACEF
PHILIPPINE

ABCDCAAEFF
PHILIPPOFF

ABCDCACEFE
CRITICISMS

ABCDCACEFG
CRITICIZED

ABCDCAEABF
ENGAGEMENT

ABCDCAEFDG
CHARACTERS

ABCDCAEFFG
CRITICALLY

ABCDCAEFGD
GEOLOGICAL

ABCDCAEFGF
GEOLOGISTS

ABCDCBCEFC
PREFERENCE

ABCDCBEDFA
SYNONYMOUS

ABCDCBEEBF
BESTSELLER

ABCDCBEECF
HELPLESSLY

ABCDCBEFGC
PREFERABLE

ABCDCBEFGH
PREFERABLY
PRESERVING

ABCDCCEFGH
PRECEEDING

ABCDCDEFBG
PETITIONED
PETITIONER

ABCDCEACFG
CLEMENCEAU

ABCDCEAEFG
SURPRISING

ABCDCEAFEA
STEVENSONS

ABCDCEBFGC
STEREOTYPE

ABCDCEBFGD
BIOLOGICAL

ABCDCEBFGF
BIOLOGISTS

ABCDCECFDC
PRECEDENCE

ABCDCECFGH
PHONOLOGIC
PRECEDENTS

ABCDCEDFGH
PRONOUNCED

ABCDCEFACD
THEREAFTER

ABCDCEFBGD
ECOLOGICAL

ABCDCEFBGH
ECONOMICAL
THOROUGHLY

ABCDCEFCAG
TRIVIALITY

ABCDCEFCGG
CLEVERNESS

ABCDCEFDGH
HOMEMAKERS
REVIVALISM

ABCDCEFFDC
FORERUNNER

ABCDCEFFEF
FORTRESSES

ABCDCEFGAB
PHONOGRAPH
PHOTOGRAPH

ABCDCEFGAD
POSTSCRIPT

ABCDCEFGAH
ELIMINATED
ELIMINATES

ABCDCEFGDC
PREVENTIVE

ABCDCEFGDG
ANTITHESIS

ABCDCEFGEE
PROKOFIEFF

ABCDCEFGEF
PROLONGING

ABCDCEFGEH
PRESENTING
PRETENDING
PREVENTING

ABCDCEFGFH
PRIVILEGED
PRIVILEGES

ABCDCEFGGH
GUARANTEED
GUARANTEES
ORIGINALLY

ABCDCEFGHA
SPIRITUALS

ABCDCEFGHB
RESISTANCE

ABCDCEFGHC
DISASTROUS

ABCDCEFGHE
PREVENTION

ABCDCEFGHG
ECONOMISTS

ABCDCEFGHI
APOLOGETIC
APOLOGIZED
CARTRIDGES
DRAMATIZES
GRADATIONS
ORIGINATED
ORIGINATES
OVEREATING
PHOTOGENIC
PORTRAYING
PROFOUNDLY
TREMENDOUS
TREVELYANS

ABCDDAECFA
EXAGGERATE

ABCDDAEFGH
ABERRATION
UNOCCUPIED

ABCDDBCABE
REAPPEARED

ABCDDBCEFD
CROSSROADS

ABCDDBEEFD
GRASSROOTS

ABCDDBEFBA
RENSSELAER

ABCDDBEFCA
STREETCARS

ABCDDBEFGB
REASSEMBLE

ABCDDBEFGH
SCREECHING

ABCDDCECDF
FLANNAGANS

ABCDDCEFGH
BRILLIANCE
UNATTACHED

ABCDDEAEDF
CLASSICISM

ABCDDEAFBG
REAFFIRMED
SLUGGISHLY

ABCDDEAFGH
REASSURING

ABCDDEBFEF
UNATTENDED

ABCDDEBFGH
SWALLOWING

ABCDDECFGD
CLASSMATES
GRASSLANDS

ABCDDEDFGH
AGREEMENTS
UNASSISTED

ABCDDEFBBG
BLISSFULLY

ABCDDEFCDG
INACCURACY

ABCDDEFCFG
STIFFENING

ABCDDEFCGA
GLITTERING

ABCDDEFCGH
INACCURATE
SHIMMERING

ABCDDEFDDC
SNELLVILLE

ABCDDEFDDG
SCHOOLROOM
SKILLFULLY

ABCDDEFEGH
CLASSIFIED
OVERRIDING
UNOFFICIAL

ABCDDEFFGD
CLASSROOMS

ABCDDEFFGH
GUERRILLAS

ABCDDEFGEF
CRITTENDEN

ABCDDEFGEH
CHALLENGED
CHALLENGES
UNAFFECTED

ABCDDEFGFH
FLATTENING

ABCDDEFGHB
SHIBBOLETH

ABCDDEFGHD
STAGGERING

ABCDDEFGHI
ASYMMETRIC
CHATTERING
FLUTTERING
QUARRELING
SCATTERGUN
SHATTERING
SHUDDERING
STUBBORNLY

ABCDEAAEFG
SUBMISSION
SUBMISSIVE

ABCDEAAFCG
OVERLOOKED

ABCDEAAFED
EIGHTEENTH

ABCDEABAFD
INDEFINITE

ABCDEABCFG
WORDSWORTH

ABCDEABDEF
WASTEWATER

ABCDEABFFG
NATIONALLY

ABCDEABFGD
HOUSEHOLDS

ABCDEABFGH
MATCHMAKER

ABCDEACDFG
ACTIVATION

ABCDEACFDG
AUTOMATION

ABCDEACFGH
ALTERATION

ABCDEADFCG
CONTACTING

ABCDEADFDF
SUPERSEDED

ABCDEADFDG
THREATENED

ABCDEADFGH
ABUNDANTLY
INVARIABLY

ABCDEAEACF
IDENTITIES

ABCDEAEFGH
TRADITIONS
WORTHWHILE

ABCDEAFACB
IDENTIFIED

ABCDEAFACG
IDENTIFIES

ABCDEAFADG
IMPOSITION

ABCDEAFAGB
INDECISION

ABCDEAFAGD
INDECISIVE

ABCDEAFAGE
EXCITEMENT

ABCDEAFAGH
IMPURITIES

ABCDEAFBGH
CARMICHAEL
CONDUCTORS

ABCDEAFCEG
INACTIVATE

ABCDEAFCGE
ALIENATION

ABCDEAFCGH
ADEQUATELY
BLACKBOARD
RECIPROCAL

ABCDEAFDGH
ABSTRACTED
ADMIRATION
ASPIRATION
INVALIDATE
NATIONWIDE

ABCDEAFEBC
CONVICTION

ABCDEAFEFA
DISORDERED

ABCDEAFEGH
DISORDERLY
WRISTWATCH

ABCDEAFGAH
AUSTRALIAN
IDEALISTIC

ABCDEAFGBC
CONDUCTION
CONVECTION

ABCDEAFGBH
ELOQUENTLY
OLDSMOBILE

ABCDEAFGCH
CONDUCTING

ABCDEAFGDE
TAPESTRIES

ABCDEAFGFD
MICROMETER

ABCDEAFGFG
HYPOTHESES

ABCDEAFGGE
VAUDEVILLE

ABCDEAFGGH
BLACKBERRY
CHEMICALLY
FAITHFULLY

ABCDEAFGHD
UNADJUSTED

ABCDEAFGHE
CITYSCAPES
CONJECTURE
SWEATSHIRT

ABCDEAFGHF
IMPATIENCE

ABCDEAFGHG
HYPOTHESIS

ABCDEAFGHH
WINDOWLESS

ABCDEAFGHI
ADVOCATING
AMBIVALENT
EVANGELISM
INFURIATED
LEGISLATOR
OVERCOMING
RICHARDSON
SOMERSAULT
SUPERSONIC

ABCDEBAFBG
SIMPLISTIC

ABCDEBAFDG
THOUGHTFUL

ABCDEBAFGH
GOITROGENS
MONTGOMERY
RECOVERING
TABULATION

ABCDEBCBFF
GENTLENESS

ABCDEBCCEF
RESTLESSLY

ABCDEBCDFG
AMENDMENTS
MAINTAINED

ABCDEBCFGH
COMPROMISE
CONFRONTED
HOMECOMING
MATURATION
SATURATION

ABCDEBDCFA
STRUCTURES

ABCDEBDCFG
STRUCTURAL
STRUCTURED

ABCDEBDFGA
STRIATIONS

ABCDEBDFGH
UNDERNEATH

ABCDEBEDFC
SANITATION

ABCDEBEFGD
AMUSEMENTS

ABCDEBEFGH
IMPLEMENTS
WHITEHEADS

ABCDEBFAGH
ENCOUNTERS
ENGLANDERS
MIDSHIPMAN
MIDSHIPMEN

ABCDEBFBCG
DENOUEMENT

ABCDEBFBEG
REFINEMENT

ABCDEBFBGA
SIMPLIFIES

ABCDEBFBGG
REMOTENESS

ABCDEBFBGH
DISABILITY
KHRUSHCHEV
MINORITIES
MORPHOLOGY
SIMPLICITY
SIMPLIFIED

ABCDEBFCGE
TRISERVICE

ABCDEBFCGH
NOTEWORTHY

ABCDEBFDCG
MONITORING

ABCDEBFDEG
LABORATORY

ABCDEBFDGA
NAVIGATION

ABCDEBFDGE
CAPITALIST

ABCDEBFDGG
TIMELINESS

ABCDEBFDGH
CAPITALISM
CAPITALIZE
DELIVERING
FEATHERTOP
RADICALISM

ABCDEBFEGH
FRUSTRATED
PUNCTUATED

ABCDEBFFBF
WEAKNESSES

ABCDEBFFBG
NEWSLETTER

ABCDEBFFEG
CHILDHOODS
FEARLESSLY
RECKLESSLY

ABCDEBFFGE
CONTROLLER

ABCDEBFFGH
CONTROLLED
HENRIETTAS

ABCDEBFGBC
RESIDENCES

ABCDEBFGBF
UNCHANGING

ABCDEBFGBH
ENCHANTING
LINGUISTIC

ABCDEBFGCH
PRESCRIBED

ABCDEBFGDE
MELANESIAN

ABCDEBFGDH
DISTRIBUTE
FRATERNITY
GARIBALDIS
MEANDERING
PILGRIMAGE

ABCDEBFGEH
FLASHLIGHT
PREMARITAL

ABCDEBFGFH
HEARTENING

ABCDEBFGGH
INTERNALLY
PUNCTUALLY

ABCDEBFGHB
DELIBERATE

ABCDEBFGHC
POLYNOMIAL

ABCDEBFGHD
OSTENSIBLE

ABCDEBFGHI
BEFOREHAND
FOREBODING
HORIZONTAL
PARLIAMENT
PRECARIOUS
PROVERBIAL
REMODELING
SCRATCHING
SURMOUNTED
WEATHERING

ABCDECAECF
CONVINCING

ABCDECAFGH
PRINCIPALS
PRINCIPLES

ABCDECBAFB
NEGLIGENCE

ABCDECBFGA
SITUATIONS

ABCDECBFGH
FOREGROUND
STARVATION

ABCDECCBFG
DISCUSSING
DISCUSSION

ABCDECDFBC
CONTENTION

ABCDECEFDB
NEGLIGIBLE

ABCDECEFGD
PLANTATION

ABCDECFAGF
STEPHENSON

ABCDECFAGH
ESCUTCHEON

ABCDECFBCG
PERFORMERS

ABCDECFBDG
CHILDISHLY

ABCDECFBFG
CONTINUOUS

ABCDECFBGD
DISGUSTING

ABCDECFBGH
HEADWATERS
WILHELMINA

ABCDECFCDG
CONTINENTS

ABCDECFDEG
UNPREPARED

ABCDECFDGH
IMPROPERLY

ABCDECFECG
CONTINUING
CONVENIENT

ABCDECFEDG
CONTINUITY

ABCDECFEGH
DISRESPECT
REDUNDANCY
WANGENHEIM

ABCDECFFCG
CHAMPASSAK

ABCDECFGBC
CONVENTION

ABCDECFGBH
HEADMASTER
PERFORATED
RECONCILED

ABCDECFGCD
CONTINGENT

ABCDECFGCE
THEMSELVES

ABCDECFGCH
DENOUNCING
UNEXPECTED

ABCDECFGDH
OFTENTIMES

ABCDECFGED
FORTHRIGHT

ABCDECFGEH
SEAQUARIUM

ABCDECFGFE
LIEUTENANT

ABCDECFGHA
GRADUATING

ABCDECFGHE
BORDERLINE
PRAGMATISM

ABCDECFGHI
ENORMOUSLY
EVACUATION
EVALUATING
EVALUATION
FREQUENTLY
FRICTIONAL
GRADUATION
INCULCATED
OVERWEIGHT
PERFORMING
POTENTIALS

ABCDEDAFGH
AUTOLOADER

ABCDEDBEFG
LIBRARIANS

ABCDEDBFCG
ALCOHOLICS

ABCDEDBFDG
INFERENCES

ABCDEDBFEG
DEFICIENCY

ABCDEDBFGH
CANDIDATES
INHERENTLY
MULTITUDES
RECIPIENTS
UNBALANCED

ABCDEDCDFG
ACTIVITIES

ABCDEDCFGH
AUTOMOTIVE

ABCDEDDFGH
FORESEEING

ABCDEDEBFG
DILATATION

ABCDEDEDFG
FEMININITY

ABCDEDFACG
ANTICIPATE
IDEOLOGIES

ABCDEDFBAG
ENVISIONED

ABCDEDFBFG
FACILITATE

ABCDEDFBGA
SOLICITOUS

ABCDEDFBGF
PERSISTENT

ABCDEDFBGH
DECISIVELY
DEFINITELY
POLYGYNOUS
SEPARATELY

ABCDEDFCDG
INTERESTED
OPTIMISTIC

ABCDEDFCGH
CHILBLAINS
QUOTATIONS
SPACECRAFT

ABCDEDFDAG
ARTIFICIAL

ABCDEDFDBG
FELICITIES

ABCDEDFDCE
POSITIVIST

ABCDEDFDCG
POSITIVISM

ABCDEDFDGB
DEFINITIVE
EMPIRICISM

ABCDEDFDGE
DEFINITION

ABCDEDFDGH
CHRONOLOGY
EXHIBITING
EXHIBITION
FACILITIES
MOBILIZING
POLITICIAN

ABCDEDFECG
CONSISTING
OBLIGINGLY

ABCDEDFEGH
PERSISTING
PRECOCIOUS

ABCDEDFFDC
PENICILLIN

ABCDEDFFEG
CARELESSLY
HOPELESSLY

ABCDEDFGBH
CAFETERIAS
PLEASANTLY

ABCDEDFGCF
CONSISTENT

ABCDEDFGCH
SHREVEPORT

ABCDEDFGEB
LEGITIMATE

ABCDEDFGED
INVETERATE

ABCDEDFGHA
SOVEREIGNS

ABCDEDFGHI
ADMINISTER
AUTOMOBILE
ESCALATION
EXCAVATION
HUMILIATED
LEGITIMACY
MEANINGFUL
POSITIVELY
RELAXATION
SEPARATING
SEPARATION
SOLICITUDE
STRIKINGLY
THEOLOGIAN
VIGOROUSLY
WAVELENGTH

ABCDEEAFEG
INFALLIBLE

ABCDEEAFGB
HEMORRHAGE

ABCDEEAFGH
IMPOSSIBLE

ABCDEEBFGH
MAYONNAISE
RECOMMENDS

ABCDEEDECF
BEGINNINGS

ABCDEEDFDG
UNFETTERED

ABCDEEDFGE
ADMISSIONS

ABCDEEDFGH
ADMISSIBLE
IMPASSABLE

ABCDEEFABG
ENROLLMENT

ABCDEEFBDG
PIONEERING

ABCDEEFBGH
ADMITTEDLY

ABCDEEFCDA
SATELLITES

ABCDEEFDGC
DISAPPEARS

ABCDEEFGCA
STRAGGLERS

ABCDEEFGHD
CARTOONIST
IMPECCABLE

ABCDEEFGHE
STRAGGLING
STRUGGLING

ABCDEEFGHI
DISAPPROVE
IMPECCABLY
PROCEEDING
STRADDLING

ABCDEFABFG
DESPONDENT

ABCDEFABGB
HEMISPHERE

ABCDEFABGG
BASKETBALL

ABCDEFABGH
ENDOWMENTS
INHOLDINGS
LIBERALISM
LIBERALITY

ABCDEFACGH
ANTIQUATED

ABCDEFADBE
CONTRACTOR
REGISTRIES

ABCDEFADGH
CONTRACTED
INTERVIEWS

ABCDEFAEBG
INGREDIENT

ABCDEFAEGD
RESTAURANT

ABCDEFAEGH
AFTERWARDS

ABCDEFAFGD
TRANSITION

ABCDEFAFGH
COMPLICITY

ABCDEFAGAF
EMBOLDENED

ABCDEFAGAH
ENCUMBERED

ABCDEFAGBF
INCLUSIONS
INTRUSIONS

ABCDEFAGBH
INFECTIONS
REINFORCED
REINFORCES
TRAJECTORY

ABCDEFAGCH
OVERFLOWED

ABCDEFAGDB
ASPENCADES

ABCDEFAGDE
INFLEXIBLE
SUBVERSIVE

ABCDEFAGFE
TURPENTINE

ABCDEFAGFH
TORMENTING

ABCDEFAGHB
SCHOLASTIC

ABCDEFAGHC
UNDISPUTED

ABCDEFAGHE
INCREDIBLE
PSYCHOPATH

ABCDEFAGHF
REGISTRANT

ABCDEFAGHI
ADJUSTABLE
CHRONICLES
COMPLICATE
EXTRANEOUS
IMPERVIOUS
IMPROVISED
INCREDIBLY
INFECTIOUS
REGULARITY

ABCDEFBABG
REGISTERED

ABCDEFBAEG
EMBANKMENT

ABCDEFBAGH
ADIRONDACK
EMBODIMENT
EMPLOYMENT

ABCDEFBCBG
LENGTHENED

ABCDEFBCDA
SENTIMENTS

ABCDEFBCDE
HANDSTANDS

ABCDEFBCEE
UNEASINESS

ABCDEFBCGH
COURTHOUSE
RANGELANDS
ROUNDHOUSE
VIOLATIONS

ABCDEFBDBG
CENTIMETER

ABCDEFBDEA
THROUGHOUT

ABCDEFBDGH
CAPTIVATED
ORDINARILY

ABCDEFBEGH
CHERISHING
VICTORIOUS

ABCDEFBFAG
SCEPTICISM

ABCDEFBFGB
PERMANENCE
PERTINENCE

ABCDEFBFGH
ATROCITIES

ABCDEFBGBF
BEWILDERED

ABCDEFBGBH
HESIOMETER

ABCDEFBGCH
STEPMOTHER

ABCDEFBGDE
PAKISTANIS
STRENGTHEN

ABCDEFBGDH
BIPARTISAN
DIRECTIVES
LIBERTINES
PORTSMOUTH
VOCATIONAL

ABCDEFBGEC
HORSEPOWER

ABCDEFBGEF
DIMENSIONS

ABCDEFBGFH
INFLUENCED
INFLUENCES

ABCDEFBGGH
BRIDEGROOM
HABITUALLY
MATERIALLY
RATIONALLY

ABCDEFBGHA
LITURGICAL
TRANSCRIPT

ABCDEFBGHC
HISTORIANS

ABCDEFBGHD
LANDSCAPED
METHUSELAH
WINDSHIELD

ABCDEFBGHE
LANDSCAPES
MARKETABLE

ABCDEFBGHF
DIVERSIONS

ABCDEFBGHG
HYDROLYSIS

ABCDEFBGHH
INWARDNESS

ABCDEFBGHI
ASTONISHED
CALIBRATED
DIRECTIONS
FASCINATED
GRAPEFRUIT
HISTORICAL
MOLESWORTH
RIGHTFIELD
SUPERHUMAN
UNFRIENDLY
VIEWPOINTS
VISUALIZED
WATCHMAKER

ABCDEFCAFA
SCIENTISTS

ABCDEFCAFC
NORTHERNER

ABCDEFCAGH
STUDIOUSLY
TRANSLATED

ABCDEFCBGH
DISPERSION
GRAVEYARDS

ABCDEFCCFA
DISTRESSED

ABCDEFCCFC
BUSINESSES

ABCDEFCCFG
UNSTRESSED

ABCDEFCDBG
MOTIVATION

ABCDEFCDED
PHENOMENON

ABCDEFCDGA
DISTRUSTED

ABCDEFCDGE
EXTINCTION

ABCDEFCDGH
ESTIMATING
ESTIMATION
MALEVOLENT
MISTRUSTED

MOTIVATING
PHENOMENAL
POSTMASTER

ABCDEFCEBG
UNITARIANS

ABCDEFCECG
MENTIONING
TENSIONING

ABCDEFCEGC
CHESAPEAKE

ABCDEFCEGH
CONSTANTLY
MICROSCOPE
MICROSCOPY
MULTIPLIED
MULTIPLIES
PATRIOTISM

ABCDEFCFCG
CONTAINING

ABCDEFCFGE
TECHNICIAN

ABCDEFCFGH
COMPLEMENT

ABCDEFCGAA
SINFULNESS

ABCDEFCGAE
SMOKEHOUSE
STOREHOUSE

ABCDEFCGAH
EJACULATED
ELABORATED
EPITOMIZED
EVAPORATED

ABCDEFCGBH
ULTIMATELY

ABCDEFCGCB
SCIENTIFIC

ABCDEFCGCD
INTERSTATE

ABCDEFCGCE
CERTIORARI

ABCDEFCGCH
CONDEMNING
UNORTHODOX

ABCDEFCGDE
DETONATION
WRONGDOING

ABCDEFCGDH
SCOREBOARD

ABCDEFCGED
LITERATURE

ABCDEFCGFH
ALTOGETHER
ORNAMENTED

ABCDEFCGGH
DIAGONALLY
DOUBTFULLY

ABCDEFCGHA
ACETONEMIA
SCULPTURES
STEINBECKS

ABCDEFCGHB
CHILDBIRTH
MEASURABLE
REASONABLE
RESPONSIVE

ABCDEFCGHC
PREVALENCE

ABCDEFCGHD
INTERSTAGE
PRESIDENTS
SCULPTURAL

ABCDEFCGHF
CHANGEABLE

ABCDEFCGHI
BLANCHARDS
CAUTIOUSLY
CHARITABLE
COMPLIMENT
CONTAINERS
DISCLOSURE
EDITORIALS
EXTRACTING
EXTRACTION
FURTHERING
HINDRANCES
PRESIDENCY
PRIVATIONS
REASONABLY
SCULPTURED
SMITHFIELD
UNIMPAIRED

ABCDEFDAAG
LOUISVILLE

ABCDEFDAGH
OVERTHROWN

ABCDEFDBAE
LAUDERDALE

ABCDEFDBDG
INTERVENED
UNLEAVENED
VOLUPTUOUS

ABCDEFDBEG
DISTORTION

ABCDEFDBGH
OBTAINABLE
PORTENTOUS

ABCDEFDDCD
TRESPASSES

ABCDEFDDCG
TRESPASSED

ABCDEFDEDG
INTERFERED
INTERFERES

ABCDEFDFAB
MIANTONOMI

ABCDEFDFBA
DEVASTATED

ABCDEFDFGH
PRACTICING

ABCDEFDGBG
DECOMPOSES

ABCDEFDGBH
PLAINFIELD

ABCDEFDGCA
SPECTACLES

ABCDEFDGCB
BREAKWATER

ABCDEFDGCH
OVERTURNED
PROTECTION

ABCDEFDGDH
MANEUVERED
UNRELIEVED

ABCDEFDGEH
GRATUITOUS
INVALUABLE

ABCDEFDGFA
SUBTLETIES

ABCDEFDGGH
PLAINTIFFS

ABCDEFDGHA
EXPANDABLE

ABCDEFDGHB
DETACHABLE
PERSUASIVE

ABCDEFDGHD
DIVERGENCE
PROTESTANT

ABCDEFDGHE
CHRISTIANS
NUTCRACKER
PROTECTIVE

ABCDEFDGHF
ABSTENTION
CONGREGATE

ABCDEFDGHG
BREAKFASTS
BROADCASTS
CHRISTIANA

ABCDEFDGHI
CENSORSHIP
CLOUDBURST
DEVIATIONS
HEMOGLOBIN
PERIODICAL
PERSUASION
PROTECTING
PROTESTING
SOCIALIZED
XENOPHOBIA

ABCDEFEABG
ENCAMPMENT
PHILOSOPHY

ABCDEFEAGH
IMPUTATION

ABCDEFEBCG
CONDITIONS
SAUERKRAUT

ABCDEFEBGD
NEWSPAPERS

ABCDEFECAE
CONFERENCE

ABCDEFECDG
HELIOPOLIS

ABCDEFECGA
SACRIFICES

ABCDEFECGD
UNBEARABLE

ABCDEFECGF
PROVISIONS

ABCDEFECGH
FLIRTATION
PRODIGIOUS
SACRIFICED
UNCRITICAL

ABCDEFEDBG
DELICACIES

ABCDEFEDCG
INTERPRETS

ABCDEFEDGB
MEDITATIVE
RECITATIVE

ABCDEFEDGD
PHYSICISTS

ABCDEFEDGH
HESITATION
LEVITATION
MEDITATING
MEDITATION
RECITATION

ABCDEFEEAG
RACKETEERS

ABCDEFEFGH
QUANTITIES

ABCDEFEGAE
COMPETENCE

ABCDEFEGBC
FERTILIZER
RESONANCES

ABCDEFEGBH
FERTILIZED

ABCDEFEGCH
RENDITIONS

ABCDEFEGDH
EXPLICITLY
IMPLACABLE

ABCDEFEGEA
DISHEVELED

ABCDEFEGEH
CONSTITUTE
PROSTITUTE

ABCDEFEGGH
WATERPROOF

ABCDEFEGHA
SPECTATORS
SYNAGOGUES

ABCDEFEGHC
FASTIDIOUS
WATERFRONT

ABCDEFEGHD
ARISTOTLES
ASTRONOMER
PHYSICIANS
UNDERWRITE

ABCDEFEGHF
PREVISIONS

ABCDEFEGHG
MACHINISTS
PORTUGUESE

ABCDEFEGHI
ABORIGINES
COMPARABLE
EXCITATORY
EXULTATION
INTERGROUP
METROPOLIS
MONTEVERDI
ORDINANCES
PATHOLOGIC
PROFICIENT
PROHIBITED
PUBLICIZED
REPUTATION
STABILIZED

ABCDEFFABG
INDWELLING
INSTALLING

ABCDEFFAGE
IMPRESSIVE

ABCDEFFAGH
IMPRESSING
IMPRESSION

ABCDEFFBDG
WITNESSING

ABCDEFFBGG
RECOILLESS

ABCDEFFCBF
PROFESSORS

ABCDEFFEBG
TRAVELLERS

ABCDEFFEGA
TOPGALLANT

ABCDEFFEGB
PERMISSIVE

ABCDEFFEGH
FORBIDDING
PERMISSION
PERMITTING
SUBMITTING

ABCDEFFGAH
COMBELLACK

ABCDEFFGBC
CONFESSION
ENGROSSING

ABCDEFFGBH
COMPASSION
UNDRESSING

ABCDEFFGCH
CONFESSING
PROCESSION
PROFESSION

ABCDEFFGDH
OUTRIGGERS

ABCDEFFGEH
FOURTEENTH

ABCDEFFGHB
PERCUSSIVE

ABCDEFFGHD
FORGETTING

ABCDEFFGHG
COSTAGGINI

ABCDEFFGHI
COMPELLING
CONSUMMATE
DISCREETLY
MISCELLANY
PATROLLING
PERCUSSION
PROCESSING
PROFESSING
TRAVELLING

ABCDEFGABH
ENRICHMENT
INCREASING
INSPECTING
INSULATING
OUTRAGEOUS
TERMINATED

ABCDEFGACH
ARTICULATE
INTERFAITH

ABCDEFGADA
SUPERVISES

ABCDEFGADB
INVOLUTION

ABCDEFGADF
TYPEWRITER

ABCDEFGADH
EMBROIDERY
SUPERVISED

ABCDEFGAEH
RHINOCEROS

ABCDEFGAFC
OBSEQUIOUS

ABCDEFGAGH
WITHDRAWAL

ABCDEFGAHA
DOWNGRADED
THERMOSTAT

ABCDEFGAHB
INCUBATION
INFLECTION
INSPECTION
INSULATION

ABCDEFGAHD
IMPERATIVE

ABCDEFGAHE
INDUSTRIES
SUPERVISOR

ABCDEFGAHF
COPERNICAN

ABCDEFGAHI
APOTHECARY
COPERNICUS
EQUIVALENT
HEADLIGHTS
INDUSTRIAL
INSECURITY
INSULARITY
OBJECTIONS
OPERATIONS
STRAVINSKY
TRANSMUTED

ABCDEFGBAE
TRANSPORTS

ABCDEFGBAH
ACOUSTICAL

ABCDEFGBBD
POCKETBOOK

ABCDEFGBBH
BLACKWELLS

ABCDEFGBCF
CONFUSIONS

ABCDEFGBCH
COURAGEOUS
DELICATELY
MANSERVANT
RELATIVELY
ROUNDABOUT

ABCDEFGBDC
UNDERLINED
UNDERMINED

ABCDEFGBDH
LOQUACIOUS
VOLUMINOUS

ABCDEFGBEC
DESTROYERS

ABCDEFGBED
DIAGNOSING

ABCDEFGBEE
JEWISHNESS

ABCDEFGBEG
TRANSVERSE

ABCDEFGBEH
DELINQUENT
PROCEDURES
RESOLUTELY

ABCDEFGBFC
POSTHUMOUS

ABCDEFGBFH
COMPANIONS
DIALECTICS
MAGISTRATE
RESPONDENT

ABCDEFGBGG
TRANSFEREE

ABCDEFGBGH
CONQUERORS
DISCERNING

ABCDEFGBHA
EARTHQUAKE
STIMULATES
STIPULATES

ABCDEFGBHB
TRANSFEROR

ABCDEFGBHC
DETACHMENT

ABCDEFGBHD
OBSERVABLE

ABCDEFGBHE
COUNSELORS
TRANSFORMS

ABCDEFGBHF
DEPARTMENT
GLOMERULAR
MASQUERADE
ORCHESTRAS

ABCDEFGBHG
INDULGENCE

ABCDEFGBHI
BALUSTRADE
CAMOUFLAGE
CARBONDALE
CATHEDRALS
COMPULSORY
CONTAGIOUS
DEBAUCHERY
DISCRETION
DISPLAYING
DISRUPTING
DISRUPTION
DISRUPTIVE
DISTURBING
FIGURATIVE
FINGERTIPS
FORMATIONS
LIBERATION
MANIPULATE
MISLEADING
NEGATIVELY
OILHEATING
ORCHESTRAL
PROCEDURAL
SIMULATION
STIMULATED
STRAIGHTEN
TRANSPIRED
VOCIFEROUS

ABCDEFGCAA
STEWARDESS

ABCDEFGCAG
CONFIDENCE
CONGRUENCE

ABCDEFGCBE
BERKSHIRES

ABCDEFGCBH
GROUNDWORK

ABCDEFGCDA
TRANSPLANT

ABCDEFGCDB
FRIENDLIER

ABCDEFGCDH
ANTISEPTIC
INTEGRATED
INTEGRATES

ABCDEFGCEH
MECHANICAL

ABCDEFGCFA
DISPLEASED

ABCDEFGCFH
ARCHITECTS
STAGECOACH

ABCDEFGCGA
GLISTENING

ABCDEFGCGH
QUICKENING

ABCDEFGCHA
EMANCIPATE
SCRIPTURES

ABCDEFGCHB
TYPOGRAPHY

ABCDEFGCHC
DISCOURSES
VIETNAMESE

ABCDEFGCHE
INADEQUATE

ABCDEFGCHF
PROLUSIONS

ABCDEFGCHH
BREATHLESS

ABCDEFGCHI
AUTHORITYS
BEAUJOLAIS
BLASINGAME
BRONCHIOLE
CONDIMENTS
CREATIVELY
DISHONESTY
EVOCATIONS
FLAMBOYANT
FUNCTIONAL
FUNCTIONED
INADEQUACY
OBITUARIES

OUTSMARTED
SANCTIONED
SCRIPTURAL
TRAGEDIANS
UNIFORMITY
UNIVERSITY
WANDERINGS
WHISPERING

ABCDEFGDAB
TYPICALITY

ABCDEFGDAE
ORDINATION

ABCDEFGDAH
ANTISOCIAL
COGNIZANCE
OBLIGATION
REPOSITORY

ABCDEFGDBE
DOMINATION

ABCDEFGDBF
INVESTMENT

ABCDEFGDBH
AUDITORIUM

ABCDEFGDCH
ARITHMETIC
FOREIGNERS
OPTIMALITY

ABCDEFGDEH
DECORATORS
DOMINATING
INTRAMURAL
SPRINKLING

ABCDEFGDFH
GOVERNMENT

ABCDEFGDHA
DISTRACTED

ABCDEFGDHC
WIDESPREAD

ABCDEFGDHE
CORINTHIAN
INSTRUCTOR
TRANSCENDS

ABCDEFGDHF
DISLOYALTY
WATERSHEDS

ABCDEFGDHH
DIRECTNESS

ABCDEFGDHI
ANTIBODIES
ARCHBISHOP
AUTHORSHIP
CONTRASTED
CULTIVATED
DARTMOUTHS
DERIVATION
EXPIRATION
HAVERFIELD
INSTRUCTED
MEDICATION
MODERATELY
OBSTRUCTED
POSTULATED
RELINQUISH
SOLIDARITY
SPRINGTIME
STRONGHOLD
SUBTRACTED
VOCABULARY

ABCDEFGEAA
SACREDNESS

ABCDEFGEAH
SPECIALIST

ABCDEFGEBH
DEPARTURES
INFREQUENT
NEGOTIATED

ABCDEFGECD
THREADBARE

ABCDEFGECH
CARPENTERS
CONFIRMING
CONSEQUENT

ABCDEFGEDA
ESCRITOIRE

ABCDEFGEDC
MAGNIFYING

ABCDEFGEDH
FURNISHING

ABCDEFGEFH
BELONGINGS
REPAINTING

ABCDEFGEGH
CUSHIONING
FASHIONING

ABCDEFGEHA
GRATIFYING

ABCDEFGEHC
PREDICTIVE
SPECIALIZE
UNDERWORLD

ABCDEFGEHF
HOPKINSIAN
POLYESTERS

ABCDEFGEHG
FRANCISCOS

ABCDEFGEHH
WICKEDNESS
WILDERNESS

ABCDEFGEHI
ADOLESCENT
CLARIFYING
CONVERSELY
DISCOMFORT
FROLICKING
HARMONIOUS
HESITANTLY
JUSTIFYING
MICROPHONE
MIDWESTERN
PREDICTING
PREDICTION
PROVINCIAL
PUBLISHING
REBUILDING
SPECIFYING
TRANSPOSED

ABCDEFGFAH
SKEPTICISM

ABCDEFGFBA
SECURITIES

ABCDEFGFBH
COMPETITOR
INCOHERENT
INDUCEMENT
UNPLEASANT
VELOCITIES

ABCDEFGFCH
BACKSTITCH
SPLENDIDLY

ABCDEFGFDH
DEPOSITION
EXPOSITION
UNFAMILIAR

ABCDEFGFEC
ORGANIZING

ABCDEFGFEH
COMPLETELY
CREATIVITY
DJANGOLOGY

ABCDEFGFEH
ELASTICITY
PLASTICITY
REACTIVITY
RELATIVITY

ABCDEFGFFB
UNFORESEEN

ABCDEFGFGH
ADULTERERS
EXPLAINING
PERTAINING

ABCDEFGFHC
PHYSIOLOGY
PSYCHOLOGY

ABCDEFGFHD
BRIDGEHEAD

ABCDEFGFHG
PROMINENCE

ABCDEFGFHH
POLITENESS

ABCDEFGFHI
ADVISEMENT
COMPREHEND
COMPRISING
DESCRIBING
DESPAIRING
DURABILITY
EQUANIMITY
EXCLAIMING
FAVORITISM
HUMANITIES
IMPROBABLE
ISOCYANATE
KILOMETERS
MAJORITIES
PREVAILING
RELATIVISM
TECHNOLOGY
WORSHIPING

ABCDEFGGBD
VERSAILLES

ABCDEFGGBE
COMPRESSOR

ABCDEFGGCH
OVERLAPPED

ABCDEFGGEH
RUTHLESSLY
WORDLESSLY

ABCDEFGGFG
COMPRESSES

ABCDEFGGFH
AFTERNOONS
CIGARETTES
COMPRESSED

ABCDEFGGHD
FALSEHOODS

ABCDEFGGHI
CARTWHEELS
CHARLOTTES
CORNWALLIS
GANSEVOORT
VOLUNTEERS
WORSHIPPED

ABCDEFGHAB
ENGLISHMEN
STAUNCHEST
THOUSANDTH

ABCDEFGHAD
CONTRADICT

ABCDEFGHAE
COUNTERACT

ABCDEFGHAF
EMPHASIZES
EXPLOSIVES

ABCDEFGHAH
MECHANISMS
THERAPISTS

ABCDEFGHAI
ADJECTIVAL
COMPLIANCE
CONSPIRACY
EMPHASIZED
ENCOURAGED
ENCOURAGES
GATHERINGS
OVERSHADOW
REGULATORY
UNGRATEFUL

ABCDEFGHBA
DEMOLISHED
DESIGNATED
DESPATCHED
MAINSTREAM
RECONSIDER

ABCDEFGHBC
CONGESTION
CONVERSION
HANOVERIAN
PARTICULAR
UNDERSTAND

ABCDEFGHBD
FOUNDATION
INSTRUMENT
PERSONAGES

ABCDEFGHBE
REPUDIATED

ABCDEFGHBF
UNDERGOING

ABCDEFGHBG
JACKSONIAN

ABCDEFGHBI
COMBUSTION
COMPARISON
COMPLETION
COMPLEXION
COMPULSION
DIAGNOSTIC
DIPLOMATIC
HELICOPTER
LEFTHANDER
MECHANIZED
MODERATION
MODULATION
ORGANIZERS
RECOGNIZED
RECOGNIZES
TECHNIQUES
UNDERLYING

ABCDEFGHCA
NEAPOLITAN
STUPENDOUS

ABCDEFGHCB
METABOLITE
PROSECUTOR
RETICULATE

ABCDEFGHCD
ELONGATION

ABCDEFGHCE
CONSTRAINT
CUMBERSOME
VULNERABLE

ABCDEFGHCF
PREJUDICED

ABCDEFGHCG
CONSULTANT
PURCHASERS

ABCDEFGHCI
CONQUERING
CONSERVING
CONSULTING
CONVERTING
DIAPHYSEAL
FRIENDSHIP

MELANCHOLY
PREJUDICES
PRODUCTION
PROJECTION
PUNISHMENT
QUESTIONED
QUESTIONER
SPECULATED
STEINHAGER
THIOURACIL
THUNDEROUS
UNEMPLOYED
UNEXPLORED

ABCDEFGHDA
EXPLICABLE
SALUBRIOUS

ABCDEFGHDB
ADVERTISED
CALIFORNIA
DEPLORABLE
INTERWOVEN
STANDPOINT
TRIANGULAR
UNDERTAKEN

ABCDEFGHDC
ASYNCHRONY
MODERNIZED
RENOVATION
UNDEPICTED

ABCDEFGHDE
COPENHAGEN
INTERLAYER
UNDERWATER

ABCDEFGHDH
WAREHOUSES

ABCDEFGHDI
ABSOLUTION
ABSORPTION
ADJECTIVES
ADVENTURES
BEHAVIORAL
BRANDYWINE
CATEGORIES
CENTRALITY
COLERIDGES
CONTRIBUTE
CONVULSIVE
COUNSELING
DECORATION
DESOLATION
GRIEVANCES
INTERFACES
INTERLACED
INTERLUDES
LAUNDERING
NEUTRALITY
OBJECTIVES
RESOLUTION

REVOLUTION
SENATORIAL
THUNDERING
UNDERTAKES
UNRESOLVED

ABCDEFGHEA
TOURNAMENT

ABCDEFGHEB
RELUCTANCE

ABCDEFGHEC
PREDNISONE
VERNACULAR

ABCDEFGHED
HOUSEWIVES
UNILATERAL
UNRELIABLE

ABCDEFGHEF
EXPANSIONS
OBLITERATE

ABCDEFGHEI
ABSOLUTELY
CATHERINES
DISHEARTEN
JUBILANTLY
MAGNETIZED
MYOCARDIAL
OUTWEIGHED
PECULIARLY
PERILOUSLY
PROSECUTED
PULVERIZED
SCHWEITZER
UNDERSHIRT

ABCDEFGHFA
DOCUMENTED

ABCDEFGHFC
AUGMENTING
ENTHUSIAST
RESULTANTS

ABCDEFGHFE
FLORENTINE
YOURSELVES

ABCDEFGHFF
SCHUYLKILL

ABCDEFGHFG
DISCONTENT
EXCHANGING
SOUTHERNER
SULZBERGER

ABCDEFGHFH
ADVENTISTS

ABCDEFGHFI
ASTOUNDING
CANTERBURY
CHANDELIER
CLOTHESMEN
ENTHUSIASM
FRAGMENTED
GLOUCESTER
HAMBURGERS
HEDONISTIC
HUMANISTIC
MANCHESTER
MANIFESTED
MIRACULOUS
MONTPELIER
OUTFIELDER
RECOUNTING
RESOUNDING
RESPONDING
WINCHESTER

ABCDEFGHGA
DISCOVERED

ABCDEFGHGD
BURGEONING
QUASIMODOS

ABCDEFGHGE
INCESTUOUS
WATERCOLOR

ABCDEFGHGF
CONSIDERED
SHOULDERED
SQUANDERED

ABCDEFGHGI
BASOPHILIC
BRIGHTENED
BROADENING
CHRISTENED
FRIGHTENED
SHARPENING
SHORTENING
SLACKENING
SPLINTERED
STRYCHNINE
WHATSOEVER

ABCDEFGHHB
MONTICELLO
SKETCHBOOK

ABCDEFGHHC
PHYSICALLY
UNDERSTOOD

ABCDEFGHHD
SOMERVILLE

ABCDEFGHHE
CAMPITELLI
MARTINELLI

ABCDEFGHHF
LONGSTREET

ABCDEFGHHG
SILHOUETTE

ABCDEFGHHI
CATHERWOOD
GRACEFULLY
GRATEFULLY
INFORMALLY
MERCIFULLY
PARENTHOOD
PERSONALLY
POETICALLY
POWERFULLY
RIGHTFULLY
SCORNFULLY
TABLESPOON
VERTICALLY

ABCDEFGHIA
DISCHARGED
DISCOUNTED
DISMOUNTED
DISPATCHED
DUPLICATED
EXHAUSTIVE
GATLINBURG
METABOLISM
SANDWICHES
SIGNATURES
SUBMARINES
SYMBOLIZES
SYMPATHIES
SYMPHONIES
SYNDICATES
TRIUMPHANT

ABCDEFGHIB
ADMONISHED
CENTRIFUGE
DECORATIVE
DEMORALIZE
ENGLISHMAN
JEOPARDIZE
LENGTHWISE
PARENCHYMA
PREDICATOR
REGULATIVE
TRANSDUCER
WHITEMARSH

ABCDEFGHIC
BETANCOURT
CREDITABLE
DELIGHTFUL
DISCHARGES
DISPATCHES
FISHERMANS
INEXORABLE
INSPECTORS
MCNAUGHTON
MYSTERIOUS
ONSLAUGHTS
PSYCHIATRY
REGULATING

ABCDEFGHID
BOLSHEVIKS
CONSTABLES
COUNTRYMAN
COUNTRYMEN
HARDBOILED
NEUTRALIST
OBSERVANCE
SYNDICATED

ABCDEFGHIE
COMPENSATE
CONGESTIVE
DEMOCRATIC
DOWNSTAIRS
HANDSPIKES
NUCLEOTIDE
PROJECTIVE
RHEUMATISM
SUBJECTIVE
TRAVELOGUE

ABCDEFGHIF
ADJUSTMENT
BURLINGTON
EXCURSIONS
GERMANTOWN
GYMNASTICS
INTRODUCED
JACQUELINE
NOTICEABLE
OWNERSHIPS
PUBLISHERS
REPULSIONS
WASHINGTON
YOUNGSTERS

ABCDEFGHIG
FLOURISHES
PROVIDENCE
WESTPHALIA
YUGOSLAVIA

ABCDEFGHIH
ATMOSPHERE
COLUMNISTS
GUIDEPOSTS
INCOMPLETE
JOURNALESE
MODERNISTS
MOUTHPIECE

ABCDEFGHII
BRIGHTNESS

Solutions to Problems

Chapter 4 Solutions

Complete Columnar Tramps

1. Why shouldn't truth be stranger than fiction? Fiction after all has to make sense. (*Mark Twain*) (SAWYER)
3. There is no expedient to which a man will not resort to avoid the real labor of thinking. (*Sir Joshua Reynolds*) (LAZYBONES)
5. Tact is the ability to describe others as they see themselves. (*Abe Lincoln*) (PRESIDENT)
7. Let me have my own way exactly in everything and a sunnier pleasanter creature does not exist. (*Thomas Carlyle*) (HISDESIRE)
9. In those days he was much wiser than he is today. He used to take my advice. (FREQUENTLY)

Chapter 5 Solutions

Incomplete Columnar Transpositions

1. A camel is a horse designed by a committee and an elephant is a mouse built to military specifications. (MODERNWORDS)
3. Its nice to be married because your wife is right there when you want her. Of course she's there when you dont want her too. (MARRIAGES)
5. Sometimes I wonder whether people become conservative because they are rich or the other way around. (LOTOFMONEY)
7. A cynic is a blackguard whose faulty vision sees things as they are rather than as they ought to be. (*Ambrose Bierce*) (EASYCOMEEASYGO)
9. It doesn't do the sheep a lot of good to legislate vegetarianism as long as the wolves are still hungry. (DEMOCRACYIS)

Chapter 6 Solutions

Double Transposition (Keys: CRAMPER + NONSENSEIS)

1. Children teach parents many things. For instance, you can learn how much patience you have.

3. The power of accurate observation is commonly called cynicism by those who do not have it.

Turning Grills

1. A diplomat is a man who always remembers a womans birthday but never remembers her age.

Skipping Tramp

1. Intelligence is the thing that allows a person to get by without an education or the other way around. (3 1 5 6 4 2)
3. The hottest places in hell are reserved for those who in time of great moral crises maintain their neutrality. (3 2 5 1 4 6)

Chapter 7 Solutions

Problems for Simple Substitution

1. (ASTRONOMY)
   Put three grains of sand inside a vast cathedral and the cathedral will be more closely packed with sand than space is with stars. (*Sir James Jeans*)
3. (CLASSICAL)
   One can't judge *Wagner's opera *Lohengrin after a first hearing, and I certainly don't intend hearing it a second time. (*Gioacchimo Rossini*)
5. (LONGYEARS)
   I detest the idea of growing old, but when you consider the alternatives available it really isn't so bad after all.
7. (SOREMOUTH)
   To the person with a toothache, even if the world is tottering, there is nothing more important than a visit to the dentist. (*G.B. Shaw*)
9. (PRESIDENT)
   I sit here all day trying to persuade people to do things they ought to have sense enough to do without my having to persuade them. (*H. S Truman*)

Chapter 8 Solutions

1. (Cherry trees grow tall—16)
   I am different from Washington; I have a higher, grander standard of principle. He could not lie. I can lie, but I won't. (*Mark Twain*)
3. (Freedom is precious—7)
   The tree of liberty must be refreshed from time to time with the blood of patriots and tyrants. (*T. Jefferson*)
5. (Fortunate ones—10)
   What can be added to the happiness of a man who is in health, out of debt, and has a clear conscience? (*Adam Smith*)

7. (Computers can be fun—6)
If everyone in the world decided to be scientists, I think I would take up plumbing and get rich charging what I pleased.
9. (Rich or poor money is nice—15)
I don't want a lawyer to tell me what I cannot do; I hire him to tell me how to do what I want to do. (*J. P. Morgan*)
11. (Degeneration—11)
America is the only nation in history which miraculously has gone directly from barbarism to degeneration without the usual interval of civilization. (*Georges Clemenceau*)
13. (Pace in terram—7)
People in general are equally horrified at hearing the Christian religion doubted, and at seeing it practiced. (*Samuel Butler*)
15. (Langhorne—8)
Satan hasn't a single salaried helper; the Opposition employs a million. (*Mark Twain*)
17. (Academia resurgans—7)
The ink of the scholar is more sacred than the blood of the martyr. (*Mohammed*)
19. (Temperature—20)
We have not lost faith, but we have transferred it from God to the medical profession. (*G. B. Shaw*)

Chapter 9 Solutions

1. MONSTER
Science fiction movies often show the ants taking over the world. I only hope that if this happens they will remember how kind we were to take them on all our picnics.
3. FUNCTIONALISM
When I am working on a problem I never think about beauty. I think only how to solve the problem. But when I have finished, if the solution is not beautiful I know it is wrong. (*Buckminster Fuller*)
5. TOYBOAT
Sometimes children get as much fun out of playing with the large expensive present you spent three days searching for as they do out of playing with the box it came in.
7. MACHINES
My favorite story about computerized translation involves the English Russian English translation of a paper on civil engineering where the term hydraulic ram came back as water goat.
9. AMBASSADOR
Diplomats are just as essential to starting a war as soldiers are to finishing it You take diplomacy out of war and the thing would fall flat in a week (*Will Rogers*)

Chapter 11 Solutions

Playfair

1. BRITISH
   You demand to be shot by a firing squad, sir. Now I know you are a civilian. Have you any idea of the marksmanship of the average soldier? (*George Bernard Shaw*)
3. BATTLES
   My child asked me how come the good guys always win. After thinking a moment I replied that to the victors belong the history books.
5. MAESTRO
   The fact that people do not understand and respect the very best things such as Mozart's concertos is what permits men like us to become famous (*Johannes Brahms*)
7. PRACTICE
   An idealist is one who on noticing that a rose smells better than a cabbage concludes that it will also make better soup (*H. L. Mencken*)
9. AMERICAN
   In Paris they simply stared when I spoke to them in French. I never did succeed in making those idiots understand their own language (*Mark Twain*)

Chapter 13 Solutions

Bifid

1. WALDENPOND 5
   If one advances confidently in the direction of his dreams and endeavors to live the life which he has imagined he will meet with a success unexpected in common hours. (*Thoreau*)
3. INCOMEOUTGO 6
   I am proud to pay taxes in the United States but it seems to me I could be just as proud even if the tax rate were half of what it is now.
5. TRYITSOMETIME 8
   Few people think more than two or three times a year. I have made an international reputation for myself by thinking once or twice a week. (*G. B. Shaw*)
7. POLITICSANDFISHING 12
   Once there were two brothers. One ran away to sea and the other became vice-president of the U.S. Nothing was ever again heard from either of them.
9. THEWEAKERSEX 6
   There is a difference between beauty and charm. A beautiful woman is one I notice. A charming woman is one who notices me. (*John Erskine*)

Bibliography

(1) Kahn, David, *The Code Breakers,* MacMillan, New York, 1967.
(A monumental—1164 pages—history of codes and ciphers from ancient Greece to the present day. Good descriptions of the mechanics of cryptanalysis, with emphasis on the people involved. Also available in paperback in abridged form from Signet, 1973.)

(2) Gaines, Helen Fouche, *Cryptanalysis,* Dover, New York, 1939.
(Originally published before the war, this is the amateur cryptanalyst's bible. Clear, concise descriptions of many ciphers and how to attack them.)

(3) Sinkov, Abraham, *Elementary Cryptanalysis,* The Mathematical Association of America, 1966.
(This book, a part of the New Mathematical Library series, is a well-written description of several ciphers. More limited range than in Gaines, but treatment is deeper, with extremely good analysis of the mathematics involved. A must for the serious amateur.)

(4) Ohauer, M.E., *Cryptogram Solving,* The Etcetera Press, P.O. Drawer 27100, Columbus, O. 43227, 1973.
(A brief, but good, discussion of solving the Aristocrat.)

(5) Barker, Wayne G., *Cryptanalysis of the Simple Substitution Cipher with Word Divisions,* Aegean Park Press, P.O. Box 2837, Laguna Hills, Calif. 92653.
(A study of the Aristocrat. Concentrates on identifying consonants and vowels. Includes lists of nonpattern words grouped by consonant-vowel distribution.)

(6) Bowers, William M., *Practical Cryptanalysis,* The American Cryptogram Association, 1960.
(Three volumes published by the ACA (see entry under *The Cryptogram* for an address). Vol. I explores the Playfair, vol. II the Bifid, and vol. III the Trifid cipher. Good discussion of the techniques of analysis for all three.)

(7) Winterbotham, F.W., *The Ultra Secret,* Futura Publications Ltd., London, 1974.
(Discussion of how the Allies broke the German ciphers in World War II. Little technical discussion, but fascinating anecdotes.)

(8) Clarke, Ronald, *The Man Who Broke Purple*, Little, Brown, Boston, 1977.

(The life of William Friedman. Not too well done with almost no technical information.)

(9) Pope, Maurice, *Decipherment*, Scribner's, New York, 1975.

(Very little analysis, but an interesting history of Champollion and other decipherers of dead languages.)

(10) Goddard, Eldridge and Thelma, *Cryptodyct*, Cryptodyct, P.O. Box 441, Marion, Iowa 52302, 1976.

(A very extensive list of pattern words that is somewhat difficult to use because of the indexing scheme.)

JOURNALS

Cryptologia, Albion College, Albion, Mich. 49224.

(*The* scholarly journal of the field, dedicated to all aspects of cryptology. Subscription currently $20 per year. If you are really interested in the field, you should probably subscribe.)

The Cryptogram, ACA Treasurer, 1007 Montrose Ave., Laurel, Md. 20810.

(This is the official publication of the American Cryptogram Association. Each bimonthly issue contains one or two articles on cryptanalysis, perhaps a book review, plus lots and lots of cryptograms of all types. If you have gotten this far, you will want to join.)

SPECIALTY PUBLISHERS

The Aegean Park Press, P.O. Box 2837, Laguna Hills, Calif. 92653, has an extensive list of publications in the area of cryptanalysis, which includes reprints of famous works, plus modern contributions.

Index

Index